Cecilia Notini Burch

# A Cold War Pursuit

Soviet Refugees in Sweden, 1945–54

Santérus
Academic Press
Sweden

Doctoral thesis in history at Stockholm University 2014

www.santerus.se



© 2014 Cecilia Notini Burch and Santérus Academic Press Sweden
ISBN 978-91-7335-037-2
*Cover art: The Prisoners* © Adolph Gottlieb/BUS 2014
*Cover profile*: Sven Bylander
Santérus Academic Press is an imprint of
Santérus Förlag, Stockholm, Sweden
academicpress@santerus.se
Printed by BOD, Germany 2014

# Contents

# Acknowledgements

What is the best way to express my gratitude as this long journey comes to an end? By recalling that dark, cold December night when I learned that Stockholm University had decided to fund my PhD application. That was some years ago and, looking back, I realise just how far I have come. I have changed in the process – for the better. And although I have written this rather long book by myself, I cannot for one moment claim that it has been a lonely journey or that I am to take all the credit for the richness it has generated to my life.

I have been lucky indeed, in so many ways. First, there is of course the Department of History, which provided me with this opportunity and has constituted a beneficial environment for academic growth. For that, I am eternally grateful. Just as important are the two supervisors who encouraged me to apply in the first place: Magnus Petersson and Karl Molin. Ever since my undergraduate days you have listened to all my outlandish ideas, read my texts and, in return, offered me your clever thoughts and insightful comments. Magnus also encouraged me to take those further steps into academic life, which I initially feared. That helped me mature both professionally and as an individual. Thank you!

Secondly, as many historians will recognise, we are sometimes helplessly lost without the shrewd support of a good archivist. This could not be truer when it comes to this study, which threw up many archival challenges. Without the diligent and conscientious assistance of archivist Lars Hallberg at the Swedish National Archives (*Riksarkivet*), this book could never have been written.

You have treated all my innumerable (and initially rather confused) questions and requests with exacting precision. You even read the first draft of the book, meticulously pointing out any mistakes and uncertainties you could find. I have appreciated your assistance enormously. A great, big, warm thank you to you and, indeed, your colleagues.

Another grand, whole-hearted thank you is due to historian Klas Åmark. He also took up the challenge of reading the first draft of this manuscript. Your intelligent, perspicacious and exceedingly knowledgeable remarks were invaluable. Thank you very much.

My warmest gratitude is also directed to all the other lovely people who read and commented on some or all of the draft submitted for my *slutseminarium* in May 2012. Leif Runefelt made a particularly prominent contribution by reading all of it, chairing the seminar and providing me with very honest and constructive criticisms. If you ever read the book again, I hope you will see that I was paying attention! Those who read, commented and assisted me in various ways on this occasion include Nevra Biltekin, Lisa Hellman, Jenny Langkjaer, Ann Hallner, Johan Bergman, Helena Tolvhed, Fredrik Charpentier Ljungqvist, Aryo Makko, Adam Hjortén, Christine Ericsdotter, Anna-Carin Stymne, Torsten Feurstein, Ingela Sjögren, Nikolas Glover, Johan Svanberg, Klara Folkesson, Kim Bergqvist and Lilita Zalkalns. As always, the ambitious participants of the PhD seminar at the Department of History provided more constructive critique than any highbrow academic conference could ever do. Thank you all! And my thanks go to all the other amazing graduate researchers that I have been fortunate to get to know during these years. I have had the time of my life! For that, and for all the fond memories, I am ever so grateful. Some of you have become friends for life.

Another inspiring group of people whose clever thoughts I have been privileged to receive is 'Flyktinggruppen' – an informal collection of historians writing about refugees in Sweden. We have shared not only good food and wine over the years, but also engaged in many constructive discussions on the issues we hold dear. I have appreciated this a great deal. So Mikael Byström, Karin Kvist Geverts, Pär Frohnert, Maija Runcis, Johan Svanberg and Pontus Rudberg (and others who have occasionally participated): thank you! I have been lucky to have you as colleagues. And I am particularly grateful to those of you who read substantial parts of the first draft of this book during the summer of 2012.

All of the above deserve a share in the credit for this research. I alone am responsible for any errors of fact.

A generous grant from The Swedish Foundation for International Cooperation in Research and Higher Education enabled me to work at LSE IDEAS at London School of Economics and Political Science in 2010–11. This enabled me to write two articles, present my work to a broader intellectual audience and taught me many useful things about the academic world. Most of all, it enabled me to discuss my work with the knowledgeable Odd Arne Westad, who discerningly reminded me that I am a historian. Thank you, Arne!

Other individuals who have in one way or another contributed to my journey are Olof Kronvall at Georgetown University in Washington, who helped me find the Ingrians already in 2006 and later read and commented on my first texts as a PhD student; David J. Smith at Glasgow University; and Roy Smith at Nottingham Trent University who provided me with the opportunity to present my work to international relations specialists. And, last but by no means least, the Swedish Ingrians who meet through the *Finsk-ingermanländska Riksförbundet* and have been cheering for me and listening enthusiastically to every word I have had to say. Toivo Flink arranged to have a summary of his well-informed book on the Ingrians in Finland translated just for me so that I could read it despite my poor knowledge of the Finnish language, and Kalervo Kähäri helped us communicate. Eric de Geer, with his passionate interest for the Ingrians, has listened, read and followed my work ever since we first got in contact. Thank you all for your whole-hearted support!

Then there is, of course, the ever so important world outside of the university, without which one would not last very long. My dear parents, Maj-Britt Höckert Notini and Thomas Notini, have always believed in me and supported me no matter what ill-considered projects and ideas I have come up with regarding my future. Your faith in my ability and sumptuous evaluation of my persona is touching, indeed, and I am very grateful for your love and support. Thomas also proof read the final version of this thesis with a keen eye for mistakes and misprints, while Maj-Britt took on a substantial load of baby-sitting. Thank you!

In addition to the highly regarded comrades I have found within Stockholm University, I am blessed with a bunch of amazing friends from before, after and outside academia. Sara Wennerström Stjärne, Maria Fahlén, Erik Myrsten, Jonna Inge, Karin Hård, Matilda Wrede-Jäntti, Christer Benktsson, Anna Sandelin, Sara Ideström, Carl-Michael Arnér, Debs Smith, Birgitta Vennström, Elisabeth Lutteman and many others. Thanks for being who you are and reminding me of what really matters. My life would be so much poorer without you. I love you all.

Thank you also to all my other friends and family in Sweden, England, Finland and Norway. Although I don't see you all as much as I would like, you are often in my thoughts. An extra great big hug goes to my nieces and nephews Sian, Eloise, Grace and Charlie Burch, and Tekla and Katja Jäntti. (Now you are in a book!)

A very special, big, loving thank you is dedicated to our remarkable Barbara Ann Burch, so very loved and painfully missed, who did not live to see this day. I finished my book Barbie! I thought you should know that.

The greatest thank you of all goes to Stuart Burch – my companion, my best friend, my great love. Your affection and support help me through when times are tough. Your unselfish devotion and belief in me make me fly higher when things are good. And, not least, your English proof reading skills make my book read better (sic)! For this, and so much more, I am forever grateful.

And then, of course, there is, and always will be, Iris. Our wonderful, funny, energetic, curious, little Iris. You interrupted me in 2012 and taught me some very useful stuff about priorities. You are what makes me the luckiest of all and I love you to the stars and back.

Wilford, January 2014.

# What Factors Determine Refugee Policies?

What factors determine refugee policies in liberal democracies? There are as many potential answers to this question as there are academic disciplines and theoretical approaches focusing in one way or another on migration and refugee issues. On a fundamental level, they all suggest something about the essence of humanitarian policies: why do states engage in them, and what determine the outcomes? In the following thesis I wish to make a contribution to this scholarly debate through an empirical study of Sweden's management of Soviet refugees during the first decade of the Cold War.

There are several reasons why this specific period, country and refugee group constitute a suitable focal point for such a study. First of all, this decade witnessed the beginning of the modern, international refugee regime that we know today, oscillating around the UNHCR and the *1951 Convention relating to the Status of Refugees* (hereafter the 1951 Refugee Convention). As such, it brought about a significant transformation in Western states' general thinking pertaining to their responsibilities for refugees. A broad overview of refugee history suggests that this development was particularly influential on Sweden's policies. From defining itself as a 'non-immigration' country and pursuing exceedingly strict policies towards Europe's fleeing populations during the 1920s, 1930s and early 1940s, the end of the Second World War witnessed Sweden hosting around 200,000 foreigners within its borders, and proudly pronouncing itself as a refugee-friendly country a few years later. Sweden's 1954 Aliens Act, which incorporated into national legislation the pioneering 1951 Refugee Convention, replaced a significantly less generous predecessor, and accredited refugees with unprecedented rights against the Swedish state.

However, the first decade of the Cold War was also characterised by increasing concerns for national security. Non-aligned Sweden had become geopolitically sandwiched between the new superpower blocs, raising security considerations which were particularly delicate and focused on the possible intentions of the Soviet Union. This brought about escalating anxieties over communism and Soviet infiltration, leading to, among other things, heavy surveillance of left wing movements. At the same time, however, Sweden's neutrality policies necessitated more or less friendly Swedish-Soviet relations throughout the whole conflict, which sometimes resulted in a radical adaptation of Swedish domestic political affairs. It is thus not unlikely that concerns of national security – expressed through fears of spies and agents and/or concerns for bilateral relations – might have influenced the management of refugees in some way or another. This is because the refugees who knocked on Sweden's doors during these years were fleeing almost exclusively from Eastern European communist countries, causing significant disapproval from the Soviet administration.

The first decade of the Cold War also coincided with the establishment of the Swedish welfare state. This ushered in an alteration of the relationship between the state and the individual, entailing both elements of increasing state responsibility over the individual's well-being, as well as enhanced state control over, and intervention in, private lives. In addition, the decade was characterised by strong economic growth and a booming labour market. Thus, these developments could also have had some bearing on the management of refugees.

Moreover, as will become clear, previous research demonstrates that ethnic prejudice played a significant part in Sweden's treatment of refugees both before and after this decade. It is, therefore, reasonable to suppose that such aspects brought an influence to bear during this period.

These are thus some of the contextual aspects of Swedish society and political life that motivate a closer study of Sweden's handling of refugees, and particularly those fleeing from the Soviet Union, during the first decade of the Cold War. Taken together, they constitute a complexity which promises to provide some more thorough insights into the mechanics of refugee policies during the early stages of the modern international refugee regime, a period which was marked by severe international tensions. Thus, *the aim of this thesis is to examine what factors determined Sweden's policies towards Soviet refugees between 1945 and 1954.* It focuses on the refugees' right to reside in Sweden and on the continuous treatment of those who were granted a right to stay. This is pursued through a study of the Swedish authorities' assessment of Soviet refugees' asylum claims and the conditions of their residence permits. On a broader, theoretical level, it is my ambition to contribute to the scholarly discussion on the nature of refugee policies in modern, liberal democracies.

The design of this study is as follows. After this introductory chapter, which presents the theoretical and methodological starting points, *chapter two* is devoted to a discussion of the relevant historical background to the issues explored. It also includes a presentation of how other scholars have interpreted what is so far known about Swedish 20th century refugee policies. What, according to previous research, were the factors which determined these policies?

In *chapter three,* the empirical examination commences with an exploration of the legal and bureaucratic foundation of refugee policies during the research period. Refugees' rights and obligations according to Swedish legislation at the time are analysed, as well as the main structure of the bureaucratic decision-making process in refugee related issues. The focus here is on what room for manoeuvre this framework afforded the authorities. In other words, it seeks to ascertain the degree to which certain influential factors could impact on refugee-related decisions.

The subsequent chapters focus on the practical implementation of the legislation. Chapters four to six examine in detail situations in which refugees' right to stay in Sweden were tested and challenged. In *chapter four,* an empirical exploration of Sweden's management of Soviet *new arrivals* is pursued. Consideration is given to those who were denied the right to stay and issued either a refusal of entry or deportation decision; on the kind of circumstances that led to these decisions and on how the practices changed over time. In *chapter five,* attention turns to Sweden's management of *the unwanted*. The issuing of deportation and expulsion decisions towards individuals with previous residence permits is analysed. What circumstances did or did not lead to such outcomes? Did these practices change over time and, if so, how? In *chapter six*, Sweden's management of *the demanded* is analysed. How did Sweden handle Soviet extradition requests during the research period? Did practices change over time?

*Chapter seven* explores the continued treatment of individuals who were allowed to stay. As shall be demonstrated, residence permits were granted for different periods of time and attached with various kinds of restrictions. Thus, this chapter examines who were granted what sort of permit, and why.

Finally, in *chapter eight*, the results are summarised and discussed in relation to previous research. An exposition on how the results can contribute to a general debate on the mechanisms of refugee policies in liberal democracies in the post-war era is pursued. This includes an exploration of the relationship between refugee policies and national security in particular.

The contextual aspects that motivate the study also constitute possible influential factors for the issues that are explored. Therefore, the overall ambition in all the empirical chapters is to ascertain *if, how*, and *to what extent* they affected the treatment of the Soviet refugees. Six such aspects are identified. In the following they are presented in more detail.

## 1.1 Identifying Possible Influential Factors

When attempting to anticipate results in order to guide one's actions, the researcher undoubtedly runs the risk of leaving out important aspects, regardless of the extent to which one's hypotheses are anchored in contextual knowledge. A completely open approach to historical evidence, however, risks becoming misleading and lack the analytical capacity that gives the past meaning to the modern spectator. All analysis of bygone realities will inevitably violate them to some extent, no matter how well pursued it may be. Nonetheless, without some theoretical prejudice, the past remains an inexplicable, chaotic hotchpotch of meaningless facts. Successful historical research is best carried out through a constant dialogue between relevant research questions, historical evidence and contextual and theoretical awareness.

An attempt to pursue such a dialogue has led to the identification of six key factors that are likely to have influenced changing refugee policies in Sweden between 1945 and 1954. These are *aspects of external security*; *internal security*; *economics*; *ethnicity*; *social control and morality*; and *international juridical developments*. There are surely others that could have been examined too. A study of this kind inevitably has to be selective, however. A contextual outlook on Swedish political life and society during the 1940s and 1950s, as well as a consideration of aspects illuminated as relevant in previous research on Swedish refugee policies, has led me to these six. Two of them are intimately linked to the concept of security, in a traditional understanding of the term. Thus, particular attention will be granted towards the relationship between security concerns and refugee policies. This is further motivated by the fact that this perspective is essentially unexplored in previous research on Swedish refugee policies.

### 1.1.1 *Aspects of External Security*

On 25 January 1946, dramatic scenes were played out in the small coastal town of Trelleborg in the south of Sweden. One hundred and forty-six Baltic citizens who had fought in the German army were forced on board the Soviet ship *Beloostrov* by the Swedish police and extradited to the Soviet Union. Many were struggling for their lives and even harming themselves in order to try to escape. This occurred in plain view of onlooking members of the public and media representatives. One month earlier, 2,700 German citizens had suffered a similar fate (although without the same public attention).

The extradition was a result of the Swedish government's decision to adhere to a Soviet demand made the previous summer. In so doing, the government challenged not only international legislation, such as the so-called Geneva Convention of 1929,[1] but also significant parts of national and (Western) international opinion

---

1     *Convention relative to the Treatment of Prisoners of War.* Geneva, 27 July 1929.
      Available at: http://www.icrc.org/ihl/INTRO/305 (accessed 23 December 2013)

which hosted sentiments of commiseration for the occupied Baltic States at this time. The determinant factor in this decision was not of a legal or moral kind, however, but predominantly constituted by *realpolitik*, including concerns for future national security. The Soviet Union had grown to become an Eastern superpower through the events of the war and was now neighbouring Sweden thanks to its hold over Finland. Through its recent behaviour it had demonstrated expansionist ambitions. For reasons of stability, prosperity and – most importantly – national security, the Swedish administration, and its Minister for Foreign Affairs Östen Undén in particular, believed it needed to maintain good relations with this new giant.[2] Thus, as historian Alf W Johansson has described it, the Soviet soldiers extradited in 1946 became a 'sacrifice on the altar of [Sweden's] neutrality policy'.[3] At this time in Swedish history, therefore, there was an intimate relationship between refugee policies on the one hand, and security policies on the other.

Theoretically, the security referred to above pertains to a traditional understanding of the term, in the sense that it focuses on a state's (military) ability to defend its territory and autonomy against external threats. Within this theoretical approach, the referent object of security – in other words that which is being secured – is exclusively identified as the state, and the threats as those directed towards the state from other actors (states) within the international arena. As such, the concept is closely connected to the theory of realism and generally not centred on things such

2   Curt Ekholm, *Balt- och tyskutlämningen 1945–1946: omständigheter kring interne-ringen i läger i Sverige och utlämningen till Sovjetunionen av f d tyska krigsdeltagare*, parts 1 and 2, 2 ed., Uppsala University, Uppsala 1995 (ref: Ekholm 1995); Wilhelm Agrell, *Fred och fruktan: Sveriges säkerhetspolitiska historia 1918–2000*, Historiska media, Lund 2000, pp. 87–97 (ref: Agrell 2000); Ulf Bjereld, Alf W. Johansson, & Karl Molin, *Sveriges säkerhet och världens fred: svensk utrikespolitik under kalla kriget*, Santérus, Stockholm 2008, pp. 72–79 (ref: Bjereld, Johansson & Molin 2008). The event has also been illuminated in a Radio Documentary titled 'Baltutlämningen', 26 April 2009, P3, Sveriges Radio, http://sverigesradio.se/sida/artikel.aspx?programid=2519&artikel=3587226 (Accessed 30 April 2012) and in a novel, P.O. Enquist, *Legionärerna: en roman om baltutlämningen*, Norstedt, Stockholm 1968.

3   Alf Johansson, 'Regeringen och tysk- och baltutlämningen 1945–1946' in *Säkerhet och försvar: en vänbok till Kent Zetterberg*, Gunnar Artéus, Karl Molin & Magnus Petersson (eds), Abrahamsson, Karlskrona 2005, p. 137.

as refugee issues at all, but strictly on foreign policy relations.[4] Even so, however, with such a concept it is still possible to imagine situations in which refugee policies become bargaining chips in foreign policy discussions. The threat the host state might perceive is, then, not connected to any specific traits or aspirations of the refugees in themselves as individuals, but has instead all to do with its relationship with the refugees' home country. A hostile state can threaten to take actions that would damage the security of the host state if the refugees residing there are not returned to their country of origin. Similarly, the designated host state could wish to ease international tensions and/or create more amicable relations between itself and the country of origin of the refugees by cooperating with this state in refugee matters (including, for example, not allowing refugees entry). Such was indeed the case when Sweden extradited the above-mentioned Balts and Germans to the Soviet Union. The question here, however, is whether there are grounds to assume that similar security concerns based on bilateral foreign policy relations could have continued to influence refugee policies during the following years.

Hypothetically, the answer should be affirmative. Sweden remained geopolitically squeezed between the new conflicting superpowers throughout the Cold War. During the first two-to-three post-war years, Sweden tried to reduce tensions in the Scandinavian area by acting like a bridge builder between East and West and by treating the Soviet Union like any other actor on the international stage. Its efforts to foster amicable relations with the Soviet Union included, among other things, granting it a substantial credit contract for buying Swedish goods over a five year period. This was a way of trying to invest in Scandinavia's

---

4    This approach is in line within the so-called *traditional school*, which was predominant during the Cold War. Despite receiving substantial criticisms since the early 1990s, it still represents an influential perspective within international relations and security studies. See, for example, Hans J. Morgenthau, *Politics among nations: the struggle for power and peace*, McGraw-Hill, New York 1993; Stephen M Walt, 'The Renaissance of Security Studies' in *International Studies Quarterly*, 1991 (35):2, pp. 211–239. For a more thorough discussion on the theoretical foundations of the concept of security, see, for example, Barry Buzan & Lene Hansen, *The evolution of International Security Studies*, Cambridge University Press, Cambridge 2009, ch.1, (ref: Buzan & Hansen 2009).

future economic stability as well as its military security.[5] Making a discernible political statement about the Soviet Union by granting asylum to its citizens could thus potentially have been counterproductive to these aims. In addition, there was an initial admiration for the Soviet Union within the Swedish political administration after the war, in large part due to the fact that it had done so much to help defeat the Third Reich.

As the bipolar Cold War tensions grew, however, Sweden's ambition of sustaining harmonious Scandinavian-Soviet relations gradually failed. In 1947–48, the Swedish administration finally abandoned its most Soviet-friendly bridge building intentions and, like the rest of the Western world, started to view the superpower in more negative terms. The Soviet Union's aggressive behaviour in Eastern Europe had influenced this change of attitudes. However, in opposition to its Scandinavian neighbours, Denmark and Norway, Sweden tried to handle this new situation by remaining non-aligned and employing a neutrality policy. The aim of this position was to be able to stay outside a future conflict. Alignment would have made this impossible since it implied a more or less automatic involvement in a new war.[6]

With the Soviet Union's tight grip on Finland (formally

5   Olof Kronvall & Magnus Petersson, *Svensk säkerhetspolitik i supermakternas skugga 1945–1991,* 2 rev. ed., Santérus Academic Press Sweden, Stockholm 2012, pp. 27–29 (ref: Kronvall & Petersson 2012); Bjereld, Johansson & Molin 2008, pp. 79–82.

6   With the argument of trying to keep the tensions in the Nordic area to a minimum, Sweden also strove to stop Norway and Denmark from joining the Atlantic Pact in 1948–49 through negotiations on the establishment of a Scandinavian Alliance. The plans went far, but ultimately failed due to disagreements regarding the Alliance's relations with the West. Whereas Sweden wished for it to engage in neutrality policies, Norway and Denmark – countries which both held painful memories of wartime occupation – found US guarantees indispensable. On the general development of Swedish Cold War policies, see Kronvall & Petersson 2012; Bjereld, Johansson & Molin 2008; Stefan Ekecrantz, *Hemlig utrikespolitik: kalla kriget, utrikesnämnden och regeringen 1946–1959,* Santérus, Stockholm 2003 (ref: Ekecrantz 2003); Olof Kronvall, *Den bräckliga barriären: Finland i svensk utrikespolitik 1948–1962,* Försvarshögskolan, Stockholm 2003 (ref: Kronvall 2003); Magnus Petersson, *"Brödrafolkens väl": svensk-norska säkerhetsrelationer 1949–1969,* Santérus, Stockholm 2003 (ref: Petersson 2003); Ann-Marie Ekengren, *Sverige under kalla kriget 1945–1969: en forskningsöversikt,* Göteborg 1997.

established in 1948 through the YYA Treaty[7]), plus Norway and Denmark's membership in the Atlantic Pact in 1949, Sweden thus became a 'neutral' (at least in its general meaning) and officially unbiased ground in between the two superpowers' spheres of influence. With time, this state of affairs became regarded as keeping in check the region's power balance. It was thought that if Sweden should change its policies in any direction and approach one of the blocs, the other would take action and tension would increase. Similarly, it was believed that if one of the blocs would intensify its policies in the area, the other would do the same. This analysis of status quo was indeed confirmed during a number of crises during the Cold War.[8]

In line with this reasoning the 1950s saw the so-called 'Finland argument' added to the debate: should Sweden become more Western-orientated, then Finland would suffer from Soviet demands for cooperation according to the YYA Treaty. Apart from bringing negative consequences to Finland's sovereignty, such a move would have disrupted the balance in the whole region. With this argument, the Social Democratic government managed to achieve a unique long-standing consensus between Sweden's political parties on security issues during the Cold War.[9]

However, Sweden's chosen position required that both superpowers trusted its neutrality ambitions. This was especially the case regarding the Soviet Union, which was, after all, the only one of the two that was regarded as a possible aggressor, and which constituted the main threat to Swedish security at the time. If this new giant neighbour was to doubt Sweden's neutral credentials, and, for example, think that Sweden would indeed allow itself to become a tool in the hands of the United States during a third world war,

7    The Agreement of Friendship, Cooperation, and Mutual Assistance (from the Finnish *Ystävyys-, yhteistyö- ja avunantosopimus*).

8    Jerker Widén, *Notkrisen och dess efterspel: USA:s relationer med Sverige under en av kalla krigets höjdpunkter, oktober 1961–mars 1962*, Göteborg University, Göteborg 2004; Bjereld, Johansson & Molin 2008; Kronvall & Petersson 2012; Kronvall 2003; Petersson 2003.

9    Kronvall 2003; Ulf Bjereld & Marie Demker, *Utrikespolitiken som slagfält: de svenska partierna och utrikesfrågorna*, Nerenius & Santérus, Stockholm 1995; Fredrika Björklund, *Samförstånd under oenighet: svensk säkerhetspolitisk debatt under det kalla kriget*, Uppsala University, Uppsala 1992 (ref: Björklund 1992); Bjereld, Johansson & Molin 2008; Kronvall & Petersson 2012.

it was more likely to assault it militarily. Therefore, evidence of Sweden's non-aggressive intentions was required.[10]

Similarly, though, Sweden did not want to become a 'lost country' in the eyes of the US. It did, after all, hope for support of some kind from the Americans in the event of a military assault from the Soviet Union. Despite public announcements suggesting otherwise, the Swedish military defence, although comparatively strong, could not have endured many days of a full Soviet attack. Western support would have been desperately needed, and due to Sweden's strategically important geopolitical position, it would have been likely to arrive. As a way of trying to secure this support, however, top secret cooperation plans with the US involving arms trading, intelligence cooperation and detailed plans of military collaboration were pursued. Too friendly relations with the Soviet Union, however, could potentially make the Americans lose interest.[11]

This tension was to characterise Swedish foreign policies during the whole of the Cold War, and led to several adjustments of domestic policies too. It resulted, for example, in a practice of political silence around security issues. An open debate between

10    Later research has revealed that substantial parts of Sweden's defense plans and secret cooperation with the West was in fact known to the Soviet administration, however. See Bo Petersson, *Med Moskvas ögon: bedömningar av svensk utrikespolitik under Stalin och Chrusjtjov*, Arena, Stockholm 1994 (ref: Bo Petersson 1994).

11    Sweden's stance towards the superpowers during the Cold War has thus been interpreted as a matter of balancing between policies of *reassurance* and *deterrence* towards the Soviet Union, and *screening* and *integration measures* towards the US. The non-alignment in itself could be regarded as a policy of reassurance directed at the Soviet Union – a 'proof' of its trustworthiness and friendly ambitions. This also regards its economic assistance to the Soviet Union established already in 1946, and several other political decisions made during the Cold War. At the same time, Sweden invested heavily in its national defence during these years – a measure that could be interpreted as a policy of deterrence. In terms of its US relationship, the non-alignment similarly constituted a policy of screening, whereas the secret arms trading and intelligence cooperation can be understood as measures of integration. See Kronvall 2003; Kronvall & Petersson 2012. See also Robert Dalsjö, *Life-line lost: the rise and fall of "neutral" Sweden's secret reserve option of wartime help from the West*, Santérus Academic Press Sweden, Stockholm 2006; Mikael Holmström, *Den dolda alliansen: Sveriges hemliga NATO-förbindelser*, Atlantis, Stockholm 2011; Ekecrantz 2003; and Mikael Malmborg, *Den ståndaktiga nationalstaten: Sverige och den västeuropeiska integrationen 1945–1959*, Lund University, Lund 1994.

the opposing parties would have risked making the Soviet Union distrust the stability of Sweden's neutrality ambitions.[12]

This state of affairs could hypothetically have had varying consequences for the Soviet refugees that arrived in Sweden. Acknowledging and protecting their refugee rights could provoke the Soviet Union, whereas a refusal to do so could damage Sweden's relations with the Western community. Both outcomes could, therefore, potentially have had national security implications. Even so, the possible impacts of foreign policy and national security concerns on Sweden's refugee policies during the Cold War remain hitherto unexplored in previous research.

Internationally, the relationship between these two areas of policy has been illuminated to a considerably higher degree. Gil Loescher and John A. Scanlan, for example, argue that in the United States, the bestowing of asylum on East European refugees became a political weapon in the struggle against the communist world. This meant that refugees from communist states were welcome to the US to a greater extent than refugees from right-wing dictatorships, with which the Americans sometimes cooperated on military and financial issues. US asylum legislation specifically identified the rights of refugees from the communist bloc until 1980. Additionally, American presidents sometimes used loop holes within the legislation in order to be able to open and close borders in accordance with its foreign policy aims during the Cold War. However, this also meant that, when foreign relations between the US and the Soviet Union temporarily improved, and the US engaged in policies more aiming at mutual understanding, the door for Eastern European refugees became harder to open.[13]

As a 'neutral' part in the Cold War conflict, Sweden could obviously not make political use of Eastern European refugees in the same way as the United States and other NATO countries. There

12    On the personal consequences for individual politicians attempting to publicly question Sweden's chosen position towards the Soviet Union, see Ulf Bjereld, *Hjalmarsonaffären: ett politiskt drama i tre akter*, Nerenius & Santérus, Stockholm 1997; Björklund 1992.

13    Gil Loescher & John A. Scanlan, *Calculated kindness: refugees and America's half-open door 1945 – present*, Free Press, New York 1986 (ref: Loesher & Scanlan 1986); See also, Carl J. Bon Tempo, *Americans at the Gate: the United States and refugees during the Cold War*, Princeton University Press, Princeton 2009 (ref: Bon Tempo 2009).

were no obvious political or strategic gains to make against the Soviet Union through granting asylum to its citizens. If anything, the opposite was true. In relation to the West, however, there were potential advantages. As the Second World War came to an end, the Swedish administration perceived a need to improve the country's international reputation. Its lenient behaviour towards Germany had damaged its standing. Taking an active role in refugee policies might, thus, have been recognised as a means of improving its international (Western) prestige.[14]

However, Sweden's sensitive geopolitical position and chosen foreign policy stance is likely to have made it more vulnerable to Soviet pressure than most other Western countries. The extradition of the German and Baltic soldiers in the winter of 1945–46 constitutes a clear example of this. It is likely that similar demands were presented later on by the Soviet authorities. The question is, of course, how did Sweden respond? And how did it handle the general strains on its relationship with the Soviet Union that the arrival of new Soviet refugees is likely to have caused? Did such aspects influence the treatment of Soviet asylum seekers?[15]

14  On Sweden's foreign policy during the Second World War, see Wilhelm M. Carlgren, *Svensk utrikespolitik 1939–1945*, Allmänna förlaget, Stockholm 1973. On attaining 'good-will' through refugee polices, see Mikael Byström & Karin Kvist Geverts, 'Från en aktivism till en annan: hur ska Sveriges agerande i flyktingfrågan under andra världskriget förklaras?' in *Sverige och Nazi-Tyskland: skuldfrågor och moraldebatt,* Lars M. Andersson & Mattias Tydén (eds), Dialogos, Stockholm 2007.

15  The question focuses on possible negative effects of external security concerns on refugee management. However, the opposite was also a matter of fact. The Swedish security police used Baltic refugees – many with conspicuously dubious pasts as former assistants of the Nazi occupation regimes in their home countries – as informants, starting already during the Second World War. During the following Cold War years, the intelligence services of the Swedish Armed Forces secretly trained Baltic refugees as agents and sent them to the Soviet Union in order to try to infiltrate society and send valuable military information back to Sweden through radio signals. As such, refugees were actively used in order to *strengthen* Sweden's external security. Research has demonstrated that the enterprise failed, however, as Soviet intelligence services managed to infiltrate and manipulate the Swedish activities already during the late 1940s, leading to the killing or imprisonment of most of the agents upon arrival, and to the sending of false reports to Sweden for several years. Mats Deland, *Purgatorium: Sverige och andra världskrigets förbrytare,* Atlas, Stockholm 2010, pp. 318–324; Peter Kadhammar, *De sammansvurna*, 2 ed., Fischer, Rimbo 2002.

### 1.1.2 *Aspects of Internal Security*

One of the most dominant features of Cold War security policies was constituted by espionage and infiltration. All involved states engaged in it, and persistently worried about and watched out for their counterpart's equivalent activities. Unlawful intelligence operations were, as both scholars and former intelligence officers have pointed out, an integral part of the psychology and strategy of the Cold War.[16]

Spies constituted a threat to national security if, for example, they engaged in military sabotage and/or gathering and transferring vital information about the military defence capabilities of the state to its opponents. This gave rise to a substantial amount of surveillance of suspected individuals, including several violations of personal integrity. Individuals believed to harbour left wing world views were particularly exposed in Western countries as potential traitors. Individuals proven to have engaged in unlawful intelligence activities were imprisoned or even executed.[17] They were also exposed to massive media attention, since espionage constituted a drama of its own during the Cold War, portrayed in numerous forms in popular culture.[18]

The fear of espionage activities could influence Western states' treatment of refugees too. It was a well-known fact that the Soviet Union and its satellite states endeavoured to send agents disguised as refugees to Western countries, and suspected refugees were often subject to severe control.[19]

---

16   Christopher M. Andrew & Vasilij Nikitič Mitrochin, *The sword and the shield: the Mitrokhin archive and the secret history of the* KGB, 1. ed., Basic Books, New York, 1999; Tore Forsberg, *Spioner och spioner som spionerar på spioner: spioner och kontraspioner i Sverige*, 2 ed., Hjalmarsson & Högberg, Stockholm 2004; Wilhelm Agrell, *Konsten att gissa rätt: underrättelsevetenskapens grunder,* Studentlitteratur, Lund 1998 (ref: Agrell 1998); Wilhelm Agrell, *Underrättelseanalysens metoder och problem: medan klockan tickar,* Gleerup, Malmö 2009; John Earl Haynes & Harvey Klehr, *Early Cold War spies: the espionage trials that shaped American politics,* Cambridge University Press, Cambridge 2006 (ref: Haynes & Klehr 2006);

17   For example in the US, see Haynes & Klehr 2006.

18   Marie Cronqvist, *Mannen i mitten: ett spiondrama i svensk kallakrigskultur,* Carlsson, Stockholm 2004 (ref: Cronqvist 2004); Kim Salomon, *En femtiotalsberättelse: populärkulturens kalla krig i folkhemssverige*, Atlantis, Stockholm 2007 (ref: Salomon 2007).

19   John Radzilowski, 'Ethnic anti-communism in the United States' in *Anti-Communist minorities in the United States: political activism of ethnic refugees,* ed. Ieva Zake, Palgrave Macmillan, New York 2009.

For a country like Sweden, the importance of preventing Soviet agents from acquiring national defence secrets was just as urgent as in other Western countries. Its non-alignment and neutrality policies rendered it absolutely essential to keep the military administration free from Soviet infiltration. For example, a (public) revelation of the secret cooperation with the West would have ruined Swedish security policies, since Swedish neutrality ambitions would no longer have been credible.[20]

There were also other reasons to fear Soviet infiltration. The Soviet Union doubtlessly constituted the most serious threat to Sweden's territorial security during these years. This was particularly the case during the early 1950s, when international tensions increased dramatically and the Swedish political administration anticipated a third world war followed by a possible Soviet invasion. Thus, anxieties about spies, agents and fifth columnists were as substantial in Sweden as in many other countries – perhaps even more so due to its proximity to the Soviet Union. The transferral of Sweden's defence capabilities to the Soviets could seriously damage Sweden's territorial security. As in other Western countries, therefore, substantial surveillance over left wing movements took place as a result.[21]

<hr>

20  Bjereld, Johansson & Molin 2008; Ekecrantz 2003; Kronvall & Petersson 2012; Petersson 2003. On what the Soviet administration actually knew of Sweden's defense plans and secret cooperation with the West, see Petersson 1994.

21  Ann-Marie Ekengren & Henrik Oscarsson, *Det röda hotet: de militära och polisiära säkerhetstjänsternas hotbilder i samband med övervakning av svenska medborgare 1945–1960*, Nordic Academic Press, Lund 2002 (ref: Ekengren & Oscarsson 2002); Säkerhetstjänstkommissionen, *Rikets säkerhet och den personliga integriteten: de svenska säkerhetstjänsternas författningsskyddande verksamhet sedan år 1945: betänkande*, SOU 2002:87, Fritzes offentliga publikationer, Stockholm 2002 (ref: SOU 2002:87); Ulf Eliasson, *Politisk övervakning och personalkontroll 1945–1969: säkerhetspolisens medverkan i den politiska personalkontrollen: forskarrapport till Säkerhetstjänstkommissionen*, SOU 2002:88, Fritzes offentliga publikationer, Stockholm 2002; Magnus Hjort, *Den farliga fredsrörelsen: säkerhetstjänsternas övervakning av fredsorganisationer, värnpliktsvägrare och FNL-grupper 1945–1990: forskarrapport till Säkerhetstjänstkommissionen*, SOU 2002:90, Fritzes offentliga publikationer, Stockholm 2002; Magnus Hjort: *Hotet från vänster: säkerhetstjänsternas övervakning av kommunister, anarkister m.m. 1965–2002: forskarrapport till Säkerhetstjänstkommissionen*, SOU 2002:91, Fritzes offentliga publikationer, Stockholm 2002; Magnus Hjort, *"Nationens livsfråga": propaganda och upplysning i försvarets tjänst 1944–1963*, Santérus, Stockholm 2004 (ref: Hjort 2004);

Potential spies and agents among the refugees thus represent another close link between refugee and security issues during the Cold War. From a theoretical point of view, this relation oscillates between *internal* and *external* security. Just as with the above-mentioned external security concerns, the referent object is the state. The threat, however, is constituted by a mixture of the intention of an individual, residing within the state's territory (an internal threat), and his or her link to another actor on the international arena with possible hostile intentions (an external threat). As such, this relation, hypothetically at least, falls within the area of traditional security studies.[22]

A speculative outlook on possible state perceptions of threats linked to Cold War refugees provides some other aspects of internal security, however, which challenge a strictly traditional understanding of the concept of security. There was an escalating fear of communism in Sweden during this decade, similar to that in other countries. Regardless of its non-aligned position in military matters, Sweden was culturally and politically a component of the Western world. The spread of communism in Sweden was as likely to endanger political stability (or, as some modernisers of the concept of security would frame it, *political security*) there as in other countries, and therefore as likely to be perceived as a threat to national security by the main political and administrative state actors. Communists were, additionally, perceived as possible future fifth-columnists.[23]

---

Lars Olof Lampers, *Det grå brödraskapet: en berättelse om* IB: *forskarrapport till Säkerhetstjänstkommissionen*, SOU 2002:92, Fritzes offentliga publikationer, Stockholm 2002; Karl Molin, *Övervakningen av "SKP-komplexet": forskarrapport till Säkerhetstjänstkommissionen*, SOU 2002:93, Fritzes offentliga publikationer, Stockholm 2002 (ref: SOU 2002:93); Sverker Oredsson, *Svensk oro: offentlig fruktan i Sverige under 1900-talets senare hälft*, Nordic Academic Press, Lund 2003 (ref: Oredsson 2003); Werner Schmidt, *Antikommunism och kommunism under det korta 1900-talet*, Nordic Academic Press, Lund 2002 (ref: Schmidt 2002); Cronqvist 2004.

22 A similar relation can characterise international terrorists, for example, if they are linked to an international organisation or country.

23 Ekengren & Oscarsson 2002; SOU 2002:87; SOU 2002:93. On the various definitions of the concept of 'security' within modern scholarly research, see Buzan & Hansen 2009, ch. 1; Barry Buzan, Ole Wæver & Jaap de Wilde, *Security: a new framework for analysis*, Lynne Rienner, Boulder Colorado 1998 (ref: Buzan, Wæver & de Wilde 1998).

Existing research demonstrates that surveillance of Swedish citizens suspected of holding communist world views was initiated already during the First World War and the Russian Revolution.[24] The intensity of that surveillance then varied over the following decades. A peak was reached during the initial years of the Second World War, which among other things witnessed the monitoring of millions of letters and phone calls by the security services, and the confinement of communist conscripts.[25] Foreigners with suspected communist sympathies were also interned.[26] During the final stages of the war and the initial post-war years, surveillance of communist movements and individuals decreased. From 1948 onwards, however, when international tensions intensified and communism began to be interpreted as an acute threat in the West, Swedish state surveillance of suspected communists became resurgent. Research has revealed that the monitoring of left wing movements constituted a constant factor of Swedish security policies during the Cold War. Over the course of the following two decades the security services registered more than 100,000 individuals as potential communist sympathisers, sometimes 'on flimsy grounds'.[27] The intensity of the perceptions of the communist threat varied in accordance with the events on the international arena. As a result, several civil liberties and

24   Ulf Eliasson, *I försvarets intresse: säkerhetspolisens övervakning och registrering av ytterlighetspartier 1917–1945*, Nordic Academic Press, Lund 2006 (ref: Eliasson 2006); Jenny Langkjaer, *Övervakning för rikets säkerhet: svensk säkerhetspolisiär övervakning av utländska personer och inhemsk politisk aktivitet, 1885–1922*, Acta Universitatis Stockholmiensis, Stockholm University, Stockholm 2011 (ref: Langkjaer 2011).

25   The security services' surveillance operations during the Second World War were directed both towards suspected Nazis and communists, although its intensity fluctuated strongly with the developments of the international conflict and Sweden's foreign policy ambitions. Janne Flyghed, *Rättsstat i kris: spioneri och sabotage i Sverige under andra världskriget*, Federativ, Stockholm 1992; Karl Molin, *Hemmakriget: om den svenska krigsmaktens åtgärder mot kommunister under andra världskriget*, Tiden, Stockholm 1982; Eliasson 2006.

26   Klas Åmark, *Att bo granne med ondskan: Sveriges förhållande till nazismen, Nazityskland och förintelsen*, Bonnier, Stockholm 2011, pp. 556–565 (ref: Åmark 2011).

27   Such registration of political opinions was rendered unlawful in 1969. However, documentation continued in other forms, testing the limits of legality. SOU 2002:87, pp. 24–29, 241–287.

individual rights were violated in the name of national security.[28]

Popularly held anxieties might very well have influenced Sweden's handling of Soviet refugees. The possibility that some refugees were in fact communist infiltrators or agents sent on a mission by their home countries is just as likely to have been perceived as a threat to Swedish national security as elsewhere – particularly from 1948 onwards. And they could potentially have been perceived as such in more ways than those pertaining exclusively to the state's ability to defend itself from external military aggression. As possible communists, regardless of whether or not they actively cooperated with the Soviet Union, they could be viewed as endangering both the military and the political integrity of the state. As such, they posed *internal* threats towards both territorial and political security.

Such a definition of the concept approaches a more 'modernist' understanding of security. Advocates of this school argue that state actors identify more aspects than those pertaining directly to bilateral relations as threats towards the state. They also identify and react to perceived threats directed towards the *societies* they represent (such as, for example, economic threats, health threats, cultural threats and/or environmental threats). Consequently, they utilise a wider interpretation of the concept than traditionalist security thinkers.[29]

### 1.1.3 Economic Aspects

One commonly pronounced scholarly interpretation of modern refugee policies is that they are predominantly determined by

---

28  Ekengren & Oscarsson 2002; SOU 2002:87–95.

29  There is, however, an expansive spectrum of opinions within this group in terms of how far this widening should go. See, for example, Barry Buzan, *People, states and fear: an agenda for international security studies in the post-cold war era*, 2. ed., Harvester Wheatsheaf, London 1991 (ref: Buzan 1991); Buzan, Wæver & De Wilde, 1998; Buzan & Hansen 2009; Christopher Rudolph, *National security and immigration: policy development in the United States and Western Europe since 1945*, Stanford University Press, Stanford California 2006, (ref: Rudolph 2006); Ann J. Tickner, *Gender in international relations: feminist perspectives on achieving global security*, Columbia University Press, New York 1992 (ref: Tickner 1992); *Gendered states: feminist (re)visions of international relations theory*, Peterson, V. Spike (ed.), Lynne Rienner, Boulder, Colorado 1992 (ref: *Gendered states* 1992).

economic considerations. Scholars often point out that in times of economic growth liberal democracies tend to welcome immigrants (including refugees) to a significantly higher degree than during times of economic stagnation.[30]

That there is such a connection is difficult to question. In post-war Sweden, for example, migration policies have tended to be more generous when the labour market has been in need of work force, than during times when it has not. The first two decades after the war were characterised by substantial economic growth. One direct result of this was an extensive importation of foreign labour. Thus between 1950 and 1967 refugees only constituted about five percent of the total influx of immigrants. The other 95% were working migrants, mainly from the Nordic countries but also Turkey, Italy, Yugoslavia and West Germany. Some researchers claim that the beneficial economic circumstances during these years meant that refugees were also welcomed.[31]

General economic developments are only apparent with the benefit of hindsight, however. The first years of the period under examination were characterised by a fear that the armistice would be followed by a post-war depression like that which distinguished the aftermath of the First World War. The material needs of the European continent were immeasurable and the Minister for Trade Gunnar Myrdal believed that the Swedish economy would suffer for a considerable time.[32] If economic considerations determine refugee policies to such an important degree, it is, therefore, not unlikely that these initial post-war fears had a restrictive influence on the treatment of the first Soviet refugees to arrive during the early Cold War years.

Previous research has suggested such causal relations regarding the 1930s and the first years of the Second World War. As in the rest of Europe, refugee policies were characterised by severe con-

---

30   See, for example, Rudolph 2006; Christer Lundh & Rolf Ohlsson, *Från arbets-kraftsimport till flyktinginvandring*, 2 ed., SNS, Stockholm 1999 (ref: Lundh & Olsson 1999).

31   Lundh & Ohlsson 1999; Nelhans, Joachim, *Utlänningen på arbetsmarknaden: de rättsliga förutsättningarna för utlännings tillträde till den svenska arbetsmarknaden*, Studentlitteratur, Lund, 1973 (ref: Nelhans 1973).

32   Gunnar Myrdal, *Varning för fredsoptimism*, Bonnier, Stockholm 1944 (ref: Myrdal 1944); Örjan Appelqvist, *Bruten brygga: Gunnar Myrdal och Sveriges ekonomiska efterkrigspolitik 1943–1947*, Santérus, Stockholm 2000.

straints. The refugees who were allowed entry were generally those who could prove to the Swedish authorities that they were fully accounted for financially by relatives or organisations.[33] Regarding the Cold War years, historians Malin Thor and Norma Montesino have demonstrated that economic factors still mattered when Swedish authorities decided which refugees from the protracted European refugee camps were to be allowed to come and live – and work – in Sweden.[34]

It is therefore possible, if not likely, that this mentality characterised refugee handling in other ways too during the Cold War, even though Sweden had by then begun to take more responsibility in refugee matters compared to the 1930s and early 1940s. Thus, economic aspects constitute a factor to include when analysing the determinant mechanisms of refugee policies.

Soviet refugees in Sweden during the first decade of the Cold War can be considered against the backdrop of two general circumstances. Firstly their limited number and, secondly, the nature of the Swedish economy during this period. Such an overview suggests that economic considerations ought at least not to have actively hindered a positive assessment of their asylum applications – in any case not from around 1946 onwards when the Swedish economy boomed. However, even if this presumption is correct (a matter which obviously needs to be examined empirically in order to be verified), it does not of course exclude economic considerations from an assessment of their cases. Potentially, economic factors might even have increased their chances of being granted asylum.[35]

33   Åmark 2011, p. 469. See also Karin Kvist Geverts, *Ett främmande element i natio-nen: svensk flyktingpolitik och de judiska flyktingarna 1938–1944*, Acta Universitatis Upsaliensis (AUU), Uppsala University 2008, Uppsala 2008, chs. 2 and 6 (ref: Kvist Geverts 2008).

34   Malin Thor 'Det är billigare att bota ett TBC-fall än att uppfostra en svensk' in Jan Ekberg (ed.) *Sveriges mottagning av flyktingar – några exempel. Årsbok 2007 från forskningsprofilen Arbetsmarknad, migration och etniska relationer (AMER) vid Växjö universitet*, Växjö University Press, Växjö 2007 (ref: Thor 2007); Norma Montesino & Malin Thor, 'Migration och folkhälsa. Tuberkulos i den svenska flyktingmottagningen under 1940- och 1950-talen', unpublished paper presented at *Svenska Historikermötet i Lund*, Maj 2008.

35   Economic factors can, of course, also be interpreted in terms of security, if applying a modernist understanding of the concept. A state requires a solid economy to maintain a strong defence system, but also to ensure political stability. In line with this argument, refugees and other immigrants are some-

However, during recent decades several researchers have pointed out that such macro-economic analyses tend to produce an over-simplified reading and that other factors also influence policies. The *place* of emigration, for example, has perennially been relevant when it comes to immigrants, including refugees.

### 1.1.4 *Aspects of Ethnicity*

Previous research has demonstrated that, just as with other Western countries, Sweden was characterised by xenophobia during the first half of the twentieth century. Ideas on racial biology and nationalism influenced policies and debates. Not surprisingly, this had a bearing on Sweden's migration policies. Anti-Semitic notions led to discrimination towards Jewish refugees. Other groups were also targeted, such as Eastern Europeans and members of Roma societies.[36]

Such patterns of thought and behaviour can be identified and analysed with help from a broad variety of concepts and definitions. Different academic disciplines tend to construct their own theoretical frameworks when analysing similar phenomena. The concept of *ethnicity* has become pervasive over the past two decades. Its meaning has, however, shifted. Two schools of thought are separated by those arguing that it refers to essential characteristics

---

times portrayed as threats towards their host society, particularly if they are not regarded as contributors to the national economy. An inverted version of that argument also allows for an interpretation of immigrants as potentially strengthening a country's economic security if they become employees and tax payers. Rudolph 2006; Buzan 1991.

36  Tomas, Hammar, *Sverige åt svenskarna: invandringspolitik, utlänningskontroll och asylrätt 1900–1932*, Stockholm University, Stockholm 1964 (ref: Hammar 1964); Hans Lindberg, *Svensk flyktingpolitik under internationellt tryck 1936–1941*, Allmänna förlaget, Stockholm 1973 (ref: Lindberg 1973); Lars M. Andersson, *En jude är en jude är en jude: representationer av "juden" i svensk skämtpress omkring 1900–1930*, Nordic Academic Press, Lund 2000 (ref: Andersson 2000); Carl Henrik Carlsson, *Medborgarskap och diskriminering: östjudar och andra invandrare i Sverige 1860–1920*, Acta Universitatis Upsaliensis, Uppsala 2004 (ref: Carlsson 2004); Heléne Lööw, *Hakkorset och Wasakärven: en studie av nationalsocialismen i Sverige 1924–1950*, Göteborg University, Göteborg, 1990 (ref: Lööw 1990); Mikael Byström, *En broder, gäst och parasit: uppfattningar och föreställningar om utlänningar, flyktingar och flyktingpolitik i svensk offentlig debatt 1942–1947*, Acta Universitatis Stockholmiensis, Stockholm 2006 (ref: Byström 2006); Kvist Geverts 2008.

of certain groups, and those who interpret ethnicity as socially and culturally constructed. Anthropologists, sociologists and historians are some of the scholars whose disciplines frequently apply the latter concept.

The definition of ethnicity is not always separated from such concepts as nationalism and racism, which tend to focus on similar, but not identical, ideas and practices. However, a common scholarly definition, which has its origins in social anthropology, understands it as 'aspects of relationships between groups which consider themselves, and are regarded by others, as being culturally distinctive'.[37] The lived experience of ethnic identity, regardless of whether referring to one's own group or that of another, varies across time and space. Ideas on a common descent often constitute the core of a group's identity. Sometimes, but not always, perceptions on 'race' constitute a cornerstone. However, as anthropologist Thomas Hylland Eriksen points out, 'racial' or religious groups can also become 'ethnified'. The construction of 'African-Americans' as a culturally distinct ethnic group constitutes a case in point. Another is the increasingly common reference to European Muslims as 'Muslims', rather than by their national categorisation as 'Ethiopians' or 'Iranians' and so forth. Irrespective of designation, the most fundamental function of this 'relationship between groups' is the cognitive separation between 'us' and 'them'. It is only through the definition of 'others' that a group of people constructs what is significantly 'them'.[38]

Within other disciplines the concept of 'identity' is more commonly used to describe similar phenomena. One such is modern security studies. In 1993, Buzan, Kelstrup, Lemaitre and Wæver published the book *Identity, migration and the new security agenda in Europe*, in which they predicted that the main security issues of the post-Cold War world would be generated by notions of identity

37 Thomas Hylland Eriksen, *Ethnicity and nationalism: anthropological perspectives*, 3rd ed., Pluto Press, London 2010, p. 5 (ref: Hylland Eriksen 2010).

38 Hylland Eriksen 2010, p. 7–8. In previous editions of this book, Hylland Eriksen identified race as a form of ethnicity. In the third edition, however, he states that he has 'come to believe in the necessity of keeping the two concepts apart'. Hylland Eriksen 2010, p. 7. See also an elaborate discussion on the relationship between ethnicity and nationalism in Christina Johansson, *Välkomna till Sverige?: svenska migrationspolitiska diskurser under 1900-talets andra hälft*, 1. uppl., Bokbox, Malmö 2005, pp. 31–49 (ref: Johansson 2005).

and culture, which were to be challenged by increasing migration flows. The concept 'societal security' was introduced to scholars of international relations and political science, which in its turn triggered the beginning of critical security studies.[39]

Regardless of from which academic discipline these phenomena are approached, it is patent that notions of ethnicity and identity are important to analyses of refugee and migration matters during the 20th century. A strong racist discourse in the Western world, in which immigrants and refugees, and especially Jews, were portrayed as deviant and, indeed, as *threats* to both the domestic 'race' and the social stability of the host countries, curtailed hundreds of thousands of asylum seekers during the 1930s and 1940s, thereby facilitating the Holocaust.[40] And despite substantial changes to international law and practices since then, perceptions of identity and ethnicity have continued to influence pursued policies. Certain groups have been stigmatised, described as accommodating specific characteristics, and subject to discriminatory state practices as a result.[41]

Human societies' strong habits of classifying and categorising people, deeming certain conducts more socially acceptable than others in certain times and places, applying certain character-

39  *Identity, migration and the new security agenda in Europe*, Ole Wæver *et al.* (eds), Pinter, London 1993 (ref: *Identity, migration and the new security agenda* 1993).

40  See, for example, Richard Breitman & Alan M. Kraut, *American Refugee Policy and the European Jewry, 1933–1945*, Indiana University Press, Bloomington 1987; Kvist Geverts 2008; Louise London, *Whitehall and the Jews, 1933–1948: British immigration policy, Jewish refugees and the Holocaust,* Cambridge University Press, Cambridge 2000.

41  *Nationalism and exclusion of migrants: cross-national comparisons*, Gijsberts, Mérove Isabelle Léontine, Hagendoorn, A. & Scheepers, Peer (eds) Ashgate, Aldershot, Hants, England 2003. One group particularly exposed to this has been Europe's Roma population. Certain African minorities have also been targeted, as have, in later years, Europe's Muslim communities. Johansson 2005; *European Union non-discrimination law: comparative perspectives on multidimensional equality law,* Dagmar Chiek & Victoria Chege (eds), Routledge-Cavendish, London 2009; Helen O'Nions, *Minority Rights Protection in International Law: the Roma of Europe,* Ashgate, Aldershot England 2007. On other ways in which collective grounds such as refugees' national and ethnical origin matter for the outcome of their asylum claims, see, for example, Charles B. Keeley, 'The International Refugee Regime(s): The End of The Cold War Matters' in *International Migration Review,* Spring 2001(35):1, Special Issue: UNHCR at 50: Past, Present and Future of Refugee Assistance, pp. 303–314 (ref: Keeley 2001).

istics to various perceived categories of individuals, and, most importantly, differentiating between 'us' and 'them', makes this perspective an important one to consider when analysing matters pertaining to refugees and foreigners.[42] In this study, the concept 'ethnicity' will be utilised in line with previous research on Swedish refugee policies during the 20th century.[43]

The question relevant to this examination is, therefore, if and to what extent ethnic prejudice influenced the treatment of Soviet refugees in Sweden between 1945 and 1954. As will be further demonstrated in chapter two, previous research has emphasised the importance of aspects of ethnicity in Swedish refugee policies during the 20th century, and especially its first half. In addition, it has identified a specific scepticism towards Eastern Europeans. Research on popular culture has also revealed a particular antipathy towards Russians at this time, rooted in at least two centuries of prejudice. This included the interpretation of them as culturally and morally inferior.[44] It is thus likely that such aspects have at least partly determined the policies during the period under scrutiny in this study.


### 1.1.5 Social Control and Morality

With industrialism came the modern state's escalating interest in the 'quality', well-being and behaviour of its population, as well as its enhanced ability to monitor it. Increasingly the state began to assist those of its citizens that were considered to be in most need. Simultaneously, however, it began to try to manipulate aspects of people's lives that hitherto were left to the individual and/or to local representatives of power such as, for example, the clergy.

In Sweden this process commenced during the second half of the 1800s. During the early twentieth century its intensity mounted

---

42  Classifications that indeed also constitute *constructions* by modern society, rather than something given by nature. Hylland Eriksen 2010.

43  See chapter two, part 2.2 and 2.5.

44  Sture Nilsson, *Rysskräcken i Sverige: fördomar och verklighet*, Samspråk, Örebro 1990 (ref: Nilsson 1990); Kristian Gerner 'Svenskars syn på Sovjetryssland: myten om antisovjetismen' in *Östersjö eller Västerhav? Föreställningar om tid och rum i Östersjöområdet*, Klas-Göran Karlsson & Ulf Zander (eds.), Östersjöinstitutet, Karlskrona 2000 (ref: Gerner 2000); Salomon 2007, ch. 4

as the social-liberal political regime formulated more active social policies. Policies such as health insurance reforms, state pensions and maternity benefits were gradually introduced. At the same time, however, demands were placed on its recipients. State assistance was regarded as a way to persuade the individual to change his or her behaviour. Social insurances were to promote the individual's own responsibility for her own well-being and persuade her to live an 'orderly' life.[45] The financial assistance provided by the state pension system of 1935, for example, excluded alcoholics, 'vagrants' and individuals who had led an 'offensive' life.[46] Similarly, laws were initiated which increased the authorities' right to punish behaviours interpreted as deviant and/or asocial. A law instituted in 1885 granted the authorities the possibility to detain 'vagrants' and 'wanderers' and subject them to forced labour.[47] This legislation was to become assiduously applied not only to individuals who could not or did not want to support themselves through work, however, but also to prostitutes.[48]

The sort of life the authorities endeavoured to make its citizens pursue was centred on ideas of *'skötsamhet'* – a Swedish word meaning roughly 'steadiness' or 'conscientiousness'. Several researchers have illuminated how this ideal characterised both the working and middle classes (although in slightly different ways) during the twentieth century.[49] It has been summarised by historian Mattias

45  Anders Berge, *Socialpolitik och ansvarsmoral*, Bertil Ohlin-institutet, Stockholm 1995; Klas Åmark, *Hundra år av välfärdspolitik*, Boréa, Umeå 2005, ch. 2–3 (ref: Åmark 2005); Mikael Sjögren, *Fattigvård och folkuppfostran: liberal fattigvårdspolitik 1903–1918*, Carlsson, Stockholm 1997; Yvonne Hirdman, *Att lägga livet tillrätta: studier i svensk folkhemspolitik,* 2 ed., Carlsson, Stockholm 2000; *Familjeangelägenheter: modern historisk forskning om välfärdsstat, genus och politik,* Helena Bergman & Peter Johansson (eds), B. Östlings bokförlag Symposion, Eslöv 2002; Mattias Tydén, *Från politik till praktik: de svenska steriliseringslagarna 1935–1975,* 2 rev. ed., Almqvist & Wiksell International, Stockholm, 2002, ch. 2 (ref: Tydén 2002); Jenny Björkman, *Vård för samhällets bästa: debatten om tvångsvård i svensk lagstiftning 1850–1970,* Carlsson, Stockholm 2001, ch. 1 (ref: Björkman 2001).

46  Björkman 2001, p. 236.

47  SFS 1885:23, 1885 års lag om lösdrivares behandling; Hans Wallentin, *Lösdriveri och industrialism: om lösdriverifrågan i Sverige 1885–1940*, Högskolan i Östersund, Östersund 1989 (ref: Wallentin 1989).

48  Tomas Söderblom, *Horan och batongen: prostitution och repression i folkhemmet*, Gidlund, Stockholm 1992 (ref: Söderblom 1992).

49  See, for example, Ronny Ambjörnsson, *Den skötsamme arbetaren: idéer och ideal*

Tydén as including norms regarding the constitution of the family (including the man as the breadwinner and the woman as a good-natured carer of the household with an 'appropriate' number of children), orderliness, tidiness, sobriety, hygiene, temperance and expressions of sexuality within the marriage only.[50] The accepted behaviour for women was notably stricter than that for men, focusing predominantly on sexual morals.[51] The ideal of *skötsamhet* was thus intimately linked to aspects of *morality*.

From 1945 onwards, more far-stretching social policy initiatives were introduced as the welfare state was established by the social democratic government. Ideas of universality and common solidarity gradually replaced previous ideas on means-tested, restrictive benefits targeted at only the most unfortunate members of the society. The introduction of the child allowance in 1948, accessible to all families regardless of financial status, constitutes one such example. Obligatory health insurance constitutes another.[52]

Although having changed in character, social policies of the 1940s and 1950s were still characterised by the elements of social control which had been developed during previous decades. Historian Johan Edman has demonstrated, for example, how the compulsory psychiatric treatment of alcoholics particularly during the 1940s and 1950s was motivated by strong moral directives and ideas. Although evidence proved the method to be unsuccessful from a medical point of view (since few alcoholics were actually cured within these detainment clinics), practices continued. Their main aim was not to break the addiction, argues Edman, but to protect society from the deleterious influence of these individuals'

*i ett norrländskt sågverkssamhälle 1880–1930*, 4 ed, Carlsson, Stockholm 2001 (ref: Ambjörnsson 2001); Jonas Frykman & Orvar Löfgren, *Den kultiverade människan*, Liber Läromedel, Lund 1979; Jonas Frykman & Orvar Löfgren, 'På väg – bilder av kultur och klass' in *Modärna tider: vision och vardag i folkhemmet*, Jonas Frykman (ed), Liber Förlag, Malmö 1985, pp. 20–139.

50  Tydén 2002, p. 125.

51  Johan Edman, *Torken: tvångsvården av alkoholmissbrukare i Sverige 1940–1981*, Almqvist & Wiksell International, Stockholm 2004, ch. 3 (ref: Edman 2004); Hirdman 1990; Söderblom 1992.

52  Jobseeker's allowances remained organised according to corporative principles, however, and state pensions became income-related. Åmark 2005, ch. 4. See also Tydén 2002, ch. 2; and Bo Rothstein, *Vad bör staten göra?: om välfärdsstatens moraliska och politiska logik*, 3 ed., SNS förlag, Stockholm 2010 (ref: Rothstein 2010).

inappropriate behaviour; to deter others from conducting themselves in the same way; and to seek to compel the population to
become diligent, orderly and conscientious. It was regarded as
more important to punish the improper and rowdy behaviour that
these individuals pursued, than to actually try to improve their
health.[53]

The same logic was applied within institutions for the compulsory psychiatric treatment of individuals perceived to be mentally
deranged. Historian Jenny Björkman demonstrates how the main
motivation for the detainment of the patients was to protect society at large from their deviant behaviour. '*Skötsamhet*' was often
cited as grounds for discharge from such institutions.[54]

Another example is constituted by the state's treatment of
homosexuals. Homosexual activities between adults were decrimi-
nalised from 1944 onwards. Nevertheless, the early period of the
welfare state was characterised by escalating efforts to control and
medically treat what was then understood as a disease leading to
morally inferior behaviour.[55]

The component of this social control system that has been most
heavily criticised subsequently is, however, the practice between
1935 and 1975 of forced sterilisations of individuals perceived to
be mentally deranged. Historian Tydén has demonstrated that, in
addition to the so-called mentally retarded, these practices extended to the forceful treatment of other individuals – mostly women –
who were regarded as leading asocial or improper lives. Sometimes
it was presented as a condition of, for example, maternity benefits
or discharge from care institutions.[56]

These interventionist ideas and practices have critically been
called examples of 'social engineering'. Some have argued that they
were integral to the ethos of the Swedish welfare state.[57] Others

53  Edman 2004, ch. 2–4.

54  Björkman 2001.

55  Jens Rydström, 'Piska och morot. HBT mellan stat och folkrörelse' in *Staten som
    vän eller fiende?: individ och samhälle i svenskt 1900-tal.*, Marika Hedin *et al.* (eds),
    Institutet för framtidsstudier, Stockholm 2007, pp. 157–92; *Criminally queer:
    homosexuality and criminal law in Scandinavia 1842–1999*, Jens Rydström & Kati
    Mustola (eds), Aksant, Amsterdam 2007.

56  Tydén 2002; Maija Runcis, *Steriliseringar i folkhemmet*, Ordfront, Stockholm
    1998 (ref: Runcis 2008).

57  See, for example, Hirdman 2000; Runcis 1998.

have claimed that they predominantly characterised the thinking of social policy during the 1930s, but that the practices of the welfare state that eventually were implemented from 1945 onwards had removed such ideas from the political agenda and were chiefly based on a good-natured ideology of collective responsibility.[58]

Regardless of how the phenomenon is explained and interpreted, however, it is clear, as Tydén has argued, that the concept of *'skötsamhet'* is central to an understanding of Swedish social policies during the 1900s.[59] Research also clearly demonstrates that interventionist practices continued during the early phases of the welfare state period. Apart from increasing living standards and offering social security to its citizens, the state also continued to try to monitor behaviour. This aspect thus constituted an important part of the relationship between the state and the individual during this period.[60]

For this thesis, which deals with the relationship between the state and the *foreign* individual (that is the non-citizen refugee), this complexity thus constitutes another interesting perspective. Although the study is not centred on the various welfare benefits that were offered to refugees, but focuses exclusively on refugees' rights to reside in Sweden and the conditions of their residence permits, the essence of the welfare state's interest in its citizens' way of life suggests that similar strictures on personal behaviour and morals might have been placed on refugees. They might even have been presented as conditions for asylum.[61]

The state practices described above are referred to as aspects of 'social control' in this study. This concept is admittedly diffuse and features extensively within such academic disciplines as criminology, psychology and sociology. It can refer both to surveillance

---

58  Rothstein 2010.

59  Tydén 2002, p. 125.

60  For a further discussion on the relationship between the state and the individual, see Urban Lundberg & Mattias Tydén, 'Stat och individ i svensk välfärdspolitik' in *Staten som vän eller fiende? Individ och samhälle i svenskt 1900-tal,* Marika Hedin *et al.* (eds), Institutet för framtidsstudier, Stockholm 2007, pp. 17–39.

61  For a thorough discussion of the welfare state's treatment of foreigners in terms of social rights and benefits, see Mikael Byström, *Utmaningen: den svenska välfärdsstatens möte med flyktingar i andra världskrigets tid,* Nordic Academic Press, Lund 2012 (ref: Byström 2012).

measures pursued by the state of its citizens in order to influence their behaviour, and to the monitoring of individuals within social groups and personal relationships.[62] In this thesis, the term is used with reference to the former. Stanley Cohen's classic definition from 1985 will guide the understanding further. He understands social control as:

> those organized responses to crime, delinquency and allied forms of deviant and/or socially problematic behaviour which are actually conceived of as such, whether in the reactive sense (after the putative act has taken place or the actor been identified) or the proactive sense (to prevent the act). These responses may be sponsored directly by the state or by more autonomous professional agents in, say, social work and psychiatry. Their goals might be specific as individual punishment and treatment or diffuse as 'crime prevention', 'public safety' and 'community mental health.[63]

Theoretically, these issues could potentially also be included in a *societal security* perspective. It is possible to imagine situations in which the authorities have perceived the traits of certain individuals (citizens or non-citizens) as *threats*, prompting state representatives to take action. An illustration of this was the above-mentioned detainment of alcoholics and the mentally deranged with the aim of protecting society from their bad influence. They were portrayed as *dangerous*; as a threat that needed to be neutralised by way of removal from society.[64] A similar logic could of course also have been applied to foreigners such as refugees. This inevitably includes individuals whose criminal activities challenged law and order and thus presented a threat to societal stability.

62  *Social kontroll: övervakning, disciplinering och självreglering*, Bengt Larsson & Oskar Engdahl (eds), Liber, Malmö 2011 (ref: *Social kontroll*).
63  Stanley Cohen, *Visions of social control: crime, punishment and classification*, Polity press, Cambridge 1985, p. 3.
64  Björkman 2001; Edman 2004.

### 1.1.6 International Juridical Developments

The sixth contemporary development that is likely to have influenced Swedish refugee management is the development of human rights – and refugee rights in particular – that took place during this period under the stewardship of the United Nations, of which Sweden was a member from November 1946 onwards. In refugee studies, the early Cold War period is considered to mark the foundation of the international refugee regime. This regime has been described as

> the collection of conventions, treaties, intergovernmental and non-governmental agencies, precedent, and funding which governments have adopted and support to protect and assist those displaced from their country by persecution, or displaced by war in some regions of the world where agreements or practice have extended protection to persons displaced by the general devastation of war, even if they are not specifically targeted for persecution.[65]

The cornerstones of this regime are the above-mentioned 1951 Refugee Convention, its additional 1967 Protocol, and the primary agency the *United Nations High Commissioner for Refugees* (UNHCR), established in December 1950. Apart from endeavouring to assist refugees materially and administratively, the regime defines refugees legally and recognises them as holders of *rights* against states of which they are not citizens. Although often criticised for not achieving enough, more significant efforts have been made in order to reach collective solutions to refugee crises during its existence than ever before.

In contrast to previous refugee legislation, the 1951 Refugee Convention is both a status and rights-based instrument.[66] It defines a refugee as someone who 'owing to well-founded fear of being persecuted for reasons of race, religion, nationality, membership of a particular social group or political opinion, is outside the country of his nationality and is unable or, owing to such fear, is

---

65  Keeley 2001. Citation from p. 303.

66  James C. Hathaway, *The rights of refugees under international law*, Cambridge University Press, Cambridge 2005, pp. 83–91 (ref: Hathaway 2005).

unwilling to avail himself of the protection of that country'.[67] And it prohibits the signatory states from expelling such refugees to territories 'where his life or freedom would be threatened', unless there are 'reasonable grounds for regarding [the refugee] as a danger to the security of the country in which he is'. This is called *the principle of non-refoulement.* [68] It also specifically articulates that states must 'apply the provisions of this Convention without discrimination as to race, religion or country of origin',[69] and that refugees must not be penalised for breaking immigration laws when entering the host country.[70] Furthermore, it defines several juridical and socioeconomic rights. Thus, the 1951 Refugee Convention established, in a previously unprecedented way, that states have responsibilities towards fleeing and persecuted individuals holding other citizenships.[71]

Seen in a historical perspective, this was indeed ground-breaking. Only a few years earlier, no such wide-ranging and compelling principles had existed within international law. The few exceptions that had been codified in law were mostly a response to the First World War's refugee crisis and had either been non-applicable or widely contravened as Europe faced the unprecedented refugee chaos of the Second World War. As a result, millions of refugees had had to find their own way back to what was possibly left of their homes, or to resettlement. They were obliged to move unassisted through a bomb-wrecked Europe during the last year of the war as the Allied powers fought on two fronts to force the prostrate German army to retreat to its original borders. To make matters worse, new groups of refugees were also created during this most destructive phase of the war as the Red Army's liberation of Eastern Europe was combined with swathes of looting, rape, incineration and material annihilation. Thus, as the war came to an end in May 1945, some 15–20 million refugees of all European

---

67   *1951 Convention relating to the Status of Refugees*, Article 1. Available at: http:// www.unhcr.org/3b66c2aA 10.html (accessed 1 December 2013).

68   *1951 Convention relating to the Status of Refugees*, Article 33. (Individuals who had committed war crimes, crimes against humanity or other, serious non-political crimes were also exempt from the regulations of the Convention, according to Article 1 F)

69   *1951 Convention relating to the Status of Refugees*, Article 3.

70   *1951 Convention relating to the Status of Refugees*, Article 31.

71   Hathaway 2005, pp. 83–91.

nationalities were still scattered across the continent, posing an acute problem for the Allied powers. Additionally, as the brutal truth of the Nazi extermination programmes were fully revealed, the Western world realised that its reluctance to assist the fleeing Jewish population had facilitated the genocide, leaving those former bystanders horrified.[72]

In light of this, many have argued that the developments of human rights that followed were a direct result of the international community's determination to never allow such atrocities and human suffering to reoccur. The war-time experiences had indeed brought about a substantial modification in general political thinking. The deep-rooted principle in international relations of non-intervention in other state's internal affairs, including the notion that a single state's treatment of its own citizens was no business of the international community, had proven disastrous. Thus, as the new foundation of an international society was constructed in the aftermath of the war, the ideas of collective responsibility and the existence of universal human rights played a more central role. This was expressed in the establishment of the United Nations in 1945, and particularly in the Declaration of Human Rights in 1948. In terms of refugees, these ideas were institutionalised within the 1951 Refugee Convention.[73]

### 1.1.6.1 Cold War Influences

Humanitarian concerns, it has been argued, were not the only purported motivation for the development of the international refugee regime. Several researchers have argued that it was in fact built on the foundations of the Cold War, rather than on purely altruistic grounds. They claim that the conflict, which had a profound impact on countless aspects of social, political and economic life the world over, determined international refugee policies too, and that the 1951 Refugee Convention became a political and

---

72   Michael Robert Marrus, *The unwanted: European refugees from the first world war through the cold war*, 2 ed., Temple University Press, Philadelphia 2002, pp. 296–345 (ref: Marrus 2002).

73   The Convention is grounded in Article 14 of the *1948 Declaration of human rights* which recognizes individuals' right to seek asylum from persecution in other countries. UNHCR, http://www.unhcr.org/3b66c2aA 10.html (Accessed 4 December 2013).

ideological tool used by the West against the communist bloc.[74]

There are several reasons for this interpretation. One regards the way in which the international refugee regime came into existence. During the final years of the Second World War the Allied Powers had attempted to cooperate in matters pertaining to refugees. The Soviet Union was, for example, involved in the work of the *United Nations Relief and Rehabilitation Administration* (UNRRA, 1943–47) which became the first large scale international organisation to provide tangible material help and protection to refugees.[75] The collaboration was, however, not only beneficial for Europe's refugees. The Western powers' wish to maintain the comradely relations with the Soviet Union that the common efforts against Nazi Germany had instigated them to agree to several Soviet aspirations regarding Eastern European refugees. It also made them consent to the conditions of the Yalta agreement in February 1945, which included the Soviet Union's demand for influence over Eastern Europe as well as its claims over those Soviet citizens outside its borders. During the months following the armistice, therefore, Europe witnessed the largest mass repatriations in history as around five million Soviet refugees were returned to Soviet territory. Around one million of them were soldiers who had fought among the German armed forces. Individuals who had not been Soviet citizens before 1939 were, however, excluded.[76]

The European refugee crisis was far from solved by these mass repatriations. When UNRRA's mandate was about to expire in 1947, there were still at least one and a half million refugees, mostly Eastern Europeans, residing in European camps. Additionally, new

74  See, for example, Loescher & Scanlan 1986; Keeley 2001; Kim Salomon, *Refugees in the Cold War: toward a new international refugee regime in the early postwar era,* Lund University Press, Lund 1991 (ref: Salomon 1991).

75  UNRRA helped around 8 million fleeing individuals to find refuge, including food and shelter. It did not, however, engage in any resettlement issues, partly due to the Soviet Union's resistance towards such measures. Cecilia Ruthström-Ruin, *Beyond Europe: the globalization of refugee aid,* Lund University Press, Lund 1993, ch. 1 (ref: Ruthström-Ruin 1993); Salomon 1991, pp. 17–42.

76  Nicholas Bethell, *The last secret: forcible repatriation to Russia 1944–7,* Deutsch, London 1974 (ref: Bethell 1974); Nikolai Tolstoy, *Victims of Yalta,* Hodder and Stoughton, London 1977 (ref: Tolstoy 1977); Anders Berge, *Flyktingpolitik i stormakts skugga: Sverige och de sovjetryska flyktingarna under andra världskriget,* Centre for Multiethnic Research, Uppsala University, Uppsala 1992 (ref: Berge 1992).

refugees were arriving from the East.[77] It was obvious that there was a continuing need for a fresh and more efficient refugee administration. Therefore, the *International Refugee Organisation* (IRO, 1947–51) was created within the newly established United Nations' framework, with a more distinct mandate to help refugees. By then, however, the hopes for future cooperation and friendly relations between the Allies that had characterised the final stage of the war and immediate months after the armistice had evaporated with the emerging political and ideological conflict of the Cold War. The Truman Doctrine speech in 1947, the Berlin blockade and the communist overthrow of Czechoslovakia in 1948 all put an end to any hope of mutual understanding between East and West and intensified the growing tensions between the blocs. As a consequence the Soviet Union and its satellite states withdrew from the cooperation already during the planning stages of the new refugee organisation. The Soviet leadership strongly opposed the organisation's plans to resettle refugees, rather than just provide temporary shelter and organise repatriations. As a result, none of the final eighteen member states of the IRO were from the Eastern bloc. Once they had withdrawn from the initial preparation process, the administration and operationalisation of the new refugee organisation became an easier task for the Western countries to accomplish.[78]

After a couple of years of the IRO's operation, which had resettled more than one million refugees (primarily to the United States, Australia, Israel and Canada), it became obvious that the needs of refugees were going to exceed even this organisation's provisional mandate. In addition to the remaining war refugees within the European camps (mainly the elderly and sick who had been rejected by the West as unlikely assets to its national economies) new refugees kept arriving from the communist states of Eastern Europe.[79] Therefore, in addition to preparing a fresh refugee convention, plans for a new, permanent organisation were discussed within the UN already in 1949–50. Again, the debates

77  The figure 1,5 million refers to the number of individuals that fell under IRO's mandate in 1947. Ruthström-Ruin 1993, p. 17. See also Mark Wyman, *DPs: Europe's displaced persons, 1945–1951*, Cornell University Press, Ithaka 1998 (ref: Wyman 1998).
78  Salomon 1991, pp. 13–42.
79  Wyman 1998.

were marred by entrenched antagonisms between the two blocs. This was exacerbated by the West's evident intentions of providing protection not only to the remaining war refugees, but also to the new arrivals from the Eastern bloc. The Soviet Union and its satellite states continued to contest all kinds of international cooperation that jeopardised their ultimate goal of repatriation. The fact that the Soviet bloc constituted a minority within the UN General Assembly meant that it could not influence the outcome of the discussions. And after five years of increasing tensions, the Western bloc no longer attempted to try to include it in refugee relief activities – particularly not since this collection of states now constituted the refugee producing countries in Europe. As a result, the Soviet Union had little authority over the creation of the UNHCR in December 1950. Thus, perhaps somewhat counterintuitively, the termination of cooperation between East and West in refugee matters meant that Eastern European refugees were protected to a significantly higher degree once they had reached Western territory. Granting such individuals asylum now constituted a chance for the West to make a political and ideological statement in the on-going conflict.[80]

Another argument pointing towards the Cold War's influence on the international (by now, Western) refugee regime was the way in which it came to include and exclude certain kinds of refugees. In terms of eligibility and identification, the foundation of the IRO and the UNHCR constituted an important step forwards for refugee rights. As Cecilia Ruthström-Ruin has pointed out, the refugee definition that was elaborated during the early Cold War required individual assessment of refugees' personal history and background, focusing on the causes of flight. As such, it constituted a break from the collective definitions of previous legislation and the 'ad hoc eligibility criteria based on national origin' that had been customary within the international community up to that point.[81] Drawing on the stipulations of the IRO, the UNHCR asserted that its 'competence' would extend to any person who 'as a result of events occurring before 1 January 1951 and owing to well-founded fear of being persecuted for reasons of race, religion, nationality,

---

80    Ruthström-Ruin 1993, pp. 18–22; Salomon 1991, pp. 13–42.
81    Ruthström-Ruin 1993, pp. 16–17, citation from p. 17.

or political opinion' was unwilling or unable to return to his home country.[82] This definition would be reiterated and further developed in the 1951 Refugee Convention.

As such, however, it included some refugees at the expense of others. It made Eastern Europeans, including Russians, eligible for asylum in Western countries – just a few years after the mass repatriation. Non-Europeans, on the other hand, were effectively excluded through the temporal restriction. This omitted millions of individuals fleeing around the world at that time such as, for example, the approximately fourteen million people on the move in India and Pakistan. Attempts by these and other countries of the Developing World to be included in the UN's refugee definitions were not adhered to within the General Assembly. Additionally, the initial definition focused on individuals escaping political oppression, rather than, for example, war, internal conflicts and natural disasters. Consequently, the majority of the Developing World's refugees were disqualified. It would take another one-and-a-half decades before the international community, as it was represented within the UN, would start to pay attention to the plight of refugees in places other than Europe.[83] In 1967, an additional protocol removed the temporal restriction of the 1951 Refugee Convention, making it universally applicable.[84] Up to that point, however, the international refugee regime's definition of a refugee had been more or less identical with an individual fleeing from the communist regimes of Eastern Europe.

A third reason to suspect a stronger influence from the Cold War conflict on the developments of the international refugee regime than official narratives often maintain, is the various ways in which that regime was employed by the political administrations

---

82  It also recognised any person who had been acknowledged as a refugee under previous international conventions. *Statute of the Office of the United Nations High Commissioner for Refugees*, 14 December 1950, A/RES/428(V), UN General Assembly. Available at: http://www.unhcr.org/refworld/docid/3ae6b3628. html (accessed 16 September 2011). See also Ruthström-Ruin 1993, pp. 18–22; and Salomon 1991, pp. 40–42.

83  The crisis in Algeria constituted one of the first non-European countries with which the UNHCR engaged. Ruthström-Ruin, 1993, pp. 59–66.

84  In December 2010, 147 states had signed one or two of these documents. UNHCR, http://www.unhcr.org/3b66c2aA 10.html (accessed 4 December 2013).

of the West during this period. The United States' usage of East European refugees as a political weapon in the Cold War conflict was mentioned previously. This practice meant that refugees from the communist world were granted protection to a greater extent than refugees from right-wing dictatorships, even after the removal of the temporal restriction in 1967.[85] It also included active usage of Eastern European refugees as propaganda tools in the on-going conflict. Through the 1951 Refugee Convention, the Western powers were targeting citizens of the communist regimes as potential holders of rights in their own states. And as Eastern European refugees sought and were granted asylum in the West, the Soviet Union seceded valuable prestige to its ideological rival.[86]

Throughout the rest of the Cold War, this became an easily recognizable pattern. For this reason, Charles B. Keeley has described the international refugee regime as being split into two parallel systems. One regime concerned 'normal' refugees, mostly originating from the Developing World. Its aim was to try to stabilise the situation that had caused the uprooting and find permanent solutions for the refugees, preferably through temporary protection and, wherever possible, repatriation. Resettlement was not an option. The alternative regime concerned refugees from the communist bloc. It, in Keeley's opinion, served other purposes. Here, foreign policy rather than international law determined who was to be regarded as a refugee. The main aim in this system was to *de*stabilise and embarrass the communist regime from which the refugees had fled. Thus, temporary protection was never a matter of consideration. Refugees from communist countries were quickly resettled in the West, and were used as political propaganda – directed both at the domestic political arena and at the communist bloc.[87]

Therefore, scholars studying these aspects of the international refugee regime tend to suggest that the political value of the Eastern European refugees was a determining factor in its construction. They interpret the regime as being built on the foun-

---

85   Loescher & Scanlan 1986; Bon Tempo 2009.

86   Ruthström-Ruin 1993, pp. 18–22; Salomon 1991.

87   Keeley 2001. See also Guy S. Goodwin, 'The Politics of Refugee Protection' in *Refugee Survey Quarterly,* 2008 (27):1, pp. 8–23; James C Hathaway, 'A Reconsideration of the Underlying Premise of Refugee Law', in *Harvard International Law Journal*, 1990(31):1, pp. 29–183.

dation of the Cold War rather than on a sense of moral obligation after the conflict of 1939–45.[88]

Whatever the most imperative motives for the construction of the refugee regime were, however, it is obvious that the Cold War represents a period in international history when refugees' rights were significantly strengthened, and that the conflict in itself seems to have influenced the development of these rights. As a result, some refugees were unmistakably valued more than others, and treated accordingly. Another insight is the fact that foreign policy and self-interest played a definite part in the process. As such, these aspects are connected to the external security concerns that were outlined in part 1.1.1.

### 1.1.6.2 Possible Outcomes for Swedish Refugee Policies?

Although Sweden as a 'neutral' part in the Cold War conflict could not make political use of Eastern European refugees in the same way as NATO countries, as an active UN member it undoubtedly constituted a component in the development of refugee rights. The general trajectory of Swedish refugee policies during these years also suggest that it did indeed have influence. Apart from being among the first to sign the 1951 Refugee Convention, it was among the earliest to ratify and incorporate it into national legislation. In 1955 it was acknowledging political refugee status to practically all Eastern Europeans fleeing from communist countries, as is attested by previous research.[89] It was now also proudly pronouncing itself as a country which pursued generous refugee policies – a reputation it still seeks to maintain today.[90]

Before this first post-war decade, however, Sweden had taken a far from active or decisive role in the establishment of the international refugee regime. In fact, in terms of legislation, Sweden was among the *last* Western European countries to ever sign an inter-

88   Salomon 1991.
89   Göran Melander, *Flyktingar och asyl*, Norstedt, Stockholm 1972 (ref: Melander 1972a); Göran Melander, *Asyl: svensk praxis i ärenden om politiskt flyktingskap: undersökning utförd på uppdrag av utlänningsutredningen*, Allmänna förlaget, Stockholm, 1972 (ref: Melander 1972b); Göran Melander, *Politiskt flyktingskap enligt utlänningslagen* 1969 (unpublished report) (ref: Melander 1969).
90   Första Kammarens Protokoll, nr 26, onsdagen den 9 november 1949; Interview with Anders Danielsson, general director of the Migration Board, in *Dagens Nyheter*, 10 May 2012.

national document relating to the rights of refugees. Sweden was a signatory to neither the *1933 Convention relating to the International Status of Refugees* nor the *1938 Convention concerning the Status of Refugees coming from Germany.* It was not a member of UNRRA or IRO, or their predecessor organisation *Intergovernmental Committee of Refugees* (IGCR, 1938–47). Whilst acknowledging the Nansen Passport during the First World War, it did not undertake to grant asylum to its holders. Thus, when it comes to the refugee question, Sweden demonstrated a substantial unwillingness to tie itself to restrictive laws or codified regulations prior to 1951.[91]

The development of the international (Western) refugee regime during the first Cold War decade thus raises questions regarding Swedish refugee policies during these years. To what extent, and in what way, were they influential? And how did non-aligned Sweden handle the Westernised Cold War framing of international refugee policies during these years?

## 1.2 Delimitations

The most imperative reasons for opting to study Sweden during the first Cold War decade were outlined in the introduction. A longer period could of course have been chosen in order to enable a continued analysis of possible developments as the Cold War progressed. However, a deliberate choice has been made to study separate cases and decisions *in depth* instead. Thus, the study concentrates on a ten-year period – a decade that appears to have been the most transformative during the 20th century when it comes

---

91    *Convention relating to the status of refugees*, League of Nations, 28 October 1933, available at: http://www.refworld.org/docid/3dd8cF 374.html (accessed 4 December 2013); *Convention concerning the Status of Refugees Coming From Germany*, League of Nations, 10 February 1938, available at: http://www. refworld.org/docid/3dd8d12a4.html; *Agreement for United Nations Relief and Rehabilitation Administration*, UNRRA, 9 November 1943, available at: http:// www.ibiblio.org/pha/policy/1943/431109a.html (accessed 2 December 2013); *Constitution of the International Refugee Organisation*, United Nations, 15 December 1946, available at: http://www.refworld.org/docid/3ae6b37810.html. See also Åmark 2011, p. 469; Tommie Sjöberg, *The powers and the persecuted: the refugee problem and the Intergovernmental Committee on Refugees (IGCR), 1938–1947*, Studentlitteratur, Lund 1991, ch. 1; Hathaway 2005; Ruthström-Ruin 1993.

to Swedish refugee policies. The timeframe ends in 1954, the year when Sweden's new and significantly more refugee-friendly Aliens Act was established.

As mentioned, the focus here is the Swedish state's treatment of Soviet refugees. A study of this nature could also have been pursued regarding *all* Eastern European refugees entering Sweden at this time. Apart from Soviet citizens, there were refugees from, for example, Poland, Hungary, Czechoslovakia, Romania and East Germany/GDR. There are two principal reasons, however, for an exclusive study of Soviet refugees and their treatment. Firstly, if concerns for security influenced Sweden's treatment of refugees during the Cold War, this is likely to be most evident in the case of refugees from the Soviet Union. The superpower was, evidently, the actor on the international scene which posed the greatest threat to Swedish territorial security during the research period. Secondly, the focus on Soviet refugees facilitates a detailed study of ethnicity since the Swedish authorities identified three distinct categories within this group, namely Balts, Ingrians and Russians. In addition, because their social status (in terms of education as well as financial and social capital) often varied, it becomes possible to address socio-economic aspects too.

The Swedish authorities' categories or 'classifications' of Soviet refugees are as follows:

1) '*Balts*'.  In this group were included anyone originating from Estonia, Latvia and Lithuania (as defined by their pre-war borders). Inclusion in this category did not pay attention to whether they had left their home country and/or arrived before or after the Soviet annexation. Nor did it pay heed to the date of the Swedish recognition of this occupation (which took place already in 1940). Around 30,000 Balts fled to Sweden during the autumn of 1944 when the Soviet Union reoccupied their countries. During the following years, at least 2,000 more arrived from various destinations.

2) '*Ingrians*'. This group were Finnish-speaking Lutherans. They came from Ingria, an area around St Petersburg to which their ancestors had moved when this district belonged to Great Power Sweden in the 17th Century. When Sweden

ceded the area to Russia in 1721, many Ingrians stayed in their new home territory, even though this meant being subjected to attempted russification. In the Soviet period such harassments increased: many Ingrians had their land confiscated, were treated as political opponents and/or were deported to Siberia. In 1941, following the German occupation, they were collectively transported to Finland. Many then assisted the Finns in the war effort, including joining the Finnish army in their fight against the Soviet Union. In the 1944 armistice agreement with Finland, however, the Soviet Union demanded their return. Many dreaded this, knowing that they would be severely punished as traitors. As a result, around 5,000 fled to Sweden throughout the study period.[92]

3) *'Soviet Russians'*. This category, broadly speaking, incorporated Russian speaking individuals from any area under direct post-1945 Soviet control (excluding the 'satellite states') that were not included in either of the first two categories. Separate ethnic categories within this group, such as, for example, Georgians, were rarely recognised or acknowledged.[93] Only a few hundred of the around 3,000 Russians (mainly soldiers) that fled to Sweden during the war remained in the country after the armistice. During the research period, fewer than 1,000 new Russians arrived.

In keeping with the contemporaneous practices of the Swedish authorities, these categories will be studied separately and any apparent differences in treatment will be scrutinised.[94]

The third reason for not including more categories of refugees

---

92   Eric De Geer, *Ingermanland, vad är det och vilka är ingermanländarna?* Finsk-ugriska seminariet, Göteborgs universitet, Göteborg 2000; Uno Hammarström, *Ingermanländarna som flydde till Sverige: en minnesberättelse*, Finsk-ingermanländarnas centralförbund, Borås 1984 (ref: Hammarström 1984).

93   However, on occasion the label 'Carpatho-Ukrainian' would be used for somebody from that particular area.

94   It should be noted that Ingrians were sometimes accounted for as a separate group, and occasionally referred to as Russians. Balts, however, were generally categorised separately.

relates to the nature of the source material and the methodological approach. As will become apparent in the following section, the empirical analysis pursued in this thesis includes the detailed examination of 260 individuals' personal files within the archive of the National Alien Commission (*Statens utlänningskommission*). Studying these in depth places limitations on the quantity of individuals that can be feasibly included. This reinforces the decision to focus on the category most apposite for the chosen research questions – the Soviet citizens.


## 1.3 Methodological Issues

The main part of the empirical study focuses on the Swedish authorities' assessment of Soviet citizens' asylum and residence permit applications, and the practices pursued regarding various kinds of what I have chosen to call 'removal decisions'. As such, the study can be described as a *practice analysis*. I have studied the outcome of asylum applications, residence permits and removal decisions based on the applicants' personal files within the National Alien Commission's archive (described below). This information has been used in an effort to establish the grounds on which decisions were reached. I have attempted to examine explicit causes (those specifically mentioned by the responsible authorities) and those that can be inferred (reasons that, whilst not overtly stated, can be strongly suspected to have been decisive). Applicants' personal circumstances, as revealed in their personal files and which constituted the basis for the authorities' decisions, have been studied in detail and analysed in relation to the conclusions reached. These include issues such as social status (education, financial position, work experience and so forth), ethnicity, personal background, arrival date, and any possible so-called 'uncomplimentary information' accrued by the authorities in relation to the individual in question. Removal decisions have been studied in extra detail, in order to try to identify the kinds of circumstances that led to a given outcome, and how the concept 'political refugee' was interpreted and implemented. Special attention has also been given to the variations of residence permits in terms of lengths and geographical restrictions, focusing on the sorts of circumstances that led to certain kinds of permits and conditions. Government instructions, correspondence between responsible authorities and other types of material revelatory of the law-interpretative principles perceived and pursued by the authorities during these years have also been examined.

The results have then been compared and discussed in relation to the six possible influential factors. This poses some specific challenges. How does one 'know' that a decision was determined by one factor or another, or any at all? In some cases the causes might appear obvious. The authorities might highlight a specific motivating cause, such as insufficient financial support or a suspicion of espionage as the reason for a shortened residence permit, a geographical restriction or a deportation decision. In other cases, the causes might be more opaque. Nevertheless, comparison with other decisions of a similar kind, and the circumstances surrounding them, might provide a closer understanding, provided that there were identifiable patterns of behaviour in the authorities' decision-making.

In order to reveal possible influential aspects relating to *ethnicity* I have searched for occasions when the authorities' decision regarding an individual seem to have been determined by their understanding of his or her inclusion in a certain category of people with particular culturally definable characteristics. In other words, ethnic prejudice is considered to be in evidence when perceptions of a certain group's features, behaviours or way of thinking is projected onto an individual and allowed to determine the outcome. Sometimes, this might be apparent only when comparing the results of a whole category with that of another.

When determining whether or not *economic aspects* have influenced the outcomes, a natural starting point is to look at some constituent factors of the individuals' social status and employment, as well as any direct comments by the authorities regarding a refugee's financial position and/or usefulness on the Swedish labour market. If such considerations influenced the outcomes, then economic concerns are interpreted as determinant.

Aspects of *social control and morality* are best found within various descriptions of an individual within their personal files. If a certain kind of behaviour (such as, for example, homosexuality, mental health problems, alcoholism, prostitution, a 'wandering' lifestyle, etc) have led to a negative outcome regarding an asylum or residence permit application, then aspects of social control and/or morality are deemed to have influenced the authorities' treatment of the individual in question.

When it comes to *security* influences, the discussion is inspired by constructivist thinking. According to this understanding, generally speaking, security is what the main state actors interpret as such at a specific time and place.[95] This entails that if the state representatives have perceived Soviet refugees as *threats* against the state and/or the society in some way or another, and based their decisions regarding these individuals upon that perception, then security concerns are understood as having influenced the pursued policies. In some cases, relating to external and internal security threats in particular, the analysis can be rather straightforward. The consequences for the residence permit of a suspected spy or communist undoubtedly fall within these categories. In other cases, it might be more difficult to determine. With a constructivist understanding, all of the perspectives stated above (ethnicity, economics and social control) might be included in the concept provided that the main state actors have perceived the individual as a potential threat to the state and/or society, and reached their decision accordingly. A prostitute might be interpreted in terms of a threat to societal security (as a potential carrier of venereal disease and/or challenger of general sexual morality, for example). An alcoholic could be regarded as being similarly disruptive, as previously mentioned. Individuals perceived as non-contributors to the national economy could also be interpreted as possible threats (to 'economic security', supposedly), as could individuals understood as belonging to an ethnic group too 'deviant' from Swedish culture and customs. Allowing several individuals of that group to reside

---

95  For a more thorough discussion on constructivism within international relations and security studies, see Alexander Wendt, *Social theory of international politics,* Cambridge University Press, Cambridge 1999 (ref: Wendt 1999); *Constructivism and international relations: Alexander Wendt and his critics,* Stefano Guzzini & Anna Leander (eds), Routledge, London 2006; *The culture of national security: norms and identities in world politics,* Peter J. Katzenstein (ed.), Columbia University Press, New York 1996 (ref: *The culture of national security* 1996); David L Rousseau, *Identifying threats and threatening identities: the social construction of realism and liberalism,* Stanford University Press, Stanford California 2006 (ref: Rousseau 2006).

in Sweden could thus be interpreted as a possible danger to societal stability and 'identity', just as was the case during the Second World War.[96]

Whether or not such situations ought to be understood in terms of security is thus determined by the general framing of the case by the authorities. Had the individual been interpreted as a threat due to his or her perceived ethnic identity, social or economic behaviour? Did this interpretation determine the outcome? If so, it is reasonable to construe the management of that case not just in terms of ethnicity, morality and economics, but in terms of societal security too.

### 1.3.1 *Analysing Removal Decisions*

It has already been mentioned that chapters four to six will explore Soviet refugees' rights to reside in Sweden. I have chosen to do this by paying particular attention to those individuals who were denied this right, through a study of the authorities' practices regarding removal decisions. This gave rise to four legal instruments: refusal of entry (*avvisning*); deportation (*förpassning*); expulsion (*utvisning*); and extradition (*utlämning*).[97] I believe that it is through studying cases where asylum rights were denied that we can best understand where the dividing lines fell and conflicting interests met. This, in turn, enables a fuller understanding of the rationale behind the pursued policies.

Apart from illuminating the general principles regarding how and why some refugees were refused residence, an analysis of the usage of the four instruments listed in the preceding paragraph can also yield a detailed understanding of how political asylum and refugees' rights were perceived at this time. Because, whereas all these instruments in broad terms were to generate the same outcome – the removal of a foreign citizen from Swedish territory – they still entailed different things, as will be further demonstrated in chapter three. Refusal of entry, for example, could for obvious reasons only be directed towards new arrivals, whereas deportation decisions could be issued against both newcomers and individuals who had

---

96   Buzan & Hansen 2009, ch. 1; Buzan, Wæver & de Wilde 1998; Rudolph 2006.
97   For a more detailed explanation of the meaning of these concepts see chapter 3.

been in Sweden for a longer period. A study of these decisions and the circumstances that led to them can, hopefully, illuminate the main components of the Swedish authorities' underlying ideas and perceptions of refugees and other foreigners at this time.

Expulsion and extradition decisions, on the other hand, were both results of a specific process – the former often a consequence of a committed crime, and the latter an affirmative response on Sweden's part of another state's demand for a foreign citizen on Swedish territory. Both these instruments are likely to have generated situations where opposing values came into conflict. The political refugee's right to protection from being deported to a country where his life and security were at risk, and the Swedish state's supposed interest to support this right, is likely to have been challenged by its interest in removing criminals from its territory, and/or its aim of maintaining amicable relations with a foreign power, in this case the Soviet Union. Thus, a study of these situations is likely to reveal the state's priorities, and its hierarchy of values.

Another important difference determining which of the four legal instruments were invoked regards the matter of *where* foreign citizens were to be sent should they be removed from Swedish territory. The normal consequence of a refusal of entry decision was a forced return to the country of departure. Deportation and expulsion decisions included no such specification. In terms of political refugees, the supposed destination of a removed individual was, however, a highly relevant question and is central to the understanding of political asylum and its associated policies. Statistical information on the number of Balts, Russians or Ingrians that were refused entry, deported or expelled will not reveal much about Swedish policies unless we know where these individuals were sent. Sending a Soviet refugee to Denmark, Germany or Austria was an altogether different matter than sending him or her to Finland, Poland or the GDR. That, in its turn, differed again from sending an individual directly to the Soviet Union, as will be further demonstrated in chapter four.

The potential influential factors identified above are also likely to have had an impact on the issuing of residence permits. Therefore, the analysis of the removal decisions (which concerns refugees' right to reside in Sweden) is complemented by a study of the conditions attached to residence permits (which illuminates the continuous treatment of those who were granted a right to stay).

### 1.3.2 *Finding Removal Decisions within the Swedish Archives*

As will be further demonstrated in chapter three, removal decisions could be reached by at least four different bodies within the bureaucratic structure. Refusal of entry decisions were made either by the police or the National Alien Commission which also assessed residence permit applications and implemented deportation decisions. Expulsion decisions were generally made by the County Administrative Board *(Länsstyrelsen)*, whereas extraditions were decided by the government.

As a consequence several archival deposits need to be examined in order to reconstruct as comprehensive a picture of the pursued policies regarding removal decisions as possible. In what follows, the archival sources examined for this thesis will be presented in more detail. First of all, however, a decision made within the National Archives *(Riksarkivet)* in 1971 needs to be commented on since it has had a profound impact on the design, selection of source material and methodological approach for this study – and is likely to influence all similar kinds of future research too.

### 1.3.2.1 An Unfortunate Rationalisation Decision

In 1971 it was decided that the archival remains of the defunct National Alien Commission were to be moved. Some of it was to follow the newly established Swedish Immigration Board (*Invandrarverket*), whereas documents now regarded as being of no immediate interest for the authorities were to be archived at the Swedish National Archives. To save space, the National Archives decided to rationalise the extensive material. Among other things, it was decided that the Commission's so-called 'table protocols' (*tabellprotokoll*) were to be destroyed. These protocols contained information, presented in chronological order, on all decisions made by the Commission regarding foreign citizens. Information could be gathered from these protocols on who had been granted a residence permit and who had not; a person's country of origin; the date a decision had been reached, and so forth. The official reason for the destruction of these protocols was that the information gathered in them was still kept in all the foreign citizens' individual dossiers and register cards. This is indeed the case. The information *can* be found in all the individual dossiers and register cards. The problem is, however, that in order for a researcher to actually get hold of these documents, one must know the names of the individuals in question. These names were to be found in those protocols.[98] From a researcher's perspective, thus, this constitutes a problem that is best described as a 'Catch 22'.[99]

The consequences that the destruction of these protocols has had on all future research in this field cannot be underestimated. It is impossible to make a complete quantitative estimation of detailed refugee policies pursued at that time, and it is therefore also impossible to examine comprehensively and quantitatively the practical implementation of the immigration legislation.[100]

It *is* possible to find most of the negative decisions, since they are often recorded in other parts of the archive, and/or at some of the other bureaucracies' archival remains. Finding all the positive determinations is, however, impossible. An analysis of, for example, *all* asylum applications during a certain period, is not therefore feasible. This is, of course, to say the least, a deeply problematical chapter in Sweden's archival history.

## 1.3.2.2 Alternative Approaches

Despite the difficulties of establishing comprehensive quantitative analyses, alternative research routes into the practical implementation of Swedish Cold War refugee policies do exist. They are,

98  The information is garnered from the register to the National Alien Commission's archive, kept at the Swedish National Archives in Stockholm, and from conversations with archivist Lars Hallberg. See also Lars Hallberg, *Källor till invandringens historia i statliga myndigheters arkiv 1840–1990*, Riksarkivet, Stockholm 2001, p. 181 (ref: Hallberg 2001).

99  Joseph Heller's 1961 novel has prompted the *Oxford English Dictionary* to define a Catch 22 as 'a set of circumstances in which one requirement, etc., is dependent upon another, which is in turn dependent upon the first'.

100  That is unless you have the time and the resources to go through the individual files or central register cards of all foreigners who arrived in Sweden during the years covering the National Alien Commission's existence. By accessing them all, every Soviet citizen entering Sweden's border during the Cold War could – at least theoretically – be traced. However, anyone familiar with the realities of research would know that such resources are not normally available when conducting a study of this nature.

nevertheless, both longer and more complicated to take. When predominantly analysing pursued principles and policies, rather than exact quantities, however, these approaches still offer many opportunities.

In terms of *refusal of entry decisions*, there is no unassailable way to trace all *issued* decisions of that kind. The various local police offices' own archives containing information of refusal of entry decisions are spread out over the country and, within the National Alien Commission, no collected documentation of such decisions has been saved at the archives of the Passport Bureau *(Passbyrån)*, which until 1953 was the principal department that handled such cases once they had been forwarded by the police. Only refusal of entry decisions that were sent on to the next level – the plenary meetings – have been methodically documented, as well as those which went to appeal. These too were sent to the government.[101]

Tracing *implemented* refusal of entry decisions, however, is significantly more straightforward. It was the police's duty to implement decisions of refusal of entry, regardless of which authority had decreed it, and to report back to the Commission afterwards. These reports are found in the so-called 'refusal of entry files'. They consist of hundreds of volumes containing accounts of accomplished refusal of entry decisions. Sometimes they also include information on withdrawn decisions (provided that they were communicated between the police and the Commission). An estimation of the files reveals that around half of the thousands of decisions documented in these files (regarding all nationalities) have been made by the Commission whereas the other half was issued by the police. Consequently, one can tend to these files in order to examine the behaviour of both these authorities. Thus, these files have been scrutinised in order to find the refusal of entry decisions whereas the motives behind them have been sought from within the refugees' personal files (see below).[102]

---

101 'Pleniprotokoll', vol. 1–4, A 1 A, Kanslibyrån, SUK, Ra; 'Hemliga pleniproto-koll', vol. 1, A 1, Hemliga arkivet, SUK, Ra; 'Föredragningslistor', vol. 1–8, A II, Inrikesdepartementet, Ra.

102 Vol. 34–56, F 11 A, Hemliga arkivet, SUK, Ra. Regarding the first post-war year, something called the 'Soviet investigation' can be examined too. It was a special examination, pursued by the National Alien Commission, on

In terms of quantitative reliability, there is no overt reason to believe that the files contain significant lacunae (apart from normal human mistakes which always constitute a factor to take into account). The files contain information on refusal of entry of thousands of individuals, including numerous Eastern Europeans. This strengthens the assumption that purposeful removal of reports for political or other reasons was not a common habit. Moreover, the number of refusals of entry seems to correspond with the internal statistics of the National Alien Commission.[103]

The refusal files also often contain some information about the individual and the reasons for rejection. Crucially for this examination, however, they provide *names* of the refused individuals, which can be used in order to access the individuals' personal dossiers within the National Alien Commission's archive. These generally contain additional details about the individual and the causes for refusal of entry and thus constitute the second major source for this study.[104]

Another source is the archived statements of the Aliens Appeals Board (*Utlänningsnämnden*).[105] These were generally required for all removal decisions issued by the Commission. In addition, documents from the National Alien Commission's plenary meetings have been used in order to find traces of such decisions that for various reasons were considered principally important or difficult, and therefore reached this highest bureaucratic level.[106] Similarly, appeals to the government have been traced through a study of cases raised within the Ministry of the Interior (*Inrikesdepartementet*).[107] Additional use has been made of various pools

---

the decisions made about Soviet citizens between May 1945 and May 1946. 'Sovjetutredningen 8/5 1945–15/5 1946', nr 250, vol. 10, F 4, Hemliga arkivet, SUK, Ra.

103 However, the National Alien Commission's statistics on refusals relied in part on reports from the police. Vol. 1, H 1, Kanslibyrån, SUK, Ra; vol. 1–2, H 4, Kanslibyrån, SUK, Ra; vol. 1, F 3, Kontrollbyrån, SUK, Ra;

104 Some refused individuals have no personal dossiers or even register cards in the Commission's archive – particularly not those who were refused directly at the border without ever reaching the assessment of the Commission. In such cases, one has to make do with the information in the refusal of entry files.

105 Vol. 1–5, A 2, Utlänningsnämnden, Ra; vol. 3–12, B 1, Utlänningsnämnden, Ra; vol. 4–6 and 22–24, F2A, Utlänningsnämnden, Ra.

106 'Pleniprotokoll', vol. 1–4, A 1 A, Kanslibyrån, SUK, Ra; 'Hemliga pleniprotokoll', vol. 1, A 1, Hemliga arkivet, SUK, Ra.

107 'Föredragningslistor', vol. 1–8, AII, Inrikesdepartementet, Ra.

of correspondence and special collections of themed documents. These also often reveal general attitudes and interpretations of Soviet refugees by the authorities, as well as names of individuals who were never issued a removal decision but who the authorities found troublesome for some reason.[108]

For the analysis of *deportation decisions,* the same kind of material has been addressed. However, instead of the refusals of entry files, protocols from the Passport Bureau and the Control Bureau (*Kontrollbyrån*) within the National Alien Commission have been analysed. These were the bureaus that were in charge of such decisions, unless they were referred to the plenary assembly and/or the government. The protocols include both names and motivations for the decision, as well as reference to the decisive paragraph in the legislation. These series thus constitute the main source for the exploration of the policies of deportation decisions, together with the analysis of the personal dossiers and register cards of those affected.[109] From 1953 onwards, after the reorganisation of the National Alien Commission, the details are to be found in the archives of the First and the Second Bureau.[110]

Even though *expulsion decisions* were generally not made by the Commission, traces of them are to be found within its archive. This is not least because the implementation of them was in general referred to the Commission. However, the Commission was often involved in the process at an earlier stage as well. Statements of

108 The secret correspondence of the Control Bureau, vol. 2–4, E 4, Hemliga arkivet, SUK, Ra; Letters to the government, vol. 1, B 1, Kontrollbyrån, SUK, Ra; vol. 1, E 1 A, Kontrollbyrån, SUK, Ra; vol. 1, B 1, Andra byrån, SUK, Ra; Secret correspondence of the Second Bureau, vol. 1, E 8, Hemliga arkivet, SUK, Ra; Statements from the Armed Forces, vol. 1–2, F 8, Hemliga arkivet, SUK, Ra; Official instructions, vol. 1, B 4C, Kanslibyrån, SUK, Ra; vol. 1, E 1 A, Kanslibyrån, SUK, Ra; vol. 1, B 4, Kontrollbyrån, SUK, Ra; vol. 1–2, B 2 B, Kontrollbyrån, SUK, Ra; vol. 1, B 2 C, Kontrollbyrån, SUK, Ra; Themed volumes, vol. 4–6 and 9–10, F 2 B, Hemliga arkivet, SUK, Ra; vol. 1 and 9–10, F 4, Hemliga arkivet, SUK, Ra.

109 Vol. 2–8, A 2, Kontrollbyrån, SUK, Ra; Vol. 1–11, A 2, Passbyrån, SUK, Ra. In terms of quantitative reliability, however, the study has indeed revealed that sensitive deportation decisions were not documented in these files during the first post-war year. Through an analysis of various other sources, such as correspondence material, they have been traced anyway. Nevertheless, no guarantees can be made that no other deportation decisions escaped also from these accounts. This will be further discussed in chapter four.

110 Vol. 1, A 2, Första Byrån, SUK, Ra; Vol. 1, A 2, Andra Byrån, SUK, Ra.

various kinds were frequently gathered from the National Alien Commission. Again, the plenary meeting protocols are useful in this regard. However, statements and various communications regarding these cases are also to be found in the various correspondence files of the Commission. Thus, communication material from the varying bureaus has been analysed for this, as well as affected individuals' appeals to the government. So too has archival material from the Aliens Appeals Board which generally produced a statement before expulsions of foreigners were implemented.[111] In addition, as with all the removal decisions, attention has been given to the personal dossiers of the individuals concerned.

Matters regarding *extraditions* are found within the archives of the Ministry for Foreign Affairs (*Utrikesdepartementet*).[112] Additionally, some general series on Soviet refugees within that particular Ministry have been studied, as well as communications between it and the National Alien Commission and various themed series within the secret archive of the Commission.[113]


### 1.3.3 The Personal Dossiers

The most abundant aspect of the source material for this study is constituted by the individual refugees' personal dossiers within the National Alien Commission's archive. In these files, the Commission collected all information they had about an immigrant. This included general matters such as copies of police interrogations held upon his or her arrival, communications with the immigrant, all applications and decisions and so on. But it could also feature private information such as hospital records, health

---

111  Vol. 1–4, A 1 A, Kanslibyrån, SUK, Ra; vol. 1, A 1, Hemliga arkivet, SUK, Ra; Föredragningslistor, vol. 1–8, AII, Inrikesdepartementet, Ra; Vol. 3–12, B 1, Utlänningsnämnden, Ra; The secret correspondence of the Control Bureau, vol. 2–4, E 4, Hemliga arkivet, SUK, Ra; Vol. 1, B 1, Kontrollbyrån, SUK, Ra; Vol. 1, E 1 A, Kontrollbyrån, SUK, Ra; Vol. 1, B 1, Andra byrån, SUK, Ra; Vol. 1, E 8, Hemliga arkivet, SUK, Ra.

112  Vol. 204, R 70 Er, 1920 års dossiésystem, UD, Ra.

113  Vol. 67–69, P 40 I, 1920 års dossiésystem, UD, Ra; Vol. 77–80, P 40 R, 1920 års dossiésystem, UD, Ra; Vol. 40–42, R 58 Er, 1920 års dossiésystem, UD, Ra; Vol. 47, R 58 Eö, 1920 års dossiésystem, UD, Ra; vol. 2–4, E 4, Hemliga arkivet, SUK, Ra; Vol. 3, 9–10, F 4, Hemliga arkivet, SUK, Ra; vol. 9–10, F 2 B, Hemliga arkivet, SUK, Ra; Vol. 1, B 4, Kontrollbyrån, SUK, Ra.

reports, private letters, information gathered from other individuals including neighbours, employers, other refugees and even ex-spouses. The files vary in size – between approximately fifteen and 500 pages – depending on the circumstances.

Another important component of the dossiers consists of information from the security police (*Statspolisens Tredje rotel*). This organisation mapped the refugee population in Sweden. It had several informers among them, and collected various sorts of data. Of particular interest was information regarding political matters, such as the names of people who had been involved in Nazi or communist activities in their home countries, and/or who might be suspected of spreading such opinions in Sweden. Individuals who might be engaging in unlawful intelligence activities were, for obvious reasons, specifically examined and watched over. The security police communicated regularly with the National Alien Commission and shared information regarded as relevant. Sometimes it was also asked to provide a personal statement prior to the Commission reaching a conclusion.[114]

All information gathered in the personal dossiers was examined when the National Alien Commission was to make a decision regarding an individual's right to reside in Sweden, regardless of how long the foreigner had lived there. It is important to note that, since permanent residence permits did not exist at this time, every foreigner had to apply for periodic renewals of his or her permit. However, as I shall demonstrate further in chapter seven, the length of the permits varied considerably, which in turn had an impact on the frequency of renewal applications. These could come with various restrictions attached. The information gathered in the personal dossiers constituted the grounds for all decisions.

The files were of two kinds. Every immigrant in Sweden during these years had a 'central dossier' (*centraldossié*) in which all 'normal' documents were gathered (such as applications and decisions, personal information of any sort, letters, references and statements from other authorities). The final page of the file was coloured

114 The Department of Counter-Intelligence of the Swedish Armed Forces (*Försvarsstabens Inrikesavdelning*) similarly held their own archive of information about Eastern European refugees, and sometimes communicated with the National Alien Commission. Consequently, reports from this organisation are sometimes also included in the personal files.

yellow and used to register minor crimes and a notable array of 'uncomplimentary information' (*ofördelaktiga uppgifter*) of a non-political nature. This could range from minor traffic violations (such as faulty parking of a car or even a bicycle), to drunkenness in public, failure to pay tax for a dog and offensive language used on a train. Individuals whose reputations were besmirched by matters of a more serious nature, including political activities and more severe criminal behaviour, were likely to also feature in a 'control dossier' (*kontrolldossié*). This was classified as strictly secret and often contained reports from the security police and/or documents from a court of law. Additionally, there were register cards where information about the various decisions made about the immigrants was collected. These cards were also of two kinds: 'central register cards' (*centralregisterkort*) and 'control register cards' (*kontrollregisterkort*). In this study, the central register cards are scrutinised in order to ascertain what sort of decisions were reached regarding the refugees. The central dossiers, the control dossiers and the control register cards are used to try to determine why certain decisions were reached.[115]

### 1.3.4 *Making a Selection of Individuals*

Careful analysis of the various source material mentioned above has made it possible to identify individuals by name. This has enabled me to examine their personal dossiers. The methods deployed have compelled me to make a selection of individuals, however, based on certain criteria.

*All* individuals have been included in the study if they were subject to removal decisions, and whose removal has left a trace within the archive in places other than in their personal dossiers (the existence of which enabled me to find them in the first place). Sometimes, they have lacked personal dossiers and the details of

---

115 The files kept within various places of the National Alien Commission's archive. *Central dossiers* are archived in F 1 ABC, F 1 AC and F 1 B, Kanslibyrån, SUK, Ra. *Central register cards* are placed in D 2 BA and D 2 AD, Kanslibyrån, SUK Ra. *Control dossiers* are kept in F 2 A, Hemliga arkivet, SUK, Ra; and *control register cards* in D 2 A and D 2 B, Hemliga arkivet, SUK, Ra. Their position in the archive is dependent on, among other things, the foreigners' nationality, whether or not they became Swedish citizens before 1971, and whether or not they had left the country before that date.

their removal have not been possible to examine. In such cases, I have had to make use of the information available. In other cases, information has been in plentiful supply.

Random selections of individuals who for various reasons caused the authorities obvious concerns, but were never subject to a removal decision, have been studied in detail too. Individuals suspected of espionage constitutes one such category. Criminals and other persons regarded as problematical for whatever reason form another. Apart from the archival places mentioned above, their names have been gleaned from various themed volumes within the archives of the Swedish security police and the Secret Archive (*Hemliga arkivet*) of the National Alien Commission. One such example is archived within that Commission, but pursued mainly by the security police. This pertains to a special examination of Balts accused of war crimes during the Nazi occupation. Others concern, for example, Soviet citizens in particular or Soviet activities in Sweden.[116] However, ordinary protocols from plenary meetings within the National Alien Commission and the Aliens Appeals Board have been useful for this purpose, as have various series within the National Alien Commission's Control Bureau and the Second Bureau, as well as documents from the Ministry for Foreign Affairs and the Ministry of the Interior.[117]

The specific focus on 'problematical' individuals enables a closer analysis of lines of conflict within Swedish refugee policies during these years. They are likely to have caused situations where opposing interests met – such as the (supposed) ambition to protect refugee rights set against a desire to remove unwanted individuals from Swedish territory. It also facilitates the analysis of the security dimension. However, individuals who were granted a right to stay with little hindrance, who never caused the authorities any

116 P 4818, SÄPO, Ra; vol. 493–501, 10.1, SÄPO, Ra; Themed volumes, vol. 4–6 and 9–10, F 2 B, Hemliga arkivet, SUK, Ra; vol. 1 and 9–10, F 4, Hemliga arkivet, SUK, Ra.

117 'Pleniprotokoll', vol. 1–4, A 1 A, Kanslibyrån, SUK, Ra; 'Hemliga pleniprotokoll', vol. 1, A 1, Hemliga arkivet, SUK, Ra; vol. 1, E 1 A, Kontrollbyrån, SUK, Ra; vol. 1, B 4, Kontrollbyrån, SUK, Ra; vol. 1, B 1, Kontrollbyrån, SUK, Ra; vol. 1, B 1, Andra byrån, SUK Ra; vol. 67–69, P 40 I, 1920 års dossiésystem, UD, Ra; vol. 77–79, P 40 R, 1920 års dossiésystem, UD, Ra; vol. 40, R 58 Er, 1920 års dossiésystem, UD, Ra; vol. 47, R 58 Eö, 1920 års dossiésystem, UD, Ra; 'Föredragningslistor', vol. 1–8, A II, Inrikesdepartementet, Ra.

concern, and against whom no 'uncomplimentary information' existed within their personal files, need to be studied too in order to pursue a comparison and illuminate differences – if, indeed, there were any. However, these 'non-problematical' individuals often left no archival footprint other than their own personal dossiers. Identifying the names of such individuals has thus been somewhat more challenging. However, through various lists, correspondence material and principal discussions, such individuals have also been traced. Moreover, those individuals discussed at times when the Commission was on the brink of changing its previously pursued policies – often through government involvement – have proven particularly insightful.[118]

Following the Commission's restructure in 1953 the identification of new arrivals is somewhat easier, since at least those issued 'non-refusal' by the National Alien Commission are gathered within the First and Second Bureau's so-called 'special protocols'. From these, it has been possible to pick a random selection without time-consuming detours.[119]

The manner of selection might raise questions of representativeness, particularly with regards to the so-called 'non-problematical' individuals. Indeed, had the aforementioned 'table protocols' been available, the making of a random selection would have been a more straightforward method. However, given that this possibility no longer exists, such a non-deliberate grouping from other kinds of sources – communications, protocols etc. – provides the next best alternative. The fact that every case is studied in depth further compensates for any potential shortcomings.

118 Individuals could of course belong to both these categories ('problematical' and 'non-problematical' – author's terminology), at different times. An individual who, for example, became suspected for communist world views or unlawful intelligence activities in the 1950s might have been regarded as a normal case in the 1940s. Thus, he or she would be included in both groups, but at different points in time. In total, however, the 'non-problematical' individuals included in the study outnumber the 'problematical' somewhat. This particularly regards the Ingrian group, within which few 'problematical' individuals and 'uncomplimentary information' have been found at all.

119 These protocols include removal decisions of foreigners and some 'non-refusal' decisions of new arrivals. They do not, however, contain information on residence permits apart from with regard to individuals subject to postponed removal decisions. Vol. 1, A 2, Första byrån, SUK, Ra; vol. 1, A 2, Andra byrån, SUK, Ra.

Additionally, any uncertainties regarding the quantitative comprehensiveness that the sources might contain are at least partly counteracted by the fact that the ambition of this study is to understand the *contents* of the policies – that is the principal ideologies and beliefs that determined them – rather than to make exact quantitative statements about how many individuals were treated in a certain way or other. Therefore, every decision is analysed in its own specific context. Quantitative predications are established too, but these emphatically constitute a secondary aspiration. Overall, I believe that enough material has been gathered to establish the types of circumstances that prompted the authorities to issue particular kinds of decisions, both in terms of removal/non-removal, and in terms of the kinds of residence permits that were issued. 'Problematical' and 'non-problematical' individuals are found within all three categories examined in this study, as well as each different sort of decisions.

In total, 260 individuals have been chosen for closer analysis. Of these, 120 are Balts. Their quantitative dominance is motivated by the fact that they were far more numerous than Ingrians and Russians in Sweden at this time. As a result, they have left more traces in the archives as the number of 'problematical' individuals was higher. Additionally, special focus has been paid to individuals accused of Nazi war crimes. A total of 33 such individuals have been chosen for analysis. Others, however, have been randomly chosen out of other sorts of material, mentioned above, and treated as 'normal cases'.

Ingrians make up 50 of the total. This is because they have left few traces in terms of 'uncomplimentary information'. In comparison with Balts, a smaller proportion of Ingrians in the study group were regarded as 'problematical' individuals. Due attention is paid to this when normal treatment is to be analysed.

The remaining 90 are Russians. This is despite the fact that they constituted a smaller group in total than both the Ingrians and the Balts. However, for reasons that will become clear, Russians left many traces in the archives of 'uncomplimentary information'. Therefore, a greater number of Russians merit analysis. In addition, a number of 'un-problematic' cases from this cohort have been selected from various lists of new arrivals.

### 1.3.5 'Lies, Damned Lies and Statistics'[120]

Although quantitative estimations are of secondary relevance in this study, some statistical claims are made for reasons of clarification. The aim with these accounts is normally to provide contextual information to the issues explored in the thesis. (Most of these estimates are made in chapter four.) The source material to support these claims is constituted by various kinds of official and unofficial statistics. However, providing answers to quantitative questions on Swedish migration matters during the 1940s (and, indeed, earlier) is challenging. As a new and relatively inexperienced bureaucracy, with tasks novel to Swedish society, the National Alien Commission's archival and statistical techniques and routines were not yet that well developed. Indeed, during the first two years of its existence, it was not even responsible for the production of official statistics of foreign citizens. Instead, the National Board of Health (*Socialstyrelsen*) continued to manage this task using information supplied by the Commission (which in its turn partly based this information on entry reports from the police). Not until 1 October 1946 was the administration of official statistics production fully transferred to the National Alien Commission.[121]

As a result, the statistics available during the Commission's first five years of existence are inconsistent, fragmentary and, at times, contradictory. Moreover, most (but not all) estimates of foreign citizens residing in Sweden are based on the number of residence permits issued at a specific time. Consequently no distinction is drawn between refugees and other foreign nationals. Meanwhile, refugees who were placed in refugee camps and had not yet been granted a permit are not included. In addition, those who were kept in camps for military staff during the last years of the war are often missing from the statistics. As a result, the approximately 2,500–3,000 Russian soldiers resident in camps partly administered by Soviet officials, and who were forcibly repatriated to the Soviet

---

120 The headline refers to a phrase that Mark Twain claimed was said by the British statesman, Benjamin Disraeli: 'There are three kinds of lies: lies, damned lies, and statistics.' (Not verified). Mark Twain, 'Chapters from My Autobiography', *North American Review*, 7 September 1906.

121 The statistics continued to be published by the National Board of Health, however, in the series *Sociala Meddelanden*. See *Sociala Meddelanden* 1946 nr 12, p. 965.

Union between 1944 and 1946, were never accounted for in any official statistics.[122] Furthermore, children under the age of 16, and, from August 1945 onwards, citizens of countries from which entry visas were abolished, are not included either.[123] From the end of 1946, Soviet citizens (excluding Balts) are, for some reason, no longer accounted for in the residence permit statistics at all.[124]

At the same time, however, the official statistics reveal a notable wish to count and calculate foreign nationals' whereabouts in Sweden. A range of variables were included in the official statistics, which were published several times per year.[125] Two examples are the accounts of the number of first residence permits that had been recently issued, as well as the number of journeys to and from Sweden that had been pursued. However, within the former, Soviet Russian and Ingrian individuals are missing. This is despite the fact that, as we shall see, over 3,000 individuals belonging to one of these two categories were granted initial residence permits during these years. Instead, these persons are, it is to be presumed, included in the category 'other nationalities'. Balts, however, are accounted for meticulously, with distinctions drawn between Estonian, Latvian and Lithuanian nationals.[126] Within the latter, 'Soviet Russian' citizens are registered, but not Balts. The somewhat incompatible nature of these and other accounts thus renders it necessary to handle them with extra care in terms of reliability.[127]

122 This might have been an intentional exclusion, however, given the secrecy surrounding Swedish policies regarding these soldiers. See chapter two.

123 That is, provided that they did not intend to stay for more than three months and had applied for a residence permit. See, for example, *Sociala Meddelanden* 1945, nr 12 p. 1072; and *Sociala Meddelanden* 1946, nr 6, p. 489.

124 *Sociala Meddelanden* 1946, nr 12, p. 966; *Sociala Meddelanden* 1947, nr 5, p. 433–438.

125 *Sociala Meddelanden* was published twelve times per year. Around half of the numbers included information on foreign citizens in Sweden. *Sociala Meddelanden* 1945–54. The Central Bureau of Statistics (*Statistiska Centralbyrån*) also included information on foreign citizens and migrants in their yearly publication of statistical information. *Befolkningsrörelsen* 1945–54.

126 *Sociala Meddelanden* 1945, nr 5, p. 434; *Sociala Meddelanden* 1945, nr 8, p. 706; *Sociala Meddelanden* 1945, nr 12, p. 706; *Sociala Meddelanden* 1946, nr 3, p. 224; *Sociala Meddelanden* 1946, nr 6, p. 493; *Sociala Meddelanden* 1946, nr 12, p. 968; *Sociala Meddelanden* 1947, nr 3, p. 216; *Sociala Meddelanden* 1944, nr 5, p. 437; *Sociala Meddelanden* 1947, nr 9, p. 837; *Sociala Meddelanden* 1947, nr 11, p. 975; *Sociala Meddelanden* 1948, nr 2, p. 111.

127 See, for example, *Sociala Meddelanden* 1946, nr 3, p. 225; *Sociala Meddelanden* 1946, nr 12, p. 969; *Sociala Meddelanden* 1947, nr 3, p. 217.

The migration statistics produced by the Central Bureau of Statistics (*Statistiska Centralbyrån*) suffer from similar problems of vagueness.[128] Emigration and immigration matters were carefully documented in terms of age, marital status and local municipality of the migrants. However, only countries of departure and arrival were documented – not the nationalities of the migrants. In post-war Europe, however, the nationality and departure country of roaming refugees far from always coincided.[129] Additionally, the fact that these statistics were based on figures from the parish registration offices mean that significant delays are built in to them as these registration procedures were a lingering affair. At least for the first post-war years, therefore, these statistics are difficult to use if one is to examine the number and nationalities of newly arrived refugees.[130]

Another problem, relevant for this particular study, is the chosen categorisations used by the authorities within the official statistics. Whereas Balts generally were listed separately, Ingrians were most often not. Instead, they were (possibly) included in the category 'Soviet Russian', if and when this category was represented. This is despite the fact that the Ingrians, according to internal statistics within the National Alien Commission, outnumbered the Russians – at least from 1946 onwards.[131] Only in internal quantitative accounts were Ingrians accounted for separately.[132] As shall be demonstrated, however, they were treated as a specific

128  The Central Bureau of Statistics still exists. Its current name (in 2013) is Statistics Sweden (*Statistiska Centralbyrån*).

129  From 1949 onwards, information on citizenship was indeed included in the statistics, however only regarding those who *emigrated* from Sweden – not the immigrants. *Befolkningsrörelsen* 1945–54, Statistiska Centralbyrån, Stockholm. See also Åke Nilsson, *Efterkrigstidens invandring och utvandring*, Demografiska rapporter 2004:5, Statistiska Centralbyrån, Stockholm, p. 3, 11, 17.

130  As a result, the more than 30,000 immigrants that were registered in 1946 and 1947 respectively stem from the refugee movement of 1944 and 1945. *Befolkningsrörelsen* 1945, p. 33; *Befolkningsrörelsen* 1946, p. 58; *Befolkningsrörelsen* 1947, p. 29; *Befolkningsrörelsen* 1948, p. 24.

131  By the end of 1945, at least 1500 Ingrians resided in Sweden. Five years later, that number had more than doubled. 'Uppskattning av antalet vuxna flyktingar i Sverige den 1 september 1950', vol. 1, H 1, Kanslibyrån, SUK, Ra.

132  See, for example, 'Till Konungen, ang. vissa rysk-ingermanländska och ryska flyktingar', 16 september 1947, vol. 4, E 4, Hemliga ark, SUK, Ra; undated 'P.M. ang "ingermanländare" i Sverige', central dossier of I46.

category by the Commission and distinguished from the Soviet Russians.

The *internal* statistical information of the National Alien Commission is somewhat better adjusted to the types of quantitative questions that are relevant for a study of this nature.[133] However, it too presents challenges of consistency and completeness. From 1949 onwards, however, the statistical and archival routines of the Commission improved. Consequently, no apparent contradictory quantitative statements have been found from this date onwards.[134]

Yet another problem is constituted by the varying practices regarding the inclusion or exclusion of children in the statistical accounts. Minors had no legal documents of their own, but were generally included in their parents' passports and permits. Similarly, in the statistical accounts they are mostly, but not always, invisible. This can obviously cause confusion in terms of the quantitative reality of refugees and other foreign citizens during these years.

Presenting a detailed, accurate quantitative statement of newly arrived refugees and other migrants during the first four post-war years is, therefore, challenging. Nevertheless, by comparing and adding together different statistical accounts, information can still be found and outline estimations reached.[135] The statistical information presented in this thesis – predominantly so in chapter four – is thus most often compiled in this manner.


### *1.3.6 Legislation and Norms*

A more straightforward kind of source material for this study is constituted by the legislation, public investigations and propositions used principally for the examination of the juridical and

---

133  Most of it is deposited in H 1–4 (7 volumes), Kanslibyrån, suk, Ra. However, statistical accounts are found in other parts of the Commission's archive as well, such as within the collections of correspondence material. See, for example, vol. 1, E 8, Hemliga arkivet, suk, Ra; and vol. 2–4, E 4, Hemliga arkivet, suk, Ra.

134  It is clear that 'gaps' remain, however, given that I have been unable to find complete statistical accounts for the years 1950 and 1951 regarding refusals of entry.

135  Many of the statistical accounts produced by the National Alien Commission are indeed called 'estimations' (*uppskattning*).

bureaucratic structure of Swedish refugee administration pursued in chapter three. Some documents from the archive of the National Alien Commission are also used, such as messages and directives to police authorities and passport controls, and various internal documents regarding the structure of this organisation.[136]


## 1.4 Research Ethics

Swedish Law prohibits the publication of information gathered from personal files in the National Alien Commission that date back fifty years or less.[137] This means that it would not contravene legal regulations to publish the names of individuals included in this study. However, many of the files examined include information of a very private nature such as crimes, marital difficulties, sexual diseases and mental problems. In some cases, such information has influenced the Commission's decision and is therefore included in the thesis. Due to reasons of research ethics, therefore, I have decided to not publish any names of individual refugees. The identities per se cannot be considered a matter of public interest. They are, however, a matter of scientific importance. In order to assess the quality and correctness of my work, names of the individuals included in this work must be accessible. Therefore, I have chosen to implement a system of footnoted letters and numbers which function as aliases.[138] A list of the real names behind these pseudonyms has been deposited at the Swedish National Archives in Stockholm. A copy can also be solicited from the author of this thesis, as well as from the Department of History at Stockholm University.


136 Vol. 1, B 4 C, Kanslibyrån, SUK, Ra; vol. 1, B 2 A, Kontrollbyrån, SUK, Ra; vol. 1–2, B 2 B, Kontrollbyrån, SUK, Ra; vol. 1, B 2 C, Kontrollbyrån, SUK, Ra; vol. 1, B 1, Kontrollbyrån, SUK, Ra; vol. 1, E 1 A, Kontrollbyrån, SUK, Ra. For the structure of the organisation, see also some documents from vol. 1–4, A 1 A, Kanslibyrån, SUK, Ra.

137 SFS 2009:400 *Offentlighets- och sekretesslag;* SFS 1990:782 *Arkivlag.*

138 B1–B120 represent the Balts; I1–I50 the Ingrians; and R1–R120 the Russians.

## 1.5 Definitions

Some terms need to be defined in more detail before the examination proceeds. The first pertains to the term 'refugee'. Today, in learned debate there is an effort to differentiate between refugees and non-refugees. 'Convention-refugees' are those who are considered political refugees according to the 1951 Refugee Convention. Since the establishment of this convention, however, more categories of fleeing people have been included in the definition 'refugee' according to international law. People fleeing from wars, for example, are called 'de-facto refugees', and can be granted asylum on humanitarian grounds. Generally speaking these juridical distinctions tend not to be adhered to in common parlance or within the language of the media. Here 'refugees' are often synonymous with 'fleeing people' or 'asylum seekers'.

During the period under examination, the juridical terminology was not as developed. Indeed, when it comes to the first half of the research period, there was not even a common international definition to refer to, let alone a Swedish one. Towards the end of the Second World War and the immediate post-war years, there were efforts to differentiate between 'refugees' and 'displaced persons', where the latter simply meant someone who the authorities believed would (or should) return to his or her home country as soon as it was practically possible. Within the National Alien Commission, however, the general discourse included any asylum seeker in the concept. There, the difference was instead between 'refugees' and 'political refugees' in which only the latter were to be granted the right to stay.

In light of this, in the following study the word 'refugee' will be used in the broad sense of the term to mean any individual who has left his country due to oppression, war, conflict and so forth. In other words, it is used regarding individuals who see themselves as refugees. 'Political refugee', however, will only be used regarding individuals who have been granted this status by the authorities.

The second definition that needs some clarification is the usage of the terms 'Soviet refugee' and 'Soviet citizen' in relation to the Balts. The reason this necessitates attention is purely political – even today the question of the Baltic refugees' nationality during the Cold War can incite upset feelings.

This thesis examines refugees fleeing from the Soviet Union. From 1944 onwards, the Soviet Union included the Baltic States. In a controversial act by the Swedish government, Sweden had recognised the Soviet annexation of the Baltic States already during the first occupation in 1940. Consequently, the Baltic refugees were regarded as Soviet citizens in Sweden. However, the Balts were accounted for separately in the immigration authorities' statistics. In addition, as shall be demonstrated, they were treated differently than other 'Soviet' citizens. According to the majority of the Baltic refugees themselves, they were *not* Soviet citizens and were offended when they were labelled as such. They had fled to Sweden as Baltic citizens and once there acquired so called Swedish Alien's Passports (*främlingspass*).

In this thesis, there is no intention to aggravate the historical memory or consciousness of this émigré group. In referring to the Balts as 'Soviet refugees', or, sometimes, 'Soviet citizens', no political or emotional evaluation is to be inferred regarding their nationality at that time. However, as individuals fleeing from the Soviet Union, they are included in this examination and, as such, they are on occasion referred to as 'Soviet refugees' and/or 'Soviet citizens'.

Another term which is used in this thesis is self-constructed. The label 'grey zone country' and 'grey zone area' is used to refer to countries other than the Soviet Union in which Soviet refugees faced risks (such as expatriation to the Soviet Union, political oppression and/or imprisonment) should they be obliged to return. This included European countries which came under the direct purview of, or were indirectly governed by, the Soviet Union. This includes, for example, Poland, GDR and Finland.

Finally, the terms *Western* and *West Europe* on the one hand, and *non-Western, Eastern* and *East Europe* on the other, will be used somewhat differently, following the traditional, however time-specific, political border between communism and liberal democracy evident in Europe during the Cold War. Countries that were incorporated into the Soviet Union at this time, as well as those that were governed by a Soviet-friendly communist regime, are thus characterised as East Europe, whereas independent countries that were governed by democratically elected governments are labelled as West Europe.[139] In most cases, the epithet 'East

---

139  This should not, however, be interpreted as a statement of any current labelling
    of Europe in the 21st century.

European' coincides with 'grey zone'. One country, however, does not. Finland constituted the exception of an independent country with a democratically elected government that still constituted a so-called 'grey zone' in terms of the safety of Soviet refugees during these years.

# Early 20th Century Swedish Refugee Management

The first time the modern state of Sweden came into contact with refugees on a significant scale was during the First World War and the Russian Revolution. As other Western countries at this time, it reacted by trying to obstruct such unwanted immigration. An assembled set of explicit prohibitions preventing foreigners from residing in Sweden was instituted in 1914. As such, they abruptly severed a 50-year long period that had been characterised by the principle of free movement of people, during which there had been no passport obligations. Sweden had been a poor agrarian country during that period, subject more to emigration than immigration.[1]

In 1927, Sweden brought in its first comprehensive Aliens Act. This document was deeply influenced by contemporary nationalism, racial biology and xenophobia. Its official aim was to protect the Swedish labour market from foreign competition, as well as to 'protect the Swedish race'.[2] The immediate historical background to the issues explored in this thesis was thus to a significant degree characterised by both protectionism and racism. In this chapter, I will present this background in some more detail through a summary of what is so far known about Swedish refugee policies during the 1930s, 1940s and, to some extent, the 1950s. I will also examine how scholars have interpreted these developments and the putative factors governing Sweden's refugee policies at this time. The sec-

---

1 Hammar 1964.
2 Hammar 1964, pp. 365–382; Kvist Geverts 2008, pp. 48–51; Lindberg 1973, p. 48; SFS 1927:333 *Lag om utlännings rätt att här i riket vistas.*

ond part of the chapter explores more specifically the management of Soviet refugees in Sweden during the Second World War.


## 2.1 Maintaining Room For Manoeuvre For The Swedish State

In the Aliens Act of 1937, any overt reference to the Swedish race had disappeared. However, the regulations were formulated in such a way that they basically provided the authorities with the right to decide as they wished. Every foreigner who arrived in Sweden had to carry a passport. If one was to stay for more than three months, one needed to apply for a residence permit. Residents of countries to which there was a visa requirement – which at this time included mainly Eastern Europe – had to apply for entry visas before arriving. However, the law did not provide directions regarding how applications should be assessed.[3]

Similarly, regulations regarding political refugees existed, however without any suggested definitions as to how the concept was to be interpreted. The imprecision of the term was deliberate, as historian Karin Kvist Geverts has highlighted. In the preparatory works leading up to the law, the legal experts who had constructed it stated that 'an absolute (...) definition of the concept political refugee cannot be maintained. The determination has to vary somewhat with regard to changing times and circumstances, different countries' juridical opinions and international relations'.[4] The idea was to grant the authorities maximum freedom of action. Thus, law should not be formulated in such a way that it would constrain the behaviour of the state.

In this way, Sweden effectively ensured that its refugee policies could be constantly adjusted to its own current goals and needs. Very few 'rights' were granted individual foreigners, be they refugees or not. And those rights that *were* ascertained could be overlooked according to the Aliens Act's 54th paragraph, which explicitly granted the government the right to deviate from any

3    SFS 1937:344 *Lag om utlännings rätt att här i riket vistas* (ref: SFS 1937:344); Kvist Geverts 2008, pp. 53–56.
4    Kvist Geverts 2008, p. 55. Kvist Geverts's citation from SOU 1936:53, pp. 56–57.

regulations in the law in the event of war or threat of war.[5] The law thus granted the authorities an almost unlimited room for manoeuvre. Consequently, outcomes were not foreseeable, as is generally the idea in a state founded on law.

## 2.2. Categorising Refugees

Despite the deliberate obfuscation, the preparatory works of the 1937 Aliens Act still specified some conditions that could *not* be included in the concept 'political refugee'. It stipulated that individuals 'feeling discomfort' in their home countries due to their 'race' were not to be included. This formulation was specifically aimed at excluding from eligibility the German Jews, who were increasingly trying to escape from the Nazi regime during the 1930s. Only those who risked being punished for political *crimes* could, according to the prescriptive terminology, be included. As a result, the legal grounds for denying asylum to European Jews, and several other categories of refugees, were reinforced.[6]

The singling out of a specific group – in this case the German Jews – in this manner was symptomatic for Swedish refugee policies during the 1930s and 1940s. The authorities' separated clearly between assorted categories of refugees and set up 'quotas'. Different groups were allocated differently sized quotas. The government simply decided how many refugees of a certain category it found acceptable to introduce to the Swedish society. This logic was predominantly racist, and had very little to do with the varying wants of the existing refugees at that time. Instead it had everything to do with the perceived needs of the Swedish state, whose representatives believed that ethnic homogeneity was crucial for Sweden's well-being.[7]

During the 1930s, this led to a conspicuously restrictive refugee policy which drastically discriminated against those who were in strongest need of protection, namely the German Jews. When the Second World War broke out, Sweden gradually introduced visa

5    SFS 1937:344, § 54,
6    Kvist Geverts 2008, pp. 54–55.
7    Åmark 2011, ch. 14.

requirements for all war-effected countries, thus efficiently ensuring that asylum applications had to be made through visa requests from abroad. However, since the protectionist labour market policies in most cases prohibited them from taking employment during the 1930s, only such Jewish refugees who could prove they had financial guarantees from relatives or organisations in Sweden were allowed entry. The Swedish state was not prepared to assist refugees financially, but left the maintenance burden to various voluntary organisations. Individuals who could provide evidence of travel arrangements to another country were also allowed entry according to certain transit migration quotas. Such arrangements still offered no guarantee of a positive assessment. The quotas available to Europe's fleeing Jews were mostly in the order of a few hundred at that time.[8]

## 2.3 The 1942 Watershed

From 1942 onwards, Swedish refugee policies opened up. During the first two years of the war, no more than 2,000–5,000 refugees in total had been allowed to reside in Sweden. Subsequently, however, practically all refugees who managed to reach the borders of Sweden were allowed to stay. The state also started to provide the necessary financial support. By the end of 1943, over 40,000 refugees resided in Sweden. The Swedish administration even actively helped Danish Jews to cross the border when the deportations there began. In May 1945, around 200,000 foreigners resided in Sweden, out of which more than half were categorised as refugees. The majority of them were Nordic citizens. Some 30,000 were of Baltic origin who had fled in haste to Sweden when the Soviet Union reoccupied their countries in the autumn of 1944. But there were also some German, Russian, Ingrian, Polish and other Central and East European refugees. Around 80,000 of the remaining group

---

8   Åmark 2011, ch. 14; Kvist Geverts 2008; *En problematisk relation?: Flyktingpolitik och judiska flyktingar i Sverige 1920–1950,* Lars M. Andersson & Karin Kvist, Karin (eds), Historiska Institutionen, Uppsala Universitet, Uppsala 2008 (ref: *En problematisk relation* 2008). See also *Betänkande angående flyktingars behandling,* vol. 1, Parlamentariska undersökningskommissionen angående flyktingärenden och säkerhetstjänst, SOU 1946:36, Stockholm 1946 (ref: SOU 1946:36).

(not referred to as 'refugees') were classified as Finnish evacuees, half of which were children temporarily cared for by Swedish families.[9] In addition, the spring and summer of 1945 witnessed Sweden, in collaboration with UNRRA, collectively transfer to its territory around 30,000 former concentration camp refugees for medical treatment (of which in total around half eventually remained in Sweden).[10]

That policies changed during the final years of the war is indisputable. Some researchers interpret this as an indication that the Swedish authorities had finally realised the seriousness of the situation by becoming more refugee friendly.[11] Others have interpreted it differently, pointing towards the fact that the majority of the refugees who sought refuge in Sweden from that date onwards were Nordic citizens, rather than Central and Eastern Europeans. In addition, they were regarded as temporary visitors, rather than aspirants for permanent settlement like the previous asylum seekers. At this point in time, Central and Eastern Europeans could, generally speaking, no longer leave their home countries due to the development of the war. And their Jewish populations had either already been deported and/or murdered, or were actively hindered from escaping by a Nazi regime which had by then initiated its 'final solution'. Thus, Sweden's new policy did little to help the Central and Eastern European Jews. The change should thus instead be understood as an expression of how Sweden favoured and felt obliged to some refugees (the Nordic citizens) rather than others (the non-Nordic citizens).[12]

9    In the interests of full disclosure, it should be noted that my own mother numbered among this group.

10   Åmark 2011, p. 523–538; *Sociala Meddelanden* 1945, nr 1. The Swedish authorities used a different system of categories for refugees ('refugees' and 'evacuees') in this statistical series than the Allied countries on the European continent at the same time ('refugees' and 'displaced persons'). In the Swedish statistics, the term 'refugees' included individuals who on the European continent would have been regarded as both 'refugees' and 'displaced persons'.

11   Steven Koblik, *The stones cry out: Sweden's response to the persecution of the Jews 1933–1945*, Holocaust Library, New York 1988; Lindberg 1973; Sverker Oredsson, *Svensk rädsla: offentlig fruktan i Sverige under 1900-talets första hälft*, Nordic Academic Press, Lund 2001, p. 357.

12   Byström 2006; Åmark 2011, ch. 15; Kvist Geverts 2008. See also Paul Levine, *From indifference to activism: Swedish diplomacy and the Holocaust, 1938–1944*, Uppsala University, Uppsala 1998 (ref: Levine 1998).

## 2.4 Administrative Challenges

One fact which scholars examining the specific circumstances of Swedish refugee policies during the Second World War all agree on is that the refugee management that the authorities eventually did organise during the last years of the war brought novel experiences to Swedish society. First of all, the demographics of Sweden suddenly changed. Never before had so many foreigners resided in the country. Moreover, it was the first time the Swedish state had organised and financed such a large scale operation. Several hundred refugee camps were set up during a relatively short period of time, and extra staff was quickly employed at the various bureaucracies that became involved. Hostels, schools, churches, theatres and various other public premises functioned as temporary collecting points, but large camps were also specifically built for the purpose. Voluntary organisations helped provide newcomers with food and clothing.[13]

Refugees were assigned various types of work, often manual labour such as forestry or agricultural work for men, or household or factory work for women. In contrast to the logic that had characterised refugee policies during the 1930s, it was now regarded as crucial to try to make refugees self-supporting as soon as possible.[14] In 1945 Sweden also began to offer health care to ill, undernourished refugees who were brought to Sweden from liberated concentration camps in cooperation with the International Red Cross and UNRRA. Around 30,000 individuals arrived in this way. This further increased the range and number of nationalities present in Sweden.[15]

As a consequence, Sweden's administration of immigration

---

13   Carl Göran Andræ, *Sverige och den stora flykten från Estland 1943–1944*, Gustav Adolfs akademi, Uppsala 2004, pp. 166–172 (ref: Andræ 2004).

14   According to Byström, the new policy regarding refugees' maintenance was established in 1941. Byström 2012, chs 3–7 and 15; Lars Olsson, *På tröskeln till folkhemmet: baltiska flyktingar och polska koncentrationslägerfångar som reservarbetskraft i skånskt jordbruk kring slutet av andra världskriget*, Morgonrodnad, Lund 1995 (ref: Olsson 1995); Andræ 2004, pp. 99–121; Åmark 2011, ch. 15.

15   Around 20,000 individuals came to Sweden through the efforts of the Swedish Red Cross and its vice chairman Folke Bernadotte during the spring of 1945 aboard the so-called 'white buses' (*vita bussarna*). Approximately 9,000 additional individuals came during the summer of 1945 as a result of Sweden's cooperation with UNRRA. Åmark 2011, p. 546–554; Sune Persson, *Vi åker till Sverige: de vita bussarna 1945*, Fisher & Co, Rimbo 2002.

matters developed. Before and during the early stages of the war, refugee matters had not been regarded as constituting a coherent policy area. Mirroring the common approach undertaken by the international community at that time, such matters were merely treated as being composed of separate, temporary and time-specific challenges. Responsibilities for refugees had thus rested among different parts of the Swedish bureaucracy. Following the outbreak of war, the Ministry for Foreign Affairs took over the outward-facing control of refugees – that is the assessment of visa permits. Meanwhile the Foreigner's Bureau of the National Board of Health and Welfare (*Socialstyrelsens utlänningsbyrå*) administered the inner control and handled the various permits pertaining to foreigners on Swedish ground. The numerous refugee camps, both open and closed, were primarily administered by the National Board of Health and Welfare (*Socialstyrelsen*), the Civil Defence Board (*Statens utrymningskommission* – from October 1944 *Civilförsvarsstyrelsen*), the Swedish Armed Forces (*Försvarsstabens inrikesavdelning*) and the Board of Medicine (*Medicinalstyrelsen*). In some cases the legations of the refugees' home countries partly administered the camps. In addition, the National Labour Market Commission (*Arbetsmarknadskommissionen*) was responsible for refugees' work placements, whereas both the civil and military security services were involved with the control of individuals believed to be politically untrustworthy.[16]

The need for a more centralised organisation was soon felt, and in July 1944 the National Alien Commission (*Statens Utlännings-kommission*) was established. The main inner and outer administration of foreigners was now gathered together under one bureaucracy. The organisation quickly became substantial in size, employing several hundred members of staff.[17] Most of the leading positions were allocated to former representatives of the defunct Foreigner's Bureau. And during the following Cold War years, refugee policies would increasingly become perceived as a specific, coherent policy area, rather than a collection of temporary challenges.[18]

16   Hallberg 2001, pp. 139–148; Kvist Geverts 2008, pp. 61–71; Åmark 2011, ch. 15; Andræ 2004, pp. 111–121. See also SOU 1946:36.
17   In the summer of 1946, the staff consisted of circa 550 members. 'Protokoll', 24 September 1946, § 1, bilaga 1, vol. 2, A 1 A, Kanslibyrån, SUK, Ra.
18   Byström, 2012; Kvist Geverts 2008.

To date, scholarly research presents a consistent picture of the administrative developments during the 1930s and 1940s. However, interpretations vary regarding the size of the room for manoeuvre for individual bureaucrats within this administrative structure. The law undoubtedly provided the state with substantial autonomy to behave as it wished. But who wielded this autonomy? Who 'made' refugee policies? The government or the bureaucrats? One historian, Karin Kvist Geverts argues that policies were mainly created by officials at the administrative level of the state bureaucracy; Klas Åmark, however, claims that policies were made at the political level by the politicians, and mainly implemented by the civil servants. This latter scenario does not exclude the possibility for individual bureaucrats to influence certain decisions according to their own beliefs, however, as was the case with a few apparently Anti-Semite bureaucrats during the war. One obscuring fact is that directions and principles, when they existed, were often unofficial, held secret, and communicated orally rather than in print. This obviously renders it more difficult for historians to reconstruct the political and administrative procedures of Swedish refugee policies several decades hence.[19]

The administrative and political structures of post-war Swedish refugee policies will be examined in greater detail in chapter three. The subsequent chapters will also, at least indirectly, reveal some more about these procedures. The results will, it is hoped, shed light on this discussion.

## 2.5 Scholarly Interpretations

Already during the 1960s and 1970s, historians Tomas Hammar and Hans Lindberg revealed that xenophobia, racial biology and nationalism had characterised Sweden's policies towards refugees and other immigrants during the early 20th century.[20] Towards the end of that century, historians began to look more closely into

19   Kvist Geverts 2008, chs 3 and 9; Åmark 2011, ch. 14–15, particularly pp. 483-485. See also Byström 2012, pp. 221-223 on the room for manouvre for the Labour Market Commission (*Statens arbetsmarknadskommission*) and the Government Board of Refugee Relief (*Statens flyktingsnämnd*).
20   Hammar 1964; Lindberg 1973.

Sweden's refugee policies during the Second World War. Several of them found that ethnic prejudice had exerted a powerful influence. Historian Mikael Byström, for example, examined the general discourses of immigrants and refugees during the 1940s and expounded what he has called the 'Nordic prerogative'. Perceptions of a shared identity and historic past with their Nordic 'brothers' generated a sense of responsibility on the part of the Swedish authorities – a duty that did not extend to other Europeans. The Nordic prerogative also included the notion that Nordic citizens were more able to adjust and integrate within Swedish society than other ethnic groups, and an identification of Jews as a culturally definable group that was particularly resistant to integration. Thus, the Danish and Norwegian Jews numbering among those Scandinavians seeking refuge were rescued *despite* their Jewishness, due to the fact that they were Nordic citizens.[21]

Kvist Geverts comes to a similar conclusion in her examination of Sweden's discrimination of Jewish asylum seekers during the Second World War. She argues that the administration was influenced by Anti-Semitism. This was again based on the belief that Jews would be difficult to integrate into Swedish society, and that they would be the cause of ethnic and religious tensions should they be allowed to settle. This would in its turn create a similar societal problem – a 'Jewish issue' – as was believed to have occurred in Central European countries. This, in its turn, led to a substantial discrimination of Jewish asylum seekers.[22]

Åmark, who has summarised the existing research on Sweden's refugee policy during the Second World War in his extensive work on Sweden's encounter with Nazi Germany during the 1930s and 1940s, agrees that xenophobia and ethnic prejudice was a central constituent factor of Swedish refugee policies during these years. He points out that the 'quotas' for Nordic refugees, regardless of whether they were official or informal, were of a completely different order than the quotas for other refugees. Nordic citizens, also including Nordic Jews, were regarded as a far more acceptable foreign element within Swedish society than other ethnic categories.[23]

---

21　Byström 2006.
22　Kvist Geverts 2008.
23　Åmark 2011, ch. 14–15.

The importance of aspects of ethnicity has also been emphasised by scholars examining other aspects of immigrants' and refugees' encounters with Swedish political life and society, particularly during the first half of the 20th century. One such example relates to workplace relations. Historian Johan Svanberg, for instance, has demonstrated that ethnic prejudices influenced refugees' and working immigrants' experiences within Swedish factories and unions during the first post-war years.[24] Similar conclusions are drawn by Björn Horgby in his study on xenophobia within working class culture in Sweden during the 20th century. Swedish workers tended to view immigrants – including, for example, Estonian refugees who remained in Sweden after 1945 – as potential threats to their working conditions and salaries, resulting in xenophobic ideas expressed in terms of culture and ethnicity.[25] Historian Carl-Henrik Carlsson, who examines the Swedish authorities' assessment of citizenship applications between 1860 and 1920, reached similar findings when it came to discriminatory policies directed against Eastern European Jews.[26]

Researchers examining Swedish refugee policies during the second half of the 20th century, such as historian Christina Johansson, have gone on to argue that ethnicity has continued to play a significant role in policy formation. In her work *Välkomna till Sverige? Svenska migrationspolitiska diskurser under 1900-talets andra hälft*, Johansson counters an official explanation based on economics by showing that perceptions of ethnicity were the more important motivation for both the decision to stop foreign labour immigration at the end of the 1960s, and the sudden and drastic restrictions placed on refugee immigration introduced by the Social Democratic government in 1989. Similarly, Johansson demonstrates how the voluntary repatriation programme which was initiated in the 1990s particularly targeted two ethnic groups that were considered to be particularly 'deviant' and 'difficult to

24  Johan Svanberg, *Arbetets relationer och etniska dimensioner: Verkstadsföreningen, Metall och esterna vid Svenska stålpressnings AB i Olofström 1945–1952*, Linnaeus University Press, Växjö 2010 (ref: Svanberg 2010).

25  Björn Horgby, *Dom där: främlingsfientligheten och arbetarkulturen i Norrköping 1890–1960*, Carlsson, Stockholm 1996 (ref: Horgby 1996).

26  Carlsson 2004. See also *En problematisk relation* 2008.

integrate', namely Bosnians and Somalians (despite the fact that a civil war was still going on in Somalia).[27]

Alternative perspectives have been advanced, however. Joachim Nelhans' early work on the legal foundations for foreigners in the Swedish working market emphasised the importance of labour market policies on the development of immigration legislation up until 1954.[28] Economic concerns are also interpreted as the main influential factor in Lundh and Olsson's macro analysis of Swedish post-war immigration policies. They point towards the fact that during times of economic growth Sweden has, just like many other Western liberal states, welcomed migration to a more significant degree than during times of economic stagnation.[29] Rudolf Tempsch's work on the Sudeten German immigration to Sweden between 1938 and 1955 is comprehensive but mainly descriptive and lacks an explanatory ambition, but can be said to remain close to an economic analytical framework as well.[30]

Historian Malin Thor takes a more analytical approach when examining the National Labour Market Board's selection of Sweden's yearly UN quota for refugees coming from the protracted refugee camps in Europe during the 1950s. National interest in terms of economic concerns clearly guided the authorities in their selection of which refugees to bring to Sweden for permanent settlement. Those who were thought to be able to contribute to the working market were welcomed, whereas the 'hard core' – such as the elderly, terminally ill or orphans – were left behind. Even when complying with the UN's plea to allow tuberculosis patients to migrate to Sweden, the authorities were careful to choose only such individuals who were regarded as curable – and whose working skills were considered to have future benefits.[31]

A more purely juridical perspective is presented by the jurist Göran Melander. He contends that Eastern European refugees were assiduously acknowledged right to protection in Sweden between 1955 and 1967. He omits, however, to compare these poli-

---

27   Johansson 2005.
28   Nelhans 1973, particularly chs 2–3.
29   Lundh & Olsson 1999.
30   Rudolf Tempsch, *Från Centraleuropa till folkhemmet: den sudettyska invandringen till Sverige 1938–1955*, Göteborg University, Göteborg 1997.
31   Thor 2007.

cies with earlier practices and, thus, does not offer any explanatory suggestions regarding how or why they came about.[32]

A distinct explanatory perspective is also missing from Anders Svensson's thesis which describes carefully the Swedish authorities' reception procedures of the Hungarian refugees in 1956–57. However, as with Tempsch's work, this study is of value to researchers examining Cold War refugee policies due to its meticulous and detailed description of how various parts of the Swedish bureaucracy – such as the National Labour Market Board and the County Labour Boards – selected refugees from the refugee camps in Austria and Yugoslavia, and strove to integrate them into Swedish society.[33]

Only a few scholars have examined national security-related factors such as foreign policy and international relations. Historian Anders Berge's work on Sweden's treatment of Soviet refugees during the Second World War explores how foreign policy relations influenced Sweden's management of the Russian and Ingrian refugees who fled to Sweden during and slightly after the Second World War. As a result, Sweden adjusted to several of the Soviet Union's demands regarding these individuals. Soviet representatives were provided with contact details of Russian refugees, were allowed to co-administer the refugee camps, and received substantial Swedish assistance in the repatriation procedures. It was a matter of a 'Swedish-Soviet power game' in which the Swedish administration tried to balance between a positive and negative assessment of Soviet demands. The tactics were, according to Berge, to 'not refuse certain Soviet demands without simultaneously assent to others'. Thus, it is reasoned, refugee policies became a tool of Swedish-Soviet bilateral foreign policy relations.[34]

Similar *realpolitik* aspects of Swedish refugee policies during these years are to some extent explored by historian Curt Ekholm in his meticulous study of the extradition of 2,700 German and Baltic military personnel in 1945–46, already described in chapter

---

32   Melander 1972a; Melander 1972b, Melander 1969.

33   Anders Svensson, *Ungrare i folkhemmet: svensk flyktingpolitik i det kalla krigets skugga,* Lund University Press, Lund 1992.

34   Berge 1992, citations from p. 87. On Sweden's foreign policy in relation to its responses to the situation of Europe's Jewish population during the Second World War, see Levine 1998.

one. Concerns for future stability and security, in the form of Swedish-Soviet relations, determined the outcome of this controversial decision.[35]

Historian Mats Deland has examined Sweden's reluctance to take action against the Nazi war criminals that fled to Sweden during and after the Second World War, despite a responsibility to do so which came with its UN membership from 1946 onwards. A general lack of enthusiasm to engage Swedish resources in such politically sensitive processes, combined with a significant portion of 'foreign policy compliance', is given as the explanation.[36]

Despite the particular foreign policy relations of Sweden during the Cold War, there is a conspicuous scarcity of scholarly work that examines the relationship between Swedish foreign and security policy on the one hand, and its refugee and immigration policy on the other. Political scientists Cecilia Malmström and Marie Demker have explored some aspects of this relationship in their work *Ingenmansland? Svensk immigrationspolitik i utrikespolitisk belysning*. However, the analysis is drawn exclusively from a migrant push-and-pull factors perspective. In other words, it examines how a country's official foreign policy stance influences the size and the constitution (in most cases the nationalities) of the migrant groups that seek residence permits in that country. The kinds of bilateral foreign policy influences tackled in the current work remain, however, unexamined.[37]

One work that explicitly connects the concepts 'national security' and 'refugees' and/or 'migration' within a Swedish context is Elisabeth Abiri's *The securitization of migration: towards an understanding of migration policy changes in the 1990s*. In this study, Abiri examines the discourse and practices of Swedish migration policies during the last decade of the 20th century, and argues that this period was when security and immigration were intertwined in Sweden.[38] As such, she is arguing in a similar vein as many

---

35  Ekholm 1995.

36  Deland 2010, citation from p. 411.

37  Marie Demker & Cecilia Malmström, *Ingenmansland? Svensk immigrationspolitik i utrikespolitisk belysning*, Studentlitteratur, Lund 1999.

38  Elisabeth Abiri, *The securitisation of migration: towards an understanding of migration policy changes in the 1990s: the case of Sweden*, Göteborg University, Göteborg 2000 (ref: Abiri 2000).

other international researchers which tend to see the Cold War as a period in history when migration and security matters – as well as internal and external security issues – were clearly separate.[39]

There are also a number of publications focusing on the specific experiences of certain refugee groups in Sweden during the Second World War and the following decade. The refugee camps, a range of refugee-related organisations and the personal experiences of specific categories of refugees are some examples of issues that have been examined.[40]

In general, however, research on post-war Swedish immigration policies still contains several gaps. Regarding the 1950s, one potential explanation is the fact that, in comparison with other decades of the second half of that century, few refugees came to Sweden. However, as has been previously emphasised, this decade constitutes such an important period of apparent change, particularly during the first years. This is reason enough to justify its study. The complexity of the early Cold War constitutes a further motivation.

## 2.6 Soviet Refugees In Sweden During The Second World War

Among the non-Nordic nationalities that came to Sweden during the Second World War, the more than 30,000 Balts constituted by far the largest component. However, other Soviet citizens also arrived – both individuals who had recently gained this civic status and persons who had held it all their lives. This included about 1,500 Ingrians and around 3,000 Russians. In the following section, attention will be given to these three refugee categories and their experiences in Sweden during the Second World War.

Apart from providing an historical context, this exposé is moti-

39   See chapter 8, part 8.5.
40   See, for example, Nils Andrzej Uggla, *I nordlig hamn: polacker i Sverige under andra världskriget*, Centrum för multietnisk forskning, Uppsala Universitet, Uppsala 1997; Malin Thor, *Hechaluz – en rörelse i tid och rum: tysk-judiska ungdomars exil i Sverige 1933–1943*, Växjö University Press, Växjö 2005; Andræ 2004; Wirginia Bogatic, *Exilens dilemma: att stanna eller att återvända*, Linneus University Press, Växjö 2011; Hammarström 1984; Tobias Berglund & Niclas Sennerteg, *Svenska koncentrationsläger i Tredje rikets skugga*, Natur & Kultur, Stockholm 2008.

vated by the fact that both refugees who arrived during and after the Second World War fall within the remit of this thesis. In the analysis of decisions of refusal of entry, only those who arrived after this work's chronological starting point are examined. However, in the analysis of decisions of deportation, expulsion and extradition, as well as the continuous treatment of refugees in terms of the conditions to their residence permits, both individuals who arrived before and after the war are included, since such decisions obviously concerned foreign citizens in Sweden regardless of their specific arrival date.

### 2.6.1 Baltic Refugees

Aside from the Nordic refugees, Balts constituted the largest national group to arrive in Sweden during the war. According to official statistics, approximately 34,000 Baltic citizens were situated in Sweden at the beginning of 1945.[41]

Around 6,500 of these were so called 'Estonian-Swedes' (*Estlandssvenskar*) – Swedish speaking people from the north west coast of Estonia, believed to be descendants of Swedish settlers from the Middle Ages and the 17th century (the so-called 'Great Power Period' of Swedish history). Almost the entire Estonian-Swedish colony in Estonia was gathered and transferred to Sweden already in 1943 as a result of joint efforts by the Swedish state and private organisations. Again it was their ethnicity – the fact that they were regarded as 'Swedish' or 'almost Swedish' – that motivated the authorities' endeavours.[42] A further group that came during the earlier stages of the war consisted of Estonian intellectuals who had been transported to Sweden as a result of American efforts.[43]

The majority of the other Baltic citizens that came to Sweden, however, fled on their own initiative in the autumn of 1944 when the Soviet Union reoccupied their homelands. Most of them travelled from their home countries across the Baltic Sea but some also came via Finland. Around 7,000 Balts had fled there during the war, and many of the young men had joined the Finnish army in

---

41  *Sociala Meddelanden* 1945, nr 1, p. 35; SOU 1951:42 *Betänkande med förslag till utlänningslag m.m.*, p. 253 (ref: SFS 1951:42).
42  Andræ 2004, pp. 21–50.
43  Andræ 2004, pp. 124, 51–90.

the struggle against the Soviet Union. As such, they became traitors in the eyes of their new occupier, and were to be extradited according to the regulations in the Finnish-Soviet peace agreement of the autumn of 1944. As a result, many sought refuge in Sweden.[44]

In total, then, around 25,000 Estonians, 6,500 Estonian-Swedes, 3,700 Latvians and 300 Lithuanians came to Sweden during the war according to official statistics.[45] On Swedish territory the Baltic refugees were initially transported to various refugee camps. Altogether they were spread out in over 250 different camps.[46]

Careful medical examinations ensued upon the refugees' arrival at the camps, organised by the Board of Medicine (*Medicinal-styrelsen*). Sick individuals were put in quarantine.[47] Rumours of Nazi perpetrators among the Baltic refugees resulted in an investigation by the security police. All refugee camps housing Baltic citizens were included in this process. In January 1945, the examination was completed. According to the police, the results demonstrated that, out of the total Baltic refugee population, 139 individuals had cooperated with the Germans and 74 with the Russians whilst a further 17 individuals had had dealings with both Germans and Russians. Most of these people were then moved to a specific closed camp in Baggå in the province of Västmanland where they underwent another round of inspection. After some time, however, most were released. Further action was in most cases not undertaken. Some of the accused were even employed by the Swedish military intelligence services, since they held information of great value to this organisation.[48]

Most of the refugees on Swedish territory – and particularly the Nordic citizens – could and did return to their home countries

---

44   About 5,000 of them were Estonians according to Andræ 2004, pp. 51–98.

45   *Sociala Meddelanden* 1945, nr 1, p. 35.

46   Andræ 2004, pp. 166–172. See also Kerstin Hellner, *De landsflyktiga och Sverige*, Bonnier, Stockholm 1952; *De första båtflyktingarna: en antologi om balterna i Sverige*, Eriksson, Lars-Gunnar (ed.), Statens invandrarverk (SIV), Norrköping 1986 (ref: *De första båtflyktingarna* 1986).

47   Andræ 2004, p. 106.

48   It is, of course, impossible to verify the numbers. The preceding investigation was mostly pursued through interviews with Baltic refugees and a significant amount of the resulting documentary evidence has been destroyed. Andræ 2004, pp. 122–129. On a thorough examination of the management of the Nazi-accused Balts in Sweden, see Deland 2010.

after the war. Balts, however, constituted the largest group who wished to stay. This fact put a strain on the resources of the Swedish administration. Maintaining the refugee camps was a costly affair, and a post-war depression with concomitant levels of unemployment were anticipated at this time.[49]

A perhaps even more important source of tension were Soviet attitudes. The massive repatriation process of its citizens had been launched on the European continent, and pressure was put on Swedish officials in the matter. The return of the Balts was a matter of prestige for the Soviet Union, and Soviet representatives attempted to persuade their Swedish counterparts by alluding to potential future Swedish-Soviet relations.[50] In June 1945 a formal complaint was also issued.[51]

Internal discussions were undertaken within government as to how this 'delicate' issue should be tackled. Newspaper editors were urged to keep a low profile on the matter, for the sake of both the refugees and Swedish-Soviet relations.[52] Already in January 1945, however, a closed meeting of the parliamentary council on foreign affairs (*Utrikesnämnden*) had decided in secret that, even though the Swedish authorities wished to see the Baltic refugees return, no civilians would be forced so to do.[53]

As a result, most of the Baltic refugees were soon allowed to leave the refugee camps and settle in various parts of Sweden. The authorities were keen to ensure that refugees could support themselves financially as soon as possible. Since the Balts were expected to stay, they were excluded from the obligation placed on non-Nordic foreigners of having a work permit already during

49  Andræ 2004; Myrdal 1944.

50  Andræ 2004, p. 133. An examination of records from the Ministry for Foreign Affairs also reveals that this matter was raised frequently by delegations of Soviet representatives, and tied to the question of future Swedish-Soviet relations. See, for example, 'P.M.', 19 november 1945, del VI, vol. 77, P 40 R, 1920 års dossiésystem, UD, Ra; 'P.M. angående baltiska flyktingarna', 21 november 1945, del VI, vol. 77, P 40 R, 1920 års dossiésystem, UD, Ra; 'P.M', 22 november 1945, del VI, vol. 77, P 40 R, 1920 års dossiésystem, UD, Ra; 'Moskva den 4 januari 1946', strängt förtroligt, del VI, vol. 77, P 40 R, 1920 års dossiésystem, UD, Ra.

51  'Moskva den 5 juni 1945', strängt förtroligt, del IV, P 40 R, 1920 års dossiésystem, UD, Ra. This seems to have been ignored, however. See also Ekholm 1995.

52  Andræ 2004, pp. 122–136.

53  Andræ 2004, p. 134.

the autumn of 1944. Initially, however, they were rarely allowed to seek employment on their own initiative. Instead, it was a task for the National Labour Market Board or the County Labour Boards to place the refugees at a range of low-skilled positions where need was greatest. Thus occupations in forestry, agricultural and factory work became common for the Balts.[54]

It became an important principle that refugees should not compete for jobs with the indigenous population. The so-called 'intellectuals' of Baltic nationality thus posed problems. They were generally not keen on being placed in agricultural or forestry work, and after some time the authorities sought to find other sorts of occupation for these individuals, especially for those over 30–35 years of age. Within the Baltic group, however, as many as 20% were characterised as belonging to this category. For these, placement in so called 'archival work' became common. These positions included mainly administrative tasks at various places such as universities or refugee organisations and were paid for and administered by the state through the Government's Board of Refugee Relief (*Statens Flyktingsnämnd*) in cooperation with the National Alien Commission. According to Mikael Byström, these archival engagements were both a labour market measure and a subsidy scheme. However, individuals suspected of having a politically questionable past (in other words Balts who were believed to have cooperated actively with the Nazi regimes in their home countries) were prohibited from archival work.[55]

Overall though, the provision of employment and housing arrangements for Baltic (and other) refugees occurred with greater rapidity in Sweden than in those other European countries that suffered greatly during the war and which received many times more refugees. In October 1945 only around 900 Baltic individuals were still housed in refugee camps.[56] Some of this number consisted of individuals deemed by the authorities to require extra surveillance.

---

54   Olsson 1995. See also Byström 2012, particularly chs 3–5; Horgby 1996. For a detailed study on Baltic refugees working at Swedish factories from 1945 onwards, see Svanberg 2010.

55   Byström 2012, pp. 113–133. See also Olsson 1995, p. 80. On the refusal to accord archival work to individuals considered dubious, see examples from the examination in this thesis, for example the central dossiers of B111 and B116.

56   'Protokoll', 2 oktober 1945, § 9, bilaga 3, vol. 1, A 1 A, Kanslibyrån, SUK, Ra.

They represented a mixture of suspected former agents, Nazis, communists or ordinary 'trouble-makers' who the authorities wanted to discipline. As such, they were kept in closed camps such as Baggå for observation, just as other suspected foreigners had been during the war. Within a year, however, most of them had been released and allowed to settle in various parts of Sweden.[57] In other European countries, such as Denmark and Germany, however, it would be several years before the protracted refugee camp situation was solved.[58]

It needs to be noted, however, that the government's official attitude towards the Baltic refugees was not all that warm and welcoming. In June 1945, Baltic refugees were informed by the Swedish authorities that they could return cost-free to the Soviet Union, and that it was the wish of the Swedish government that they should do so. It was also pointed out that it was prohibited to try to persuade a Baltic refugee *not* to return, and that any other forms of political propaganda were prohibited. This prohibition included, for example, political meetings, radio broadcasting and publishing activities that involved criticising the new regime in the Baltic countries.[59] These measures were clearly made with Swedish-Soviet relations in mind. The Balts were, to use the words of a contemporaneous Swedish diplomat, a 'constant matter for irritation' due to the strain they placed on Swedish-Soviet relations.[60]

Another adjustment to Soviet demands was expressed during the spring of 1945, when Soviet authorities were permitted to visit the Baltic refugee camps. They were also allowed to publish notes in Swedish newspapers and within the camps, urging the refugees to return and making promises that no one would be punished for his flight. This led to strong protests within the Baltic refugee group. However, as we shall see, in contrast to its treatment of

57  Åmark 2011, pp. 556–565.
58  Wyman 1998; Marrus 2002, pp. 296–345.
59  The letters that were sent for distribution at the refugee camps can be found at various places within the National Alien Commission's archive. See, for example, the following two documents within the central dossier of B53: 'Meddelande' (undated) and 'Till statens utlänningskommission', 15 juni 1945.
60  'P.M.', 21 april 1945, strängt förtroligt, vol. 67, P 40 I, 1920 års dossiésystem, UD, Ra. See also 'Protokoll', 23 augusti 1950, § 1, Bilaga 1, vol. 3, A 1 A, Kanslibyrån, SUK, Ra.

Ingrian and Russian refugees, the Swedish administration did not provide the Soviet authorities with contact details and names of individuals residing in the camps. In this way, it was harder for the Soviet authorities to bring pressure to bear on the Baltic refugees than it was to intimidate the Russians and the Ingrians.[61]

Overall, however, the Baltic civilians were granted a *collective* status as political refugees. In other words, asylum had been bestowed on them not because of their own, personal experiences, but based on their nationality and on the fact that their respective home countries had been occupied (despite the fact that Sweden had been among the first to publicly acknowledge the Baltic countries as Soviet states already in 1940). This behaviour thus corresponded with the norms of interwar international law outlined in chapter one.

Just as important, however, was the fact that Balts were not regarded as being as foreign as other Eastern Europeans. As such, a quota of 30,000 was, after all, regarded as an 'acceptable' portion to integrate into Swedish society, despite the resistance of certain elements of society.[62] And although they were not positively regarded everywhere (particularly not within the working classes who feared competition and decreasing salaries as a result of the Baltic immigration, as well as interpretations of them as being Nazi-friendly[63]), the Balts still had some vocal supporters among the Swedish population. A deportation of 30,000 Baltic civilians to the Soviet Union would have caused outraged protests.[64] Additionally, a forced deportation of the civilian Balts would also have represented a serious contravention of the Western Allied repatriation principles which only identified Soviet citizens according to the borders of 1939. It is highly likely that a refusal to grant the civilian Balts asylum would have prompted a harsh rebuke from the United States.

However, the collective political refugee status that was granted these civilians did little to help the 146 Baltic soldiers who were expatriated to the Soviet Union during the winter of 1945–46 as a result of Sweden's reluctance to provoke its new superpower neighbour. Consequently, a rather contradictory situation arose. Some

61    See part 2.6.2 and 2.6.3. See also Andræ 2004; Berge 1992.
62    Åmark 2011, ch. 15.
63    Horgby 1996; Svanberg 2010.
64    Ekholm 1995, ch. 12.

of those individuals who had fought against their new occupier, and who would under other circumstances have been considered as definite political refugees, were extradited; whereas civilians were granted the right to stay, without too many questions being asked. This included, for example, a number of Nazi perpetrators.[65] Again, this constitutes an example of how the interpretation of the term 'political refugee' varied in tandem with Sweden's geopolitical relations and the current intentions of the political administration.

The mass expatriation of soldiers left many Baltic citizens in Sweden concerned for their own future security. They feared that Sweden would eventually succumb to pressure from the Soviet Union by enacting the forced return of more Soviet and Baltic citizens. These prompted many to leave. According to some statistics, around 5,000 Balts left Sweden for the USA and Canada in the immediate post-war years. Others travelled to Argentina and the United Kingdom.[66]

Were their fears justified? Were Baltic citizens 'safe' on Swedish ground once they had been granted their first residence permit, or did they in fact risk expatriation? What happened to those persons the Soviet Union demanded be extradited? And what about those Balts who for various reasons (including criminal activities) became regarded as unwanted? How strong were their asylum rights? And did the collective political asylum function as a precedent for Balts who arrived later? Chapters 4 to 7 will examine these issues in more detail.

Overall, however, the majority of the Baltic refugees who arrived in 1944 stayed in Sweden. And by the start of the period under review, most had already received a residence permit, a work placement and had settled down. As we shall see, though, things were not so straightforward for the Ingrian and Russian refugees who knocked on Sweden's doors during the war.

65 Deland 2010.
66 *Svensk invandrar–och flyktingpolitik,* Arbetsmarknadsdepartementet, Stockholm
  1988, p. 27.

### 2.6.2 *Ingrian Refugees*

Towards the end of the Second World War, more than 60,000 Finnish-speaking Ingrians resided in Finland as a result of the collective transportations initiated by the Germans a few years earlier. By the time that the Finnish-Soviet armistice agreement was reached in 1944, however, the Soviet Union aimed for their return.

Initially, some confusion regarding the legal status of the civilian Ingrians prevailed. This related to whether or not they were to be included in the regulations of the tenth paragraph of the armistice agreement, which stated that all 'interned and compulsory transferred' Soviet citizens were to be repatriated to the Soviet Union. In the end, it was agreed that most of these civilians were not to be included in this definition, since many of them had moved voluntarily. However, according to some calculations, as many as 53,000 did return to the Soviet Union. Some did so out of free will. Many had lived under unsatisfactory conditions in Finland and wished to return to their homes. Others, however, were forced, threatened or persuaded by the Russian-led Allied Control Commission which operated in Finland at this time. Its primary purpose was to ensure compliance with the armistice agreement. This included, among other things, the repatriation of Soviet citizens. Upon their return to the Soviet Union, however, the Ingrians were forbidden from returning to their homeland. Instead they were transported to areas like Pskov, Novgorod, Jaroslavl and Tver in the middle of Russia.[67]

However, many Ingrians had joined the Finnish army in the field against the Soviet Union. Others had worked in the Finnish war industry. As such, they were considered traitors according to Soviet Law and were to be extradited according to paragraph nine of the armistice agreement. This meant that Finland had to extradite all the Ingrians (and Balts) who had fought on their side against the Soviet Union during the war. Many Finns felt deeply concerned over the fate of these individuals, and eye-witness accounts tell of

---

67 Finnish archival research project: http://www.narc.fi/Arkistolaitos/inkerilais-siirtolaiset/statistik.html and http://www.narc.fi/Arkistolaitos/inkerilaissiirto-laiset/flyttar.html and http://www.arkisto.fi/se/news/228/358/Nya-uppgifter-om-ingermanlaendarnas-repatriering-efter-fortsaettningskriget (accessed 3 October 2011); Toivo Flink, *Kotiin Karkotettavaksi: Inkeriläisen siirtoväen palautukset Suomesta Neuvostohiittoon 1944–1955,* Suomalaisen Kirjallisuuden Seura, Helsinki 2010 (ref: Flink 2010).

trains loaded with Ingrian 'traitors' moving slowly through the Finnish woods towards the Soviet Union – slowly enough to enable some of them to flee.[68]

As a result, around 1,500 Ingrians fled to Sweden in 1944–45 – often with help of Finnish citizens. Some hid among the Finnish evacuees in the north of Sweden and pretended to be Finnish citizens before revealing their true identities to the authorities. Many also tried to hide in Finland through the acquisition of new identities.[69]

Most of the Ingrians who arrived in Sweden during these last months of the Second World War were allowed entry. The National Alien Commission received directions from the government stating that they should allow entry even to those Ingrians who could 'propose even very insignificant reasons for political asylum'.[70] After spending some time in refugee camps, subject to the standard investigation procedure, many were transferred to various workplaces across Sweden, just as the Balts had been.[71]

In contrast to the Balts, however, this did not mean that they were going to be allowed to stay in Sweden permanently. Even so, the Soviet authorities had been informed by the Swedish government that it would not force any Soviet refugees to return to their home country. In January 1945 this standpoint was reiterated.[72] It is difficult to determine whether this was a matter of legal semantics (the statement excluding individuals which the authorities believed should *not* be considered 'political refugees'), or whether it was an example of interstate diplomatic strategic communication (keeping a hard line in order to avoid being subject to official demands). Berge has rightly pointed out that refugee policies had two separate dimensions during those years, and, consequently, respondents – the refugees on the one hand, and their home coun-

---

68 Hammarström 1984; Gerhard Hafström, 'Ingermanländarna och asylrätten' in *Svio-Estonica: Studier utg. av svensk-estniska samfundet,* vol. xx, Stockholm 1971; Berge 1992.

69 Regarding the statistics, see 'Antalet ingermanländare i Sverige per den 2/2 1946', vol. 68, P 40 I, 1920 års dossiésystem, UD, Ra. See also, Flink 2010.

70 'Till Konungen', 26 juni 1945, vol. 67, P 40 I, 1920 års dossiésystem, UD, Ra. See also Berge 1992, p. 76.

71 'v.p.m' (undated, though probably June 1945), vol. 67, P 40 I, 1920 års dossiésystem, UD, Ra; See also Hammarström 1984; Berge 1992, p. 76.

72 'p.m.', 22 januari 1945, vol. 67, P 40 I, 1920 års dossiésystem, UD, Ra.

try on the other.[73] However, he has also argued that in the case of the Soviet refugees/displaced persons during the Second World War, the government chose to adopt an official attitude that was more Soviet-friendly (with the Soviet authorities as respondents), and a more refugee-friendly attitude in practice (aimed towards the refugees as respondents). In the case of the Ingrians, nonetheless, it can be speculated if the reverse was true. That said, however, no general decision regarding the Ingrians' fate had yet been reached.

Be that as it may, it was clear that they were not going to be handled in the same generous way as the Balts. One reason for this was that the Ingrians were considered as legitimate Soviet citizens in a way that Balts were not. In a letter to the Ministry of the Interior, the National Alien Commission set out Sweden's' asylum principles regarding Soviet citizens, as formulated by the government. It explains the *differences* between its handling of Baltic citizens on the one hand, and Ingrians on the other, as being based on the status of their home countries. Whereas the Ingrians had been 'Russian citizens' since the 18th century, the Baltic citizens had belonged to previously independent countries that had only recently been occupied. Unlike the Ingrians, the Balts' shared experience of recent occupation thus constituted a ground for collective political asylum.[74]

Thus, there was no collective asylum status available for the Ingrians as there was for the Balts. Even so, some were indeed to be regarded as political refugees. The Commission, as well as the government, appreciated that those Ingrians who had, for example, actively fought against the Soviet Union in the Finnish army were under considerable risk of punishment upon their return to the Soviet Union. They also realised that Finland would have little opportunity to protect them, given the regulations stated in para-

---

73   Berge 1992, ch. 1.

74   *Ingermanländarna ha icke liksom estländarna, letterna och litauerna varit självstän-*
     *diga vid tiden för det sista världskrigets utbrott utan ha sedan 1700-talet varit ryska*
     *medborgare. Det motiv, som gör att Sverige icke velat tvångsförpassa de baltiska flyk-*
     *tingarna till deras hemländer, föreligger alltså icke beträffande ingermanländarna.*
     'Till Konungen', 26 juni 1945, vol. 67, P 40 I, 1920 års dossiésystem, UD, Ra.
     Such attitudes are also structurally in evidence when it comes to the arrange-
     ment of the associated archives. Balts were categorised as Estonians, Latvians
     and Lithuanians as well as collectively as Balts. Ingrians, however, were only
     sometimes accounted for separately. At other times, they were included in the
     group 'Soviet-Russian'.

graph nine of the armistice agreement. Thus, it was soon realised that a set of criteria was needed in terms of the Ingrians, in order to determine their refugee status. In other words, their asylum applications were to be *individually assessed* to another extent than the Balts. This process did not begin in earnest until the summer of 1945. (Thus, it will be further explored in chapter four.)

Before the matter of the Ingrians' right to reside in Sweden after the war was settled, however, there was another, more urgent issue to be tackled. As mentioned above, in January 1945 the Soviet Embassy demanded the names and addresses of all Soviet citizens in Sweden. As a response to this, the government granted Soviet personnel permission to visit the Baltic refugee camps, but were refused the personal information – the names and contact details – of the individuals residing there. The Ingrians, however, who were regarded as 'legitimate' Soviet citizens, now experienced the first substantial consequence of this Swedish attitude. It was decided that some of them were indeed going to have their personal contact details revealed to the Soviet legation. After some discussion between the government and the Commission, the selection criteria were established. Those who would *not* have their personal contact details revealed included persons who had participated in war activities against the Soviet Union, or had a close relative who had done so; who had been members connected to German 'Hilfswilligen' organisations; who had been punished for 'political reasons' in the Soviet Union or was threatened by such a punishment upon return; or who had worked within the Finnish war industry. Those who did not meet any of these criteria would not be afforded the same anonymity.[75]

In total, 784 Soviet citizens residing in Sweden had their names and addresses revealed to the Soviet authorities. Around

---

75   Berge 1992, pp. 57–67. See also, for example, 'P.M.', 16 januari 1945, vol. 67, P 40 I, 1920 års dossiésystem, UD, Ra; 'P.M.', 22 januari 1945, vol. 67, P 40 I, 1920 års dossiésystem, UD, Ra; 'ang. behandling av vissa flyktingskategorier', 26 januari 1945, hemlig, vol. 67, P 40 I, 1920 års dossiésystem, UD, Ra; 'Stockholm den 27 februari 1945', vol. 67, P 40 I, 1920 års dossiésystem, UD, Ra; 'P.M.', 21 april 1945, strängt förtroligt, vol. 67, P 40 I, 1920 års dossiésystem, UD, Ra; 'P.M.', 9 augusti 1945, vol. 77, P 40 R, 1920 års dossiésystem, UD, Ra. Both vol. 67 in P 40 I, 1920 års dossiésystem, UD, Ra, and vol. 77 in P 40 R, 1920 års dossiésystem, UD, Ra contain numerous documents describing these events.

500 of these were Ingrians.[76] Many of them had, however, been subjected to persecution and harassment, or even imprisonment, within the Soviet Union for other reasons than those defined as 'political' by the government (such as, for example, their class status or Lutheran religion). Some were known as political opponents to the regime, but had never been imprisoned. Some had had their land confiscated, and had been forced to settle elsewhere. Many had worked for the Germans or the Finns, but in other kinds of industries than those directly relating to the war effort. Additionally, all stood accused of having committed crimes against the state in the eyes of the Soviet Union by virtue of the fact that they had left the Soviet Union. This was compounded by allowing themselves to be given over to the enemy and by their reluctance to return. As such, they were as unwilling to re-enter the Soviet Union as many of those included in the first group. And, they were often just as unwilling to receive visits from Soviet representatives. None of this, however, was acknowledged as justification for protection.[77]

The dispatch of addresses had consequences, as is testified by the numerous letters sent to the National Alien Commission and the Ministry for Foreign Affairs during the spring of 1945. Soviet representatives travelled the country in order to try to persuade its citizens to return to the Soviet Union. The usage of various threats was common. One method was to mention an individual's family members and relatives. They could promise that, for example, an elderly mother would be better looked after should an individual choose to return. Alternatively, it was insinuated that family members still in the Soviet Union would suffer should an exile refuse to return voluntarily. Rumours that Sweden would soon repatriate by force all Soviet citizens was a common refrain. So too were guarantees that those who returned of their own volition would be treated far better than those who were forcibly repatriated later. This amplified the apprehensions of many and prompted several to return. Although the precise reactions of each individual are impossible to fathom, it is not unlikely that a significant portion of them did go back out

76   Berge 1992, pp. 66, 79.
77   See chapter four.

of fear for their own security and that of their relatives.[78]

A similar situation faced some of those other Soviet citizens – including Balts, Ingrians and Russians – whose names and addresses had not been supplied to the Soviet authorities. This is because the latter had other means of sourcing the contact details of sought-after individuals. Thus even Soviet citizens who had been shielded sometimes received visits from Soviet representatives.[79]

In the end, around one third of the Ingrians in Sweden had their contact details passed on to the Soviet authorities. By the summer and autumn of 1945 the destiny of these individuals was to be determined. The decision to protect only those individuals categorised as 'political refugees' would have a bearing on their fate. This will be further explored in chapter four together with the continuing practices regarding new arrivals of Ingrian origin.


### 2.6.3 Russian Refugees

In contrast to the Balts and the Ingrians, many of the Russians that came to Sweden did so during earlier stages of the war. Most of these were military personnel, in flight from various German prisoners of war camps. In total, about 3,000 Soviet-Russian citizens crossed the border to Sweden during the war.[80]

As mentioned above, the Soviet aim was to repatriate all these individuals using a tactical blend of formal and informal pressures. Anders Berge identifies four main formal Soviet demands exerted on the Swedish authorities regarding the Russians in Sweden. These were similar to those exercised in other countries, such as, for example, France. The first was *information* regarding names and details of every Soviet citizen that had arrived in Sweden. The second was *concentration*. The Soviet authorities demanded that the Russian refugees that came were to be gathered in separate camps in order to forestall their integration into the Swedish society. The third was *control*, and included, among other things, a wish to administer these camps. This also facilitated the fourth demand –

---

78   See various letters in vol. 67, P 40 I, 1920 års dossiésystem, UD, Ra. See also
     Berge 1992, pp. 68–72; Notini 2006; Hammarström 1984.
79   *Ibid.*
80   Berge 1992; Hans Lundgren, *Krampen: ryssläger i Sverige under andra världskriget*, Västmanlands läns museum, Västerås 2008 (ref: Lundgren 2008).

*individual treatment* – which included being able to access refugees in order to fulfil their repatriation aims.[81]

These demands were met to a considerable extent. For example, more or less closed wartime camps containing Soviet-Russian citizens only, with extensive Soviet control, were established. This enabled the Soviet administration in Sweden to achieve its goal of mass repatriation. By not presenting the refugees with any real opportunities to apply for asylum, the Swedish authorities assisted the Soviet authorities in their endeavours. In a number of secret operations during October and November 1944, more than 1,000 Soviet-Russian refugees were repatriated with help from the Swedish police. In total almost 2,500 Soviet citizens were repatriated to the Soviet Union between 1944 and 1946.[82]

Some Russian citizens managed to escape from the camps and applied for political asylum. A few hundred were successful and were granted political refugee status. In general, though, Soviet Russians were collectively considered as displaced persons rather than refugees – and, consequently, as a responsibility for the Soviet rather than the Swedish authorities. The fact that the Soviet legislation deemed many of them as traitors, since they had 'allowed' themselves to be taken prisoners of war, did not influence this assessment.[83]

Sweden offered assistance in ways that went beyond concentrating and repatriating Soviet citizens, however. During 1943 and 1944, the Soviet embassy received information about newly arrived Soviet citizens directly from the Ministry for Foreign Affairs. The arrivals were almost exclusively Russian soldiers, often fleeing from German prisoners of war camps in Norway. The information assisted the Soviet authorities in their aim to control the Soviet refugees/displaced persons under Swedish jurisdiction, and keep

---

81   Berge 1992, p. 40.

82   Berge 1992, pp. 41–57; Lundgren 2008. Most of them never appeared in the official statistics. *Sociala Meddelanden*, 1944–46.

83   The Swedish authorities also actively assisted the transportation through its territory of more than 60,000 Soviet prisoners of war from Norway to the Soviet Union. Individuals who tried to flee during the journey were captured by the Swedish police and handed over to the Soviet authorities. Berge 1992, p. 56; Lundgren 2008. See also documents dated 9 juni 1945, 12 juni 1945 and 15 juni 1945, vol. 1, E 4, Hemliga arkivet, SUK, Ra; and 'Protokoll', 10 juli 1945, vol. 1, A 1 A, Kanslibyrån, SUK, Ra.

them within the allocated camps.[84] When the Soviet legation officially demanded the names and addresses of all Soviet citizens in Sweden in early 1945, thus, it already had contact details for most of the Russians. For those residing outside of the Soviet camps, the same categories as those being applied to the Ingrians were utilised by the Swedish authorities. In other words, Russians who had been members of German 'Hilfswilligen' organisations, fought against the Soviet Union, suffered punishment for 'political reasons' or had aided the Finnish war effort were protected. All others – numbering around 250 individuals – had their personal contact details revealed. They faced a similar treatment as that issued to the Ingrians.[85]

### 2.6.4 A Comparison

Thus, in comparison with the treatment of Baltic and Ingrian refugees during the Second World War, the Russians clearly emerge as the refugee group who were least favourably treated by the Swedish authorities. Whereas the Balts were granted collective asylum, the Russians were most often collectively denied the possibility of even applying. The minority who managed to stay did so by both avoiding the Soviet administrated camps and convincing the Swedish authorities of their political refugee status.

Of course, one should not assume that they actively wished to stay. Many surely wanted to return to their families, hoping that their 'crime' (imprisonment by the enemy) should not be looked upon so badly. In practice, however, the government's attitude, which collectively identified the Russians as displaced persons rather than refugees, provided them with little choice.

84 See, for example, 'P.M.', 16 januari 1945, vol. 67, P 40 I, 1920 års dossiésystem, UD, Ra.

85 Berge 1992, pp. 57–67. See also, for example, 'P.M.', 16 januari 1945, vol. 67, P 40 I, 1920 års dossiésystem, UD, Ra; 'P.M.', 22 januari 1945, vol. 67, P 40 I, 1920 års dossiésystem, UD, Ra; 'ang. behandling av vissa flyktingskategorier', 26 januari 1945, hemlig, vol. 67, P 40 I, 1920 års dossiésystem, UD, Ra; 'Stockholm den 27 februari 1945', vol. 67, P 40 I, 1920 års dossiésystem, UD, Ra; 'P.M.', 21 april 1945, strängt förtroligt, vol. 67, P 40 I, 1920 års dossiésystem, UD, Ra; 'P.M.', 9 augusti 1945, P 40 R, vol. 77, 1920 års dossiésystem, UD, Ra. Both vol. 67 in P 40 I, 1920 års dossiésystem, UD, Ra, and vol. 77 in P 40 R, 1920 års dossiésystem, UD, Ra contain numerous documents describing these events.

Ingrians seem to have occupied a 'middle position'. Like the Russians they were regarded as legitimate Soviet citizens. In contrast, however, some of them were regarded as political refugees due to their specific backgrounds and experiences in Finland during the war. Thus, in contrast to both the Balts and the Russians, specific guidelines were established regarding the assessment of the refugee status of Ingrian refugees.

In general, however, deciding who was to be considered a political refugee or not was clearly determined along national, collective lines, rather than by being based on an assessment of a given individual. Even the assessment of the Ingrians was similarly characterised. Their special treatment was granted collectively, probably due to their Finnish-Ingrian ethnicity and heritage. Thus, somewhat paradoxically, a collective estimation of this group led to the conclusion that individual assessments were necessary. Russians, however, were in general collectively regarded as displaced persons rather than refugees.

How does this varying and nationality-specific treatment correspond with the Swedish authorities' treatment of refugee groups in subsequent years? As shall be demonstrated, the monitoring activities of the National Alien Commission extended far beyond a refugee or foreigner's right to stay. Furthermore, new groups of Balts, Ingrians and Russians reached Sweden in the years that ensued. What was the response of the Swedish authorities? And what influences were brought to bear on this affair by the prevailing context of the Cold War, the developing international refugee regime, Swedish-Soviet relations, ethnic considerations, the boosting labour market and the fluctuating relationship between the private lives of individuals and the role of the state?

# CHAPTER THREE

# The Juridical and Institutional Framework

Sweden was among the first countries to sign the UN's 1951 Refugee Convention. From that point onwards it agreed to grant asylum to individuals defined as refugees by this ground-breaking document. Three years later, in 1954, Sweden ratified the Convention through incorporating it into its new national Aliens Act.[1] Prior to this, however, Sweden was not tied to any international regulations regarding refugee related matters, as it had never signed any of the previous conventions. During the first Cold War years, therefore, national legislation still took precedence.

In this chapter, the legislation pertaining to refugees during the research period will be examined in more detail, as well as the authorities that were accountable for its implementation. What room for manoeuvre were the authorities afforded by these frameworks? What were the responsibilities of the various official organs? And what were the main steps of an asylum application process?

## 3.1. The 1945 Aliens Act – Identifying the Rights of the Swedish State

The Swedish Aliens Act of 1945 came into force on 1 July and was intended to last for two years. It was prolonged several times,

---

1    Sweden opted out of certain regulations concerning the labour market, social security and administrative assistance, however. The reservations concerned §§ 8; 12 (1); 17 (2); 24 (1)b; 24 (3) and 25. See http://www.humanrights.gov.se/ dynamaster/file_archive/040414/65628456c55c5444dfc7beca3d6f26f6/konventioner_komplett.pdf (accessed 19 September 2012)

however, until 1954 when it was exchanged for a new, permanent Aliens Act. Like its predecessors of 1927 and 1937, the 1945 Aliens Act stated that only Swedish citizens had an unconditional right to enter and reside in Sweden. It asserted the Swedish state's right to turn away, expel and/or deport foreign citizens. It also regulated such individuals' obligations to the Swedish state while on Swedish territory. This included reporting to the police whenever required as well as holding proof of identity and all other obligatory permissions regarding where to reside and work.[2]

In other words, unlike subsequent international and national legislation, the aim of the law was not to establish individuals' rights against the state. Instead, it identified the state's right – in relation to other states – to grant or refuse asylum. Thus, individual asylum seekers were only to a limited extent supported by this piece of legislation.

As such, the 1945 Aliens Act bears a marked resemblance to other European countries' immigration legislation of this period. Overall, individuals had very few rights against states of which they were not citizens.[3] 'Right of asylum' was still predominately interpreted as a juridical field which concerned states' relationships with each other rather than individuals' well-being. It established that states had the right to grant asylum to other states' citizens and that this should not be understood as an offensive action. This juridical perception stemmed from the general legal principle within international relations of the 19th and early 20th centuries that states should not interfere with another's domestic affairs and/or citizens.[4] Thus, the Aliens Act of 1945 was a child of its time.

---

2   SFS 1945: 315, *Lag om utlännings rätt att här i riket vistas (utlänningslag)* (ref: SFS 1945:315); SFS 1954:193, *Utlänningslag; given Stockholm slott d. 30 april 1954* (ref: SFS: 1954:193). Prolongations of the former law, see SFS 1947:312; SFS 1951:106; prop. nr 207/1947; and SOU 1951:42, pp. 39–40.

3   There were exceptions, however. The French constitution, for example, provided individuals 'fighting for freedom' the right to asylum on French territory. SOU 1951:42, p. 160.

4   See chapter 1, part 1.1.6.

### 3.1.1 *Three Principal Removal Instruments*

For the purpose of establishing the Swedish state's right to exclude foreigners from Swedish territory, the 1945 Aliens Act provided three primary legal tools. These were supported by one chapter each within the law.

The first was constituted by the *refusal of entry at the border* (*avvisning*). The regulations regarding this instrument identified the various reasons by which the authorities had the right to refuse an individual entry to Sweden. An individual of Roma origin, for example, could be denied entry wholly based on his or her ethnic identity. Individuals believed not to be able to support themselves economically, or thought to be aiming at supporting themselves by travelling through the country and playing music, showing animals 'or other similar occupation', could be treated in the same way. A person convicted of criminal activities (such as, for example, 'sexually immoral manner of living', theft or forgery) could similarly be removed. However, this also applied to individuals who did not hold the necessary identification documents, and/or had not obtained the obligatory permission to enter.[5] Refusal of entry decisions were issued either by the police or the Commission. Only in some cases could they be appealed, as will become clear below.

The second instrument of disposal according to the 1945 Aliens Act was *deportation* (*förpassning*). The main difference between a decision of refusal of entry and deportation was that the latter in general was issued against individuals who had already resided in Sweden for some time. It was issued by the National Alien Commission, and normally delivered as a consequence of a negative response to an application for a renewed residence permit. It could however also be issued to new arrivals applying for their first residence permit, thus equalling a refusal of entry decision. Sometimes it stemmed from a foreigner exceeding his or her leave of stay, and it was often formulated as a future consequence should the foreigner not leave the country willingly within a stipulated time period. (Such limits could vary in time between 'immediately' and 90 days.) It could also be issued to a foreigner who had provided the authorities with false information or not observed the

---

5    SFS 1945:315, §§ 19–24, 31.

regulations within the Aliens Act. Apart from this, however, little guidance was provided regarding what sort of circumstances gave rise to a given decision – particularly in cases where it constituted a negative response to a residence permit application. Before issuing a notice of deportation, however, 'reasonable consideration' had to be paid to the individual's family situation and the time which he or she had spent in the country.[6]

The third instrument was *expulsion* (*utvisning*). This was normally issued by the County Administrative Board as a juridical consequence of various criminal offences. The implementation of such decisions was referred to the National Alien Commission. Expulsions could also be issued on 'racial' grounds to Roma people; to prostitutes, pimps and other 'sexually immoral' individuals; professional gamblers; people guilty of illicit distilling; poor relief dependants; individuals suspected of vagrancy or, again, people supporting themselves through itinerant showmanship. In these cases they were issued by the National Alien Commission. In addition, paragraph 37 granted the government the right to expel an individual with reference to the 'security of the state' or other reasons concerning the 'state's interest'. No detail as to what this might include were provided, however. Nonetheless, just as in the case of deportations, the law stated that regard should be paid to the individual's family relations and duration of stay.[7]

All these three legal instruments also granted the authorities' the right to take individuals, of whom such removal decisions had been made, into custody, should the prevailing circumstances warrant such action. This referred to, for example, situations when the authorities believed the individual might escape, or cases when the implementation was hindered for some reasons.[8]

---

6  SFS 1945:315, §§ 25–30. Regarding the 'reasonable consideration', see § 26.
7  SFS 1945:315, §§ 31–38.
8  Gustav Lindencrona, *Utlänningshandbok: utlänningslagen och därmed sammanhängande författningar jämte anvisningar och förklaringar*, Årg. 1949, Norstedt, Stockholm 1949, pp. 7–14 (ref: Lindencrona 1949).

### 3.1.2 Regulations of Political Asylum

Although mainly observing the state's right to remove foreigners from its territory, the Aliens Act also acknowledged some rights for those individuals generally characterised as political refugees.[9] It stated that the authorities could not remove an individual to the country he had come from if he had fled for 'political reasons'. Neither could it send him to another country where there was a risk that he might be transported to his point of origin. For new arrivals, this meant that if a foreigner claimed to have fled to Sweden for 'political reasons' and these claims were not 'evidently untrue', the police had to refer his application to the Commission.[10]

Removal decisions could thus encounter obstacles. In such cases, the matter of their implementation was referred to the Commission, which could attach to the decision a so-called 'home country proviso' (*hemlandsklausul*). This barred an individual from being forwarded to their homeland (or another risk country). This, in its turn, could necessitate the issuing of a respite, if no other country was willing to receive the individual. Such postponements could be attached to deportation and expulsion decisions, but generally not refusal of entry decisions.

However, just as its predecessor from 1937, the 1945 Aliens Act did not define the meaning of 'political reasons'. This was a deliberate omission, aimed at enabling Sweden to tailor its refugee policies to current circumstances. In the preparatory work for the law, legal experts advised that the flexible definition remain unchanged. They maintained that the policies pursued during the war had been continuously modified with regard to both humanitarian and foreign policy-related considerations. A more exact definition would have rendered this impossible. The experts also anticipated that Sweden might be compelled to proceed to a 'relatively restrictive refugee policy' if, due to changing political conditions in other countries, the near future would witness 'new refugee categories' of a 'character non-desirable' to Sweden. Such a policy could also prove indispensable when it came to the labour market. Alternatively, they argued, 'our [Sweden's] relationship towards other states' might demand this. Therefore, they con-

---

9   The term 'political refugee' was not used in the legislation, however.
10   SFS 1945:315, §§ 24, 30, 36.

cluded that the law should continuously be formulated in such a way as to grant the state substantial freedom of action to manage matters pertaining to refugees.[11]

The new 'non-desirable' refugees that the commission had in mind were, first and foremost, war criminals and Nazi perpetrators. Sweden had officially declared already in 1944 that it would not grant asylum to those individuals 'who had challenged the conscience of the civilised world', with foremost in their minds being Danish and Norwegian Nazi collaborators. Through the flexibility of the Aliens Act, Sweden had been able to pursue 'generous' policies towards refugees in need, state representatives argued, while at the same time refusing entry to traitors and war criminals.[12]

It is also a matter of fact, however, that the legislative plasticity was used in order to adapt policies to current foreign policy ambitions, as well as the state's interest in preventing particularly Central European Jewish refugees from settling in Sweden.[13] The continuous emphasis on flexibility within the 1945 Aliens Act meant that refugees were in fact guaranteed few juridical rights. Instead, it granted the authorities a significant room for manoeuvre. As a consequence, a refugee's 'right' to protection continued to be dependent on the authorities' current interpretation of the term 'political reasons'. The pursued *practices*, thus, were presumably to a large degree influenced by factors other than the specific regulations within the Aliens Act. Such factors could, obviously, render the practices in the direction of leniency as well as strictness.


### 3.1.3 *The Residence Permit*

In order to be allowed to reside in Sweden for more than three months, foreigners had to apply for a residence permit. All permits were temporary, and could according to the eighth paragraph of the Aliens Act be attached with 'such reservations that are required

---

11   SOU 1945:1 *Betänkande med förslag till utlänningslag och lag angående omhändertagande av utlänning i anstalt eller förläggning*, pp. 61–66, citations from p. 65–66 (ref: SOU 1945:1). On the previous legislation, see chapter two and Kvist Geverts 2008, pp. 53–56.

12   SOU 1951:42, pp. 159–183, citation from p. 165. See also SOU 1945:1.

13   See chapter two.

by the circumstances'.[14] The 'circumstances' and the measures that should be taken were not defined in the law, however.

Some indication of the types of measures in question was, however, provided in the special directions appended to the law. Paragraph 42 read: 'Residence permits may be restricted to a certain district or area and may be attached with other reservations necessitated by the interests of the public.'[15] Geographical restrictions, in other words, could be attached to residence permits. As will be further demonstrated in chapter seven, they existed in two main forms. A permit with a 'normal' main city restriction prohibited its holder from residing in Stockholm, Gothenburg and Malmö. Meanwhile permits with 'strict' geographical constraints compelled recipients to reside within a narrowly prescribed area, such as a county district or a small town.[16] The permits also varied in terms of duration. The decision-making basis for issuance of these permits remained ill-defined in the law. This is further evidence of the room for manoeuvre, enabling the authorities to decide according to their own beliefs and/or principles.


### 3.1.4 The 'Security Paragraphs'

Although matters pertaining to asylum seekers were to be handled primarily by the central immigration bureaucracy, the government was still able to have the final word. Paragraph 48 established, first of all, that the central immigration bureaucracy could, if it found 'specific reasons' for so doing, refer a specific case to the government for assessment. Again, no definitions as to the nature of these reasons or circumstances was provided.[17]

---

14   *Uppehållstillstånd skall meddelas för viss tid samt må förbindas med de förbehåll som finnas påkallade.* SFS 1945:315, § 8. The permanent residence permit was not introduced until 1976. From 1954 onwards, however, foreigners who had resided in Sweden for more than five years could apply for a 'settlement permit' (*bosättningstillstånd*), which was not time restricted. SFS 1954:193, § 10.

15   *Uppehållstillstånd må begränsas till viss ort eller visst område samt må förbindas med de förbehåll i övrigt, som med hänsyn till det allmännas intresse finnas påkallade.* KK 15 juni 1945 med föreskrifter i anledning av utlänningslagen (utlänningskungörelse), § 42.

16   See chapter seven and Lindencrona 1949, pp. 26–28.

17   SFS 1945:315, § 48.

Somewhat more forthcoming were the above-mentioned paragraph 37, which established that the government could expel an individual if there were reasons for this pertaining to national security or other issues regarding the interests of the state. However, as with the other removal decisions the paragraph also stated that deportation should not lead to an individual being expelled to a country from which he had fled for political reasons, or to a country from which the individual risked being rendered to such a country.[18]

However, all above-mentioned regulations were conditioned by paragraph 56, which maintained that the government in case of 'war or threat of war or due to the defence of the realm or specific circumstances' had the right to issue 'specific necessary provisions' regarding foreign citizens' right to 'enter or reside in the country or dwell in a specific region or hold employment'. Similarly, during such situations the government had the right to block or remove foreign citizens as circumstances dictated.[19] Thus, just as previous immigration legislation had stipulated, any regulations within the Aliens Act – including those pertaining to political asylum – could be discarded should paragraph 56 come into force.

Few changes were made to the 1945 Aliens Act while it remained in force.[20] Thus, the legal room for manoeuvre of the political and administrative authorities to make decisions regarding removal and residence conditions on arbitrary or other grounds not based on law in refugee matters remained a reality until at least 1951, if not until 1954. This implies that the potential impact of the six factors identified in chapter one was considerable.

18   SFS 1945:315, § 37.

19   *I händelse av krig eller fara för krig eller där sådant för rikets försvar eller eljest på grund av särskilda omständigheter prövas erforderligt, äger Konungen, med avseende å utlännings rätt att inkomma eller uppehålla sig i riket eller att vistas å viss ort inom riket eller att här i riket antaga eller inneha arbetsanställning, meddela de särskilda bestämmelser som må finnas nödiga. I fall varom i denna paragraf sägs må Konungen i fråga om utlännings avvisning, förpassning ur riket eller utvisning förordna efter omständigheterna. Med avseende å utlännings omhändertagande i anstalt eller förläggning så ock utlännings hållande i förvar under längre tid gäller vad därom är särskilt stadgat.* SFS 1945:315, § 56.

20   The most important changes regarded paragraphs concerning foreigners' taken into custody in 1946 (see part 3.3), and some administrative changes introduced in 1947 when the assessment of residence and work permits were decentralised. SFS 1947:312; SFS 1951:106; SFS 1952:191.

## 3.2 The 1954 Aliens Act – Introducing the Right of the Individual Foreigner

Thus far, this examination has demonstrated that there was a significant difference in general juridical thinking between the Swedish 1945 Aliens Act and the international 1951 Refugee Convention. The former predominantly sought to establish the state's right to remove (or not remove) foreigners from its territory, whereas the latter defines the rights of the refugee to be granted protection by states of which they were not citizens.

Given the fact that Sweden's new Aliens Act of 1954 incorporated the 1951 Refugee Convention into national legislation, it is clear that it must have differed significantly from its predecessor. Indeed, a comparison of the two documents suggests that attitudes towards individual foreigners' rights had undergone considerable change during the intervening years. The first paragraph of the 1954 Act established a foreigner's right to not have his freedom restricted in any other way than the law prescribed, and not to any further extent than was absolutely necessary.[21] This can be compared with the previous Aliens Act which contained no such formulations, and its first paragraph which had stressed the immigrant's obligation to hold all necessary identification documents.

Paragraph two established the right of political refugees to not be refused asylum without 'particular reasons'. This section also contained a definition of a political refugee as someone who 'in his home country risks being subjected to political persecution'. Moreover, it *defined* 'political persecution' as that which was based on an individual's '[ethnic] origin, belonging to a certain social group, religion or political opinion'.[22] In other words, it focused on the risk the individual faced upon returning to his or her home country. (The previous legislation had only, without any further specifications, mentioned the reasons for flight.) These formulations were equivalent to the refugee definition in the 1951 Refugee Convention.

The new law contained other novelties such as the 'settlement permit', which granted its holder the right to enter and reside in

21   SFS 1954:193, § 1.
22   SFS 1954:193, § 2.

the country without any geographical or temporal restrictions. The permit could be granted to foreign citizens who had been residents of the country for some time.[23] There were, however, no prerequisites or directions defining the sorts of circumstances that might lead to the granting of this permit. No individual had the 'right' to receive such a document. Conversely, the special directions attached to the law stated that it was *not* to be granted to any individual of whom there was 'doubt' regarding his 'conduct or trustworthiness from a security point of view'.[24]

The new law no longer allowed deportation or refusal of entry of foreign citizens solely on the grounds of their ethnic origin or occupation. Criminal behaviour, however, still constituted a reason for deportation and refusal of entry. A few novel categories were also added, such as suspicions of spying activities and alcoholism.[25] Detention without a court sentence was not abolished, but restricted to a total maximum of three months, and a new government assessment was required every month.[26]

Furthermore, all individuals subject to expulsions were now to be given the chance of a plea hearing. They also had the right to be informed of the reasons for the decision.[27] Political refugees' rights to not be deported or expelled to a country where their life and freedom was at risk was emphasised clearly.[28] The only exception to these regulations that the law identified was, as before, those situations pertaining to the security of the state, and/or if the individual had committed a serious crime.[29]

In general, therefore, the 1954 Aliens Act recognised the rights of the foreigner – and in particular the refugee – to a significantly higher degree than hitherto. Just as in the 1951 Refugee Convention, there was no *unconditional* right for a political refugee to receive asylum. However, as long as there was no direct and acute security risk entailed in allowing the individual to reside in the country, that person was entitled to protection in Sweden if he or she met


23   SFS 1954:193, § 10.
24   SFS 1954:194, *KM:ts utlänningskungörelse 4 juni 1954*, §§ 34–35.
25   SFS 1954:193, §§ 18–19, 29.
26   SFS 1954:193, §§ 35–38.
27   SFS 1954:193, §§ 31–33.
28   SFS 1954:193, § 53.
29   SFS 1954:193, § 34, 54, 70.

the requirements of political asylum established in the Convention.

The formulations of the 1954 Aliens Act thus suggest that they were influenced by contemporaneous international juridical developments. That this was indeed the case is also evident from the examination that was pursued by the committee that presented a first draft of the law in 1951. References to the on-going work with the 1951 Geneva Refugee Convention were made, as well as to the general stipulations regarding refugee rights within the UN Declaration of Human Rights and the universal values established through the foundation of the United Nations. 'Western ideas' and 'West-European democratic principles' regarding political refugees' right to asylum were also emphasised. It was argued that Sweden's *practices* regarding political asylum had been pursued in accordance with such principles during the first post-war years, and that they as such had been more generous than were actually stipulated by the regulations of the 1945 Aliens Act. The committee thus suggested that the new law ought to be adapted to better reflect these changed practices.[30]

Nelhans has pointed out, however, that the committee's most liberal ambitions had been substantially downplayed in the legislative document that finally became the 1954 Aliens Act. The original preamble was to have included the lawmakers' desire of seeing a return to the old principle of 'free movement of people'. This came in for heavy criticism from, among others, the police, the Labour Market Board and members of the National Alien Commission. This was also the case for several other of its suggestions and, after a couple of years of further discussions and consideration, the end product was far less generous in granting refugees and other foreigners rights towards the Swedish state than the committee had initially envisaged.[31] Melander, arguing along similar lines, opined that the new Aliens Act (as well as the committee that prepared it) only took the 1951 Refugee Convention into 'limited consideration'.[32]

Even so, however, the international imprint on the final document is still unmistakable. And the preparatory committee's work strongly demonstrated that general thinking on refugee rights had

30   SOU 1951:42, particularly pp. 159–179 and 285–302.
31   Nelhans 1973, pp. 15–54.
32   Melander 1972a, p. 23.

changed during the first post-war years. The acknowledgement of refugees as holders of rights against states of which they were not citizens had been bolstered. Thus, refugee policies seem to have been increasingly reinterpreted as a matter of *law*, rather than predominately about *politics*. This, in its turn, suggests that the international juridical developments taking place within the UN during these years had exerted a strong influence.

## 3.3 Other Immigration Related Laws

The impact of the Second World War led the Swedish government to pursue a careful and initially very strict border control policy. It also prompted it to make use of another instrument of control over foreigners. Foreigners suspected of political untrustworthiness had been taken into custody. This had been carried out through an administrative direction from the government, which leaned on the above-mentioned security paragraph. Foreigners labelled as untrustworthy were held in closed camps without trial. As an expression of Sweden's changing foreign policy concerns, the first war years witnessed the interment of suspected communists and even Nordic members of the resistance against the Nazi occupation regimes, whereas the final years of the conflict saw the confinement of mainly Nazi collaborators.[33]

In 1945, the administrative direction was exchanged for a separate law, the *1945 Law regarding taking foreigners' into custody*. The first paragraph of this law stated that a foreigner whose removal presented practical obstacles could be incarcerated. The same was applicable to any foreigner who for reasons of 'general order and security, or other reasons pertaining to the security of the state', ought not to be able to move freely. Every four months a hearing and a renewed examination was to be pursued. The law stipulated no requirements of court trials or guilty verdicts in order to keep a foreign citizen in confinement. Nor did it specify what sort of behaviour could lead to this measure.[34]

---

33    § 54 of the 1937 Aliens Act (SFS 1937:344) equalled § 56 of the 1945 Aliens Act (SFS 1945:315). See SOU 1946:36 and Åmark 2011, ch. 15

34    SFS 1945:316, *Lag 15 juni 1945 ang. utlännings omhändertagande i anstalt eller för-läggning*, §§ 7–9.

The law was revoked in 1946 according to schedule and by which time several of the interned foreigners had returned home. This reflects the fact that it was, after all, intended as a temporary war-time control measure. Some adaptations were then made to the Aliens Act, however, supporting the regulations that stipulated that foreigners that were to be removed from the country could be placed in custody while awaiting implementation.[35]

Another legal removal instrument was the 1913 Extradition Law.[36] The only time this law could come into force was when another state demanded that one of its own citizens be extradited from Sweden. The law stated that such a request had to be presented through diplomatic channels, and was only to be assessed if the misdeed under consideration was regarded as a crime according to Swedish legislation.[37] Moreover, it had to have been committed in another country, and evidence thereof, as well as a decision of either detention or a verdict of guilty, had to be provided by a court or a similar authority. Extradition could not, however, occur if the crime of which the individual was accused was of a political character or if he or she had fled from the country for 'political reasons'.[38]

This law was subject to only minor changes during the period that it remained in force. These mostly concerned administrative changes, or bilateral agreements with other countries, and did not challenge any of the major regulations.[39] In 1957, it was superseded entirely in order to comply with the new European Convention on Extradition, stipulated by the Council of Europe.[40]

35 SFS 1945:315, § 49; SFS 1946:360 *Lag om ändring i utlänningslagen den 15 juni 1945.*

36 SFS 1913:68, *Lagen den 4 juni 1913 angående utlämning av förbrytare* (ref: SFS 1913:68).

37 SFS 1913:68, §§ 4 and 14.

38 SFS 1913:68, §§ 7–8.

39 See, for example, SFS 1948:451, *Lagen den 30 juni 1948 angående införande av lagen om ändring i strafflagen*; SFS 1946:817, *Lagen den 20 december 1946 om bevisupptagning vid utländsk domstol*; SFS 1952:644, *Kungörelsen den 25 september 1952 angående skyldighet för myndighet att i vissa fall meddela underrättelse till brittisk konsul.* See also SFS 1951:42, p. 40 and 203–236.

40 SFS 1957:668, *Lagen om utlämning för brott*; *European Convention on Extradition*, Paris 13 December 1957, CETS No. 024. Sweden signed this convention in 1957. It was ratified in 1959 and came into legislative force in 1960. See http://conventions.coe.int/treaty/Commun/ChercheSig. asp?NT=024&CM=8&DF=&CL=ENG (accessed 17 September 2012)

The fact that the 1913 Extradition Law was not cited when the German and Baltic soldiers were extradited in the winter of 1945–46 is indicative of the flexible treatment of foreigners at this time. Had it been so, the regulations regarding political reasons would have presented a significant obstacle. Instead, however, the extradition was managed as a purely administrative issue.[41]

In addition to the 1913 Extradition Law, Sweden was bound by separate extradition treaties with a number of countries. The Soviet Union, however, was not one of them.[42]

## 3.4 The Institutional Framework

Institutional frameworks often bring a stronger influence to bear on pursued policies than initial indications suggest. Bureaucracies' design, habitual patterns and culture can have a substantial impact on the outcome of political decisions. It is therefore important to pay attention to bureaucratic structures, especially in circumstances in which executive officers are accorded considerable room for manoeuvre.[43]

### 3.4.1 *The National Alien Commission*

The origins of the institutional framework of refugee policies in Sweden during the Cold War are to be found within the bureaucratic solutions that were reached during the Second World War. The National Alien Commission was constructed in 1944 as a response to the critical refugee situation that then loomed large. As with other state measures during the war years, it was supposed to be a temporary solution to challenges that would abate after the fighting ceased. However, as it turned out, refugees kept arriving in Sweden, albeit in smaller numbers. And as the fast growing economy soon inspired increasing work immigration, the

41  Ekholm 1995.

42  SOU 1951:42, pp. 203–236.

43  On such factors' influence on security and surveillance policies, see, for example, Langkjaer 2011 and Didier Bigo, 'Security and immigration: toward a critique of the governmentality of unease' in *Alternatives* 2002: 27, Special Issue, pp. 63–92 (ref: Bigo 2002).

numbers of foreigners in Sweden grew once again. Thus, despite far reaching plans to replace it with an organisation with even more central authority towards the end of the 1940s, it remained in existence until 1969. During its 25-year life span, it did undergo a series of reorganisations, the most significant of which took place in 1953.[44]

The Commission was a sizeable authority. In the summer of 1946 it boasted 550 employees.[45] During the greater part of the time period examined in this study, it was divided into three main bureaus and one secretariat. The Passport Bureau (*Passbyrån*) assessed visa and residence permit applications for 'normal' foreigners. It also administered entry permits and work permits, and could issue deportation decisions. The Control Bureau (*Kontrollbyrån*) managed refusal of entry decisions and deportations, and decided when to take foreigners into custody. It was also responsible for control measures, and handled residence permit applications and various other matters concerning 'less desirable foreigners'. It kept a substantial register with 'uncomplimentary information' (so called 'control dossiers') on foreigners, and worked closely with both the military and civilian security services. Any individual thought to be requiring more careful investigation and monitoring ended up in the Control Bureau's registers, and his or her applications would be assessed by staff from this office.[46]

Some cases were perceived as requiring even greater attention, however. The reasons for this could be case specific, for example uncertainties regarding how to interpret the legislation. Or it could be in order to establish a precedent. It might also be due to doubts regarding an individual's background, or possible consequences for Swedish national interests should that person be allowed to enter and/or stay. Someone could be thought of as a possible security risk, for example, and/or as a person of importance to Sweden's

---

44 'Protokoll', 17 februari 1948, including attachmets, vol. 2, A 1 A, Kanslibyrån, SUK, Ra; and numerous documents within vol. 1, E 1 A, Kanslibyrån, SUK, Ra.

45 'Protokoll', 24 september 1946, bilaga 1, vol. 2, A 1 A, Kanslibyrån, SUK, Ra. See also Hallberg 2001, pp. 179–188.

46 In addition, the Social Bureau (*Socialbyrån*), closed down in 1947, administered the refugee camps and oversaw the distribution of financial help to refugees. In this study, however, it is the Passport Bureau and the Control Bureau that are of most interest. Hallberg 2001, pp. 179–188; SOU 1946:36, p. 20.

foreign relations. If so, the case was often transferred to the plenary assembly. This was constituted by the Board of Directors which included the chairman of the Commission and the directors of the three bureaus, plus secretaries and other prominent members of staff. The assembly held weekly meetings at which various sensitive cases were decided. Some of these gatherings were classified as secret. Separate minutes were kept at both the normal and the secret meetings. If uncertainties arose or the plenary assembly could not agree, a case would be forwarded to the government for arbitration.[47]

Apart from determining which foreigners were to be allowed to reside in Sweden, the Commission's executive officers decided how long and with which possible restrictions residence permits would be renewed. Additionally, they assessed or gave statements regarding applications for other sorts of additional permits required by these foreign citizens. Examples of these included travel documents (enabling someone to re-enter Sweden after travelling abroad), permission to buy property, to attend higher education and to take a driving licence. Thus, the staff at the Commission held sway over the lives and well-being of foreign citizens in Sweden. With time, the number of activities requiring the permission of the Commission decreased. With the signing of the 1951 Refugee Convention, Sweden had to assure that it would not treat refugees in any other way than the national population in terms of freedom of movement, labour, social security etc. Aside from the few reservations Sweden attached to the ratification of this Convention, it had to live up to the equality regulations of this document from 1951 onwards.

As a step towards this modernisation, the National Alien Commission went through a substantial restructuring in 1953. The previous bureaus were dissolved, and a tighter, more centralised organisation was launched. Only the secretariat remained mostly intact under its new name of the Third Bureau. The Passport Bureau and the Control Bureau, however, were disbanded and the First and Second Bureau established. They shared responsibility over all immigration related matters relating to the

47   Normal plenary meeting protocols, see vol. 1–4, A 1 A, Kanslibyrån, SUK, Ra; Secret plenary meeting protocols, see vol. 1, A 1, Hemliga arkivet, SUK, Ra. See also SOU 1946:36, pp. 21–31.

nationalities of the foreigners in question. The First Bureau took charge of Nordic, Baltic, German and Austrian citizens, whereas the Second managed all foreigners descending from Eastern Europe and the rest of the world.[48]


### 3.4.2 Other Bureaucracies

Despite the 1944 centralisation, other parts of Sweden's state bureaucracy remained involved in the management of foreigners and refugees in various ways. Some had decision-making responsibilities, others provided statements to the Commission in a consultative capacity.

Aside from the National Alien Commission, the authority most involved in refugee matters was the police. Local police officers most often constituted the first contact refugees had with Swedish society. As new arrivals without entry permits (so-called 'illegal' immigrants), they were taken into custody by the police and interrogated. The police officers then decided whether to refuse entry to the foreigner and send him or her back immediately, or forward the case to the National Alien Commission for assessment. If the foreigner claimed to have fled his country for 'political reasons' and this claim was not 'obviously incorrect', the police had to refer the case to the Commission for assessment. While awaiting the Commission's judgement, the individual was to be kept in custody by the police.[49]

The local police was also the authority which normally received foreigners' applications for prolonged residence permits. They were supposed to make sure that the application was complete, gather a statement from the County Administrative Board and pursue an examination of the applicant, sometimes including a hearing, and write a report before sending it to the Commission for assessment. Similarly, they received other types of applications, such as for travel documents, and had to pursue the compulsory interrogation before transferring the documents to the Commission. Other

---

48 Hallberg 2001, pp. 179–188. See also *Riksarkivets beståndsöversikt. D. 5, Centrala myndigheter och domstolar, internationella organ, Bd 2, Myndigheter M–Ö, internationella organ*, Riksarkivet, Stockholm 1999.

49 SFS 1945:315, §§ 19–24, citations from § 20. See also Lindencrona 1949, pp. 7–11.

police duties included control over the border and other routine matters, such as ensuring that foreigners complied by their geographical restrictions. For its part, the National Alien Commission posted regular directives and other kinds of information to the police authorities.[50]

From December 1947 an effort was made to reduce the Commission's workload by decentralising the assessment process and granting the police more responsibility over immigration matters. From then on, local officers could prolong residence permits of 'unproblematic' individuals without involving the Commission. Those deemed to be more troublesome or in receipt of a strict geographical restraint continued to be sent to the Commission. A list was regularly updated and dispatched to all local police offices, including information on which individuals belonged to this category. Their permits were also specifically marked. In addition, all applications for residence permits longer than two years were assessed by the central immigration authority.[51]

The security services – that is the civilian security police (*Statspolisens tredje rotel*) and the Department of Counter-Intelligence of the Swedish Armed Forces (*Försvarsstabens Inrikesavdelning*) – pursued surveillance and various control measures over all immigrants in Sweden. They held their own registers and archives of information on refugees and other foreigners. As the Cold War continued, their focus turned specifically towards the Eastern Europeans. Both these organisations cooperated closely with the National Alien Commission, and its Control Bureau in particular. If an application was considered to impinge on national security (regarding, for example, an individual perceived as politically untrustworthy) one or both of these bureaucracies would be heard before a decision of renewed residence was made (the security police more often than the Department of Counter-Intelligence

---

50   Cirkulär och utlänningsmeddelanden till polismyndigheter, vol. 1, B 4 C, Kanslibyrån, SUK, Ra.

51   SFS 1947:20, Kungl. Maj:ts kungörelse angående ändring i utlänningskungörelsen den 15 juni 1945 (nr 317); *Råd och anvisningar rörande förfarandet hos polismyndighet med ärenden om uppehålls- eller arbetstillstånd för utlänningar*, SUK 1947, p. 5, vol. 1, B 4 C, Kanslibyrån, SUK, Ra; 'Till samtliga polismyndigheter', 5 december 1947, vol. 1, B 2 C, Kontrollbyrån, SUK, Ra.

of the Swedish Armed Forces, however).[52] Additionally, for some years during and after the war, there were strict guidelines regarding the kinds of work that were prohibited for foreigners. This included, for example, the weapons industry and other companies that produced goods that in some way or another could be used for the defence of the country. However, it also included several kinds of state jobs. Employment that could entail increased knowledge of Sweden's infrastructure was forbidden. Thus, foreign citizens were not allowed to work on the national rail network, for example. If a company which was regarded as important to Sweden's defence capabilities wished to employ a foreigner, it had to apply for a specific permission from the National Alien Commission. The Commission then requested a statement from the Department of Counterintelligence of the Swedish Armed Forces.[53]

Another important instance was the Aliens Appeals Board (*Utlänningsnämnden*). According to the 1945 Aliens Act, the National Alien Commission was to obtain the Board's opinion before issuing a removal decision, except in cases of an 'exceedingly urgent nature'. Likewise, the right to appeal a negative decision made by the Commission was only granted individuals whose cases had either not been reviewed by the Board, or when the Board had not been unanimous in its evaluation. The Board consisted of three members and their deputies. One had to be a legal judge, and one had to have experience of international law. The main purpose of the committee was to function as an extra juridical 'safety net' for political refugees.[54]

Work permits were issued by the National Alien Commission and, from 1947 onwards, also by local police officers, after hearings from the National Labour Market Commission (*Arbetsmarknads-kommissionen*, 1940–48) or its successor the National Labour Market Board (*Arbetsmarknadsstyrelsen*, 1948–2007). This bureau-

---

52  Control dossiers of B1-B120, I1-I150 and R1-R90.

53  The statements which are included in the source material for this study suggest, however, that the defence authorities rarely gave their approval. None of the Soviet refugees who came into question for such a position (mostly Balts) were granted permission. See Control dossiers of B1-B120. *KCirk 15 juni 1945 till statliga myndigheter angående utlännings anställande i statens tjänst* (attachment to SFS 1945:315, § 13)

54  Hallberg 2001, pp. 198–199; SFS 1945:315, §§ 46–47.

cracy, or, alternatively, local Labour Market Offices (*länsarbets-nämnder*), then normally provided jobs for the immigrants. Baltic and Nordic citizens, however, were excluded from the necessity of holding a work permit.[55]

In order to be allowed to work within certain high-skilled professions, such as medical doctors, dentists or veterinary physicians, foreigners needed special work permits. They were issued by the Ministry of the Interior (*Inrikesdepartementet*), thus in effect by the government. The same authority assessed appeals against the National Alien Commission's removal decisions, and made final settlements. Citizenship applications, on the other hand, were handled by the Ministry of Justice (*Justitiedepartementet*).[56]

Apart from these main state bureaucracies, there were a number of official and semi-official organisations providing material assistance to refugees. The Government's Board of Refugee Relief (*Statens flyktingsnämnd*), for example, provided loans to refugees to help them finance their settlement. A number of voluntary organisations were also engaged with helping refugees to establish new lives for themselves.[57]

### 3.4.3 The Government's Power

As the law-making authority, the political administration had the highest political jurisdiction over refugee issues. It also had far-reaching powers to intervene in matters concerning the interpretation of this legislation. Apart from settling appeals, in practice the government had a final say in all matters pertaining to foreigners' right to reside in Sweden, should it wish to exercise this option.

The main juridical tools that provided the government with this room for manoeuvre were the above-mentioned paragraphs 37, 48 and 56 of the Aliens Act. Particularly paragraph 48 was used to exercise this power, as the government made *precedential assessments*. A test case could consist of a group of individuals from the same ethnic group but with varying backgrounds. The Commission

---

55   SFS 1945:315, §§ 13–18; Hallberg 2001, pp. 195–198; and chapter two, part
     2.6.1.
56   Hallberg 2001, pp. 81–108. See also Föredragningslistor, vol. 1–8, AII,
     Inrikesdepartementet, Ra.
57   Byström 2012, in particular chs 12–13.

provided the government with details of the individuals and requested its interpretation of how to evaluate their political refugee status, and, thus, how to assess their asylum applications. Based on the government's reply, the Commission was then supposed to judge future cases according to the same principles. These procedures, which will be further illuminated in chapter four, thus reinforces the view that the 1945 Aliens Act still regarded refugee policies as a predominantly political rather than juridical affair. The bureaucracies were to implement not only the government's desires in terms of legislation, but also its current wishes in terms of its interpretation.[58]

In order to clarify further the interplay between the institutional and the juridical frameworks, the following section provides a demonstration of the normal course of events for newly arrived refugees.

## 3.5 The Asylum Seeking Process

During the 1940s, asylum could be sought in two principal ways. One was to apply for legal permission to enter the country, the so called '*entry permit*' or '*entry visa*' (*inresetillstånd, inresevisum*). The other was to arrive 'illegally' without such a permit and apply for a residence permit citing political grounds.

Entry visas were compulsory for citizens of all countries from which Sweden had not removed the general visa requirements. During the research period, Sweden made such visa-free agreements with more than twenty countries, starting with Denmark and Norway in 1945. A similar arrangement was made with Finland in 1949. No other grey zone countries were included in the visa-free zone, however.[59]

---

58   See chapter four and the following examples: 'Till Konungen', 26 juni 1945, vol. 67, P 40 I, 1920 års dossiésystem, UD, Ra; Protokoll', 10 september 1946, vol. 1, A 1, Hemliga arkivet, SUK, Ra; 'Protokoll', 8 november 1946, vol. 1, A 1, Hemliga arkivet, SUK, Ra; 'Till Konungen', 9 november 1946, vol. 3, E 4, Hemliga arkivet, SUK, Ra; 'Till Konungen', 16 september 1947, vol. 4, E 4, Hemliga arkivet, SUK, Ra.

59   The abolition of visas for Danes and Norwegians in 1945 constituted a return to pre-war conditions, as Sweden had temporarily set up visa requirements for all foreigners during the war. The reason for the late inclusion of Finland

Entry visas were applied for from abroad, normally at Swedish legations, consulates and embassies. These entitled an individual to enter the country and reside there for a limited period of time, normally three months. One needed to specify one's reasons in order to receive such a permit. Business and tourist visas were often granted without question, as well as visas to foreigners who wanted to visit their relatives in Sweden. However, individuals suspected of wishing to settle in Sweden (such as potential refugees) were normally not granted entry visas. Additionally, individuals fleeing from their home country – especially the Soviet Union – rarely risked having their plans revealed to the Soviet authorities through making official applications.[60]

Thus, the normal *first step* in a refugee's asylum seeking process was to enter the country illegally and make claims to a right to stay. If the police did not refuse entry to the individual directly at the border, the case was transferred to the National Alien Commission. (And if the refugee had been refused entry by the police, he or she could appeal this decision to the Commission within eight days.)

The *second step* of a refugee's journey into Swedish society thus took place at the National Alien Commission. Depending on the circumstances, the Passport Bureau, the Control Bureau or the Plenary Assembly assessed the case. Normally, the first decision regarded whether or not the individual was going to be refused entry. A decision of 'refusal' or 'non-refusal' was made. While awaiting this, the individual was to be kept in police custody.

If granted a right to stay, the refugee was thereafter urged to apply for a residence permit, and, most often, a Swedish Alien's Passport, assuming these applications had not already been submit-

---

in the visa-free zone was probably the presence of Soviet citizens in Finland during the first post-war years. In 1952, however, Sweden, Finland, Norway and Denmark abandoned passport control for travels between these countries. Thus, the Nordic countries (apart from Iceland, Greenland and the Faroe Islands, which were included a couple of years later) now constituted both a visa and passport free zone. Other nationals still needed to carry a passport, however. Additions to SFS 1945:317: *KK 10 aug 1945 ang. viseringfrihet för norska medborgare; KK 17 aug 1945 ang. viseringsfrihet för danska medborgare; and sfs 1952:525 ang. ändring i Utlänningskungörelsen den 15 juni 1945.* See also 'Meddelande till rikets samtliga polismyndigheter', 16 december 1949, vol. 1, B 4 C, Kanslibyrån, SUK, Ra; and SFS 1954:194, § 20.

60  'Protokoll', 23 oktober 1945, § 9, vol. 1, A 1 A, Kanslibyrån, SUK, Ra; 'Protokoll', 13 november 1945, § 1, vol. 1, A 1 A, Kanslibyrån, SUK, Ra.

ted. A 'non-refusal' decision almost always meant that a residence permit would be granted. Its temporal duration and whether or not it was going to be attached with a geographical restriction were, however, matters for individual assessment. In coming to judgement, the Commission normally used the interrogation protocols that the police attached to the application. These contained information on personal background, reasons for flight, political activities and so forth. When the individual was granted a residence permit, he or she was often also assigned a place of work arranged by the labour market authorities.[61]

If the Commission was in doubt as to whether the person should be refused entry or not, the *third step* was to consult the Aliens Appeals Board. This assessed the case and delivered a statement. Based on this, the Commission now made a decision. This constituted the *fourth step*. If the Board had declared that an individual should *not* be removed from the country, the Commission was obliged to give him or her permission to stay. However, if the Board 'saw no hinder' for removal, the Commission could decide either to grant a permit to stay, or to deport or refuse entry. If the Board declared that it found 'strong reasons' for refusal of entry or deportation, however, the Commission decided accordingly. The implementation of a negative decision was transferred to the police in cases of refusal of entry, and to the County Administrative Board in cases of deportation.[62]

Sometimes the Aliens Appeals Board recommended that the case should be transferred to the government for a statement. If so, the Commission acquiesced. It could also refer cases to the government without going via the Board, even though this was unusual. This might involve a case of specific importance to international relations or security, or if it was being used to establish a precedent. The statement that the government then made was not legally formulated as a final decision. However, as the highest authority the Commission always abided by its opinion.

As mentioned above, the foreigner could in some cases appeal a negative decision to the government through the auspices of the

---

61 Sometimes, however, refugees managed to enter Sweden unnoticed by the police and applied directly for a residence permit after settling down with friends or relatives, thus skipping this first step.

62 SFS 1945:315, §§ 46–47.

Ministry of the Interior. The ensuing verdict was final and could not be appealed. This part thus constituted the *fifth and final step* for a refugee's application for asylum.[63]

The process is illustrated in Figure 1 below. The deportation procedure was identical to this, with the exception that such decisions were generally initiated by the National Alien Commission rather than the police. As mentioned above, other bureaucratic bodies were sometimes consulted in specific cases, such as the security services.[64] These organisations are, however, not included in the flowchart, the aim of which is to provide a simplified clarification of the asylum process.

## 3.6 Conclusion

This chapter has demonstrated that the institutional and juridical frameworks afforded considerable room for manoeuvre to the authorities when assessing individual refugees' applications for asylum and residence permits. The law provided only limited guidance as to whom was to be regarded a political refugee, and no directions when it came to determining the lengths and geographical restrictions of residence permits.

The government's possibilities to intervene in individual cases were also significant. Paragraphs 37, 48 and 56 gave the political administration leeway to determine individual cases as it wished – *if* it wished. Similarly, the deliberate lack of clarity within the 1945 Aliens Act considering the definition of 'political reasons' provided the government (and the central immigration authority) with considerable flexibility. Thus, the institutional framework positioned refugee policies as a predominantly political and administrative matter rather than a legal issue.

The framework that succeeded in 1954, however, was characterised by other principles. The new Aliens Act defined the individual's right against the state more extensively, and constituted

63   SFS 1945:315, § 47.
64   And, in cases of immigrants *other* than political refugees, the National Labour Market Board would sometimes be consulted, as well as, in certain cases, trades unions. (Additionally, these bodies were consulted in all applications for work permits.)

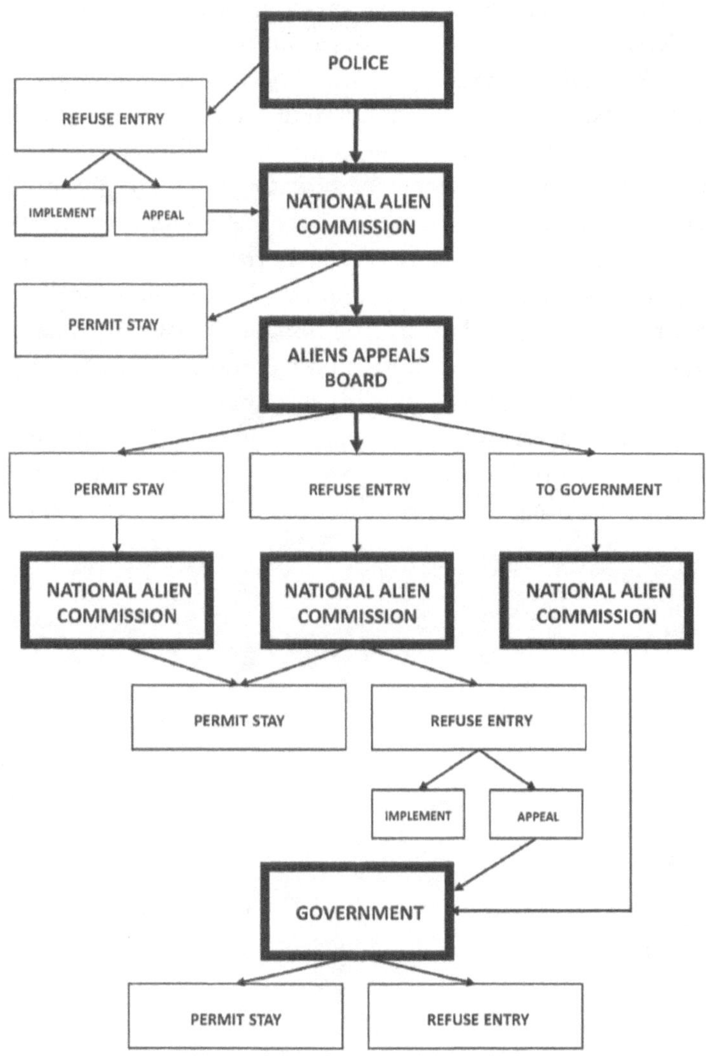


*Figure 1: The asylum seeking procedure, as regulated by the 1945 Aliens Act, for newly arrived refugees.*

a ratification of the 1951 Refugee Convention. The formulations in this law, as well as the work of the committee that prepared the new Aliens Act, suggest a substantial influence from *international juridical developments* on refugee thinking during these years.

The extensive room for manoeuvre that the legal and institutional framework granted the authorities during the research period means, however, that there was significant potential for influential factors other than those based on law to affect the pursued practices. This was particularly true when it came to the issuing of residence permits. Indirectly, the examination has thus far also re-emphasised that refugee policies in Sweden during the research period ought to be understood as being constituted by two main, but diverse, fields that benefit from being studied separately. One relates to determinations over 'asylum', including who was and was not allowed to reside in Sweden. The other concerns the continuous treatment of those who were granted leave to stay.

# The New Arrivals

In 1949, the Minister for the Interior, speaking in a parliamentary debate, addressed the question of individuals who had illegally arrived in Sweden from Eastern Europe. He claimed that, in recent years, only persons who had 'fled solely because they felt uncomfortable with the social and economic circumstances in their home country' or because they 'yearned for better possibilities to support themselves financially', had been refused entry.[1] In other words, such individuals had not been categorised as political refugees and could therefore be sent back to where they had come from.

Two years later, a similar statement was delivered by a specialist committee charged with drawing up a new Aliens Act. They maintained that the refugee policies of the Swedish authorities had been 'humanitarian'. The interpretation of the legal concept 'political reasons' had been extensive, and political refugees had been granted asylum. They also claimed that this policy had been supported by the Swedish public.[2]

Certain Eastern European refugees *had* been refused entry, however. In the aforementioned 1949 parliamentary debate, the Minister for the Interior explained one of the main reasons why this had to be so:

One needs to take into consideration that an uncontrolled refugee flow could possibly be so substantial in number that

---

1   Första Kammarens Protokoll 1949, nr 26, onsdagen den 9 november 1949, p. 8. (Also quoted in SOU: 1951:42, p. 163.)

2   SOU 1951:42 pp. 163–64.

it could become difficult to master even from a labour market perspective. Would it become known in the Eastern zone that we – in contrast to Denmark – do not send any refugees back to the Eastern zone, it is likely that a large number of individuals who only search for an improved livelihood will attempt to enter our country. In all probability, all these refugees would not be able to be placed in work and find a place to live.[3]

Thus, the Minister for the Interior argued that some refugees needed to be sent back to the 'Eastern zone' in order to deter other, 'non-political' persons from making a similar journey.[4] Economic concerns relating to the labour market were presented as the main motivation. A similar argument was made by the Head of the Legal Department at the Ministry for Foreign Affairs, Gösta Engzell. In 1948 he wrote a letter to the Swedish representative in Berlin in which he stated that refugees arriving from the Russian zone of Germany who 'cannot be considered political refugees' were refused entry, since the Swedish authorities were 'of course rather worried that the unregulated refugee flow would continue' and that they wanted to 'state a few examples which should function as a deterrent'.[5] He also claimed, however, that they had supposed that those who were returned were 'not subject to any particular difficulties, but were freed after interrogations and allowed to mind their own businesses'. This estimation, he argued, was based on reports from the refugees themselves.[6]

3   *När man skall taga ställning till vår flyktingpolitik, måste man bl.a. taga hänsyn till att en okontrollerad flyktingsström kan komma att få en sådan storleksordning, att den även ur arbetsmarknadspolitiska synpunkter kan bli svår att bemästra. Blir det bekant i östzonen, att vi – i motsats till Danmark – inte skickar tillbaka några flyktingar till östzonen, kan det tänkas, att ett stort antal rena försörjningsfall söka sig till vårt land i förhoppning om en bättre utkomst. Sannolikt skulle icke ens med nuvarande läge på arbetsmarknaden samtliga dessa flyktingar kunna placeras i arbete och erhålla bostäder.* Första Kammarens Protokoll 1949, nr 26, onsdagen den 9 november 1949, pp. 10–11.

4   The 'Eastern zone' (östzonen) here refers to the Soviet zone of Germany, later the GDR.

5   *Man är ju ganska orolig för en fortsatt oreglerad flyktingström av detta slag och vill gärna statuera några exempel, vilka nog verka avstyrande.* 'Stockholm 11 september 1948', vol. 4, E 4, Hemliga arkivet, SUK, Ra.

6   *Vi utgå emellertid från att de återsända i allmänhet ej råka ut för särskilda svårigheter utan bli efter förhör frigivna och få sköta sig själva'* 'Stockholm 11 september 1948', vol. 4, E 4, Hemliga arkivet, SUK, Ra.

However, another document reveals that, at least during the summer of 1949, the National Alien Commission and the Ministry for Foreign Affairs were well informed that refugees who were sent back to the Russian zone of Germany were at substantial risk of various forms of punishment for their illegal departure. Imprisonment and even deportation to various parts of the Soviet Union were not uncommon. The information was provided by the Displaced Persons Branch at the British military government's political department in West Germany, and the International Red Cross.[7]

Similarly, the Swedish authorities were informed that persecutions of individuals attempting to leave Poland without permission were increasing. Imprisonment now awaited most of them. Overall, in the critical year of 1948, when international tensions between the superpowers accelerated, the Soviet Union and the satellite states it indirectly governed implemented severe enhancements to their border controls. This included the use of draconian punishments as a means of making examples of those individuals who, by attempting to leave the country without authorisation, had demonstrated an antipathy toward the regime.[8]

Thus, as legal experts sometimes pointed out, all refugees from the communist, Soviet-influenced countries of Eastern Europe could in fact be regarded as political refugees, since their flight in itself had made them criminals against the state in the eyes of the regimes from which they were fleeing, regardless of their initial motivations for leaving.[9] The official representatives' declarations on Swedish asylum policies around the turn of the decade nonetheless suggest that the authorities disregarded this fact in order to safeguard its interest in preventing more Eastern European refugees from arriving. The argument cited above is strikingly similar to the 'domino effect logics' which characterised the Swedish administration's interpretation of refugee movements during the 1930s. This was formulated by a representative of the Swedish Ministry for Foreign Affairs in 1938 in the following manner: 'for every German refugee that is allowed entry in Sweden, several oth-

---


7    Berlin den 7 juni 1949, vol. 4, E 4, Hemliga arkivet, SUK, Ra.

8    'Stockholm 25 januari 1949', vol. 69, P 40 I, 1920 års dossiésystem, UD, Ra.

9    See, for example, a juridical examination by Dr. Gerhard Hafström, 'P.M.', 14 februari 1946, vol. 68, P 40 I, 1920 års dossiésystem, UD, Ra.

ers arrive'.[10] Although perhaps not as robustly pursued as during the beginning of the Second World War, the Swedish authorities still seem to have prioritised domestic concerns over the refugees' need of protection.

The minister's statement about the capacity of the Swedish labour market can, moreover, be questioned. In 1949, the year of his speech, around 24,000 individuals migrated successfully to Sweden according to official statistics.[11] Less than five per cent of these – around 1,100 individuals – had arrived illegally as refugees (mostly from the GDR and Poland). The bulk of the others were economic migrants, travelling to Sweden to fill labour shortages in the booming Swedish post-war economy. The refusal to admit approximately 1,300 individuals that same year (1949) – including at least 140 refugees arriving directly from communist East European countries and many of the others Eastern Europeans coming from Central European refugee camps – seems somewhat incoherent. It suggests that ethnic considerations – namely a wish to regulate the number of Eastern European residents in Sweden – might have played an as important, if not *the* most imperative, part in this decision.[12]

How, then, does this relate to the management of Soviet refugees? In this chapter, Swedish asylum policies between 1945 and 1954 are examined in more detail. Special attention is paid to negative responses to Soviet refugees' asylum applications. The juridical tools examined are, thus, *refusal of entry* decisions, and those *deportation decisions* that were used in a similar manner (in other words directed at new arrivals).[13] What factors determined these policies? And how can they be understood in relation to the potential influential aspects that were identified in chapter one (*external* and *internal security, economics, ethnicity, social control and morality,* and *international juridical developments*)? In order to place the results in their contemporaneous context, it is first, however, necessary to comment on the general quantitative situation concerning Swedish

10   Åmark 2011, p. 479.
11   *Befolkningsrörelsen* 1948, pp. 24–25.
12   'Illegalt anlända utlänningar under år 1949', vol. 1, H 1, Kanslibyrån, SUK, Ra; vol. 1, F 11 A, Hemliga arkivet, SUK, Ra; *Befolkningsrörelsen* 1949.
13   Deportation could be issued to both new arrivals and individuals who had resided in Sweden for some time. See chapter 3.

refugee policies during the period under investigation, and the specific conditions of the fleeing Soviet citizens.


## 4.1 Refugee Migration to Sweden, 1945–54

By the end of the Second World War in May 1945, a peak of 200,000 foreigners resided in Sweden. Shortly afterwards, the size of the population of foreign nationals decreased. The most significant reason for this drop was the homeward migration of Nordic refugees. From 1947 onwards, however, the number of foreign citizens in Sweden increased again. Roughly speaking, 20,000–30,000 individuals migrated to Sweden annually between 1946 and 1954, reaching its zenith in 1948. In total, the foreign population of Sweden rose from 120,000 in 1946, to approximately just under 300,000 in 1954.[14]

The majority of these immigrants were not refugees, however, but economic migrants. Nordic citizens in particular travelled to Sweden to find employment after the war. The fact that they needed neither a visa nor a work permit to do so meant that they encountered significantly fewer obstacles than other nationals.[15] The removal of the passport requirement in 1952, and the establishment of a common Nordic labour market in 1954, facilitated still further the Nordic citizens' access to Sweden's strong post-war economy.[16]

In addition the Swedish state started to arrange collective transportation of workers from European countries in order to meet the needs of the booming economy. For two decades starting in 1947 this was to become a regular pattern for Swedish migration policies. Businesses in need of labour could contact the National Labour Market Board and apply for batches of European workers. Thus, the close of the 1940s saw the Board transport workers from Italy,

14   The fact that Nordic citizens could travel to and from Sweden without passports from 1952 onwards makes the statistics from that year onwards somewhat uncertain. SOU 1951:42 p. 251; *Sociala Meddelanden* 1945, nr 10, p. 858; *Sociala Meddelanden* 1946, nr 4, p. 323; *Sociala Meddelanden* 1946, nr 12, p. 965; *Befolkningsrörelsen* 1946–1954, in particular 1946, p. 57; Lundh & Olsson 1999, p. 27.
15   The visa requirement for Finnish citizens was not removed until 1949, however.
16   *Befolkningsrörelsen* 1946–1954; SOU 1951:42, pp. 251–253; Lundh & Olsson 1999, pp. 30–32, 55–58.

Hungary and West Germany to Sweden. During the 1950s, these were joined by Austrians, Belgians and Dutch nationals.[17] Although the collectively transferred workers were not supposed to stay in Sweden on a permanent basis, many eventually did.[18]

Statistically speaking, thus, the approximately 19,000 refugees who came to Sweden and were granted a right to stay between 1946 and 1954 only constituted about ten per cent of the total influx of migrants. Almost exclusively, they held Eastern European nationalities.[19]

About half of these arrived illegally. Apart from Balts, Russians and Ingrians, many of them were Poles and East Germans. Some fled directly from their home countries. Others came from Central European refugee camps (in, for example, Denmark, West Germany and Austria), in which they had resided since the Second World War.[20] Germany's food shortages of 1947 brought an increase of both Germans and other 'displaced' refugees of various nationalities still resident there.[21] And although there was a more or less constant influx of Poles during the second half of the 1940s, it

17   In the 1960s, Greeks and Yugoslavs were transferred too.

18   The transportations also involved exiled Sudeten Germans. *Befolkningsrörelsen* 1946–1954; SOU 1951:42, pp. 251–253; Lundh & Olsson 1999, pp. 58–59; Tempsch 1997; Thor 2007; Åke Nilsson, *Efterkrigstidens invandring och utvandring,* Statistiska centralbyrån, Stockholm 2004, pp. 19–22.

19   Between 1945 and 1948 the refugees made up approximately 25% of the total number of new arrivals. During the following years, that number fell to about 5%. *Befolkningsrörelsen* 1948, pp. 24–25; Lundh & Olsson 1999, pp. 77–81 and the following source material: 'Illegalt anlända utlänningar under år 1949', vol. 1, H 1, Kanslibyrån, SUK, Ra; 'PM angående det europeiska flyktingproblemet', 1951, vol. 1, H 1, Kanslibyrån, SUK, Ra; 'Stockholm den 17 december 1953', attached table 2: 'Illegalt anlända, vilka godtagits såsom flyktingar 1946–1952', vol. 1, H 1, Kanslibyrån, SUK, Ra; 'Av Statens utlänningskommission meddelade beslut i avvisnings- och förpassningsärenden även som av polismyndighet meddelade avvisningsbeslut år 1952', vol. 1, H 1, Kanslibyrån, SUK, Ra; 'Av Statens utlänningskommission meddelade beslut i avvisnings- och förpassningsärenden även som av polismyndighet meddelade avvisningsbeslut år 1953', vol. 1, H 1, Kanslibyrån, SUK, Ra; 'Av Statens utlänningskommission meddelade beslut i avvisnings- och förpassningsärenden även som av polismyndighet meddelade avvisningsbeslut år 1954', vol. 1, H 1, Kanslibyrån, SUK, Ra; SOU 1951:42 p. 254.

20   'Illegalt anlända utlänningar under år 1949', vol. 1, H 1, Kanslibyrån, SUK, Ra; SOU 1951:42, p. 253; 'PM angående det europeiska flyktingproblemet', 1951, vol. 1, H 1, Kanslibyrån, SUK, Ra.

21   West Germans were most often turned away at the border, though, according to 'PM angående det europeiska flyktingproblemet', 1951, vol. 1, H 1, Kanslibyrån, SUK, Ra.

reached a peak in 1948 when Cold War tensions intensified and the Soviet Union tightened its grip over its satellite states (exemplified by, among other things, the Berlin crisis, the Soviet intervention in Czechoslovakia and the establishment of the Finnish YYA treaty).[22] Similarly, the intensified search for Soviet citizens in Finland by the Russian Control Commission in late 1947 and early 1948 led to a new wave of arrivals of Soviet citizens as approximately 2,000 Ingrians and Russians sought asylum in Sweden.[23]

Increased border surveillance by Soviet, Polish and East German authorities towards the end of the 1940s meant that fewer individuals managed to escape. In addition, harsher rules were introduced within the Soviet satellite states. Attempts at illegal departure led to more severe punishments as a means of deterrence. In addition, the Swedish authorities made their own efforts to hinder migration from Eastern Europe. Shipping companies transporting goods between Sweden and Poland, for example, were made to take responsibility for the repatriation of any refugees that had hidden on their merchant vessels. As a result, refugee migration to Sweden decreased significantly.[24]

Refugees arrived in other ways too. Some managed to obtain entry permits from other Western countries, often in order to reunite with close relatives. Others were collectively transported

22  SOU 1951:42, p. 254; 'Stockholm den 25 januari 1949', vol. 69, P 40 I, 1920 års dossiésystem, UD, Ra; 'Illegalt anlända utlänningar under år 1949', vol. 1, H 1, Kanslibyrån, SUK, Ra.

23  'PM nr 5 angående vissa ryska flyktingar från Finland', 15 september 1947, vol. 68, P 40 I, 1920 års dossiésystem, UD, Ra; 'VPM' by N. Hagelin, attachment to 'Protokoll', 27 april 1948, vol. 1, A 1, Hemliga arkivet, SUK, Ra. (According to this memorandum, 1,500 Ingrians arrived during the first four months of 1948 alone. According to SOU 1951:42, however, only 1,036 Ingrians were issued a 'non-refusal' decision in 1948. However, no refusal decisions have been found at all regarding Ingrians from 1948. How these contradictory numbers should be interpreted has not been possible to determine with certainty. The most plausible explanation, however, is that a substantial number of these Ingrians applied for residence permits before the authorities had issued a refusal or non-refusal decision, thus cutting short one step in the asylum seeking process.)

24  'PM angående det europeiska flyktingproblemet', 1951, vol. 1, H 1, Kanslibyrån, SUK, Ra. See also 'Till Kungl. Utrikesdepartementet', 5 juli 1946, vol. 3, E 4, Hemliga ark, SUK, Ra; 'Protokoll', 23 augusti 1950, vol. 3, A 1 A, Kanslibyrån, SUK, Ra. See also several statements on the matter in vol. 1, B 4, Kontrollbyrån, SUK, Ra and in vol. 69, P 40 I, 1920 års dossiésystem, UD, Ra (particularly from February and March 1949).

to Sweden from Central European refugee camps. Between 1946 and 1951, 3,400 refugees were transported to Sweden through the efforts of the IRO.[25] Although a collaboration between the Swedish state and international refugee organisations, this process was not too dissimilar from the importation of European workers. The individuals were picked out on location by representatives of the National Labour Market Board, whose task it was to find suitable workers among the refugees who could fill labour shortages in Sweden. In the beginning of the 1950s, the cooperation with the international refugee organisations became institutionalised as Sweden promised the newly established UNHCR that it would accept a quota of 1000 refugees annually. Thus, between 1950 and 1967, 17,000 refugees, mostly Eastern Europeans, came to Sweden as part of this deal.[26]

### 4.1.1 The Soviet Asylum Seekers

The Second World War shattered ethnic and national groups. Soviet citizens were by no means immune from these changes and, by the time the armistice was declared, they were to be found across

25   'Uppskattning av antalet vuxna flyktingar i Sverige den 1 september 1950', vol. 1, H 1, Kanslibyrån, SUK, Ra.

26   As a response to the pleading of international refugee organisations, Sweden soon started to accept individuals in need of medical care too. However, the National Labour Market Board, assisted by Swedish doctors, only chose individuals with curable diseases and suitable labour skills, in the expectation that they would become serviceable to the Swedish economy after undergoing medical treatment. Similarly, when selecting children with tuberculosis, only those whose parents were healthy and suitable to the needs of the Swedish labour market were picked. Orphans were left out. The collective transfer of refugees from European refugee camps was therefore, as Thor has noted, another kind of labour recruitment, governed by economic interests. As such, it did not differ all that much from the policies of other Western countries. As Wyman has demonstrated the old, infirm, sick or disabled who were not regarded as possible contributors to the national economies of the recipient states had to spend up to ten years in European refugee camps. Thor 2007; Wyman 1998. See also Sune G. Dufwa, 'Våra systrar snart här', and Norma Montesino, 'Flyktingmottagning en fråga om hälsa och arbete' in *Sveriges mottagning av flyktingar – några exempel. Årsbok 2007 från forskningsprofilen Arbetsmarknad, migration och etniska relationer (AMER) vid Växjö universitet,* Jan Ekberg (ed.) Växjö University Press, Växjö 2007; and Anders Berge, 'Sveriges politik mot de ungerska flyktingarna 1956–1959', in *Historisk tidskrift* 1993: 113, pp. 332–349.

the European continent. *Estonians, Latvians* and *Lithuanians* had continuously fled in various directions during different stages of the war, as their states were occupied on no less than three occasions (by the Soviet Union in 1940, Germany in 1941 and again by the Soviet Union in 1944). Those who had escaped were to be found in, for example, West Germany, Denmark and Sweden in 1945. But there were also those who had been trapped within the Eastern zones of Europe, such as Poland and the Soviet zone of Germany (from 1949 onwards the DDR – *Deutsche Demokratische Republik*, in English translated to GDR – *German Democratic Republic*). Therefore, those Baltic refugees that arrived in Sweden after the war came principally from three directions: from Western countries such as Denmark and West Germany; from the Soviet Union; and, occasionally, from Soviet satellite states such as Poland and the GDR. Some also came via Finland.

*Ingrians* were not as spread out. They came almost exclusively from Finland where they had been transferred by the Germans in 1942–43. The *Russians*, on the other hand, were even more dispersed than the Balts when the armistice came in May 1945. However, due to the forced mass repatriation movement that occurred on the European continent during the succeeding months, not that many managed to stay behind on Western territory. Thus, those Russian refugees that came to Sweden after the war usually came from the Soviet Union, Finland or, occasionally, from Poland and Germany. During the first post-war year, some also arrived from Norway where Soviet prisoners of war had been kept by the Germans during the occupation.

In consequence, whilst removal decisions in all probability constituted uncomfortable experiences to most individuals who were exposed to them, they had very different ramifications for those sent back to, for example, Denmark or West Germany, compared with those returned to the Soviet Union. In war-torn Denmark and parts of West Germany and Austria, Baltic refugees were held in refugee camps for several years after the war, with little possibility of finding employment or accommodation outside of the camps – a situation which obviously caused frustration. Rumours of the superior living conditions of Baltic refugees in Sweden spread throughout Western Europe. Consequently, Balts reaching Sweden from Western European refugee camps were often in search of a better and more independent life, a position of work, and, sometimes, a lost relative. A forced return thus cost the individual considerable disappointment and further frustration.[27]

A return to the Soviet Union, on the other hand, was likely to cost an individual significantly more than that. After the chaos and confusion of the final year of the war, the Soviet Union once again tightened its grip over its (new) borders. Leaving the Soviet Union without permission was considered a crime according to Soviet Law and severe punishments often awaited failed escapees. In addition, they often risked not only their own lives and security, but that of their relatives too, since their flight frequently led to state persecution of their family members.

Reappearance in the grey zones such as Poland and the Soviet zone of Germany/GDR could also be deeply problematic. These countries' close political and administrative ties to the Soviet regime meant that refugees faced similar risks upon return as those arriving from the Soviet Union.

Finland constituted a special case. Although it escaped direct 'Sovietisation' and a communist overtake, it was held in a tight grip by the Soviet Union during most of the Cold War. This was particularly so during those first years, due to the regulations in the armistice agreement of 1944, which forced many unwelcome conditions upon the Finns. Apart from having to accept responsibility for the material losses the Soviet Union had endured through the Finnish-Soviet War and provide substantial reimbursements as 'compensation', it was obliged to send several Finnish national politicians and military staff to the Soviet Union to stand trial for war crimes. Similarly, the agreement entailed the extradition of Soviet citizens who had 'violated their national law by treason or collaboration with the enemy during the war'.[28] This included thousands of individuals – Ingrians in particular, but also Balts and Russians – who had helped the Finns fight the Soviet Union. A Control Commission was set up to ensure compliance in this matter. From 1948 onwards, the establishment of the Agreement of Friendship, Cooperation and Mutual Assistance (YYA Treaty)

---

27  The cost was sometimes financial too given that they had often paid a significant sum of money to a refugee smuggler. See, for example, central dossier of B52.

28  Finnish-Soviet Armistice Agreement, September 1944, article 9.

meant that Finland's foreign policy and defence strategies were intimately bound to the Soviet Union, thus further strengthening its dependency.[29]

Soviet refugees in Finland were therefore in a dire position – particularly those who had assisted the Finnish war effort. So too were the Finnish authorities, however, which had to extradite Finland's former soldiers-in-arms as a condition for peace. Civilian Soviet citizens were initially not explicitly demanded for extradition, yet nor could they regard themselves as safe. Soviet policy sought the return of all its citizens, and the Control Commission worked hard to implement this goal using varying methods ranging from threats and false information to propaganda and allurements.[30]

Despite these procedures, some Soviet citizens succeeded in remaining in Finland, often under false identities. The fear of repatriation hung over them for some years to come, however. In 1947, the Control Commission presented new directives regarding the civilian Russians in Finland, and demanded that most of them return.[31] It also stepped up its search for civilian Ingrians. By the end of 1947, its official activities in Finland were discontinued as the final peace agreement was signed. However, in 1948–50, Soviet citizens were still intermittently extradited to the Soviet Union according to the armistice agreement of 1944.[32] And by 1953, the Finnish authorities were continuously supplying Soviet officials with detailed registers of Soviet citizens residing in Finland. As a result, all Soviet citizens in Finland were a possible target for the activities of the Soviet authorities and its repatriation agents.[33]

29  At the same time, however, the treaty simultaneously guaranteed Finland's sovereignty in a way that the satellite states had not been granted. Flink 2010.

30  Flink 2010.

31  'PM nr 5 angående vissa ryska flyktingar från Finland', 15 september 1947, vol. 68, P 40 I, 1920 års dossiésystem, UD, Ra.

32  'Helsingfors den 12 maj 1952', del: *Avvisning av ingermanländare*, vol. 6, F 2 B, Hemliga arkivet, SUK, Ra; 'Helsingfors den 16 november 1948', vol. 4, E 4, Hemliga arkivet, SUK, Ra and vol. 69, P 40 I, 1920 års dossiésystem, UD, Ra; 'Helsingfors den 11 december 1948', vol. 69, P 40 I, 1920 års dossiésystem, UD, Ra; 'Helsingfors den 13 december 1948', vol. 69, P 40 I, 1920 års dossiésystem, UD, Ra. Flink claims that the last extradition took place in 1948 (Flink 2010). In his 1952 letter to the Ministry for Foreign Affairs, however, the Swedish representative Engzell claims that a few Ingrians had been extradited from Finland to the Soviet Union in 1950.

33  Flink 2010.

In addition, between 1945 and 1948 the communist party had a significant influence on Finnish politics, as a result of its gaining a third of the total votes in the 1945 election. The consequential appointment of the communist Yrjö Leino to the influential post of Minister for the Interior meant that the state security police became deeply influenced by communism and initiated a hunt of its own for Soviet refugees – a process escalating in late 1947 and 1948. Soviet citizens in Finland thus fled to Sweden trying to escape both the Soviet Control Commission and the Finnish state police.

Consequently, even though countries such as the GDR, Poland or Finland were not part of the Soviet Union, they could not protect Soviet refugees from forced repatriation. Nor could they hinder the activities of Soviet repatriation agents, often employed by the Soviet Repatriation Committee, established in 1944, or the Control Commission who operated freely in their countries during the first post-war years.[34] Moreover, within both the GDR and Poland, leaving the country without authorisation was considered a crime against the state that could lead to punishment.

Soviet citizens fled to Sweden in varying numbers from all the above-named territories between 1945 and 1954. The risks associated with flight or forced return both to the safety of the migrant and, sometimes, that of the families they left behind were considerable. But the exact nature of this threat depended on where their journey had begun and whether or not they had managed to act without being noticed by the authorities. Such factors establish the general context necessary to appreciate the complex issues pertaining to the refugee question in post-war Europe. It is now time to begin examining how Sweden responded to the asylum claims of Soviet citizens.


## 4.2 The Management of Baltic New Arrivals

Available statistical accounts suggest that slightly more than 1,200 Baltic refugees who reached Sweden illegally between the end of the Second World War and December 1954 were granted the right to stay. The majority of these – at least 1,000 – came

34  Berge 1992, p. 11.

between 1945 and 1948.[35] Most of them were from West Germany and Denmark, in other words countries which had normally already recognised these individuals' refugee status.

In addition to this, many Balts arrived 'legally' with a valid entry permit. According to an estimation made in 1950, 950 Baltic refugees had arrived in this manner and been granted a right to stay between April 1945 and September 1950.[36]

According to the refusal of entry files, between 20 and 50 Balts were subjected to this decision yearly between 1945 and 1948. During the following years – 1949–54 – that number varied between five and 20. This totals at least 250 refused Baltic citizens during the entire research period.[37]

35  Around 400 came during the second half of 1945 (although this number is
    unconfirmed), 90 in 1946, 350 in 1947 and 250 in 1948. In 1949 and 1950
    respectively, around 50 illegally arrived Balts were granted leave to stay.
    Thereafter, between the years 1951–54, when the traffic decreased significantly,
    no more than five to twenty per annum. See vol. 34–56, series 3418, F 11 A,
    Hemliga arkivet, SUK, Ra; 'Sovjetutredningen 8/5 1945–15/5 1946', nr 250,
    vol. 10, F 4, Hemliga arkivet, SUK, Ra; 'Illegalt anlända utlänningar under år
    1949', vol. 1, H 1, Kanslibyrån, SUK, Ra; 'Antalet flyktingar som anlänt till riket
    under år 1951', vol. 1, H 1, Kanslibyrån, SUK, Ra; 'PM angående det europeiska
    flyktingproblemet', 1951, vol. 1, H 1, Kanslibyrån, SUK, Ra; 'Stockholm den
    17 december 1953', attached table 2: 'Illegalt anlända, vilka godtagits såsom
    flyktingar 1946–1952', vol. 1, H 1, Kanslibyrån, SUK, Ra; 'Av Statens utlännings-
    kommission meddelade beslut i avvisnings- och förpassningsärenden även som
    av polismyndighet meddelade avvisningsbeslut år 1952', vol. 1, H 1, Kanslibyrån,
    SUK, Ra; 'Av Statens utlänningskommission meddelade beslut i avvisnings- och
    förpassningsärenden även som av polismyndighet meddelade avvisningsbeslut
    år 1953', vol. 1, H 1, Kanslibyrån, SUK, Ra; 'Av Statens utlänningskommission
    meddelade beslut i avvisnings- och förpassningsärenden även som av polismyn-
    dighet meddelade avvisningsbeslut år 1954', vol. 1, H 1, Kanslibyrån, SUK, Ra;
    'Uppskattning av antalet vuxna flyktingar i Sverige den 1 september 1950' vol. 1,
    H 1, Kanslibyrån, SUK, Ra; SOU 1951:42, p. 254.
36  Moreover, some 200 Balts who had been transferred to Sweden through the
    assistance of the Red Cross and UNRRA in 1945 were still in the country in
    1950. How many of the 3400 refugees who were transferred to Sweden by the
    IRO between 1946 and 1951 were of Baltic origin has not been possible to verify
    from the sources analysed in this thesis. The total number of Balts arriving in
    Sweden through collective transportation measures in the 1950s, however, was
    minor. Statistical information on legally arrived Balts *after* 1950 has not been
    found. 'Uppskattning av antalet vuxna flyktingar i Sverige den 1 september
    1950', vol. 1, H 1, Kanslibyrån, SUK, Ra; 'Till Sverige kollektivt överförda
    flyktingar 1950 – 1 juli 1959 fördelade dels på asylland, dels på ursprungligt
    hemland', vol. 1, H 1, Kanslibyrån, SUK, Ra.
37  Vol. 34–56, series 3418, F 11 A, Hemliga arkivet, SUK, Ra; 'Sovjetutredningen
    8/5 1945–15/5 1946', nr 250, vol. 10, F 4, Hemliga arkivet, SUK, Ra.

*Where*, then, were they sent – and why? What circumstances determined who could stay and who could not? And how should the apparently generous treatment of Balts arriving from Western countries be understood in comparison with what was demonstrated above, namely that some of the refugees from the GDR and Poland were indeed turned away at the border, even though they presumably had more reasons to claim political refugee status? And what about the Balts who arrived from the Soviet Union and Eastern Europe – were they all granted permission to stay?

### 4.2.1 Reassessment of the Collective Refugee Status, 1945–47

The Swedish government's clear, generous policy regarding the around 30,000 Baltic (civilian) refugees who arrived in 1944 was demonstrated in chapter two. Nevertheless, there is evidence to suggest that the National Alien Commission did not interpret these principles as fully precedential for Baltic new arrivals after the war. During the second half of 1945, the protocols from the Commission's plenary meetings reveal that cases concerning newly arrived Baltic refugees' right to reside in Sweden caused ambiguity and were often the subject of discussion at the highest level of the Commission – regardless of whether they had arrived from Western or Eastern Europe, or even the Soviet Union.[38] Similarly, an analysis of the Aliens Appeals Board's archive reveals that this body was asked to give a statement on the possibility of refusing at least thirty newly arrived Balts during the autumn of 1945 alone. Again, this concerned individuals arriving both from Western and Eastern Europe.[39]

Several concrete examples of these ambiguous attitudes among the decision makers can be found. In July 1945, for example, two Latvians arrived in a small rowing boat. It transpired that they had both resided in Sweden for a short period during the war. In late 1944, they had returned to the Soviet Union after being promised a good life back home by Soviet representatives. Their hopes had been shattered, however, as they had been sent to forced labour

38   See, for example, protocols dated 31 July 1945, 21 August 1945, 30 August 1945, 9 October 1945, 23 October 1945, 13 November 1945, 20 November 1945, vol. 1, A 1 A, Kanslibyrån, SUK, Ra.
39   Vol. 3–4, B 1, Utlänningsnämnden, Ra.

instead. Through some fortunate circumstances, they managed to escape to Sweden again via Helsinki and applied for asylum. The National Alien Commission then stated, however, that due to the fact that the foreigners had returned willingly to the Soviet Union in 1944, they should not be considered political refugees. Instead, they should be refused entry and sent back. But the Aliens Appeals Board did not agree. It claimed that the young Latvians had the same reason for political asylum as 'other Balts' and, as a result, the case was referred to the government. The government, in its turn, favoured the more generous line and declared that the Latvians could stay.[40]

One month later, in August 1945, a similar plenary discussion led the Commission to the conclusion that two newly arrived Estonians should be refused entry and sent back to the Soviet Union. The plenary assembly had been divided, however, and as a result, the implementation of the decision was referred to the government. After requiring some additional investigations, the government decided to regard them as political refugees and granted them leave to stay.[41]

A Latvian man arriving that same autumn was not as fortunate. He was refused entry by the Commission and forced to return to Finland in November 1945, despite the fact that he had worked on various tasks for the Wehrmacht, dressed in German uniform, and been taken as a prisoner of war by the Russians. He had managed to escape and flee to Finland. As a Soviet citizen, he had legitimate fears of being extradited to the Soviet Union in accordance with the regulations of the Finnish-Soviet armistice agreement. Nonetheless, the Commission did not approve his motivations for asylum. When placed on the ship that was to take him back to Finland, however, he made such violent resistance that the staff refused to accept him on board without a guard. As a result, a couple of Swedish police officers had to follow him on the ship and personally deliver him to the Finnish authorities.[42]

40 Central dossier of B85; 'Protokoll', 31 juli 1945, vol. 1, A 1 A, Kanslibyrån, SUK. See also nr 2592 and 2593, 'Stockholm den 27 juli 1945', vol. 4, B 1, Utlänningsnämnden, Ra.
41 'Protokoll', 21 augusti 1945, vol. 1, A 1 A, Kanslibyrån, SUK, Ra; 'Protokoll', 30 augusti 1945, vol. 1, A 1 A, Kanslibyrån, SUK, Ra; central dossier of B89.
42 Nr 2558, vol. 35, F 11 A, Hemliga arkivet, SUK, Ra, and central dossier of B33.

As mentioned in chapter three, new arrivals could also sometimes be issued deportation decisions. Within the National Alien Commission's 'Secret Archive' exist traces of more delicate matters regarding removals of new arrivals that were seemingly never documented in any of the usual refusal of entry or deportation series or meeting protocols. One such example is constituted by a group of nineteen Latvians, arriving directly from the Soviet Union in a small fishing boat on 31 October 1945, including some members from the former Latvian army who had fought against the Soviet Union. Seventeen of them immediately applied for asylum.[43]

Their timing was unfortunate. They arrived halfway through the sensitive extradition affair of the 146 Baltic soldiers which placed the Swedish government under severe international pressure.[44] Compounding this problem was the fact that they had arrived in a rather sizeable group, which risked arousing public attention. This, in turn, was something the government generally wished to avoid in matters concerning Soviet refugees since it could provoke the Soviet authorities into intensifying their lobbying of the Swedish government.[45]

All this probably explains why, when informed of their arrival, the Commission immediately contacted the Ministry for Foreign Affairs. The Ministry stressed the 'urgency' of this matter and the 'aspects of foreign policy' that it invoked. It therefore needed to be settled immediately. The Aliens Appeals Board was hastily convened. Its opinion was emphatic: according to the law and the situation in their home countries, the refugees ought to be granted asylum.[46]

Nevertheless, the Commission seems to have perceived that it still did not have the authority to settle the case, and decided to send it to the government according to paragraph 48 of the Aliens Act. In the Commission's enclosed remark, however, it was pointed

---

43  'Till Konungen', 2 november 1945, hemlig, part H 1021–1288, Vol. 2, E 4, Hemliga arkivet, SUK, Ra.

44  This affair is described in ch. 1, part 1.1.

45  On the relation between publicity and Soviet pressure, see, for example, 'Till Konungen', 9 november 1946, vol. 3, E 4, Hemliga arkivet, SUK, Ra.

46  'Till Konungen', 2 november 1945, hemlig, part H 1021–1288, Vol. 2, E 4, Hemliga arkivet, SUK, Ra.

out that 'no refusal of entry of Balts arriving from the Soviet Union has taken place so far'.[47]

The foreign policy concerns of the case were, however, clearly taken seriously by the government. On the very same day the letter from the National Alien Commission arrived, the government decided that the nineteen Latvians ought to be deported. The decision was referred to paragraph 56 of the Aliens Act (the 'security paragraph' which gave the government freedom to deviate from any regulations in the law in times of 'war or danger of war'). This decision is not to be found in any of the regular meeting protocols or deportation files. Nor does it appear in any of the relevant correspondence material. Instead, the only place where it is in fact documented is within the personal dossiers and register cards of the Latvians in question.[48] This substantiates further the impression that politically sensitive decisions were often deliberately left out of the official records. This makes finding evidence of their existence a particular challenge.

The deportation decision came with a time limited postponement, however, until 'further instructions from the government' were forthcoming. When this expired, the Latvians applied for a renewal of the postponement, which was granted. This was then pursued repeatedly over several years.[49] Thus, in the end, members of this group had their deportation decisions individually withdrawn by the Ministry for the Interior in 1951 and 1952. Consequently, none of these deportation decisions were carried out through transferral to the Soviet Union.[50]

Through this arrangement, the government could avoid further pressure from the Soviet authorities while at the same time safeguard the refugees from political persecution. The deportation decision presumably placated the Soviet authorities, while their repeated postponement provided the Latvians with a measure of protection. Thus, this strongly suggests that the deportation decision was motivated by *external security concerns*, similar to those which had

---

47  *Ibid.*

48  See, for example, central dossier of B79 and control register card of B95.

49  See, for example, central dossier of B79.

50  See the following documents from Föredragningslistor , vol. 3–6, A II, Inrikesdepartementet, SUK, Ra: 30 juni 1949, nr 63; 26 januari 1951, nr 44; 5 oktober 1951, nr 25; 23 november 1951, nr 25–28; and 14 mars 1952, no. 18–19.

determined the extradition decision that same year. However, the failure to implement the deportation decision evinces a wish to protect the Balts and adjust to international standards regarding this group's refugee rights at this time. Nonetheless, the Swedish state's ambiguous behaviour in this case rendered the Latvians' presence in Sweden as precarious. As shall be demonstrated in chapter seven, deportation decisions – even those postponed – resulted in several unpleasant consequences for the individuals in question.

This example is the only deportation decision that has been found regarding Balts travelling directly from the Soviet Union or the grey zone areas.[51] Similarly, the refusal of entry files and the meeting protocols of the National Alien Commission reveal no other *implemented* refusal of entry decisions regarding Balts arriving from the Soviet Union or the grey zone countries in the autumn of 1945 aside from the above-mentioned Latvian.[52] In general, thus, Balts arriving from Eastern Europe and the Soviet Union in the autumn of 1945 seem to have been granted a right to stay. This included individuals with the same sort of background as the 146 military Balts who were interned awaiting extradition during these months as a result of a direct Soviet demand.[53] However, the principles seem to have been somewhat unclear, leading to several discussions and referrals to the government.

In 1946, however, there is evidence suggesting a stricter attitude altogether towards newly arrived Balts. A number of refusals to grey zone countries took place. At least eight Balts arriving from Poland were refused entry – five by the National Alien Commission, and three by the police. Out of these, at least five claimed that they had been engaged in such activities that would have rendered them to be identified as 'traitors' and/or 'enemies of the state' in the eyes of the Soviet Union. They had, for example, worked for the Germans during the war. Therefore they feared repatriation to the Soviet Union,

---

51  As has been demonstrated, however, it is possible that similar politically sensitive removal decisions remain undetected within the personal dossiers of refugees whose names are as yet unknown due to the rationalisation of the National Alien Commission's archive during the 1970s (see chapter 1).

52  Vol. 3–4, B 1, Utlänningsnämnden, Ra; vol. 34–35, F 11 A, Hemliga arkivet, SUK, Ra; vol. 1, A 1 A, Kanslibyrån, SUK, Ra.

53  Central dossiers of B113 and B114.

as had been the fate of some of their fellow-countrymen in Poland.[54]

This was similarly the case with a Latvian arriving from Finland. In his instance, the police observed in their report that he was to be considered a political refugee in Finland, but reasoned that this was not the case in Sweden.[55] The reasoning appears somewhat illogical, however. The man was not considered a war criminal according to article nine of the Finnish-Soviet armistice agreement, since he had not been enlisted in the army. However, his alleged work for the Germans during the war still made him an enemy of the state in the eyes of the Soviet Union. A return there would have entailed a considerable risk to his personal safety. Thus, the police's argument was based on the presupposition that he was under no risk of being sent to the Soviet Union from Finland. However, the general Soviet pressure Finland was under during those years meant that no Soviet citizens could feel immune from such a risk – and particularly not an individual who had assisted Finland or Germany in the war.

The asylum principles regarding the Balts who arrived from grey zone areas in 1946 thus seem to have continued to be unclear, or, alternatively, inconsistently applied. This is further emphasised by the fact that among those who *were* granted permission to stay were, indeed, other Balts with very similar stories and backgrounds. They had, for example, worked for the Germans, either within the war industry or with other tasks.[56] Nothing in particular can be found in the various documents concerning these individuals that can explain why some of them were, and others were not, granted asylum in 1946.[57] Thus, the different outcomes do not appear to have been based on predetermined principles.

54   The lack of information concerning the others does not, obviously, mean that
     they did not present similar causes for flight – only that no such information
     was registered in their reports. Nr 2622, 2783, 2921, 3135, 3210 in vol. 35–38, F
     11 A, Hemliga arkivet, SUK, Ra.

55   Nr 3175, vol. 37, F 11 A, Hemliga arkivet, SUK, Ra.

56   See, for example, a Latvian carpenter and his friend, arriving in July 1946, presenting
     similar stories as the above-mentioned Balts. The police believed they should be
     refused entry but for some reason decided to send the case to the Commission
     anyway, which in its turn opted to let them stay. Central dossier of B14.

57   One exception is constituted by two married Latvian couples, arriving from
     East Germany in October 1946, who seem to have been granted a right to
     stay due to the two women's late pregnancies. The decision was made by the
     Commission. See central dossier of B17.

One factor, however, made an important difference in cases where it arose. Some of the Balts who arrived from Eastern European countries (other than the Soviet Union) received assistance from prominent members of Swedish society and/or trusted individuals from the expatriate elite in Stockholm, often with high positions within the Estonian and Latvian refugee help committees. If these esteemed individuals and/or organisations testified to the Commission in favour of a refugee, guaranteeing, for example, his or her political trustworthiness (in other words non-Nazi and non-communist world views and historical past) and respectable character, as well as his or her sufferings under the Soviet and/or the German regime/s, the refugee was likely to be granted asylum. All cases examined in this study, where such support has clearly been given to the individual, resulted in a positive assessment by the Commission. Personal contacts with figures of high social standing who could guarantee an applicant's excellent character thus stand out as an important factor of influence on the outcome of Baltic refugees' asylum applications during these first post-war years.[58]

In the end, two of the nine refusal of entry decisions concerning Balts arriving from grey zone countries in 1946 were withdrawn by the Commission.[59] The implementation of another two was hindered by the Polish authorities who refused to grant the Balts re-entry. These individuals were sent back to Sweden, where they later received a residence permit.[60]

Two cases protrude more conspicuously, however. On Christmas Eve 1945, two Latvian sailors aged 18 and 25, arrived in Malmö on a Polish ship. Their personal files do not contain much information. However, the protocols from the police claim that they, as reason for their flight, mentioned poor conditions on their ship; that they were being treated badly and paid and fed deficiently. In other words, according to the police they did not mention any

---

58   See, for example, central dossiers of B8, B6 and B103.

59   Nr 3135, vol. 37, F 11 A, Hemliga arkivet, suk, Ra; nr 3288, vol. 38, F 11 A, Hemliga arkivet, suk, Ra. One of the refusal decisions had been made by the police (nr 3288), and the other by the Commission (nr 3135).

60   Nr 3219 and no 3437, vol. 37, F 11 A, Hemliga arkivet, suk, Ra. In addition, in seven out of in total twenty-five withdrawn refusal of entry decisions regarding Balts, the country of destination could not be deciphered. See nr 3344, 3346, 3372, 3485, 3486, vol. 38, F 11 A, Hemliga arkivet, suk, Ra.

motives pertaining to political conditions. However, the older of the two had spent some time in Sweden in a closed refugee camp in 1944, and was at that time considered a political refugee. He had left in October of that year, however, presumably to return to his home country, which had by then been turned over from German to Soviet control. In response to a direct question from the police, they replied that they were not members of any political organisation, but that they did 'not under any circumstances want to go back to an area controlled by the Russians'. The police sent their case further to the National Alien Commission, which assessed it in January 1946. The Commission decided that the Latvians were not to be considered political refugees. As with the above-mentioned cases, the fact that they did not want to live under Russian control was not considered a compelling enough reason, even though this had constituted a criteria for political refugee status for Balts arriving one year earlier. The fact that they had left their positions illegally, and thus possibly attracted attention from the authorities, was not considered either. The Commission decided that these men were to be sent back to Poland, and on 9 January 1946, this decision was implemented.[61]

In Poland, however, the authorities refused to grant them re-entry and returned them to Sweden.[62] At that point, the Commission decided to send the two Latvian sailors to the Soviet Union, instead of granting them permission to stay, as seems to have been the chosen solution in other similar circumstances. There is no clarification for this decision to be found either in their personal dossiers or in any other protocols. The decision is in fact not even mentioned in the protocols from the plenary meetings, which is in itself conspicuous. It is unlikely that the case was not brought up within the plenary meetings, considering its unusual outcome. However, the sensitive nature of this case is probably the reason why it is absent from these protocols.

61  Nr 2622, vol. 35, F 11 A, Hemliga arkivet, SUK, Ra; Central dossiers and central register cards of B30 and B70.

62  This happened on a regular basis and constituted a diplomatic issue for concern and frequent discussion between Sweden and Poland during the late 1940s . See, for example, 'Stockholm den 25 januari 1949' and 'Warszawa den 12 mars 1949', vol. 69, P 40 I, 1920 års dossiésystem, UD, Ra. This volume consists of several other documents on the same theme.

The implementation of this noteworthy decision, however, is documented both in the young Latvians' respective central dossiers, on their central register cards and in the refusal of entry files. On 25 January 1946, the sailors were transported to the Soviet Union on the ship Beloostrov leaving from Trelleborg. In other words, they were placed on the very same ship as the 146 Baltic soldiers that were extradited to the Soviet Union on that day.[63]

Thus, in so doing, Sweden sent two civilian Balts, who claimed not to want to return to an area controlled by the Soviet Russians 'under any circumstances', to the Soviet Union. This was contrary to their previous (and, indeed, subsequent) policies regarding Baltic (civilian) refugees. These two sailors constitute the only cases that have been found, however, of Baltic citizens being sent directly to the Soviet Union as a result of a refusal of entry decision. It is thus likely that the impending extradition of the military Balts influenced this decision and was interpreted by the Commission as a sign of the government's changing principles and that Balts should no longer collectively be recognised as political refugees.[64] Still, however, other new arrivals who had assisted the German war effort in various ways, but had arrived in Sweden under other circumstances than the 146 military Balts who were to be expatriated, continued to be granted a right to stay. The expatriation of the 146 Baltic 'traitors' thus seems to have been regarded as an exception to a continued rule, namely that Balts with strong claims to political asylum were to be protected. Instead, it was individuals with less strong claims to political refugee status, such as the two refused civilian sailors, who were sent to the Soviet Union against their will. However, the fact that they constitute the only example of its kind (documented in the sources at least) makes the decision somewhat curious.

In terms of discussions, the year 1946 included at least eleven plenary meetings which involved a debate on whether or not to refuse entry to a varying number of Baltic individuals, arriving from both East and West. Opinions within the plenary assembly

63   Nr 2622, vol. 35, F 11 A, Hemliga arkivet, SUK, Ra; central dossiers and central register cards of B30 and B70.

64   Some members of staff at the Commission had, however, engaged in a protest action against the impending extradition of the military Balts. 'Protokoll', 27 november 1945, vol. 1, A 1 A, Kanslibyrån, SUK, Ra.

were often divided. As a result, some of the cases were referred to the government for a final decision.[65]

There is no evidence suggesting that the discussions – or indeed implemented refusals – examined thus far were instigated due to a specific perception of threat. As such, security concerns do not emerge as a prominent motivation behind these particular pursued practices. Nor have any direct or indirect references to the other potential influential aspects been identified. Instead, the inconsistencies and ambiguity seem to have been caused by the authorities' varying interpretations of the vague or even confusing guidelines provided by the government, regarding how the Aliens Act was to be applied to Balts. This seems to be especially the case in 1946, after the controversial extradition of the Baltic and German soldiers. A general unwillingness to pursue 'too generous' principles also obtrude, however. Like the authorities' previous line of reasoning – as historians Kvist Geverts and Åmark among others have argued – it is possible to conclude that this was founded on ethnic concerns, entailing a reluctance to encourage more Balts to come to Sweden through the adaptation of liberal border practices.[66]

One case stands out as possibly being determined by something else, however. This concerns the treatment of five Latvians who arrived in a small boat on the island of Gotland in April 1946. The Commission granted them asylum but was not united in its decision. One of the members of the plenary assembly insisted that they should have been 'immediately refused entry' and sent back to the Soviet Union. Again, this was a case of individuals who had previously resided in Sweden but had chosen to return to the Soviet Union. As a sort of a compromise, the Commission decided to grant them a geographically restricted residence permit.[67]

No further motivations for the decision have been documented.

---

65  From vol. 1, A 1 A, Kanslibyrån, SUK: Protocols dated 22 January 1946 and 19 February 1946. From vol. 2, A 1 A, Kanslibyrån, SUK, Ra: Protocols dated 16 April 1946, 24 April 1946, 14 May 1946, 28 May 1946, 27 August 1946, and 15 October 1946. From vol. 1, A 1, Hemliga arkivet, SUK, Ra: Protocols dated 19 July 1946, 20 August 1946, and 3 September 1946. For decisions brought to the government for decision, see also, for example, 'Protokoll', 31 juli 1945, vol. 1, A 1 A, Kanslibyrån, SUK, Ra; 'Till konungen', 2 november 1945, hemlig, vol. 2, E 4, Hemliga arkivet, SUK, Ra.

66  See chapter two, part 2.2 and 2.5.

67  'Protokoll', 16 april 1946, vol. 2, A 1, Kanslibyrån, SUK, Ra.

However, it can possibly be interpreted in two ways. On the one hand it could have been a result of the fear of spies. The Soviet Union's habit of sending agents disguised as refugees to Western countries was well known at this time. Sometimes their mission was to collect information on military matters of the host country. Often, however, the task was to infiltrate and spy on the Soviet refugee groups.[68] The fact that the Latvians had been in Sweden before and now returned could, according to this logic, be a sign that they were being sent back to Sweden on a mission from the Soviet authorities. The individuals could be perceived as having demonstrated feelings of solidarity with the Soviet Union as they had returned there willingly towards the end of the war. Now they had managed to leave the country – even though the borders of the Soviet Union were strictly controlled. If such suspicions constituted the reason for the division within the plenary assembly, the wish to protect the individuals from potential political persecution within the Soviet Union (for whatever reason, be it domestic/international prestige, humanitarian concerns or so forth) still took precedence.

It could also have been a question of moral principles on the part of the Commission. This study has so far revealed that members of the Commission, in 1945 at least, believed that a refugee who had left Sweden willingly to return to his country of origin had forfeited his right to asylum. According to this view, the individual's need of protection had then proved to be insignificant.

Overall, however, 1946 stands out as a year when the immigration authorities took a harsher stand towards newly arrived Balts and did indeed send some individuals back to grey zone countries.

In contrast, during 1947 evidence of only two refusal of entry decisions regarding Balts to grey zone countries has been discovered. These were made by the police rather than the Commission, and concerned two Estonian brothers who had passed the Finnish border on foot. They were found by the police when roaming around a military area in northern Sweden. According to the protocols from the police hearings, the men declared that they were former soldiers from the Finnish army. As such, they were included

68   See, for example, 'PM' [undated], vol. 4, E4, Hemliga arkivet, SUK, Ra; 'ang. Heimoveljet', vol. 5, F 2 B, Hemliga arkivet, SUK, Ra; 'ang. Ryska legationens repatrieringsverksamhet', vol. 9, F 2 B, Hemliga arkivet, SUK, Ra.

in the expatriation regulations within the Finnish-Soviet armistice agreement and had good reasons to fear a forced repatriation to the Soviet Union. Considering this, and the fact that the autumn of 1947 was when the persecutions of Soviet citizens in Finland intensified, the police's decision to send these Estonians back to Finland against their will, and without passing their case onwards to the Commission, is noteworthy. It does indeed contrast with the authorities' treatment of other Soviet citizens who had been soldiers within the Finnish army and who in general were granted asylum. Similarly, it contrasts with the 1945 Aliens Act's regulations on political asylum which stated that asylum applications in which the applicant claimed plausible political refugee status were to be referred to the National Alien Commission. The decision was implemented within two days, in other words six days before the legal appeal time had passed.[69]

The fact that the Estonian brothers had moved around a military base does not seem to have influenced the decision. Had the police suspected espionage they would have almost certainly contacted both the Commission and the security police in order to organise further hearings prior to removing the individuals from the country. No evidence of any such communication has been found. Thus, the outcome of this case appears unusual. Additionally, it is the only example from 1947 of refusals of entry of Baltic individuals arriving from Eastern Europe or any grey zone country to have been located.[70] Whether it was a deliberate decision to not adhere to current principles on the behalf of the police, or a temporary misjudgement (perhaps based on unclear principles from the Commission) remains uncertain. Had the Commission reacted negatively towards the decision, however, it is likely that it would have reprimanded the police afterwards.[71] No further documents

69  Nr 4025, vol. 40, F 11 A, Hemliga arkivet, SUK, Ra; Central dossier and central register card of B107.

70  It is, of course, not impossible that similar refusals of entry, decided by the police, took place during that year. As mentioned in the methodological considerations, reports of decisions may have been lost due to human error.

71  This interpretation is based on the numerous letters of reprimand sent to various police offices by the Commission that have been found in refugees' personal dossiers after December 1947 following the decentralisation of the residence permit process. The Commission's general complaint concerned situations when it felt that the police had acted beyond its remit.

mentioning this case have been discovered, either within the internal meeting protocols of the Commission or within its communication with the police.[72]

The plenary meeting protocols strengthen the impression that this case was atypical. In 1947, seven meetings within the plenary assembly included a discussion of a possible refusal of entry of Balts, according to the protocols. However, at that time they only regarded Balts arriving from Western countries.[73]

### 4.2.2 *The Watershed, 1948*

From 1948 onwards the sources contain no evidence of refused Balts arriving from the Soviet Union or the grey-zone countries.[74] However, in that year, 36 Baltic citizens arriving from Western countries were turned away at the border.[75] Most of the cases were determined by the Commission, signalling the principal importance of decisions concerning Baltic citizens. But some (at least nine, according to the files) were decided by the police and were thus never assessed by the Commission. Those refused entry were sent back to countries like West Germany (the British zone), Denmark, Belgium and the Netherlands. As many as 22 refusal decisions seem eventually to have been withdrawn, however, allowing the individuals to reside in Sweden after all.[76]

Similarly, the files reveal that, during the following years 1949–1954, refused Balts were only sent to West European countries. In contrast to the previous period, however, a significant percentage of these decisions were not forwarded to the Commission but were instead determined by the police.[77] Moreover, from this date

---

72  Obviously, the inexistence of such documents should not be used to infer with certainty that no such reprimand took place.

73  Protocols dated 3 January 1947, 28 January 1947, 17 June 1947, 2 September 1947, 16 September 1947, 6 November 1947 and 19 December 1947, in vol. 2, A 1 A, Kanslibyrån, suk, Ra. See also central dossier of B112.

74  Vol. 40–56, F 11 A, Hemliga arkivet, suk, Ra.

75  Vol. 40–43, F 11 A, Hemliga arkivet, suk, Ra.

76  The reasons hereto will be examined in the next section. Vol. 40–43, F 11 A, Hemliga arkivet, suk, Ra.

77  However, two refusal of entry decisions regarding Balts arriving from Finland and the Soviet Union have been found during 1953 and 1954 respectively. Both were swiftly withdrawn, however, and thus never implemented. The first

onwards, no matters concerning newly arrived Baltic citizens' right to stay in Sweden have been documented as a matter for discussion within the plenary assembly. Similarly, the sources lack any evidence of asylum cases concerning Balts being sent to the government for assessment. A stabilisation of policies, to the benefit of Balts arriving from the Soviet Union or the grey zone countries, thus seems to have taken place from 1948 onwards. This correlates with the general international juridical developments within the international refugee regime at this time, and thus suggests an adjustment of Swedish practices to these. It also coincides with the intensified tensions of the Cold War conflict, which witnessed Sweden modify its foreign policy stance towards the Soviet Union.

### 4.2.3 The Policy of the 'Western Balts'[78]

Balts arriving from Western countries were sometimes permitted to remain in Sweden but at other times not. In this section, attention shifts to the underlying policies behind these decisions in an attempt to try to explain them. Which of those illegally arriving 'Western Balts' were allowed to stay, and which were not? And, most importantly, why? What principles determined these practices?

---

regarded a Finnish woman with an Estonian citizenship, acquired through marriage, who felt harassed by her communist Finnish family in Finland. She was initially refused entry by the border police, which might not have believed that she was in fact an Estonian citizen. The National Alien Commission changed the refusal of entry decision, however, and granted her permission to stay (see central dossier and central register card of B42). The second case concerned an Estonian man arriving directly from the Soviet Union in 1954. He admitted upon arrival that he had been sent on a mission to Norway by the Soviet security services. However, he also claimed to have agreed to this only since he aimed to flee to Sweden. After an initial doubtful response from the National Alien Commission, resulting in a refusal of entry decision, the authorities believed him and granted him permission to stay. See central dossier, central register card and control register card of B68. See also nr 267, vol. 11, F 4, Hemliga arkivet, SUK, Ra.

78   This section is based on a study of the personal dossiers and register cards of the following Balts, arriving from West European countries between 1946 and 1954: B5, B6, B9, B11, B21, B22, B25, B35, B44, B46, B52, B75, B83, B91, B112; vol. 38–56, series 3418, F 11 A, Hemliga arkivet, SUK, Ra; vol. 2–8, A 2, Kontrollbyrån, SUK, Ra; vol. 1–11, A 2, Passbyrån, SUK, Ra; vol. 1–4, A 1 A, Kanslibyrån, SUK, Ra; vol. 1, A 1, Hemliga arkivet, SUK, Ra.

Balts arriving from Western countries where asylum legislation was regarded the same as in Sweden were not considered political refugees.[79] In general, therefore, if they could not present 'strongly humanitarian motives' or close family members already residing in Sweden, they were refused entry and sent back, most often to Denmark or West Germany. In these countries, they enjoyed protection from the Soviet authorities, but generally not the more beneficial living circumstances that were provided in Sweden during the first post-war years. Some of the refugees arriving in Sweden from Denmark and West Germany towards the end of the 1940s had been languishing in refugee camps for many years.

In 1947, when the traffic of Balts from Western Europe began to increase, policies in Sweden also began to change and an increasing number of Balts arriving from Western countries were now allowed to stay. What, then, made the Swedish authorities open up its doors for some of these individuals, and what determined which ones were chosen?

The examination undertaken of Balts arriving from Western countries from 1947 onwards reveals unusually transparent results. Those who could *prove* their value to the Swedish labour market were now much more likely to be granted a right to stay. This, however, was most likely to be achieved by those who, contrary to the regulations in the Aliens Act, had managed to enter Sweden unnoticed and had established themselves in the labour market before making their presence known to the authorities. Given the fact that Balts did not need work permits in Sweden at this time, this was considerably easier for this refugee group than the others. Their chances of being granted a residence permit increased still further if their employer was willing to confirm in writing that they were necessary, capable workers of upstanding social character and provided a service that no one else (a Swede, that is) could offer should they be forced to leave.

At first, in 1947, this policy was thought of as a temporary exception to a stable principle. During a plenary meeting in September a number of cases including Balts who had arrived from Denmark

---

79   'P.M. angående baltiska flyktingar i Sverige', 15 mars 1949, part XII, vol. 80, P 40 R, 1920 års dossiésystem, UD, Ra; 'Ändringar och tillägg till P.M. 15/3 1949', 18 mars 1949, by B. Åman, part XII, vol. 80, P 40 R, 1920 års dossiésystem, UD, Ra.

were discussed, and it was decided that those individuals who had already secured work would be granted a right to stay, whereas those who had been taken into custody at their arrival should be refused entry should no strong humanitarian reasons suggest otherwise. Thus, the Commission in fact decided to favour those who had acted contrary to the regulations of the Aliens Act (which stipulated that it was a foreigner's duty to report him or herself to the authorities immediately upon arrival), and refuse those who had abided by it. However, at the same time it also decided that, in the future, *all* Balts arriving from Denmark should be refused entry, regardless of whether they had been identified upon arrival or at a later stage – unless there were compelling humanitarian reasons not to do so.[80]

In January 1948, however, the National Alien Commission came to the opposite conclusion. Within a secret plenary meeting the exception principles from 1947 were now established as precedents. It was decided that those Balts who were found 'later than upon arrival' and who had a 'position of specific value to the employer' could be allowed to stay, given that the 'circumstances in general' did not include any information that could lead to a different outcome. Information on such individuals should, nevertheless, be procured from the Danish police.[81]

These new principles benefited several of the individuals included in this study arriving from 1947 onwards. Some had been refused entry in 1946 or 1947, but came back shortly afterwards and were then allowed to stay, provided that they had managed to acquire both a job and accommodation before making themselves known to the authorities. They were assisted in this by the Baltic community which, together with employers in such sectors as the textile industry, found work for whole groups of Balts and provided them with accommodation. Thus, for a capable individual with useful contacts within the Baltic exile community and/or other parts of Swedish society, gaining a residence permit from 1947–48 onwards was not that difficult, even though he or she had arrived from a Western country and were thus not regarded as a political refugee.[82]

---

80   'Protokoll', 2 september 1947, vol. 2, A 1 A, Kanslibyrån, SUK, Ra.
81   'Protokoll', 27 januari 1948, Hemliga arkivet, A 1, vol. 1, SUK, Ra.
82   B5, B6, B9, B11, B21, B22, B25, B35, B44, B46, B52, B75, B83, B91, B112.

The rationale behind these policies was thus indubitably characterised by *economic interests*. They coincided with the beginning of the unprecedented boom in the Swedish economy, and the increasing importance of economic migrants required to fill vacancies in the labour market. Thus, those Balts whose employers begged the authorities to be allowed to keep them were rarely disappointed. The less gainfully employed, however, were sent back, thus establishing the preference of 'useful' individuals who had broken the immigration legislation, to the detriment of those who had followed it.

In the same manner, the implementation of a substantial number of issued refusal of entry and deportation decisions were postponed and eventually withdrawn if the individual could confirm his or her value to the labour market. Thus, the high number of withdrawn refusal of entry decisions in 1948, demonstrated above, was constituted by such examples. A letter from an employer, certifying the refugee's indispensability, habitually constituted a ticket to a residence permit for Western Balts.

However, the second ingredient in these practices was undoubtedly constituted by *social control*. Employers were not only to guarantee an individual's usefulness at a Swedish workplace, but also his or her excellent behaviour. And permission was only given provided that no 'uncomplimentary information' existed about the individual. The Commission required careful examination of personal traits. If the employer wished to retain the employee, he or she ought to emphasise that the employee was 'ambitious', 'hard working', 'conscientious', caused 'no trouble', and did not engage in politics.[83]

Even so, however, individuals with work positions and/or offers and letters guaranteeing the quality of their characters were still, at times, refused. The principles the Commission developed regarding the Western Balts towards the end of the 1940s opened the way for arbitrary assessment practices. The analyses of a sample of these individuals do indeed reveal an inconsistency in the applications of these directives in some cases.

Towards the end of the research period, the traffic of Western Balts decreased significantly. So too did the number of removal decisions issued to new arrivals.

---

83   See, for example, central dossiers of B6, B11, B35; Nr 3958, vol. 40, F 11 A, Hemliga arkivet, suk, Ra.

## 4.3 The Management of Ingrian New Arrivals

Around 5000 Ingrians arrived in Sweden between 1944 and 1954. 1,500 of these did so during the last year of the war. Out of the other approximately 3,500 individuals who came during this decade, most did so during late 1947 and 1948 when the hunt for Soviet citizens in Finland intensified. The year 1950 saw a small increase again as some new extradition demands were presented to Finland by Soviet authorities. In 1951–54, however, the traffic lessened and only about 50–75 Ingrian adults arrived per annum. The Ingrians arrived exclusively from Finland – a country here defined as a grey zone area which could not guarantee safety from political persecution or extradition to the Soviet Union for Soviet citizens.[84]

This means that out of the total of around 7,000–8,000 Ingrians who did not return from Finland to the Soviet Union in the mass transportations of the winter of 1944–45, more than half eventually fled to Sweden.[85] How were they treated when they reached Swedish territory and applied for asylum? Were they granted the right to stay?

84    The statistical sources are unusually divergent as regards the exact number of the Ingrians. One reason is that Ingrians were generally not accounted for separately in the official statistics, but referred to as 'Soviet' or 'Soviet-Russian' citizens. Within the internal statistical accounts, a specified documentation of the Ingrians was more common. However, some of these sources present incompatible information, among other things due to the varying practices concerning the inclusion and exclusion of children in the quantitative accounts. Exact numerical information is therefore difficult to assemble. The numerical information above should therefore be regarded as estimations, based on a compilation of the statistical information within the following documents: SOU 1951:42 p. 254; 'PM angående det europeiska flyktingproblemet', 1951, vol. 1, H 1, Kanslibyrån, SUK, Ra; 'Uppskattning av antalet vuxna flyktingar i Sverige den 1 september 1950', vol. 1, H 1, Kanslibyrån, SUK, Ra; 'Flyktingar med tidigare domicil i område, som nu ingå i Sovjetunionen, vilka erhållit uppehållstillstånd i Sverige under tiden 8/5 1945 – 28/2 1947', 'Sovjetutredningen 8/5 1945–15/5 1946', nr 250, vol. 10, F 4, Hemliga arkivet, SUK, Ra; undated 'P.M. angående "ingermanländare" i Sverige' in central dossier of I46, Kanslibyrån, SUK, Ra; 'P.M. ang. till Haparanda under april månad 1947 anlända ingermanländska flyktingar', del 1, vol. 1, F 3, Kontrollbyrån, SUK, Ra; 'V.P.M.' by Nils Hagelin, 26 april 1948, attachment to 'Protokoll', 27 april 1948, § 1, vol. 1, A 1, Hemliga arkivet, SUK, Ra, pp. 2–3. See also Flink 2010.

85    Just like many other refugees in Europe fearing the power of the Soviet Union, however, some travelled elsewhere later on – for example to the US. Flink 2010.

### 4.3.1 *Two Contradictory Decisions: September 1945 and June 1946*[86]

The account of the Swedish authorities' treatment of Soviet refugees during the Second World War revealed that, in contrast to the
Balts, the Ingrians who came in 1944 were *not* considered political
refugees on a collective basis. However, it was also demonstrated
that the Commission had received (oral) directives from the government to adopt a generous policy at the border when Ingrians
arrived in 1944, and that two thirds of them were protected from
having their addresses disclosed to the Soviet authorities in 1945.
Thus, few Ingrians had been refused entry when arriving illegally,
according to the Commission's own account. It was also highlighted, however, that the non-refusals of the Ingrians did not guarantee
a right to stay once the war was over. No decision regarding their
future had yet been reached.[87]

In September 1945, the time had come for a verdict on this
matter. Talks had been preceded by discussion between the
Commission and the government, in which the former, as it sometimes did, sent the government a written account of a number of
'typical examples' of members of the refugee group in question,
representing different sorts of experiences and backgrounds.[88] The
objective of the account was to solicit a precedential statement
from the government regarding which refugees were to be granted
a right to stay, and which were not.[89]

In its request, the Commission pointed out that it had, in accordance with earlier oral directives from the government, applied generous principles at the border and not refused entry except to those
'who could not allege other reasons for their flight than that they

---

86  Some of the events related in this section have previously been described in
    Berge 1992 and Notini 2006. Thus, references both to Berge's work and to
    novel research are presented. The examinations regarding removal decisions
    constitute exclusively novel research.

87  See ch. 2, part 2.6.2.

88  This information generally originated from the police interrogations held with
    the refugees upon their arrival.

89  'Till Konungen', 26 juni 1945, vol. 67, P 40 I, 1920 års dossiésystem, UD, Ra.
    Other examples of the request of prejudicial statements from the government
    include 'Protokoll', 10 september 1946, vol. 1, A 1, Hemliga arkivet, SUK,
    Ra; 'Protokoll', 8 november 1946, vol. 1, A 1, Hemliga arkivet, SUK, Ra; 'Till
    Konungen', 9 november 1946, vol. 3, E 4, Hemliga arkivet, SUK, Ra; 'Till
    Konungen', 16 september 1947, vol. 4, E 4, Hemliga arkivet, SUK, Ra.

would get on better in Sweden, or similar reasons'.[90] Consequently, they were of the opinion that, since the Ingrians' position against the Soviet Union had 'not changed in the slightest since their arrival', those who had not been refused entry 'should not be deported either'.[91] In other words, the Commission argued that the Ingrians that now resided in Sweden ought to be allowed to stay.

There were reasons other than straightforward coherency for granting the Ingrians this permission, however. According to incoming reports from Hans Beck-Friis, the Swedish representative in Helsinki, there were indications that the Soviet Union was about to change its stance regarding the civilian Ingrians in Finland (who were not included in paragraph nine or ten in the armistice agreement), and start forcefully repatriating all members of this group that were strong and young enough to work. There were also reports revealing that Ingrian refugees were 'ruthlessly split up' upon arrival in the Soviet Union, and that all their possessions were being confiscated. Additionally, rumours spread that the Ingrians were to be used to work at the salt mines.[92]

Likewise, during the rest of the year, more troubling reports began arriving from the Swedish legation in Finland. According to these, the Finnish state police were already 'completely communist' and arrested and deported Soviet citizens on a regular basis. Refused Ingrian citizens that were sent back to Finland had been deported directly to the Soviet Union. Both members of the Ministry for Foreign Affairs and the National Alien Commission expressed concerns over what would happen to the Ingrians if they were to be expelled from Sweden.[93]

Had the government given priority to this information in their assessment in September 1945, all the Ingrians could have been granted status as political refugees. They all stood accused of at least two acts that made them criminals against the state accord-

90  *I enlighet med dessa direktiv har kommissionen meddelat avvisningsbeslut blott i sådana fall, då ingermanlänningen icke kunnat anföra annat skäl för sin flykt än att han skulle trivas bättre i Sverige eller dylikt.* 'Till Konungen', 26 juni 1945, vol. 67, P 40 I, 1920 års dossiésystem, UD, Ra.

91  *De flyktingar, som sålunda icke blivit avvisade, borde icke heller förpassas, då ju deras ställning gentemot Sovjetryssland icke blivit i minsta mån förändrad efter hitkomsten.* 'Till Konungen', 26 juni 1945, vol. 67, P 40 I, 1920 års dossiésystem, UD, Ra.

92  'Helsingfors den 17 september 1945', vol. 67, P 40 I, 1920 års dossiésystem, UD, Ra. See also Berge 1992, p. 81.

93  Berge 1992, p. 81.

ing to the Soviet legislation (leaving the Soviet Union 'illegally', and then demonstrating a refusal to return by fleeing to Sweden from Finland). Moreover, Finland's limited ability to refuse Soviet repatriation demands at this time could in principle have led them all to be granted the status of political refugees.[94]

However, in its September 1945 decision the government chose to adhere to its earlier principles. In a comment about this decision in his diary, the Minister for Foreign Affairs repeated the collective approach rationale that had explained previous disparities in treatment: 'the difference between the Ingrians and the Balts [is that] the latter have been Russians for 200 years'.[95] Thus, use was made of the same criteria as that which had been deployed a few months earlier regarding the passing on of names and addresses to the Soviet authorities. Those who had deserted from the Red Army, or actively participated in political or military actions against the Soviet Union, would be granted a right to stay. That also included their families. The others would be deported. In contrast to the interned military Balts and Germans, however, they were not to be deported collectively. The government by all likelihood wanted to avoid the public attention and outrage that was expected to accompany the coming expatriation of the interned military Balts. Additionally, the Ingrians had, after all, acquired residence permits that were still valid, and were spread out at various work positions in Sweden.[96] Consequently, the Ingrians were to be deported to Finland 'successively and individually, concurrently with the expiry of their temporary residence permits'. And the decision was to be kept secret.[97]

The judgement was looked upon as setting a precedent and,

94  As demonstrated in chapter 3, the Aliens Act stated that the Swedish authorities should not deport individuals to a jurisdiction from which they might undergo rendition to the country from which they had fled for political reasons.

95  *Underströk för övrigt olikheten mln ingermanlänningarna och balterna, i det de förra sedan 200 år varit ryssar.* Diary note by Östen Undén 7 February 1946 in Östen Undén, *Anteckningar: 1918–1952*, Kungl. Samf. för utgivande av handskrifter rörande Skandinaviens historia, Stockholm 2002, p. 131.

96  'Promemoria', juni 1945, vol. 67, P 40 I, 1920 års dossiésystem, UD, Ra. See also chapter two, part 2.6.2.

97  'Allmän beredning för flyktingfrågor', 26 september 1945, vol. 67, P 40 I, 1920 års dossiésystem, UD, Ra. (The document can also be found in vol. 77, P 40 R, 1920 års dossiésystem, UD, Ra.)

as such, it had an immediate effect. On the very same day as the verdict had been reached, the Commission decided to refuse entry to 28 Ingrians who had arrived a couple of weeks earlier and were awaiting evaluation. They were transported by train to the northern town of Haparanda and taken over the Finnish border within a couple of days. In response to a direct question from the media, the Commission answered that the decision had been taken 'according to distinct directives from the government'.[98]

The government was not united in its chosen policy, however. The Minister for Justice, Herman Zetterberg, had pleaded for the sake of the refugees on several occasions. A week later he contacted the Minister for Foreign Affairs, Östen Undén, and complained that the decision was inhumane. The categories chosen for exception from deportation were too narrowly defined, he argued. Zetterberg's own notes stored within the archives of the Ministry for Foreign Affairs indicate the nature of Undén's response: he wished that 'the suggested formulation, which had already previously been used, was preserved as an outwards principle'. Nonetheless, he claimed that he 'did not mind a somewhat more generous application in certain cases.'[99]

Whether or not this specific oral directive ever reached the Commission is difficult to ascertain. However, an investigation was initiated once again to determine which of the Ingrian refugees who already had acquired a temporary residence permit in Sweden were to be issued renewals, and which were to be deported according to the government's new directions. Those whose status as political refugees was in doubt were to be given the chance of providing new information.[100]

98   About half of these are named in the refusal of entry files. See nr 2365,
     2367, 2370, 2406, 2407 and 2408, vol. 34, F 11 A, Hemliga arkivet, SUK, Ra.
     Children are, however, unaccounted for in these statistics. (Certain other
     individuals could also be missing.) The number 28 is gathered from 'Baltiska
     flyktingar blevo avvisade' in *Svenska Dagbladet*, 4 oktober 1945, referred to in
     Hammarström 1984, pp. 37–38. (The Ingrians were wrongly referred to as Balts
     in the heading of the article.)
99   *Undén förklarade sig önska, att den föreslagna formuleringen, som redan tidigare*
     *använts, bleve bibehållen såsom en princip utåt, men han sade sig ej ha något att*
     *erinra mot en något generösare tillämpning i särskilda fall.* 'Allmän beredning för
     flyktingfrågor', 26 september 1945, vol. 77, P 40 R, 1920 års dossiésystem, UD,
     Ra. See also Berge 1992, p. 78.
100  'Protokoll', 12 februari 1946, vol. 2, A 1 A, Kanslibyrån, SUK, Ra.

In February 1946, the investigation was complete. By then, the directives had been adjusted somewhat into a list of prerequisites. Evidence of the following criteria were now used to indicate political refugee status, and thus a right to stay in Sweden:

1) Political activities in the home country

2) Desertion from the Red Army or similar withdrawal from Russian active service

3) Service – either voluntary or by force – in the Finnish or German army

4) Close relatives (father, brother, husband or son) who had fought against the Soviet Union

5) Work in the Finnish or German war effort

6) Having been punished or deported within the Soviet Union

7) A close relative who was under arrest in the Soviet Union for political reasons

This list was also to be used by the border police when interrogating newly arrived refugees, and used as a guideline to determine which refugees were to be refused entry and which were not. Ingrians who met one or more of the above criteria were to be granted a right to stay. The others were to be sent back to Finland. And when the examination of the Ingrian group already residing in Sweden was complete, 542 out of a total of 1553 Ingrian refugees (including children) had been identified as 'non-political refugees' and were to be deported. Again, this was to be kept secret.[101]

This did not prevent individuals within Swedish society from monitoring the government's behaviour regarding refugee issues. Thus, information about the planned deportations leaked out. As a

---

101 The list can be found in several places within the National Alien Commission's archive, for example in a number of Ingrian refugees' personal dossiers. See, for example, central dossiers of I17, I19 and I38. See also an undated version of the list in vol. 3, F 3, Kontrollbyrån, suk, Ra.

result, Östen Undén felt obliged to hold a 'secret' press conference. On 7 February 1946, he met with members of the Swedish media and informed them of the decision. He went on to ask them to not publish the information but keep it to themselves – out of 'concern for the refugees'.[102] In what is perhaps a significant indication of the close relationship between the media and politics during the 1940s, most of the invited representatives of the press seem to have agreed to this – with one notable exception. The newspaper *Morgon-Tidningen* decided to go against the directive and on 9 February published the story.[103]

This event deeply alarmed some of the activists that had kept a careful watch over the Ingrians' interests ever since they started to arrive in 1944. They had feared that the Swedish government would not be strong enough to withstand pressures from the Soviet Union regarding refugees and decided at an early stage to try to protect the Ingrians for whom they felt a particular affinity. The recent extradition of the military Balts and Germans had not soothed their worries. The support group consisted of, for example, representatives of the Church of Sweden, and former military officers and jurists, many of whom were Finnish-speakers. They helped Ingrian refugees apply for asylum and introduced them to the basics of the Swedish Aliens Act, including the nature of the concept 'political refugee'.[104]

When news of the decision to deport more than 500 Ingrians emerged, the response of the activist group was immediate. A campaign was initiated aimed at trying to stop the deportation. Efforts were taken to collate evidence showing that the civilian Ingrian refugees who were transported back to the Soviet Union from Finland were not sent back 'home' as they had been promised, but to various labour camps in the middle of Russia. With some difficulty, they managed to locate a surviving witness who could prove both this and the fact that severe punishment and even torture awaited many of those who had worked for the Germans or the Finns (of which numerous Ingrians were guilty). In May 1946,

---

102 Diary note by Östen Undén 7 February 1946 in Östen Undén, *Anteckningar: 1918–1952*, Kungl. Samf. för utgivande av handskrifter rörande Skandinaviens historia, Stockholm 2002, p. 131.
103 Berge 1992, p. 79.
104 Hammarström 1984.

the evidence was sent to the government in the form of a report. In addition, an extensive juridical analysis of Soviet legislation was attached, which among other things pointed out that, according to Soviet law, all Soviet citizens who left their country without authorisation were regarded as criminals against the state.[105]

Whether or not it was this campaign that made the final difference is difficult to substantiate. It is not, however, unlikely. Traces of the activists' efforts, in the form of letters and the above-mentioned reports, are found in the archives of the Ministry for Foreign Affairs.[106] These indicate that they had brought similar pressure to bear on the National Alien Commission as well, whose staff they believed was ignorant of the relevant circumstances surrounding the Ingrians' plight.[107]

Something did, nonetheless, make at least the Commission question the directives it had been given. One example of its doubts was expressed by its official executive Sven Laurell. In the central dossier of one of the supposedly non-political Ingrian refugees is a hand-written note in which Laurell laments: 'When one reads this pro memoria [about the Ingrian man in question] one cannot without difficulty free oneself from the suspicion that we adhere too closely to principles. This family wants to stay in Sweden and this must be regarded as desirable from a Swedish point of view. Why should we then send him to Russia?'[108] And in May 1946, the Commission did indeed send a new list of 'typical examples' to the government in order that they might be used to establish a precedent. They included, for example, individuals who had been stripped of all their property by Soviet authorities; who had cousins and uncles (but no closer relatives) who had been deported; who believed they would be punished for having left their country, allocated village and/or position without permission; who had worked for the Germans or the Finns in other occupations than the war

---

105 Hammarström 1984.
106 See, for example, 'P.M.' by Fil. Dr. Gerhard Hafström, 14 februari 1946, vol. 68, P 40 I, 1920 års dossiésystem, UD, Ra.
107 Hammarström 1984.
108 *När man läser denna p.m. kan man svårligen frigöra sig från misstanken att vi letar för mycket efter principer. Denna familj vill stanna här och detta måste anses önskvärt ur svensk synpunkt. Varför skola vi då skicka honom till Ryssland?* Hand-written note on memorandum, central dossier of I38.

industry; had been imprisoned during the 1920s; who believed their anti-communist opinions were known to the authorities; and other, similar circumstances. In other words, they had varying reasons to fear a return to the Soviet Union, but were not identified as political refugees according to the list of criteria that the government had established.[109]

The opinion of the Aliens' Board had been heard regarding all of these individuals. It recommended that some of them should be allowed to stay due to labour market shortages. They were young and healthy and valuable to the Swedish economy through their employment, argued the Board. They went on to add that those *not* considered valuable to the labour market ought to be deported. In addition to this statement, however, the Board had made clear that it did in fact regard a few of the persons on the 'typical examples' list as political refugees. As a consequence, it recommended that these should also be granted a prolonged residence permit. This assessment, however, was not shared by the National Alien Commission. Based on the interpretative directions it had received from the government, it concluded that none of these individuals were in fact political refugees.[110]

Thus, the Commission decided to pass these cases on to the government for its decision, in order to have a 'precedential decision from the government regarding how cases similar to these should be assessed in the future'. Added to this letter was a statement in which the Commission declared that, in its *own* opinion, all the individuals on the list should be allowed to stay on humanitarian grounds. In other words, it contended that the Ingrians should remain regardless of their specific juridical status, thus dismissing the prerequisites on the previous list.[111]

The government, in its turn, seems to have agreed with the Commission. In June 1946, it declared that all the 'typical examples' in the National Alien Commission's written account should be granted a renewed residence permit 'due to the specific circumstances'.[112] Whether or not they were to be regarded as political

109 'Protokoll', 14 maj 1946, vol. 1, A 1, Hemliga arkivet, SUK, Ra. See also central dossier and central register card of I11.
110 'Protokoll', 14 maj 1946, A 1 vol. 1, Hemliga arkivet, SUK, Ra.
111 *Ibid.*
112 'Protokoll', 18 juni 1946, vol. 1, A 1 Hemliga arkivet, SUK, Ra.

refugees was now of less importance. The government chose to adhere to the 'humanitarian reasons' that the Commission had invoked. Thus, an important policy transformation regarding the Ingrians had occurred.

What factors determined the outcome of this case, and the two contradictory decisions? The government's decision of September 1945 seems to have been governed mainly by the Minister for Foreign Affairs, Östen Undén, whose attitude appears to have been swayed by concerns for national (external) security and, possibly, considerations for future economic cooperation. A wish to maintain amicable relations with the Soviet Union had dominated his view on the handling of the extradition demand regarding the Balts and the Germans a few weeks earlier, and his opinions had been granted precedence over other concerns as the government had come to a conclusion. By granting a right to residence to some Ingrians, but not all, the government would reach a compromise. It demonstrated to the Soviet Union that it was not going to grant asylum to 'all' Soviet citizens who found their way to Sweden. At the same time, it adapted to international norms vis-à-vis those individuals who were regarded as being in most acute need of protection, namely those who had actively assisted the Finnish war effort.

It is also possible, but not likely, that the government did not wish to send a signal to Soviet refugees in Finland that 'everybody' would be granted asylum. The government had just managed to rid itself of a few thousand Soviet citizens (the Russian soldiers) and probably wanted to avoid a new flow of such individuals – perhaps both for reasons of bilateral Swedish-Soviet relations and general aversions based on ethnic concerns. The decision might thus have been influenced both by external security concerns, in terms of bilateral Swedish-Soviet relations, and ethnic considerations, as well as, of course, economic considerations.

At the time of the U-turn in June 1946, however, the government obviously perceived that, in terms of bilateral security relations at least, it had sufficient room for manoeuvre to grant the Ingrians the right to stay. It is likely that the expatriation of the Balts and the Germans six months earlier had assisted in this cause. The Swedish government had now demonstrated its amicable stance towards the Soviet Union and did perhaps therefore conclude that it had more options in this case. Additionally, no expatriation demand had in fact been presented regarding these individuals.

Nevertheless, the risk of causing another public scandal analogous to that which had characterised the removal of the Balts was probably just as important a reason. The affair had damaged the government's national standing and international reputation, and had triggered something of a public trauma. It had also been a personally distressing experienced for several members of the government. Additionally, the attention it had raised had caused the Soviet Union to increase its pressure on Sweden in the matter. In all likelihood, the government wished to avoid a repeat of this predicament. The abrupt change of policy enabling the Ingrians to stay succeeded in silencing the most vocal of Ingrian supporters whose strident protests risked provoking the Soviet Union into a new competition for prestige. It is therefore likely that indirect concerns for security, in this inverted sense, as well as a wish to avoid causing any more harm to its own reputation, influenced the government's June 1946 decision too. Be all that as it may, it is undoubtedly the case that *timing* seems to have played a significant part in this particular incident.

### 4.3.2 Precedential Influence?

Compared with the Balts, an analysis of refusal of entry decisions of Ingrian refugees is somewhat less complicated since they all arrived from Finland.[113] Similar to previous examples, a general quantitative survey of refusals of Ingrian refugees between 1945 and 1954 paints a somewhat inconsistent picture. However, in this particular case the discrepancy applies only to the very first post-war year. According to a quantitative account in the archives of the Ministry for Foreign Affairs, referred to in earlier research by historian Anders Berge, only 33 Ingrians were refused entry in 1945. The same document also asserts that no refusals of Ingrians

---

113 Of all the Ingrian cases documented in the sources included in this study, none arrived from any other country. It is possible though that a small number of Ingrians might have arrived from, for example, Germany or the Soviet Union. However, given the absence of such examples in the source material that has been selected for this study, no analysis of such a scenario will be pursued.

took place at all in the years 1943 and 1944.[114] There is, however, reason to suspect that the data relating to 1945 at least represented a substantial underestimation. First of all, another document in the same archival series suggests that in early June 1945, 39 Ingrians had already been refused entry.[115] Moreover, at least 40 Ingrian adults were refused entry during the *second half* of 1945. This is indicated by both the refusal of entry files and the 'Soviet investigation' deposited in the archives of the National Alien Commission (and which has never been analysed in previous research).[116] Thus, added together, these accounts suggest that *at least* 80 Ingrians (plus an unaccounted number of children) were refused entry in 1945 and sent back to Finland. Consequently, it seems possible that the principles established by the government in early 1945 regarding the disclosure of addresses might have been interpreted as providing guidelines for the future treatment of Ingrians at the border by the immigration authorities already before the September 1945 decision, which confirmed these principles.[117]

From 1946, however, the examined sources reveal only six refusals of entry pertaining to Ingrians. Additionally, they all occurred during the first half of that year – in other words, before the reversal brought about by the June 1946 decision.[118] It is important to note, moreover, that all refusal of entry decisions regarding Ingrians found within this study from both 1945 and 1946 were settled by the National Alien Commission rather than by the police. This is a potential indication of the principal importance of these cases.[119]

Few of the Ingrians who were refused entry left personal dossiers in the archives of the National Alien Commission. Thus, tracing

---

114 'Antalet ingermanländare i Sverige per den 2.2.1946', vol. 68, P 40 J, 1920 års dossiésystem, UD, Ra. See also Berge 1992, p. 75.

115 Undated 'v.p.m' from the National Alien Commission to the Minister of Health and Social Affairs (probably written in early June 1945, however), vol. 67, P 40 J, 1920 års dossiésystem, UD, Ra.

116 Vol. 34–35, F 11 A, Hemliga arkivet, SUK, Ra; and 'Sovjetutredningen 8/5 1945–15/5 1946', nr 250, vol. 10, F 4, Hemliga arkivet, SUK, Ra.

117 See chapter two, part 2.6.2.

118 Vol. 35–36, F 11 A, Hemliga arkivet, SUK, Ra.

119 The only cases that *were* determined by the police regarded a couple of individuals who came back after being refused entry by the Commission. Their second refusal of entry decisions were issued by the police.

the motivations for the refusal decisions is, in most cases, arduous if not impossible. There are a few exceptions, however. By studying these, some indications of the varying principles pursued in practice by the authorities can be uncovered.[120]

One such example is constituted by an Ingrian primary school teacher who arrived in the summer of 1945. He told the authorities that he had been tasked with registering Ingrians during the German occupation of his homeland. Thus, according to Soviet policy at the time, he was likely to be considered a traitor. The Commission, however, did not regard this condition as sufficient for political refugee status, and sent him back to Finland.[121]

A similar example concerns a family which was also sent back in April 1946 after being found in Sweden by the police without permits. In a police interrogation, the father of the family – a 35 year-old carpenter – declared that he had fled to Sweden from Finland because he had heard that all Soviet citizens were to be extradited to the Soviet Union. This he wanted to avoid because he 'could not exist in the Soviet Union with his family'. The reason for this, he claimed, was that living conditions were too bad. In addition he feared being parted from his family and put in prison for illegally leaving Russia'. When specifically asked about imprisoned relatives, he asserted that he had a brother who had been imprisoned in 1933 for anti-communist views, and several other relatives who were still imprisoned. However, the Commission decided to refuse entry to the carpenter, his wife and their three children. They were all sent back to Finland.[122]

Another individual was also refused entry during the first half of 1946. He was a 24 year-old pattern maker. Food shortages had

120 In certain cases the motivations are documented in the refusal of entry files. In a few other instances, refused individuals have come back at a later stage, and been reassessed. In such cases, the motivations for the earlier refusal decisions have occasionally been documented.

121 As an example of the sometimes rather complicated archival situation, most of this information has not been found in the school teacher's own dossier, but in that of one of his fellow countrymen who arrived at the same time as him the *second* time he entered in 1946. See information about 'I33' in the following documents in the control dossier of I30: 'Rapport', 31 juli 1945; 'Rapport', 2 september 1946; and 'Till Konungen', 10 september 1946. See also central dossier for I33.

122 'Polisrapport', dated 27 March 1946 in central dossier for I18.

promoted him to desert his position as an employee in a Soviet tank factory in 1942 and flee to Estonia. From there, he had been transported to Finland where he had taken up work within the textile industry. When asked for the reasons for this flight to Sweden, he declared that he feared to be deported to the Soviet Union, since he believed he might be severely punished for having left his position. The Commission, however, sent him back to Finland in early June 1946.[123]

These three examples all correlate with the directions given by the government in September 1945. The school teacher who had worked for the Germans had not been directly involved in the war effort (such as weapon construction), which at this time was the only occupation that was interpreted as constituting a prerequisite for political asylum for non-Baltic Soviet citizens. The carpenter's brother, who had been imprisoned, had indeed been subject to this persecution for political reasons. However, thirteen years had since passed, thus making the seventh criteria on the above-mentioned list non-applicable, since it was formulated in the present tense. Similarly, his other imprisoned relatives were not members of his immediate family, thereby also falling outside of the criteria. Finally, the responses given by the pattern maker during his hearing had also lacked any mention of circumstances that would meet the criteria on the list.

The Ingrians who *were* allowed entry during 1945 and the first half of 1946, however, all seem to have presented motives for asylum that correlated with the seven criteria on the list. Among those chosen for analysis in this study, everyone who arrived between February 1945 and June 1946 and were allowed entry met the criteria.[124]

Added together, these results indicate strongly that the directives that were given by the government in September 1945 were indeed followed carefully by the Commission until June 1946 when new guidelines were established. However, they also indicate that these directives were being followed *before* the September 1945 decision – indeed already from the first weeks of 1945 at the time when the government handled the Soviets' demands for names and

---

123 Central dossier and register card for I29.

124 See, for example, central dossier for I10, who was denied entry when he first arrived in March 1945, but allowed entry the second time in October 1945, at which point he presented new details of his past, thus making him eligible according to the list.

addresses. This thus seems to constitute a difference in comparison with 1944 when the (oral) directives from the government, as mentioned earlier, had been more generous.

This delineation relates well to the quantitative estimations presented above, which demonstrated that at least 80 adult Ingrians (plus an unaccounted number of children) were refused entry during 1945, and that these refusals were spread out over the whole year. There were also suggestions (gathered from claims made by the Minister for Foreign Affairs rather than an independent analysis) that no Ingrians were refused entry at all in 1944. If correct this means that Ingrians were allowed entry on collective grounds – just like the Balts – in 1944, but that policies regarding them changed in early 1945 when the names-and-addresses affair spurred the authorities into establishing some criteria on the Ingrians' political refugee status. Thus, perhaps somewhat paradoxically, it was the collective assessment of this group that led to the recommendation that they be evaluated on an individual basis. The criteria that were developed in the address matter were then interpreted by the Commission as establishing a precedent for future border control; an interpretation which the government indeed confirmed in its September 1945 statement.

Thus, for *newcomers* of Ingrian nationality, the address procedures in early 1945 in fact constituted a greater change of policy than the September 1945 decision. An analysis of some individuals who sought asylum in early 1945 reinforces this conclusion, and suggests that the change took place sometime between the end of January 1945 and early March of that year, as individuals with identical historical pasts and living circumstances were assessed differently depending on whether they arrived just after the new year (which gave rise to a positive assessment) or in March (leading to a negative outcome).[125] For Ingrians that had arrived prior to this date, however, and in particular the 542 who had been labelled as 'non-political', the September 1945 decision was, of course, of far greater significance.

The next substantial change of policies occurred in June 1946 when the government shifted their stance over the 542 Ingrian

---

125  See, for example, central dossiers for I38 who arrived in early January 1945, and I12, who arrived in March 1945.

'non-political' refugees. According to the quantitative analysis, this decision seems to have had a significant effect on newcomers too. From this date onwards, the sources reveal no more refusal of entry decisions regarding Ingrian refugees until 1952, when changing circumstances in Finland made the authorities come to the conclusion that Ingrians now faced only a minor risk of being deported onwards to the Soviet Union. Even then, however, very few individuals seem to have been refused entry, and it only seems to have been issued to those regarded as unwanted for a specific reason.[126]

Thus, when the primary teacher and the pattern maker returned to Sweden after the summer of 1946, they were both granted permission to stay, as were the around three thousand other Ingrians that were to arrive during the following years.[127] The asylum criteria pursued during 1945 and the first half of 1946 thus appear to have been abolished from this date onwards. In other words, Ingrians were now (again) granted asylum on a collective basis. There was a subtle difference, however, between their treatment and that of the Balts. The latter seem to have been assessed in 1944 on the basis of this specific group's *collective* experiences of recent occupation. The official reason now given for granting Ingrians collective asylum appears to have been an acknowledgement of their shared *individual* experiences, namely being subject to political persecution or being at risk of such a fate should they be returned to Finland.

### 4.3.2.1 The Essence of Correct Information

The above-mentioned school teacher constitutes an example of another kind of problem. Soviet refugees were fleeing from an oppressive dictatorship, in which personal information was a very

126 'Helsingfors den 12 maj 1952', vol. 6, F 2 B, Hemliga arkivet, SUK. Only one refused Ingrian has been found from the years 1952–54. See 'Protokoll', 20 maj 1952, vol. 3, A 1 A, SUK, Ra; and control register card of I24. See also vol. 1, A 2, Första Byrån, SUK, Ra. One exception has been found in the case of the pattern maker who was refused entry by the Commission in early June 1946 and who came back in August that same year. On this occasion the police refused him entry without presenting the case to the Commission. The third time he came back, however, in 1948, he was granted a right to stay, without presenting any new information. See nr 2977, vol. 36, F 11 A, Hemliga arkivet, SUK, Ra, and central dossier and register card for I29.

127 Central dossier and register card for I29 and I33.

sensitive matter. If divulged to certain recipients, such data could have very unpleasant consequences for the individual concerned. Thus, some Soviet refugees were fearful of telling their stories – in particular to men in uniform such as the Swedish police officers tasked with interviewing new arrivals. As a consequence, they sometimes withheld information that could actually have enhanced their likely status as political refugees due to an anxiety that this information would be passed on to the Soviet authorities, thus causing danger to their lives and security should they be forced to return to the Soviet Union. The Swedish activists endeavoured to inform Ingrian refugees that it was only the sensitive information – regarding political activities, beliefs or imprisonments, for example – that could furnish them with the chance of being granted asylum. Far from all refused Ingrians were beneficiaries of this assistance, however, and it is likely that individuals who could have been rendered political refugees in 1945–46, had they revealed more about their backgrounds, were sent back to Finland.[128]

Whether or not the primary school teacher received any guidance is not known. However, he reapplied for asylum when he and his family returned to Sweden in September 1946. This time he was more forthcoming with his information. The police were told that he had been imprisoned in 1938 and tortured for ten months by the Soviet authorities for illegally lending out a map to a friend while working for the military services. This, he claimed, led to his sentencing to ten years of forced labour, from which he had later managed to escape. After supplying these details the teacher and his family was allowed to stay.[129]

From 1945 onwards, however, the police interrogations that were held with newly arrived Ingrians followed more or less the same pattern, including detailed questions based on the criteria on the list. In addition to the 'normal' questions asked to most new arrivals of all categories, including things such as name, parentage, marital status, family members, education, profession, religion, criminal record and reasons for flight, the questions that were asked of the Ingrians were: Had they or any close family member

128 Hammarström 1984. See also central dossier and central register card of I38.
129 Central dossier for I33. See also 'Rapport', 2 september 1946, and 'Till Konungen', 10 September 1946, in the control dossier of I30. (The dossier of I33 lacks this information.)

deserted from the Red army, fought against the Soviet Union in the Finnish or German army, or been imprisoned for political activities? Had they worked for the German or Finnish war industries and/or been politically active against the Soviet Union? Or did they have any family members who had done so? The seven points on the list were ticked off one by one, and the refugees' answers were written down in the police report, which was then referred to the Commission as the basis for decision.[130]

### 4.3.3 *The Sensitive Continuation, 1946–47*

As mentioned, careful searches of the archives reveal no more refusal of entry of Ingrians after June 1946. This suggests that the decision the government made at that date regarding the 542 'non-political' Ingrian refugees had indeed set a precedent. However, an examination of the continued procedures shows that policies were still not quite as straightforward as they at first seem. Had they been so, the Commission would probably have perceived that it had the authority to assess all future Ingrian cases without involving the government. This, however, was certainly not the case in the autumn of 1946.

During the second half of that year at least 130 Ingrians arrived in Sweden, divided into four sizeable groups. However, only the individuals within one of these clusters (the last to arrive in December 1946) were assessed by the Commission in the final instance. The other three were all referred to the government according to paragraph 48 of the Aliens Act. These comprised of around 100 individuals in total. On the first occasion, in September 1946, the National Alien Commission stated in a plenary meeting for confidential matters that, 'according to the Commission's practice, the Ingrians would have been permitted to stay through an individual assessment. However, considering the foreign policy concerns of the matter, the case will be referred to the government

130  See, for example, interrogation protocols ('förhörsprotokoll') in central dossier of I38. The questions could also be asked at a later date, see central dossier of I19. A copy of the list of criteria can also be found in some of the newly arrived Ingrians' personal dossiers. See, for example, central dossier of I17 (arriving in November 1946).

for assessment'.[131] The same motivation was given for the second group, on 1 October 1946.[132] In the third case, the foreign policy concerns were expressed even more explicitly. On the one hand, the Commission argued, the 'refugees seem to have particular reasons to fear bad treatment in Russia'. It therefore believed that the Ingrians should be allowed to stay, adhering to the same views it had expressed in their account given in May (in the 'typical examples' list).[133] However, since the arrival of the 56 Ingrians in question had 'been given such publicity that foreign policy reasons might influence the assessment of the case', the Commission 'felt obliged to refer it to the government according to paragraph 48 of the Aliens Act'. And so it did.[134]

Several of the Ingrians included in this case claimed to have worked within the war industry (in armament factories, for example) or had close relatives who had done so. Thus, they would have been considered political refugees even before the decisions of September 1945 and June 1946. Others that did not qualify had nevertheless worked for the Finns or the Germans in some capacity. They all feared that the Russian-led Control Commission would soon demand that they be sent back to the Soviet Union.[135]

This demonstrates that, regardless of the precedents established in June 1946, the Commission still felt it lacked the authority to assess the asylum applications of these Ingrians. Their arrival was obviously understood as pertaining to aspects of foreign

131   *enligt kommissionens praxis vid individuell prövning skulle ha tillåtits kvarstanna i riket, men att med hänsyn till ärendets utrikespolitiska beskaffenhet ärendet jämlikt 48 § UtlL borde hänskjutas till Konungen för avgörande.* 'Protokoll', 10 september 1946, vol. 1, A 1, Hemliga arkivet, SUK, Ra.

132   'Protokoll', 10 september 1946, vol. 1, A 1, Hemliga arkivet, SUK, Ra.

133   *[E]när flyktingarna synes ha särskilda skäl att befara dålig behandling i Ryssland, kommissionen anser, att de synpunkter, som kommo till uttryck i ovan nämna skrivelse den 14 maj 1946, böra tillmätas avgörande betydelse även i förevarande fall.* 'Till Konungen', 9 november 1946, vol. 3, E 4, Hemliga arkivet, SUK, Ra. See also 'Protokoll', 8 november 1946, vol. 1, A 1, Hemliga arkivet, SUK, Ra.

134   *Då ovan nämnda 56 flyktingar ankommit till Sverige fått sådan publicitet, att utrikespolitiska skäl kunna tänkas inverka på bedömandet av frågan om förfarandet med dem, har kommissionen ansett sig, jämlikt 48§ Utlänningslagen, böra överlämna förevarande ärende till Kungl. Maj:ts avgörande.* 'Till Konungen', 9 november 1946, vol. 3, E 4, Hemliga arkivet, SUK, Ra.

135   'Till Konungen', 9 november 1946, vol. 3, E 4, Hemliga arkivet, SUK, Ra.

policy – in other words, Sweden's relationship with the Soviet Union – and was thus to be referred to the highest political level for adjudication. Ultimately the government decided that all these around 100 individuals were to be granted a right to stay due to the 'specific circumstances'.[136] Thus, although external security aspects influenced the management of these cases, in that they were referred to the government, such concerns were not decisive to the outcome.

Probably as a consequence of these three positive government decisions, the National Alien Commission chose to act independently over the fate of the fourth group which arrived in December that same year. It decided unanimously that none of the individuals was to be refused entry, but granted them residence permits. The matter was discussed at plenary level, however, during a meeting for confidential affairs.[137]

During the first half of 1947, these policies seem to have continued without further government involvement. Similarly, the sources reveal no other detailed discussion of Ingrians' right to asylum within the plenary assembly. Only two cases which involved Ingrians were discussed. The first related to a group of 58 who had all, although in smaller separate groups, walked over the Finnish-Swedish border, reaching Haparanda in April. As previous arrivals, their backgrounds and experiences varied. Some claimed to have fought within the Finnish army, and/or supported the war effort. Others had carried out smaller tasks for the Germans, or only worked within the 'normal' industries in Finland. A few stated a wish to reunite with close relatives in Sweden as the predominant reason for their flight. All of them wanted, however, to avoid being forced to return to the Soviet Union. The Commission decided that none of them was going to be refused entry. No specific motivations were documented, nor any discussions as to whether or not the individuals were to be regarded as political refugees. As such, the government's decision from June 1946, as well as the three autumnal decisions that followed, appear to have functioned as a precedent. The Ingrians seem to have been granted asylum on

136 'Till Statens Utlänningskommission', 4 oktober 1946, vol. 3, E 4, Hemliga arkivet, SUK, Ra; 'Till Statens Utlänningskommission', 22 november 1946, vol. 3, E 4, Hemliga arkivet, SUK, Ra.
137 'Protokoll', 14 december 1946, vol. 1, A 1, Hemliga arkivet, SUK, Ra.

(collective) 'humanitarian' grounds, regardless of their specific circumstances.[138]

Nonetheless, the policies were still not set irrevocably. In the early autumn of 1947, the changing circumstances in Finland triggered an increase in the number of Soviet refugees fleeing to Sweden. A total of 130 Ingrians had arrived during the first half of 1947, according to the Commission, but more were expected given that a few thousand Ingrians were still believed to be there. This caused the National Alien Commission to question the continuing validity of the decisions made by the government just one year earlier. In a new request for a precedential statement, it queried for 'various reasons' whether granting asylum to a 'larger number of Soviet-Russian citizens' (here referring to both Russians and Ingrians) was in 'the interest of the Swedish state'.[139] As a consequence, the assessment of 26 Soviet citizens' asylum applications – both Ingrians and Russians – was, yet again, referred to the government.[140]

The Ingrian group consisted of nine people split between two families. The adults had worked for the Germans during the occupation. After being transported to Finland, they laboured within agriculture and industry (not, however, connected directly to the war effort). They alleged that they had been urged by the Finnish state police to return to the Soviet Union several times. Since they feared punishment there, they had fled to Sweden.[141] However, the Aliens Appeals Board had stated that it 'saw no obstacle' to refusing entry to the Ingrians.[142]

The Commission decided to refer the assessment of both the Russians and the Ingrians to the government. Before doing so

---

138 'P.M. angående till Haparanda under april månad 1947 anlända ingermanländska flyktingar', 8 maj 1947, vol. 1, F 3, Kontrollbyrån, SUK, Ra; 'Protokoll', 13 Maj 1947, vol. 2, A 1 A, Kanslibyrån, SUK, Ra.

139 *Kommissionen ifrågasätter emellertid, huruvida det av olika skäl kan anses vara med landets intressen förenligt att här bereda fristad åt ett större antal sovjetryska flyktingar.* 'Till Konungen', 16 september 1947, vol. 4, E 4, Hemliga arkivet, SUK, Ra.

140 'Till Konungen', 16 september 1947, vol. 4, E 4, Hemliga arkivet, SUK, Ra; 'Protokoll', 16 september 1947, vol. 1, A 1, Hemliga arkivet, SUK, Ra.

141 'Till Konungen', 16 september 1947, vol. 4, E 4, Hemliga arkivet, SUK, Ra. Central dossier for I46; central dossier for I28.

142 'Till Statens Utlänningskommission', 5 september 1947, vol. 6, B 1, Utlänningsnämnden, Ra. See also central dossiers of I46 and I28.

it made a few comments of its own. Among other things, it was pointed out that the refugees, who all feared what would happen to them if sent back to Finland, had been forced to stay in Swedish refugee camps for 'quite some time now' since their cases were of such a 'sensitive' nature. The officials at the Commission declared as their own point of view that they were 'prepared to let the refugees stay'. However, they also wished to draw attention to the fact that a positive assessment was likely to lead to an increased refugee flow from Finland, and questioned whether this could be considered to be in line with the national interests of the Swedish state. Thus, they concluded, this was a decision that had to be made by the government. Consequently, paragraph 48 of the Aliens Act was yet again utilised.[143]

To what particular aspect the Commission was referring when alluding to Sweden's 'national interest' cannot be verified with certainty. Its continued usage of paragraph 48 as well as its description of the case as 'sensitive' suggests, however, that it implied the same kind of foreign policy concerns as had been involved in the assessment of Ingrian asylum applications in 1946. Ingrian refugees were still looked upon as challenging Sweden's foreign policy relations with the Soviet Union – in other words, aspects relating to external security.

Nevertheless, one month later, the government informed the Commission that it saw nothing to hinder the granting of residence permits to all the 26 Soviet citizens.[144] Thus, although external security concerns had continued to influence the management of the Ingrian asylum applications in 1947, they did not determine the final outcome.


### 4.3.4 *Stabilising Policies, 1948*

According to available sources, the 26 Ingrians mentioned above constituted the last case of its kind that was brought to the government for assessment, as well as to the plenary assembly's attention. From then on, matters brought up for discussion in the

---

143 'Till Konungen', 16 september 1947, vol. 4, E 4, Hemliga arkivet, SUK, Ra.
144 'Till Statens Utlänningskommission', 17 oktober 1947, vol. 1, E 1 A, Kontrollbyrån, SUK, Ra.

plenary assembly regarding Ingrians dealt only with information on numbers, problems within refugee camps or similar issues. The sudden arrival of at least 1,500 Ingrians during the following spring exemplifies this. The assessment of these individuals' asylum applications was handled within the normal assessment structure of the Commission only. No government involvement or even plenary discussions on their right to asylum have been revealed. And, according to the quantitative examinations at least, none of these Ingrians were refused entry.

Thus, although Ingrian refugees in fact seem to have been granted asylum after June 1946, it is fair to say that it was not until 1948 that policies regarding this group actually stabilised. The same conclusion can be drawn from an analysis of relevant sources from other bureaucratic bodies which were variously involved in refugee matters. The archives of the National Alien Commission's Control Bureau, the Ministry for Foreign Affairs and the Ministry of Domestic Affairs all lack evidence of any principal discussions regarding Ingrians' right to asylum from 1948 onwards. Thus, from that point Ingrians seem to have been granted asylum without any official or unofficial doubts being expressed. Consequently, this correlates to the results in the examination of the Balts, which also points to 1948 as being a watershed year in policy terms. For the Ingrians, however, the political framing of the policies seem to have lingered longer than for the Balts. Foreign policy concerns, in which aspects of external security played a significant part, delineated the management to a considerable extent, even though the outcomes were affirmative from June 1946 onwards. Even so, however, no deportation decisions regarding new Ingrian arrivals (equalling those issued to the seventeen Latvians in November 1945, for example) have been found.[145]

In the early 1950s, the Ministry for Foreign Affairs reached a new assessment of the Ingrians' situation in Finland, suggesting

---

145 The only exception being a former *Obersturmführer* in the German Waffen
ss who arrived in 1947, claiming to be an Ingrian hunted by the state police
in Finland. The Swedish authorities police did not believe him, however, and
issued a deportation decision based on the assumption that he was either Finnish
or German, and, additionally, probably a Nazi. The decision was implemented
through his transferral back to Finland. Central dossier, control dossier, central
register card and control register card of I2o; vol. 1–11, A 2, Passbyrån, suk, Ra.

that the risk of them being sent back to the Soviet Union was now insignificant. As a result, a handful of people were denied right of residence.[146]

## 4.4 The Management of Russian New Arrivals

Out of the around 3,000 Russians that arrived in Sweden during the war, approximately 440 individuals remained by the end of the summer of 1945, according to a statistical estimation. Most of these were 'expected to return to Russia' according to Social Minister Gustav Möller.[147] In addition, 730 Russian concentration camp refugees were collectively transferred to Sweden by the Red Cross and UNRRA for medical treatment in 1945. Two years later, only 70 of them were still residing in Sweden.[148]

The statistical accounts of the influx of individually arriving Russian refugees are scarce and difficult to interpret.[149] Some esti-

146 'Helsingfors den 12 maj 1952', vol. 6, F 2 B, Hemliga arkivet, SUK; Control register card of I24; Nr 7917, vol. 52, F 11 A, Hemliga arkivet, SUK, Ra; 'Protokoll', 20 maj 1952, vol. 3, A 1 A, SUK, Ra; vol. 1, A 2, Första Byrån, SUK, Ra. See also part 5.2 on deportations of Ingrians with previous residence permits.

147 'P.M.', 14 augusti 1945, vol. 67, P 40 I, 1920 års dossiésystem, UD, Ra. According to historian Hans Lundgren, the last group repatriation of Russian former soldiers took place in early 1946. Lundgren 2008.

148 The circumstances of their departure, that is whether or not they were provided with an alternative other than repatriation once their medical treatment was terminated, has not been possible to verify. It is likely that many left of their own accord to the Soviet Union, to Palestine or elsewhere. However, given Sweden's policy towards Russian refugees in general during the war it is also possible that some were forced to leave against their will. 'Uppskattning av antalet utlänningar med vistelsetillstånd i Sverige per den 17.11.1946', vol. 1, F 3, Kontrollbyrån, SUK, Ra; 'Uppskattning av antalet utlänningar med vistelsetillstånd i Sverige per den 7.9.1947', vol. 1, H 4, Kanslibyrån, SUK, Ra; and 'PM angående det europeiska flyktingproblemet', 1951, vol. 1, H 1, Kanslibyrån, SUK, Ra.

149 This is, among other things, due to inconsistencies between official statistical accounts revealing 'non-refusals' and occasional, non-comprehensive, unofficial accounts measuring the amount of granted residence permits. Particularly during the first post-war years, these two did not correlate for the Russians. Individuals arriving from Norway who were repatriated to the Soviet Union were 'non-refused' at the border, but transported directly to the shipping ports and thus never granted a residence permit. Individuals using Sweden as a transit country on their way to another destination could partly account for

mation can be made, however. Approximately 100 Russian refugees arrived in Sweden and were granted asylum during the first two post-war years. Starting in the autumn of 1947, and continuing throughout 1948, the traffic of Russians increased as the hunt for Soviet citizens in Finland escalated. Approximately 500 individuals reached Sweden.[150] In 1949 the number of new arrivals decreased. However, new Soviet extradition demands directed at the Finnish authorities in the following year triggered yet another increase, albeit smaller than before. In 1951–54, however, fewer than ten individuals arrived illegally per year.[151] In 1952 the authorities calculated than slightly over 1,850 Russians resided in Sweden, out of which only approximately 350 had Russian passports. The other 1,500 had other credentials, including Swedish aliens' passports which normally meant that they had arrived as refugees.[152]

In total, therefore, the sources suggest that fewer than 1,000 Russians arrived in Sweden illegally and were granted asylum as refugees during the research period, with a peak in 1948. Most of them came via Finland. Some, however, arrived directly from the

---

this muddled picture, as could individuals arriving on sailors' visas. Other statistical sources often exclude Russian Soviet citizens, due to their insignificant numbers, or account for them together with Ingrians. Additionally, children are generally excluded. See, for example, 'Flyktingar med tidigare domicil i område, som nu ingå i Sovjetunionen, vilka erhållit uppehållstillstånd i Sverige under tiden 8/5 1945–28/2 1947', vol. 10, F 4, Hemliga arkivet, SUK, Ra; and SOU 1951:42 p. 254. See also central dossiers of R3, R4 and R36.

150 The 'non-refusals' statistics revealed 121 non-refused Russians in 1947, and 345 in 1948. These sources do not estimate the numbers of granted residence permits, however.

151 'Illegalt anlända utlänningar under år 1949', vol. 1, H 1, Kanslibyrån, SUK, Ra; 'Uppskattning av antalet vuxna flyktingar i Sverige den 1 september 1950', vol. 1, H 1, Kanslibyrån, SUK, Ra; 'PM angående det europeiska flyktingproblemet', 1951, vol. 1, H 1, Kanslibyrån, SUK, Ra. SOU 1951:42 p. 254; 'Av Statens utlänningskommission meddelade beslut i avvisnings- och förpassningsärenden ävensom av polismyndighet meddelade avvisningsbeslut år 1952', vol. 1, H 4, Kanslibyrån, SUK, Ra; 'Av Statens utlänningskommission meddelade beslut i avvisnings- och förpassningsärenden ävensom av polismyndighet meddelade avvisningsbeslut år 1953', vol. 1, H 4, Kanslibyrån, SUK, Ra; 'Av Statens utlänningskommission meddelade beslut i avvisnings- och förpassningsärenden ävensom av polismyndighet meddelade avvisningsbeslut år 1954', vol. 1, H 4, Kanslibyrån, SUK, Ra.

152 A few hundred of the 1,850 Russians were individuals who had resided in Sweden since before the war. 'Till Konungen', pp. 2–3, 22 april 1952, vol. 4, E 4, Hemliga arkivet, SUK, Ra.

Soviet Union.[153] How did Sweden respond? Did the harsh policies practiced during the war continue, or did the increasingly more generous attitude towards the Ingrians also apply to the Russians?

### 4.4.1 Challengers to the Repatriation Policy

In chapter two, it was demonstrated that the Russian soldiers who fled to Sweden during the Second World War were generally not categorised as refugees but as displaced persons. As such, most of them were repatriated to the Soviet Union between 1944 and 1946. In this respect, Sweden's treatment of Russians was similar to the Western Allied countries, which pursued mass repatriation of millions of Soviet Russians in 1945.

Some, however, did manage to stay. Prior to turning to Sweden's management of the new arrivals from 1945 onwards, some attention will be given to these individuals. Which policies guided Swedish authorities in their assessment of asylum applications from Russian former prisoners of war during and slightly after the war?

Common for all of the Russian soldiers who managed to persuade the authorities of their right to asylum is that it was in large part something they had to achieve by their own initiative. No detailed questions were asked upon their arrival, such as was the case with the Ingrians. Many of them were only provided with an emergency visa and sent to a shipping port or to a refugee camp for Russians without having an opportunity to explain their personal

---

153  See 'Sovjetutredningen 8/5 1945–15/5 1946', nr 250, vol. 10, F 4, Hemliga arkivet, SUK, Ra; 'Illegalt anlända utlänningar under år 1949', vol. 1, H 1, Kanslibyrån, SUK, Ra; 'Antalet flyktingar som anlänt till riket under år 1951', vol. 1, H 1, Kanslibyrån, SUK, Ra; 'PM angående det europeiska flyktingproblemet', 1951, vol. 1, H 1, Kanslibyrån, SUK, Ra; 'Stockholm den 17 december 1953', attached table 2: 'Illegalt anlända, vilka godtagits såsom flyktingar 1946–1952', vol. 1, H 1, Kanslibyrån, SUK, Ra; 'Av Statens utlänningskommission meddelade beslut i avvisnings- och förpassningsärenden även som av polismyndighet meddelade avvisningsbeslut år 1952', vol. 1, H 1, Kanslibyrån, SUK, Ra; 'Av Statens utlänningskommission meddelade beslut i avvisnings- och förpassningsärenden även som av polismyndighet meddelade avvisningsbeslut år 1953', vol. 1, H 1, Kanslibyrån, SUK, Ra; 'Av Statens utlänningskommission meddelade beslut i avvisnings- och förpassningsärenden även som av polismyndighet meddelade avvisningsbeslut år 1954', vol. 1, H 1, Kanslibyrån, SUK, Ra; 'Uppskattning av antalet vuxna flyktingar i Sverige den 1 september 1950' vol. 1, H 1, Kanslibyrån, SUK, Ra; SOU 1951:42, p. 254.

circumstances. In other words, it was taken for granted that they were not political refugees but displaced persons who were to return to their home country when the war was over. As such, they were not provided with the opportunity to apply for asylum as were the Balts and the Ingrians. Those who *did* convince the authorities of their reasons for asylum generally did so by fleeing from the Russian refugee camp and contacting the Swedish authorities on their own.[154]

This was a risky strategy. Through their flight from these partly Soviet administered camps, they revealed their antipathies towards the Soviet regime. If the Swedish authorities refused them asylum, they were forced to return to the camps where Soviet officials had noted their flight. Additionally, due to the Swedish authorities' practice of reporting all newly arrived Soviet refugees to the Soviet legation during the war, the Soviets were well informed of the identities and personal circumstances of most Russians who resided in Sweden and took notice if someone suddenly 'disappeared'.[155]

If they managed to apply for it, Russians who had actively fought against the Soviet Union, either in the German, the Vlasov or the Finnish armies, were generally granted asylum. Here, the assessment appears to have been consistent. However, it is not impossible that some individuals belonging to this category were repatriated anyway, partly due to the general indifference of the Swedish authorities regarding their personal circumstances and also because access to Russian speaking translators was erratic.[156]

Other individuals were assessed in a more arbitrary manner. This includes those whose asylum applications referred to their experiences as former prisoners of war. As such, they risked punishment upon arrival in the Soviet Union since Stalin had ordered all Soviet soldiers to commit suicide rather than allow themselves be taken prisoners by the enemy. This was a criterion that encom-

---

154 'Till Konungen', 26 juni 1945, vol. 67, P 40 I, 1920 års dossiésystem, UD, Ra. See also R6, R7, R13, R21, R22, R30, R31, R40, R48, R50, R51, R56, R55, R62, R65, R67, R75, R87, R88.

155 See chapter two, part 2.6.3. See also copies of information letters to the Soviet legation in the central dossiers of, for example, R16 and R31.

156 R7, R12, R16, R21, R48, R51, R56. On language difficulties, see, for example, 'Förhörsprotokoll', 5 oktober 1944, central dossier of R48. See also 'Protokoll', 9 oktober 1945, vol. 1, A 1 A, Kanslibyrån, SUK, Ra.

passed most of the Russians soldiers in Sweden. Some of them had also disobeyed Stalin's orders in other ways – for example through deserting or fleeing from their posts. In addition, some claimed to have been persecuted in the Soviet Union for political untrustworthiness or due to their class or religion.[157]

Had these factors been acknowledged as general reasons for political asylum for the Russians, most of them would indeed have been entitled to a residence permit. However, out of the individuals who claimed one or more of the above-mentioned criteria, only some were granted permission to stay. Others were sent back to the Soviet authorities. No clear reason why some of them were granted asylum, and others were not, can be identified. Timing, luck, the official in charge of the assessment and the individual's own capacity to understand the Swedish asylum system and communicate with bureaucracies seem to have been some of the determining factors. Personal contacts definitely helped. The fact that many of these individuals had demonstrated their antipathy towards the Soviet regime by refusing to return 'voluntarily' did not constitute a criterion for asylum at this time either. In other words, anti-Soviet behaviour in Sweden was not (yet) regarded as a motivation for determining someone's status as a political refugee.[158]

Some referred to family ties in their applications. Certain men had, for example, fathered children in Sweden during their stay. As Lundgren has demonstrated, however, far from all such individuals were allowed to stay. Thus, several of the children's fathers were sent back to the Soviet Union.[159] Whether or not they were granted a right to stay seems to have been determined by, among other things, social factors such as personal behaviour, conscientiousness and *morality*. A revealing example is the treatment of a 32 year-old former prisoner of war and his 21 year-old Swedish partner. They had had a child together and wished to marry. When applying for a residence permit and a permission to leave his refugee camp to go and live with his partner, an official at the camp was asked to give a statement. He concluded that the 'girl' was 'loose and indecent' and came from a 'poor and pitiable home'. Therefore he 'advised

157  See, for example, R6, R13, R22, R30, R31, R40, R50, R55, R62, R65, R67, R75, R87, R88.
158  *Ibid.*
159  Lundgren 2008, pp. 153–196.

against a relationship' between the two parents. As a result, the
Russian's application was rejected and he was forced to stay in the
camp. After three years in custody and many letters, however, he
was finally granted a residence permit and thus managed to avoid
the mass repatriations. He then married the 'loose and indecent'
mother of his child.[160]

Some managed to stay in Sweden through going underground
– often with help from refugee-friendly Swedes – where they
remained until making a fresh appeal a couple of years later
when policies regarding Russians were, as shall be demonstrated,
softening. A case in point was a Russian man who had worked
both for the Soviet and the German intelligence services, and who
feared for his life should he be returned to the Soviet Union. The
Commission decided that his deportation was to be 'immediately
implemented'. His double agent activities (in other words aspects
relating to both internal and external security) made the authorities regard him as untrustworthy and his presence in Sweden was
therefore interpreted as undesirable. He went into hiding and did
not appear again until late 1946, at which point the authorities
chose not to refer him to the Soviet Union. Instead, he was provided with a temporary postponement. However, he was held under
daily police supervision and kept under surveillance for several
years. Moreover, the authorities refused to withdraw the decision,
and forced him to seek entry visas to other countries. Thus, in 1949,
the decision was implemented through his removal to Venezuela.[161]

Another two men escaped their deportation using the same
strategy. Both had been prisoners of war in German camps and
had several family members who had been deported to Siberia
for political reasons. They were convinced that they would be
killed or severely punished upon arrival in the Soviet Union, and
went underground to avoid this fate. One was found only a few

160 See various documents dated between 1942 and 1947 in central dossier of R73.
161 Files in his dossier suggest, however, that the decision might possibly have been
    withdrawn had he not also challenged social behavioural norms. The police and
    the Commission frequently noted with disapproval that he refused to take per-
    manent work positions, had several affairs with women, and was interpreted as
    generally unreliable, ill-mannered and uncooperative. Consequently, they kept
    pressuring him to leave Sweden. He was, however, never compelled to go to the
    Soviet Union. Central dossier, central register card, control dossier and control
    register card of R88.

months later, in late 1945. The other managed to hide until 1947. Upon their discovery they were issued postponements rather than immediate expulsion. There then followed a thorough examination which featured the testimony of several Swedes who had been in contact with them and could certify to their good characters. Their deportation decisions were subsequently withdrawn in 1948 and 1949 respectively.[162]

Another strategy was used by a Russian doctor who had practiced his profession within the prisoners of war camps in Norway, an action for which he was convinced would lead to severe punishment should he be forced to return to the Soviet Union. When informed of his deportation decision he managed to appeal to the government – despite the fact that the decision was legally 'non-appealable' – through making use of his contacts with prominent Swedes who could verify his excellent character. He made the most of his intelligence and personal drive. His proficiency at communicating with the authorities is testified by the letters he wrote and which have been saved within his dossiers. They are articulate, polite and show that he knew how to navigate the Swedish bureaucracy. As a result, in December 1945, the Minister for Justice, Herman Zetterberg wrote to the National Alien Commission to inform them that this doctor was not to be referred to the Soviet Union. The Ministry had, moreover, decided to attach a home country proviso to his deportation decision.[163]

This doctor's motives for asylum were similar to those of many other Russians who were nevertheless deported or repatriated against their own will. In this particular case, however, the individual' own capabilities and, not least, personal contacts seem to have played a decisive role, just as they did for some of the Balts arriving in 1946. Thus, he managed to remain in Sweden and within a short space of time his deportation decision was withdrawn thanks, in large part, to his 'good behaviour', which was continually scrutinised.[164] Aspects of social control and morality thus also influenced the outcome.

---

162 Central dossier and control dossier of R6, and central dossier of R50.
163 Central dossier of R75.
164 *Ibid.*

Most of the Russians who had resided in Sweden during the war were indeed repatriated, however, either as a group or on an individual basis. Among the latter were several people whose personal circumstances would have led to their asylum had they been Ingrians (or, indeed, Balts). As shall be demonstrated in the following sections of this chapter, there were also those whose experiences would become recognised as criteria for political refugee status only one or two years later. By then, however, most of the Russian war refugees had returned to the Soviet Union.

### 4.4.2 *Parsimonious ad hoc Practices, 1945–46*

During the second half of 1945, Russians continued to arrive illegally. The refusal of entry files suggest that eighteen Russian adults were refused entry and sent back to their point of departure, which in their case was Finland or Denmark. The decisions were made by the National Alien Commission and all of them were implemented.[165] None was refused entry when coming from Norway as former prisoners of war. Instead, they were generally sent directly to Russians refugee camps or shipping ports for further transportation to the Soviet Union.[166]

The authorities' management of Russian refugees after the armistice evinces a lack of consistent principles when it comes to both new arrivals and 'displaced persons' already residing in Sweden. No guidelines similar to those that had delineated the management of the Ingrians (or, indeed, the Balts) were in use. Consequently, during the summer of 1945, the Commission turned to the government and requested directives. In a letter containing typical examples for assessment, the Commission highlighted certain matters. Firstly, it repeated the principles that had been established six months earlier regarding the distribution of personal contact details of Soviet refugees to the Soviet legation. Balts had been excluded, whereas Ingrians and Russians had been selected according to certain prin-

---

165  Apart from incidents of a second return, in which case they were made by the police.

166  Nr 2356, 2369, 2406, 2409, 2421, 2432, 2485 vol. 34, F 11 A, Hemliga arkivet, SUK, Ra; nr. 2536, 2569, vol. 35, F 11 A, Hemliga arkivet, SUK, Ra. (Ingrians documented as Russians are excluded from this account. Such individuals' ethnicity has been revealed through an examination of their personal dossiers.)

ciples.[167] Secondly, it claimed that assessments of political asylum had so far been based on an estimation of what sort of treatment individuals could expect should they be returned to their home countries (a questionable statement in the light of what has been demonstrated above). However, it also reminded the government of its statement the previous year that it would not grant asylum to 'traitors', in this case referring to Danish and Norwegians who had assisted the German occupation regimes in their home countries. How, the Commission wondered, should this principle be interpreted regarding the Russians? It emphasised that the Soviet Union would of course pay attention to any deviation in the treatment of those Soviet nationals deemed to be 'traitors'. Thirdly, however, it pointed out that it found it reasonable that those individuals who had been protected from having their addresses revealed to the Soviet legation should not now be deported to their home country. (This was also the ultimate conclusion reached with regard to the Ingrians in 1945, as demonstrated above.)

So far, this attitude suggests that the Commission believed Russians and Ingrians ought to be managed according to similar principles. However, when listing the typical examples, attached with an individual assessment of the cases, the Commission gave expression to a significantly more parsimonious interpretation of the Russians' right to protection than the address criteria had established. The list included individuals who had worked within the German war effort in various ways. Some had been taken prisoners of war, but all claimed to have worked for the Germans on a voluntary basis. Some had family members who had been deported to Siberia for political reasons, or had themselves been in trouble with the Soviet authorities on political grounds.[168]

Thus, had they been Ingrians, they would have been considered political refugees. Both the Aliens Appeals Board and the Commission advocated a stricter interpretation regarding these Russians, however. Whereas the Board believed that only those who had been enlisted in the 'Organisation Todt' should be granted a right to stay, the Commission believed that none of them were eligible for

---

167  See chapter two, part 2.6.
168  'v.p.m.' (undated, though probably June 1945), vol. 67, P 40 I, 1920 års
      dossiésystem, UD, Ra.

political asylum. Moreover, it asked for the government's opinion on those who had been enlisted in the Finnish, German or Vlasov armies: should they be in continuous receipt of residence permits?[169]

In other words, criteria that granted residence permits for Ingrians were not regarded as sufficient in the case of the Russians. No explanation for this divergence was given. Soviet law, however, identified them all as traitors and administered serious punishments for the sort of activities in which they had engaged.

The government, which was to settle the case, did so with great ambiguity a few months later. In its decision it followed the evaluation made by the Commission and decided to deport all the above-mentioned 'typical examples' according to paragraph 56 of the Aliens Act (the 'security paragraph').[170] However, it attached a postponement to the implementation of the deportations. For the individuals in question, this implied temporary protection, but also considerable uncertainty regarding their future. For some of them it also entailed a prolonged stay in the closed refugee camps in which they were continuously held.[171]

Rather than establishing a precedent, this decision just reiterated the external security concerns involved in asylum cases regarding Russian refugees of this category. As a result, a number of new arrivals were also forwarded to the government a few weeks later. This time they consisted of five individuals who had variously worked for the Germans, been imprisoned and persecuted for political reasons within the Soviet Union or, in the case of one individual, had fought within the Vlasov army. Again, with reference to the 'security paragraph' 56, the government decided to deport these men. This time, however, a homeland proviso was attached to the decision, making its implementation through referral to the Soviet Union unlawful.[172]

These decisions coincided with the deportation, also under paragraph 56, of seventeen Latvians in November 1945 and the

169 *Ibid.*

170 § 56 granted the government the right to discard any regulations within the Aliens Act in case of 'war or threat of war or due to the defense of the country or specific circumstances'. See chapter three.

171 'Protokoll', 9 oktober 1945, vol. 1, A 1 A, Kanslibyrån, SUK, Ra. See also personal dossiers of R16 and R12.

172 Central dossiers and control dossiers of R71, R87, R86.

extradition affair concerning the 146 Balts and the around 2,700 Germans.[173] The subjects of the deportation decisions were classified as 'traitors' for mainly the same reasons as the extradited Balts and Germans. The results so far have demonstrated that Soviet asylum seekers with these kinds of personal backgrounds (active military service against the Soviet Union) were regarded as political refugees and granted residence permits before the armistice and prior to the Soviet extradition demand. This was true of Balts and Ingrians in particular, but also to those Russians who managed to apply for asylum. Because of the developments during the summer of 1945, however, the foreign policy stakes raised by such individuals had suddenly become much higher. Their timing was, to say the least, unfortunate. However, these particular individuals had not been specifically singled out by the Soviets for extradition like the nearly 3,000 Germans and Balts. It is possible, therefore, that the Swedish government managed to reach a compromise in their case. By issuing a deportation decision, it took foreign policy concerns into consideration and demonstrated to the Soviet Union that it was not going to grant asylum to those who were considered traitors. Yet at the same time Sweden could claim to be sensitive to humanitarian concerns too since it protected these individuals by not carrying out their deportation.

How, then, were these ambiguous decisions interpreted by the Commission regarding the continuous assessment of Russian asylum seekers? Out of the eighteen refusal of entry decisions that have been found from the autumn of 1945, six concerned individuals sent back to Finland. There exist personal dossiers for five of them. One was a Ukrainian farmer who feared being deported to Siberia like so many of his countrymen and women. After a short police interrogation, his case was sent to the Commission which decided to refuse him entry and send him back to Finland.[174] The same happened to a young Russian man who had fled to Finland when he was called up for military service in the Soviet Union. Now he feared being punished for his desertion should he be forced to return. The Commission, however, refused him entry and sent him back.[175]


173  See parts 1.1.1 and 4.2.1.
174  Central dossier and central register card of R58.
175  Central dossier and central register card of R49.

This was similarly the case with three opponents of the Soviet regime. They had heard the Russian Control Commission's exhortations on Finnish radio that all Russians were to return to the Soviet Union. They thereafter fled to Sweden in September 1945. Yet they too were refused entry.[176]

Thus far, the treatment of these individuals does not reveal any substantial differences compared to that which applied to new arrivals of Ingrian origin. Of the latter, those who did not meet the criteria on the list that had been specifically drawn up in early 1945 were also refused entry between January 1945 and June 1946. However, in one important respect the treatment diverged significantly. The Ingrians were asked specifically about whether or not they had worked within the Finnish or German war industries, had been imprisoned for political reasons, or had any close relatives who had been so (in other words whether or not they met any of the criteria on the list established to settle their refugee status). In contrast the Russians seem to have been asked only the standard questions for new arrivals regarding name, birth, occupation, political view point and so on. The police protocols documenting their interrogations are perfunctory and their refusal of entry decisions seem to have been implemented without allowing for appeals. The war-time legacy of perceiving the Russians as less eligible for political asylum than both Ingrians and Balts thus seems to have continued to influence practices in late 1945.

However, if circumstances still arose which indicated that the individual might be a political refugee (according to the criteria on the Ingrian and/or the address selection list), the Commission seems to have been prepared to grant him or her asylum. An example of this is a 33 year-old Russian film technician who had worked for the Finnish authorities (an activity which made him subject to the expatriation regulations within the Finnish-Soviet armistice agreement). Upon arrival in the autumn of 1945 he was placed in an internment camp. To the consternation of the other internees, rumours quickly spread that he might have worked for the Russian Control Commission in Helsinki. The man had good contacts within Swedish society, however. Thus after a few months of inspection and following good references from the staff

176 Central dossiers and central register cards of R72 and R53.

at the camp, he was released and granted a residence permit.[177]

Overall, however, 1945 seems to have been characterised by a conspicuously 'ad hoc' arrangement, whereby the settlement of cases depended significantly on Sweden's current foreign policy situation – as well as chance. Refugees with identical asylum motives were treated differently depending on when they arrived. And although individual experiences were increasingly accounted for when applications were assessed, the most noteworthy dividing line still went between ethnic categories. In comparison with the Ingrians and, indeed, the Balts, Russian asylum seekers were assessed significantly more parsimoniously. As such, of course, the legislation functioned as intended. The lawmakers had emphasised the Swedish state's need to adjust its pursued policies in refugee matters according to current needs and ambitions. Establishing consistent guidelines was not considered a priority, or even a necessity. As such, the management resembled the policies pursued during the war years.

In 1946, however, policies towards Russians seem to have softened somewhat. In February the National Alien Commission decided to collectively grant 29 Russians residence permits and thus permission to leave the camp in which they had been residing for a considerable time. The camp in question was *Byringe,* which at this time hosted individuals who had fought against the Soviet Union – in other words Soviet 'traitors' of the same kind as those 146 Balts who had been extradited to the Soviet Union only a couple of weeks earlier.[178]

One month later, in March 1946, the Commission raised the idea that activities in Sweden, such as flight from the Russian refugee camp Lisma, could lead to political refugee status.[179] This discussion was brought about by a formal note from the Soviet authorities which, among other things, included a demand for repatriation of individuals who had 'unlawfully escaped' from the camp. The Ministry for Foreign Affairs had requested a statement

177  Central dossier of R20.
178  'Protokoll', 12 februari 1946, vol. 2, A 1 A, Kanslibyrån, suk, Ra.
179  'Till Kungl. Utrikesdepartementetet', 26 mars 1946, vol. 3, E 4, Hemliga arki-vet, suk, Ra. The contemporary name of the locality south of Stockholm where the Soviet refugee camp was situated is Lissma.

from the Commission regarding this demand.[180] In its reply, the Commission made three important assertions. Firstly, in a direct comment to the Soviet demand, it pointed out that Lisma was an 'open camp for foreign citizens' and that 'no foreigners are forced to reside there' (a statement which, however, merited qualifying, given that it was partly administered by Soviet officials who did, of course, make notice of any expressions of opposition). Secondly, it offered the reassurance that its continuous assessment followed the directions it had been given by the government, and that any deportation decisions were carried out according to the law and would also have to be assessed also by the Aliens Appeals Board. Thirdly, however, it added that, in the opinion of the Commission, 'escape' from Lisma under 'dubious' circumstances 'should be regarded as an indication of political refugee status'. With regard to this, the Commission continued, 'one should reckon on only a few "escapees" being deported from the country'.[181]

This was an apparent change to the views expressed by the Commission about nine months earlier, when it had been of the opinion that only those Russians who had actively fought against the Soviet Union could be recognised as political refugees. The stance they now presented was significantly more generous. As a result, the around 70 Russian Lisma-escapees were allowed to stay. The handling of the case thus suggests that the government's deportation decisions of the two groups of typical examples set out a few months earlier had not been interpreted as setting a precedent for future arrivals. (The postponed implementation might have been, though.) The Commission now seems to have been provided with a greater power of influence too.

Russians were still refused entry in 1946, however, and were sent both to Finland and Poland. Fourteen Russian adults plus an unknown number of children are documented as refused entry, again both by the police and the National Alien Commission. All decisions were implemented.[182] One regarded a 22 year-old former

<hr>

180 'P.M.', 19 februari 1946, vol. 3, E 4, Hemliga arkivet, SUK, Ra.

181 'Till Kungl. Utrikesdepartementetet', 26 mars 1946, vol. 3, E 4, Hemliga arkivet, SUK, Ra. See also Berge 1992.

182 Nr 2677, 2904, 2912, 2914, 2977, 2978, 3018, vol. 36, F 11 A, Hemliga arkivet, SUK, Ra; Nr 3060, 3099, 3234, vol. 37, F 11 A, Hemliga arkivet, SUK, Ra; Nr 3360, vol. 38, F 11 A, Hemliga arkivet, SUK, Ra.

soldier arriving from Poland. He had deserted from the Red Army, a crime which he feared would lead to punishment in the event of his return. He also claimed to have carried out translating work for the Germans. Instead of sending his case further to the Commission, as stipulated in the Aliens Act, the police refused him entry twice and sent him back to Poland. (One possible factor which affected his case negatively was that he, in the police's view, told somewhat different stories on his two arrivals.)[183]

Another man also sent to Poland was a 32 year-old former soldier who had resided in Sweden for a few years during the war after his escape from a German prisoner of war camp in Norway in 1942. In 1945 he had voluntarily travelled to Poland. There, however, he had been warned that his prisoner of war experience would result in him being sent to forced labour camps should he set foot in the Soviet Union. Thus, to avoid repatriation, he had opted to return to Sweden but with the ultimate aim of continuing on to France. The police sent a report about the man to the National Alien Commission with a statement claiming that he had initially used a false identity, and 'appeared to be an adventurer'. The Commission decided to refuse him entry and he was sent back to Poland the same day.[184]

A third man, an 18 year-old, arrived from Finland in May 1946. He had resided there during the war and worked for the Germans. In 1944 he had been transferred back to the Soviet Union by Soviet officials. Mainly because of hunger, he fled two years later and managed to make his way back to Finland. Since he feared the NKVD and believed that both he and his family would be severely punished for his illegal departure from the Soviet Union, he continued on to Sweden.[185]

The police forwarded his case to the National Alien Commission, again with a statement of their own. In this they noted that it had been difficult to question the man (perhaps partly because they had used a Polish interpreter to translate from Russian), and that the 'value of his story is difficult to judge'. Additionally, they claimed that it was 'noteworthy' that he wanted to stay in Sweden given that

183  Nr 3060, vol. 37, F 11 A, Hemliga arkivet, SUK, Ra.
184  Central dossier of R41. See also nr 2912, vol. 36, F 11 A, Hemliga arkivet, SUK, Ra.
185  Central dossier and central register card of R83.

he had his family in Russia.[186] The Commission decided to refuse him entry. In the refusal of entry files it is claimed that he was sent to the Soviet Union.[187]

At least one of these above-mentioned men – the 22 year-old deserter from the Red Army who additionally claimed to have worked for the Germans with translating services – would most likely have been granted a right to stay had he been an Ingrian. The others constitute ambiguous cases. One case which contains no such doubt, however, is represented by another 22 year-old arriving from Poland in August 1946. His whole family consisted of anti-communists who had fought the Soviet regime. His father was a priest who had served within the Tsarist army, and then within the 'white army' against the communists. He himself had been extensively involved in the Russian émigré anti-communist, anti-Soviet organisation NTS (*National Alliance of Russian Solidarists*). During the war, he had pursued dangerous infiltration work both within and outside of the Soviet Union on behalf of this organisation. In Poland he had lived under a false identity and worked as a taxi driver. He feared being revealed and repatriated by the Soviet-directed communist Polish authorities. Additionally, he wanted to establish contact with his parents, which he knew resided in West Germany.[188]

Without reservation, this man was a political refugee – also according to general 1946 principles. The risk of his rendition to the Soviet Union from Poland was substantial, and the fate he would meet if returned there was obvious. In a secret plenary meeting the Commission nevertheless decided to refuse him entry and send him back to Poland.[189] The decision was implemented. Once in Poland, however, an officer controlling the Polish border realised who he was and decided to help him, rather than to deliver him to the Russian authorities which he was supposed to do. He

186 'Polisrapport', 5 maj 1945, central dossier of R83.
187 On his central register card, however, it is registered that he was sent to Finland. However, it is likely that the ship was to continue to the Soviet Union. In addition, Finnish authorities would have been likely to refer him back to the Soviet Union in case he tried to escape in Finland. Central dossier and central register card of R83; Nr 2904, vol. 36, F 11 A, Hemliga arkivet, SUK, Ra.
188 Central dossier and central register card of R79.
189 'Protokoll', 10 september 1946, vol. 1, A 1, Hemliga arkivet, SUK, Ra.

refused him entry and sent him back to Sweden again with an exhortation to leave Poland since he would be extradited and shot immediately should his identity be revealed. Thus, he was referred to the Commission again.

However, the Commission had not changed its mind. In another secret session, it decided to refuse him entry again and send him back to Poland for a second time.[190] This time they added in a note in his central dossier that 'it should be organised so that he can come to Poland as Jankowski', which was the false Polish identity he had used in Poland. 'Jankowski' himself, however, tried to assure them that this would not make any difference. His Russian nationality and background would soon become known to the Soviet authorities in Poland. The Commission ignored his pleas and in October 1946 he was once again sent back to Poland. The archives contain no further information about this man or his subsequent fate.[191]

Other Russian new arrivals were allowed to stay. Among them was a 30 year-old with a similar story as the 22 year-old NTS activist. He claimed to have worked in an underground organisation which printed illegal anti-communist propaganda material in Poland. The organisation had been discovered by the secret police, however, and he had been arrested. During his transportation he had managed to flee, and had concealed himself on a ship heading from Gdynia to Trelleborg in Sweden, where he was granted a residence permit.[192]

One possible reason for the varying treatment of the NTS activist 'Jankowski' compared to the man who had printed anti-communist propaganda in Poland can be found in the nature of the organisations of which they were members. Sweden forbade immigrants from engaging in political activities during these years in an attempt to prevent activities that could endanger Sweden's foreign

190 'Protokoll', 1 oktober 1946, vol. 1, A 1, Hemliga arkivet, SUK, Ra.
191 Central dossier and central register card of R79; 'Protokoll', 10 september 1946, vol. 1, A 1, Hemliga arkivet, SUK, Ra; 'Protokoll', 1 oktober 1946, vol. 1, A 1, Hemliga arkivet, SUK, Ra; nr 3234, vol. 37, F 11 A, Hemliga arkivet, SUK, Ra. It has not been possible to examine the other Russians who were refused entry to grey zone countries in 1946 since no personal dossiers belonging to them can be traced within the National Alien Commission's archive.
192 Control dossier of R59.

policy relations. During the early stages of the Second World War this had predominantly affected the treatment of opponents of Nazism. Foreign Nazi adversaries had been interned, including Nordic citizens.[193] Towards the end of the war and the initial post-war years, this ban was directed towards critics of the Soviet Union. Balts often had a condition stapled into their passports reminding them of this prohibition. Sweden was well aware that the Soviet Union was keen to put an end to anti-Soviet émigré movements in the West. Negative publicity about the Soviet Union was often brought to the attention of the Soviet legation in Sweden, and complaints were repeatedly directed towards the Ministry for Foreign Affairs that 'allowed' such things to be written in the Swedish media.[194] Newly arriving refugees were always asked for their political views and activities. The answers looked upon most favourably were 'apolitical', 'democratic' or 'no political engagement'. This was soon picked up by newcomers who often gave such answers, regardless of their beliefs.

The international organisation NTS was known within the National Alien Commission and the security police. From the 1950s onwards, it was watched more carefully by the authorities which suspected it of fascist tendencies.[195] Foreigners residing in Sweden who were believed to be members of it were subject to various consequences, including denial of travel documents.[196] Thus, it is possible that suspicions about the nature of the NTS had a bearing on the above-mentioned decision or that the authorities had a general reluctance about Soviet citizens who had worked for the Germans during the war – particularly within the intelligence services or more serious political organisations. Such individuals were generally regarded as particularly untrustworthy. This is despite the fact that it granted asylum to those who had actively fought against the Soviets. This, however, can be compared with the substantial number of Balts with links to the German occupation regimes of

193 See Åmark 2011, ch. 15.
194 Various documents, for example memorandums and letters dated 29 December 1944, 16 January 1945 and 7 April 1945, within vol. 67, P 40 I, 1920 års dossiésystem, UD, Ra.
195 'Ang. Ryska emigrantorganisationen NTS', no. 272, vol. 11, F 4, Hemliga arkivet, SUK, Ra.
196 See chapter 7.

their home countries, including involvement in war crimes. This did not stop them being granted residence permits in Sweden. Thus, fears of granting entry to possible fascist elements in Sweden cannot be the sole explanation for this behaviour.

Having engaged in intelligence activities for the NKVD was not looked upon favourably by the Swedish authorities either. Apart from raising doubts about the trustworthiness of the person in question, there was the likelihood of getting into trouble with the Soviet authorities. Such was the case when a NKVD-agent left his mission and applied for asylum in Sweden in September 1946. The Soviet authorities immediately demanded his extradition, which in its turn put the Swedish authorities in a difficult position. They hastily decided to deport him to Denmark (despite the fact that he had arrived from the Soviet Union) in order to 'export' this troublesome situation off Swedish territory.[197]

Another former NKVD agent applied for asylum in March 1946. Contrary to the previous example, however, this 23 year-old claimed to have been blackmailed by the NKVD into working for them as an agent in Helsinki. Nonetheless, the Commission still regarded him as untrustworthy and decided to place him in custody since they believed there were 'doubts regarding his persona'. His letters were read and his behaviour monitored. The camp's director was of the opinion that he was well behaved. A few months and several interrogations later he was released and granted a short residence permit under police surveillance. There were still fears over his character, but he was granted a right to stay. A few months later, however, he emigrated elsewhere.[198]

A few deportation decisions relating to civilians have also been found. A Russian family escaping from the Soviet repatriation committee in France arrived in 1946. They intended to stay in Sweden for only a few weeks while they arranged their tickets and entry visas to Venezuela. When their travel plans failed due to financial problems, the Aliens' Committee took urgent measures

197 Central dossier of R26. The individual is also mentioned in *Ett diplomatiskt miss-lyckande: fallet Raoul Wallenberg och den svenska utrikesledningen*, Kommissionen om den svenska utrikesledningens agerande i fallet Raoul Wallenberg, SOU 2003:18, Fritzes offentliga publikationer, Stockholm 2003, pp. 367–368 (ref: SOU 2003:18). His case will be examined in more detail in chapter 6.
198 Central and control dossiers of R38.

to have them deported before their re-entry permit to France had expired.[199]

Overall, however, the policies towards the Russians seem to have become somewhat more generous in 1946 compared to the previous year. Still, those who were refused entry or deported included persons who would certainly have been regarded as political refugees had they been Ingrians or Balts. Suspicions against some individuals – particularly former agents regardless of which side they had worked for – were obviously influenced by concerns for (external and, perhaps, internal) security. Other inconsistencies are likely to be explained more by the absence of clear principles; a legacy of interpreting Russians as *collectively* less eligible for political refugee status than Balts and Ingrians; and, perhaps, a possible general antipathy towards Russians based on ethnic principles. In this it would have reflected attitudes which had characterised the broader Swedish society of the first half of the 20th century.[200]

### 4.4.3 Guidelines and Increasing Protection, 1947–48

In late 1947, policies changed also with regard to the Russians. This led to the drawing up of new guidelines. As previously mentioned, the traffic of Russians increased that year due to the intensifying hunt for Soviet citizens in Finland. The Russian Control Commission there had now decided that all Soviet-Russian citizens were to return to the Soviet Union. This prompted the arrival of around fifty Russians in the early autumn of 1947. The Commission was firmly of the belief that this number was set to increase. Therefore, as previously mentioned, it requested new guidelines from the government in September 1947.

The Russians whose asylum applications were now sent to the government for precedential assessment had all been forcibly evacuated to the Russian part of Karelia in the 1930s, and had willingly handed themselves over to the Finnish troops when they arrived in 1941. All declared themselves opponents of the regime. Some of them had also been subject to intimidation and/or been imprisoned within the Soviet Union on political grounds, such as a refusal to

199 Central dossiers of R3 and R4.
200 See part 1.1.4.

join the communist party. Others had other close family members who had recently been deported to Siberia. Because of this, and the new directives from the Russian Control Commission, the Aliens Appeals Board had acknowledged that they risked being forcefully repatriated to Russia and subject to punishments or reprisals. Due to the 'circumstances' and the 'matter's significance for other, similar cases', however, the Board suggested that the Russians' applications ought to be referred to the government.[201]

The National Alien Commission agreed with the Aliens Appeals Board on the significance of the case and sent the applications to the government. However, within its own comments, which it attached to the referral, a new approach towards the Russian refugees is evident. It now questioned the appropriateness of maintaining the previous *difference* in the treatment of Russian and Ingrian refugees. It stated that the main rule regarding *all* (Soviet) refugees from Finland had been that individuals who had 'deserted from the Red Army or actively participated in political or military activities directed against the Soviet Union, as well as such individuals' family members' had been considered political refugees. It added, however, that, during the last year, a new tendency had developed regarding the Ingrian refugees: even those 'less politically afflicted' had been granted a right to stay. This difference should no longer be maintained, argued the Commission. The Russian refugees who were now arriving from Finland came from the same 'social environment' and had a similar 'political past' as the Ingrians. Moreover, most of the individuals' main political offence, be they Russian or Ingrian, was that they had left Soviet territory without permission and refused to carry out their 'duty' by returning there, claimed the Commission. It also confirmed that it was willing to grant all the individuals in question residence permits.[202]

In November 1947, the government acted accordingly. All the Soviet new arrivals were allowed to stay.[203] The impact of this new

---

201 'Till Statens Utlänningskommission', 11 september 1947, vol. 6, B 1, Utlänningsnämnden, Ra; 'Till Konungen', 16 september 1947 (including two attachments), vol. 4, E 4, Hemliga arkivet, SUK, Ra.

202 'Till Konungen', 16 september 1947 (including two attachments), vol. 4, E 4, Hemliga arkivet, SUK, Ra.

203 See decision on 7 November 1947 in central dossiers of, for example, R32, R43, R45, R46, R63, R64, R84, R76, R77.

approach can be traced immediately. A 28 year-old Ukrainian, for example, had arrived for the first time in early September 1947. In his asylum application he cited the intensifying hunt for Soviet citizens in Finland and to the fact that he had surrendered voluntarily to the Finns and then assisted them in highway construction. The Aliens Appeals Board and the National Alien Commission did not recognise him as a political refugee, however, and he was refused entry and sent back to Finland. He returned just three months later – at which point he was granted permission to stay.[204]

The same happened to a 24 year-old Russian car mechanic, who had first arrived in August 1947 and been refused entry. When he returned in December, possibly after hearing rumours about the Swedish government's changed attitude, he was granted a residence permit.[205]

Several others were also reassessed after the government's statement of November 1947. One of the Soviet regime's opponents, who had been refused entry in 1946, came back in late 1947 with six associates. They were all granted a right to stay.[206] So too was a Russian factory worker whose right to asylum had not been recognised by the Aliens Appeals Boards in September 1947. In this case, however, the Commission chose to await the government's decision regarding the individuals on the typical examples list before assessing his case. He too was ultimately granted a residence permit.[207]

Another Russian – an architect – was subject to a similar, but slightly longer, wait. He had arrived in July and informed the Swedish authorities about the victimisation he had faced in Finland. Someone had denounced him as an anti-Soviet propagandist. (He was keen to stress, however, that necessary caution meant that he had had to be very careful about making such remarks since his arrival in Finland.) As a result, he had been subject to lengthy

204 Central dossier of R39.
205 On that second occasion he revealed some more details about his background – such as the fact that he had assisted the Finnish military establishment. That said, however, his persecution by Soviet authorities as well as his voluntary escape to Finland in 1941 had already been mentioned in August. Central dossier of R15.
206 Central dossier and central register card of R72.
207 Central dossier of R14.

questionings by the Finnish state police. He feared that the Soviet authorities might discover the manuscript to a book he had written a few years earlier recounting the conditions for single business owners in the Soviet Union, and that this was the reason for the Finnish state police's increased interest in him. He had also been pestered by local communists in the town in which he resided.

In early September 1947, however, when the Aliens Appeals Board was to give a statement about the man, they had not believed that these circumstances constituted a prerequisite for regarding him as a political refugee. Because of the on-going government reassessment of the asylum principles for Soviet citizens arriving from Finland, however, the architect and his family was kept in custody, awaiting the settlement of the seventeen cases on the typical examples list. Once the government had given its final verdict, the architect and his dependants were granted permission to stay.[208]

Thus, the government decision did indeed function as a precedent. It established a new attitude towards the Russian refugees arriving from Finland. The reason, it seems, was recognition of the seriousness of the increasing hunt for Russians in Finland, as well as of what they were likely to be subject to upon return to the Soviet Union, even in the cases of those individuals who had not actively fought against the Soviet Union. The questioning of the previous differentiation between the treatment of Ingrians and Russians suggests that the latter were now beginning to be regarded as equally eligible for political asylum as Ingrians. This, in turn, indicates that the focus was shifting from the previous collective approach to asylum assessments to one based on individual experiences and risks. As such, it corresponds with contemporaneous international developments of refugee rights.

Another change that seems to have taken place in the treatment of Russian asylum seekers in 1947 concerns the questioning routines to which new arrivals were subjected. Several of these individuals were now, according to the police protocols, asked the same questions as those put to Ingrians since 1945 – including whether or not they had experienced any of the circumstances set out in the specific list compiled during the address affair of 1945.

208 Central dossier and central register card of R25.

And, accordingly, individuals were now granted the right to stay if they met one or two of these criteria.[209]

Individuals were still refused entry, however. Five implemented refusal of entry decisions have been found from 1947. Two of these regarded the above-mentioned individuals who were sent back to Finland but later returned. One other concerned a man arriving from Norway. Two more, however, were individuals who were sent to Poland.[210] Both of these decisions were made by the National Alien Commission. None of them were asked anything else apart from the standard questions for new arrivals, and the interrogation protocols were brief.[211] In a handwritten note in one of the individuals' personal dossiers, however, a personal statement from a police officer was attached to the existing basis for decision: 'Gramvall had personally got the impression, that [xx] is no first class sailor. He seems to be a bit of a drunkard.' It was also noted that he had required medical treatment for syphilis.[212] Social aspects, pertaining to personal behaviour, morality and '*skötsamhet*' (conscientiousness), thus seem to have held sway in this particular case.

In total, however, few refusals of this kind seem to have taken place, particularly during the last months of 1947. It is thus likely that the majority of the 121 Russians that, according to a public investigation, were issued 'non-refusal' decisions in 1947, arrived during the late autumn of that year, when persecutions of Russians in Finland increased and Swedish policies regarding their right to asylum softened.[213] This is also in all probability what lay behind the comparatively high number of Russian non-refusals in 1948 – 345 individuals. The likelihood is that most of them came from Finland, and that most of them were granted permission to stay.

This is because, from 1948 onwards, available source material

209 See, for example, police interrogation protocols in central dossiers of R15, R25, R47.

210 Nr 3596, 3960 in vol. 39, F 11 A, Hemliga arkivet, SUK, Ra; and nr 3935, 4009 in vol. 40, F 11 A, Hemliga arkivet, SUK, Ra.

211 Central dossiers of R36 and R28. No comment on what language was used during the interrogations has been found.

212 *Gramvall hade personligen det intrycket att [xx] icke var någon första klassens sjöman. Han hade förefallit ganska försupen.* Handwritten note from Rosqvist to Ernberg, 18 mars 1947, central dossier of R36.

213 SOU 1951:42 p. 254.

reveals only two refusal of entry decisions of Russians. One was of a man sent back to the Norwegian ship on which he had arrived; the other of a 28 year-old vagrant arriving from Finland whose alleged Russian citizenship was given no credence by the authorities.[214] From 1949 onwards no refusals of entry of Russians to the Soviet Union or any grey zone countries have been found. As with the Ingrians, however, from the early 1950s the grey zone countries no longer included Finland in the view of the Swedish authorities. Thus, a few civilians not regarded as political refugees were indeed sent back to Finland. A few others were sent to other Western countries.[215]

To sum up, the refugee rights of Russian new arrivals seem to have been fully protected following the government decision of November 1947. No cases were sent to the government for assessment either, according to available sources. A clear watershed can thus be revealed regarding the Swedish authorities' attitude and practices regarding Russian asylum seekers from this date onwards. The timing correlates with the results of the examinations of the Balts and the Ingrians.

## 4.5 Conclusion

One of the most conspicuous results of the examination of the authorities' management of new Soviet arrivals between 1945 and 1954 is the identification of 1948 as a *watershed* year. From this date onwards, no Soviet citizens seem to have been refused entry if arriving from the Soviet Union or a territory from which there was a risk of persecution. The principles pursued do, from that date on, appear to have been consistent and stable. Apart from the quantitative accounts, this is demonstrated by the lack of cases requiring a

214  Nr 4584, vol. 41, F 11 A, Hemliga arkivet, SUK, Ra; Nr 4683, vol. 42, F 11 A, Hemliga arkivet, SUK, Ra. See also central dossier and central register card of R69.

215  Refused Russians from 1950 onwards: Nr 6441 and 6669, vol. 47, F 11 A, Hemliga arkivet, SUK, Ra; Nr 8006, vol. 52, F 11 A, Hemliga arkivet, F 11 A, SUK, Ra; Nr 8104, vol. 53, F 11 A, Hemliga arkivet, F 11 A, SUK, Ra, Nr 8652, vol. 55, F 11 A, Hemliga arkivet, SUK, Ra; Nr 8869, vol. 56, F 11 A, Hemliga arkivet, F 11 A, SUK, Ra. See also central dossier, central register card and control dossier of R33.

statement from the Aliens Appeals Board regarding Soviet citizens arriving from non-Western countries. It is also apparent from the lack of detailed discussions regarding Soviet refugees' right to reside in Sweden both within the National Alien Commission's plenary assembly and within its discussions with other authorities, such as the Ministry for Foreign Affairs. Additionally, it is confirmed by the fact that no asylum applications presented by newly arrived Soviet refugees seem to have been forwarded to the government from that date on. This is despite 1948 constituting a peak year for the traffic of incoming Russian and Ingrian refugees from Finland. Even so, the Commission now assessed the applications without detailed government involvement and granted the individuals asylum.

This indicates an adjustment to one of the potential influential factors identified in the opening chapter, namely *international juridical developments*. There are three main reasons for this. *Firstly*, it is clear that the policies beginning in 1948 were characterised by a significantly more uncompromising acknowledgement of refugee rights, which in its turn correlates with contemporaneous developments within the international refugee regime. *Secondly*, the results demonstrate that asylum applications were increasingly assessed on individual rather than collective grounds. Rather than, as previously pursued, according refugee status to certain groups, often along ethnic lines and based on their presumed collective experiences, the individual circumstances of each applicant was increasingly acknowledged. Somewhat paradoxically, this eventually lead to the principle that 'all' Soviet refugees fleeing from Finland or the Soviet Union were to be regarded as political refugees, due to the opposition demonstrated by their flight and due to the increasing persecution of Soviet citizens in Finland. This change of attitudes correlates with the ways in which refugee rights were progressively being interpreted internationally at this time – namely as something belonging to an individual, based on certain kinds of personal experiences, rather than to groups limited to time-specific international circumstances.

*Thirdly*, the development demonstrates what can be called a *depoliticization* of refugee matters – at least on the detailed assessment level. Although the developments of the international refugee regime in the highest degree constituted a political process, its transformation of attitudes towards refugees meant that these individuals were now interpreted as holders of rights, which in their turn were a matter for bureaucrats rather than for politicians to interpret and implement. Legislation now became more specific as to who was to be regarded a political refugee and what consequences this brought about in terms of rights (for the refugee) and obligations (for the host state). As such, refugee management was reinterpreted as a matter of *law* more than politics, which further strengthened refugee rights. The fact that the Swedish government obviously stopped interfering with the National Alien Commission's assessment of individual applications for asylum from 1948 onwards is an example of such a depoliticization in process. On a general level, refugee policies were, of course, still a matter of politics (as they always are, everywhere) as the government obviously remained the law making authority, and general law-interpreting guidelines were probably still issued to some extent. However, the discontinuation of its practice of issuing specific law-interpreting directions regarding the implementation of individual cases constitutes an important amendment which ought to be interpreted as an outcome of the transformation of refugee matters in juridical terms. As such, they clearly correlate to the standards established within the international refugee regime at this time.

Before this date, however, direct government involvement on a detailed assessment level regarding newly arrived Soviet refugees was considerable. The main reason for this pertains to another of the influential factors identified in chapter one, namely *external security concerns*. The management of Soviet refugees was still at this time commonly framed as a national security issue and, as such, it needed to be governed by the highest political authority. However, this seems to have concerned the Russians and the Ingrians more than the Balts. The last named group appear to have been directly affected by this only in the autumn of 1945, when the seventeen Latvians who arrived in the middle of the extradition affair (which also, obviously, pertained to aspects of national security) were deported by the government according to paragraph 56 of the Aliens Act. (This, it will be recalled, referred to situations of 'war or danger of war'.) The government still decided to protect them, however, and postponed the implementation of the decision. Cases regarding Ingrians and Russians, on the other hand, were continually referred to the government during 1946 and 1947 – particularly so if they concerned individuals who had arrived in larger groups and could draw public attention. The reason for this was linked explicitly to the 'foreign policy concerns' that were invoked.

Despite continuous government involvement, the majority of the individuals whose applications were regarded as sensitive cases seem to have been protected. Most of the individuals were ultimately allowed to stay, either through postponement of deportation decisions or because the government simply decided to grant them residence permits. The government thus seems to have wanted to safeguard these individuals' asylum needs despite the foreign policy concerns that were involved. One explanation is probably the traumatic experience of the extradition affair of 1945–46. The government was in all likelihood keen to avoid another such scandal which would risk causing both renewed national and international criticism and, possibly, an increasing investment of Soviet prestige in those cases leading to heightened Soviet pressure. It is also possible, of course, that more purely humanitarian considerations also played a part in the outcome.

The path towards the 1948 stabilisation was far from straightforward, however, and varied significantly for the three ethnic groups included in this study. The examination of refusal of entry decisions revealed that the interpretation of Balts as collective political refugees was more or less intact during the whole research period. Most of the Balts who arrived illegally in Sweden from the Soviet Union or the grey zone countries during the research period were indeed allowed to stay. Some important exceptions were found – particularly from 1946 when some Balts were indeed refused entry and sent back to first and foremost Poland and Finland. However, external or internal security concerns do *not* appear to be the main motivation for this. Instead, vague and inconsistently applied guidelines seem to have been a determining factor. Individuals with very similar backgrounds and circumstances received different outcomes. Possibly, a general reluctance to stimulate further refugee flows from these countries through a 'too generous' stance played a part. It is also conceivable that the extradition affair was interpreted by the refugee managing authorities as a sign of harshening policies towards the Balts.

In comparison with the two other groups, however, the Balts were without doubt the most generously treated. Ingrians were not collectively interpreted as political refugees in 1944–45, and it would take until 1948 before their status as such became fully recognised by the Swedish authorities. During 1945 and the first half of 1946, many Ingrians were indeed refused entry to Finland. In contrast to the few refused Balts, however, these policies followed unusually clear guidelines. The principles that had been established by the government in early 1945 regarding the address affair were utilised as setting a precedent when the police and the National Alien Commission assessed new arrivals of Ingrian descent. Those who did not meet the criteria on the list were refused entry and sent back to Finland. In early 1946, however, there is evidence to suggest that attitudes were changing both within the government and the Commission. A campaign launched by some Swedish activists lead to the withdrawal of a deportation decision issued towards 542 Ingrians identified as 'non-political refugees'. The results suggests that, apart from a reluctance to trigger another scandal as that generated by the extradition of Balts some six months earlier, the authorities felt sympathy for the Ingrians. From this date onwards, they were generally not refused entry. However, the government continued to interfere in the assessment of new Ingrian arrivals until late 1947, and the Ministry for Foreign Affairs persisted in pointing out the 'foreign policy aspects' of the management this group.

Russian new arrivals were interpreted as challenging foreign policy concerns in the same manner as Ingrians. In contrast to both the Ingrians and the Balts, however, they were only in exceptional cases granted political refugee status in 1944–45. The Swedish authorities were not keen on hosting Russian refugees within its borders once the war had ended. Only such individuals who had actively fought against the Soviet Union were regarded as potential political refugees, and in such cases only if they themselves managed to bring this to the attention of the authorities. Considerable interpersonal skills and contacts were generally required. This strict interpretation seems to have softened somewhat already in 1946, although Russians still had to fight the hardest for their asylum compared to both Ingrians and Balts, since fewer questions were generally asked upon their arrival. This was in part because of the authorities' lingering interpretation of the Russians as a collective with less reason to political asylum than Balts (in particular) and Ingrians. Gradually, however, the same principles started to be applied to the Russians as those which had been used towards the Ingrians since 1945. Not until late 1947, however, were Russians granted refugee status on the same terms as the Ingrians.

The Swedish government's reluctance to host Russian refugees after the war should probably to a considerable extent be interpreted in terms of foreign policy relations, in which *external security concerns* played a significant part. The government's ambition to maintain friendly relations with their Eastern neighbour was not compatible with a generous refugee policy towards Russian refugees. This was particularly so in 1945 when the rest of the Western world was repatriating Russians. (Balts, on the other hand, were protected by other Western countries, thus potentially helping Sweden to depoliticise the framing of these policies in relation to the Soviet Union.) Granting asylum to some was believed to encourage more to come. This domino-effect mentality can be traced back to the 1930s and the management of Jewish refugees. The feared upshot was a likely increase in friction within Swedish-Soviet relations.

However, the results also suggest that other considerations were involved, namely those pertaining to a third influential aspect identified in the first chapter: *ethnicity*. As previous research has demonstrated, the first half of the 20th century was characterised by a perceptible antipathy towards East Europeans in Sweden. A comparison between the treatment of the Finnish-speaking, Lutheran Ingrians (with their 18th century Swedish heritage) and the Russians at this time reveals a considerably more sympathetic attitude towards the former, leading to more generous policies. It is thus likely that the treatment of the Russian refugees was influenced not only by external security concerns but also a Swedish scepticism towards Russians in general, based on ethnic prejudices. The acceptable quota for Russians within Swedish society was probably regarded as smaller than that of the Ingrians (and, indeed, that of the Balts). Even so, however, from 1948 onwards, when refugee rights in Sweden were significantly strengthened, this also included the Russians.

Two other factors that also seem to have influenced the pursued practices – particularly during the initial post-war years when policies were somewhat vague and inconsistently (or arbitrarily) applied – are *social control* and *economics*. This was particularly the case with regards to Balts arriving from Western countries, where the assessment was not dependent on estimations of the person's potential refugee status. Those who could prove their value to the Swedish economy and provide references guaranteeing their immaculate morals and social behaviour (and, sometimes, their politically impeccable past) were most often granted a right to stay. Contacts with prominent members of the Swedish society certainly helped. 'Western Balts' failing this were refused entry or deported.

The last influential aspect that has not been mentioned as yet is *internal security*. Since this pertains to the behaviour of the individual, it is likely to have made more of an impact when it comes to the issues that are to be studied in the next chapter which concerns the management of those 'unwanted' individuals that already resided in Sweden. However, it was indeed an influential factor in those cases where individuals who had worked as (double) agents were refused entry in Sweden. They were regarded as specifically untrustworthy. Thus, overall, *all* the influential aspects identified in chapter one seem to have influenced Sweden's asylum policies towards Soviet refugees, to a greater or lesser extent.

The results above raise a number of attendant questions. One such is what happened to the external security concerns, which were so intimately intertwined with refugee policies during the first post-war years, after 1948? How could the 'room for manoeuvre' in terms of foreign policy relations with the Soviet Union suddenly include such a considerable 'depoliticization' of refugee policies that the government decided to let go of its direct detailed management of the assessments?

Ideological influence from the international refugee regime is likely to have mattered. So too did by all likelihood deteriorating Swedish attitudes to the Soviet Union, exacerbated by the superpower's behaviour in Eastern Europe. However, it is also probable that this 'room for manoeuvre' was established when Sweden abandoned its previous bridge-building ambitions towards the Soviet Union in 1948 (as described in chapter one, part 1.1.1.). Although Sweden needed to maintain trustworthy relations with the Soviet Union during the entire Cold War conflict, the change of attitudes in 1948 meant that the most ambitious attempts at establishing a friendship were abandoned. Possibly, this also meant that the government no longer felt that it needed to take the Soviet Union's wishes into consideration to the same extent when managing refugees. As such, the political framing of refugee matters was alleviated.

Conversely, however, the same effect was also probably established by the reinterpretation of refugee policies as a matter predominantly of law rather than politics. When the main responsibility for the implementation of policies is transferred to the bureaucratic level, politicians can, at least officially, deny responsibility for individual outcomes. Thus, defending Swedish refugee policies to their Soviet counterparts might have been somewhat easier for the Swedish government after 1948, since it no longer interpreted itself as directly responsible for the law-interpretative decisions. (In chapter six, these aspects will be further explored as focus turns to Sweden's management of Soviet extradition demands.)

# CHAPTER FIVE

# The Unwanted

The previous chapter focused on traditional asylum policies – that is state responses to asylum seekers. In this section, a different complex of problems is analysed as attention is turned to Sweden's handling of those Soviet refugees that it for various reasons wished to remove from the country after they had been granted asylum. As was demonstrated in chapter three, applications for renewed residence permits could be rejected and superseded by a *deportation* decision if the authorities for some reason had changed their mind about the applicant since the issuing of the last permit. As such, the deportation decision constituted the most important legal tool for the authorities to remove from Swedish territory 'unwanted' foreign residents who did not meet any of the criteria for which expulsion could be issued. When it comes to deportations, the authorities' legal room for manoeuvre was considerable as few guidelines as to which circumstances would lead to this result were provided within the 1945 Aliens Act.

The issuing of the *expulsion* decision, on the other hand, was more specifically regulated within that piece of legislation. As described in more detail in chapter three, it was issued as a consequence of a committed crime. It could also, however, be delivered with reference to other circumstances such as Roma ethnicity, 'sexually immoral' behaviour and vagrancy; or, as paragraph 37 of the Aliens Act stated, to individuals who challenged 'national security or other issues regarding the interest of the state'. Political refugees were to be protected from being returned to a country in which he or she could expect political persecution. However, the government was granted the right to deviate from these regulations in times of 'war or threat of war or due to the defence of the country or specific circumstances'.[1]

How, then, did the Swedish authorities handle Soviet refugees it came to regard as 'unwanted' after they had been granted asylum? What circumstances led them to issue deportation or expulsion decisions? How was the affected individuals' political refugee status valued? Were there any differences in the treatment of Balts, Ingrians and Russians? And how does this relate to the potential influential aspects identified in chapter one (*external* and *internal security, economics, ethnicity, social control and morality,* and *international juridical developments*)?

## 5.1 The Management of 'Unwanted' Balts

A general examination of the issued and implemented deportation decisions of Balts with previous residence permits suggests that this legal tool was not practiced very often.[2] One reason might have been the fact that the only country that would accept Sweden's 'unwanted' Balts was the Soviet Union. And since the Balts were regarded as political refugees on a collective basis, this option was not available.[3]

Those Balts against whom such decisions *were* issued were individuals suspected of very serious crimes committed beyond Sweden's borders. One man from Estonia, for example, was a well-known Nazi collaborator. During the German occupation he had worked for the 'political police' and stood accused of having assaulted, arrested and murdered numerous political opponents. He was also known to have stolen significant amounts of gold from Jews and other 'unwanted' citizens within the German-Estonian regime. This former police officer was subjected to a series of rigorous interrogations and several months of detainment in a secure refugee camp following which, in November 1945, the

1   According to the 'security paragraph' 56. See chapter three.
2   Apart from some of those who had arrived from Western countries. See chapter four, part 4.2.3.
3   Vol. 2–8, A 2, Kontrollbyrån, SUK, Ra; vol. 1–11, A 2, Passbyrån, SUK, Ra; vol. 1, A 2, Första Byrån, SUK, Ra; vol. 1, A 2, Andra Byrån, SUK, Ra.

Commission issued him with a deportation order plus a prohibition on his return to the country. This was completed not by his removal to the Soviet Union, however. Instead, he managed to obtain permission to travel to Venezuela, where he moved in 1946.[4] Another man, also accused of committing serious crimes against his fellow countrymen during the German occupation, was the subject of a deportation decision issued in 1944. Nevertheless, this was never implemented.[5]

It is important to note, however, that these two examples constitute exceptions. Between 1944 and 1947, the Swedish security police pursued two extensive examinations of the Baltic community in Sweden. This was intended to identify individuals who had committed war crimes during the German occupation; had been collaborators of the Nazi regime; and/or were advocates of Nazism. This included interrogations with numerous Balts, collecting information and evidence, and the making of an ideological mapping out of the entire Baltic refugee community. The examinations resulted in the identification of a few hundred individuals who stood accused of many things. Some were strongly suspected of having committed a variety of crimes during the occupation, including murder, torture and appropriation of Jewish property. Others had held important positions within the Nazi apparatus, had assisted this regime in various ways, and/or were influential Nazi demagogues.[6]

From the names gathered in these investigations, a random selection of 33 individuals has been chosen for closer study. Within

4    B119, see 'Protokoll', 19 oktober 1945, vol. 1, A 2, Utlänningsnämnden, Ra; 'Protokoll', 29 maj 1946, vol. 2, A 2, Utlänningsnämnden, Ra; 'Protokoll', 22 januari 1946, vol. 2, A 1 A, Kanslibyrån, SUK, Ra; 'Protokoll', 7 maj 1946, vol. 2, A 1 A, Kanslibyrån, SUK, Ra ; 'Protokoll', 4 juni 1946, vol. 2, A 1 A, Kanslibyrån, SUK, Ra. See also various information on B119 in P4814, SÄPO, Ra; 'Ang. av Statens utlänningskommission begärd utredning rörande vissa balt. förhållanden', vol. 10, F 2 B, Hemliga arkivet, SUK, Ra; and in Deland 2010 where he is also mentioned.

5    Central dossier, control dossier and central register card of B87. See also various information about him in P4814, SÄPO, Ra; 'Ang. av Statens utlännings-kommission begärd utredning rörande vissa balt. förhållanden', vol. 10, F 2 B, Hemliga arkivet, SUK, Ra; and in Deland 2010.

6    'Ang. av Statens utlänningskommission begärd utredning rörande vissa balt. förhållanden', vol. 10, F 2 B, Hemliga arkivet, SUK, Ra; and P4818, SÄPO, Ra. See also Deland 2010.

this group are several individuals accused of a variety of things outlined above – from murder and torture to stealing and spreading Nazi propaganda. Out of these, however, only the two abovementioned individuals were ever issued a removal decision of any kind.[7] This correlates with the results presented by Mats Deland in *Purgatorium*, in which he demonstrates that no action was usually taken against the numerous former Baltic war criminals who resided in Sweden, despite the existence of substantial information on their criminal past.[8] Thus, even if (internal) security concerns might have motivated the security police to gather such information, this did not provide strong enough grounds to induce the immigration authorities to take any measures against these individuals.

A similar situation concerns those Balts suspected of harbouring communist views. A number of such cases arose in the early 1950s, some of which included suspicions of illegal intelligence activities. Unless such activities were proven, none of them were issued a removal decision.[9] However, other measures were also taken against them, as will be further demonstrated in chapter seven.

Deportation *was* considered, however, with regard to one man who was thought to have been implicated in a murder in his home country in 1941. Police interrogations took place including interviews with witnesses. After some further examination involving a hearing of the man's employer (who affirmed that the individual in question was well behaved and performed his work duties in a satisfactory manner), the question was dropped.[10]

Overall, however, few Balts seem to have been regarded as 'unwanted' enough to lead the authorities to take such a drastic measure as deportation. Rather, the authorities' interest in protecting them from the Soviet Union seems to have taken precedence over any possible wish to remove them from the country.

---

7   B3, B4, B15, B18, B19, B20, B27, B36, B37, B39, B40, B49, B56, B58, B62, B64, B65, B71, B72, B73, B76, B87, B88, B92, B94, B96, B97, B102, B105, B108, B111, B115, B116.

8   Some of the above-mentioned individuals are also included in Deland's study. Deland 2010.

9   These cases are discussed in more detail in part 5.1.2.

10  Central dossier for B53.

### 5.1.1 *Criminal Balts – Expelled and Protected*

Around forty *expulsion* decisions pertaining to Balts with a criminal record have been found. The crimes included things such as bank robbery, theft, fraud, receiving stolen goods, shoplifting, damage, violent behaviour and assault, and rioting within refugee camps. Almost all expulsion decisions were, however, attached with a so-called 'homeland proviso'. This in effect rendered their completion impossible, since no other countries were generally willing to receive foreigners with a criminal past. As a result, most of these individuals remained in Sweden. (That said, however, a limited number of them managed to leave for Venezuela and Argentina.)[11]

Thus, Baltic individuals with criminal records were continuously regarded as political refugees and were protected from the Soviets. Nonetheless, expulsion decisions were still issued. As a consequence, their implementation had to be postponed repeatedly. Some individuals had to apply for postponement twice a year for as long as twenty years before the expulsion decision was finally withdrawn.[12] As such, the authorities clearly signalled to Balts with criminal records that they were 'unwanted' in Sweden, while still protecting their right to asylum.[13]

11  This examination is based on the following: a study of minutes from the Ministry for the Interior in which removal decisions were challenged and, sometimes, withdrawn; meeting protocols from the National Alien Commission where more complicated expulsion decisions were discussed; protocols from the First Bureau where all postponements of expulsion and other removal decision were issued from 1953 onwards; and, finally, an examination of the personal dossiers and register cards of a randomly chosen selection of Baltic individuals issued expulsion decisions between 1945 and 1954. From Föredragningslistor, vol. 1–6, A II, Inrikesdepartementet, sᴜᴋ, Ra: 21 november 1947 nr 40, 9 juli 1948 nr 42, 16 juli 1948 nr 32, 28 april 1949 nr 2, 14 oktober 1949 nr 14, 9 december 1949 nr 37, 28 april 1950 nr 23, 1 september 1950 nr 18 and 41, 6 oktober 1950 nr 29, 1 december 1950 nr 22, 26 januari 1951 nr 45, 16 mars 1951 nr 1, 6 april 1951 nr 19, 10 augusti 1951 nr 29, 7 september 1951 nr 18, 30 juni 1952 nr 42, 3 oktober 1952 nr 34; from vol. 1, A 2, Första Byrån, sᴜᴋ, Ra: Protocols from 1953 nr 1005, 1129, 1133, 1205, 1206, 1254, 1296, 1301, 1324, 1327, 1332, 1409, 1434, 1484, 1512, 1512, 1540, 1558, 1583, 1582, 1614, and from 1954 nr 10, 48, 54, 87, 116, 124, 189, 216, 226, 238, 257, 273, 299, 307, 318, 354, 359, 403, 429, 448; plenary meeting protocols in vol. 1–4, A 1 A, Kanslibyrån, sᴜᴋ, Ra and vol. 1, A 1, Hemliga arkivet, sᴜᴋ, Ra; central dossiers and cards and control dossiers and cards for the following individuals: B1, B10, B13, B29, B34, B41, B45, B50, B55, B74.

12  See, for example, central dossier of B45.

13  The consequences a postponed expulsion decision had on an individual's life will be examined more closely in chapter 7.

A few exceptions have been found, however. Some Baltic refugees did in fact lose their refugee status as a consequence of crimes committed, and were expelled to the Soviet Union or Finland. The felonies for which they were convicted all involved espionage or other unlawful contacts with Soviet authorities – in other words offences considered to be damaging to the national security of the Swedish state.

The first such example concerns a 42 year-old Estonian, imprisoned in 1949 for being a Soviet spy. He had been watched by the security police for some time, and was discovered exchanging bags and files of documents with representatives of the Soviet legation in Sweden at various places, such as by a remote lake in a rural suburb north of the Swedish capital. The files had contained, among other things, information about refugees residing in Stockholm. Data on some other Swedish matters had also been collected and transferred. When his prison sentence expired, his expulsion decision was carried out through his referral to the Soviet Union.[14]

A similar situation occurred in 1954 in relation to a 26 year-old Estonian man. Due to his unlawful spying activities, he had been sentenced to eight months imprisonment followed by expulsion. The espionage he had conducted, however, appears to have been less significant in terms of both quantity and quality than that perpetrated by his older compatriot. It also seems to have been less ideologically motivated. Over the course of a month, he had collected information about Baltic refugees in Sweden and provided them to the Soviet Embassy in Stockholm. In exchange for this he had received money. During interrogations, as well as in his pleas to the authorities, he claimed that he had not realised that this behaviour was illegal or harmful, and that he regretted it deeply. He blamed a prolonged overconsumption of alcohol that had impaired his power of judgement, and explained to them that his mind had been manipulated by a group of Italians whom he had started to socialise with since moving to Gothenburg a couple of years earlier. They had made him believe that the quality of life was superior in the Soviet Union, and it was this factor alone that had prompted him to contact the Soviet representation in Sweden

---

14	Various documents dated between 1 and 15 March 1949, del XI, vol. 80, P 40 R, 1920 års dossiésystem, UD, Ra; and control register card of B106.

in the first place with view to a possible return. As a consequence, he had been 'duped' into the information transfer affair. Now, however, he claimed that he realised in full that he had made a terrible mistake and was very repentant. His mother also pleaded to the authorities and pointed out that her son had behaved very well until this unfortunate episode of his life, and that he had been much appreciated by his employers.[15]

The veracity of the explanations offered by the Estonian and his mother regarding the affair is obviously difficult to determine. However, according to his own testimony and that of his family, he had as a teenager fought against the Soviet Union as a war-time volunteer in the Finnish army. As such, he now feared what would happen to him if he returned to the Soviet Union. Several close family members had already been deported to Siberia, he argued. Thus, he begged to be allowed to stay in Sweden, or at least be granted the chance to apply for an entrance permit to Finland should the authorities still want him out of the country.

When the implementation of the expulsion was to be settled by the Commission, however, it was decided that he was to be referred to the Soviet Union. The Estonian and his mother appealed the decision, both to the Commission and to the government, but without success. He was refused any pardon. The Ministry for Foreign Affairs was granted the task of arranging with the Soviet Embassy for all his necessary documents, such as passport and entry permit.

Shortly before his scheduled departure the Soviet Embassy had formally agreed that he was to be transported on the ship *Beloostrov*. On the day of his departure, however, he was barred from boarding the ship. This compelled the Ministry for Foreign Affairs to contact the Embassy again and try to persuade them to accept the Estonian, who still appeared very unwilling to leave. A few days later suspicions arose that this individual might have been involved in more espionage activities than the authorities had previously been aware. A prisoner with whom the Estonian had shared a cell, claimed to have found a drawing of a planned power station under the suspect's bed. Thus, the security police now wanted to

15   Various documents within the control dossier of B41. See also 'Protokoll', 26
     april 1954, and 'Protokoll', 4 september 1954, vol. 1, A 2, Första Byrån, SUK, Ra.

arrange more interrogations with the Estonian, and, therefore, the Prosecution Authority of Gothenburg requested that the expulsion should be postponed temporarily.[16]

No more information on the fate of this Estonian has been found. However, he is not mentioned again in the protocols of the First Bureau (which have been examined up until the year 1960), nor in any other source material consulted.[17] This suggests that the implementation of his expulsion decision was not postponed, but in fact carried out.

An examination of other sources could probably reveal more.[18] However, for this study, which focuses on the Swedish authorities' principles and ideas, what actually happened to this man in the end is of comparatively less significance. The most important result reached here, is the fact that the Commission, the government *and* the Ministry for Foreign Affairs refused his appeals and took several measures to remove him from the country through sending him to the Soviet Union. Together with the example of the above-mentioned 42 year-old, it illuminates the types of crimes and circumstances that led the authorities to seek to expel Baltic refugees to the Soviet Union. They were without exception associated with certain types of espionage activities. This was even if it was 'only' restricted to one month's duration; pertained to other refugees rather than, for example, Swedish military secrets; and was supposedly influenced by drunkenness. An individual's previous status as a political refugee – even one based on military activities against the Soviet Union – was eroded when it transpired that he or she had unlawfully passed information to the Soviet Union. The individual's motives seem to have mattered less. As Soviet collaborators, these individuals were regarded as a threat to Swedish national security who had forfeited their right to asylum. (It is also possible, of course, that the authorities reckoned that such individuals would not be too unfavourably treated within the Soviet Union. Sending

---

16   Various documents within the control dossier of B41; 'Protokoll', 26 april 1954, and 'Protokoll', 4 september 1954, vol. 1, A 2, Första Byrån, SUK, Ra.

17   Vol. 1–3, A 2, Första Byrån, SUK, Ra.

18   Apart from the archives of the Migration Board (*Migrationsverket*) in the city of Norrköping, which probably includes his central dossier, archives of the police, the Country Administrative Board of Gothenburg or other legal records, as well as population census registers, might elicit more information.

them back was thus not regarded as inhumane.) The study so far suggests that proven espionage, no matter how substantial, was the only crime that actually led to the fully implemented expulsion of Balts to the Soviet Union.

Few rules come without an exception, however. In this particular case, it comes in the form of a young, troublesome Estonian-Swede, who arrived from Finland in 1946. He had never attended school, but learned to read a little as a child thanks to his mother and through the Bible to which he, as a deeply religious man, often referred during his numerous encounters with the Swedish authorities. In one of the reports on him the County Administrative Board of Östergötland states somewhat scornfully: 'he believes that he knows more about Life and Truth than most people'.[19] Parts of his childhood he had spent as a member of a travelling Roma circus company. He feared the Soviets intensely, and claimed to have fled to Sweden to avoid being forced to return to the Soviet Union. However, he refused to reveal his true identity to the Swedish authorities, claiming that this was a matter between only him and God. During the twenty years he resided in Sweden before he died, he moved in and out of prison numerous times following sentencing for, among other things, theft, robbery (sometimes armed), drunkenness in public and domestic burglary. During interrogations he sometimes portrayed himself as a modern-day Robin Hood and that, as a poor man, he was granted the right by God to take from the rich.[20]

The authorities did not agree. The question of his expulsion was raised already in 1947. In 1948, after yet another court sentence, an expulsion decision was indeed issued. He was not to be sent to the Soviet Union, however, but to Finland, from whence he had arrived. Thus, in early September 1948, he was transferred to the Finnish city of Turku and placed in temporary custody by the Finnish police.[21]

Within a short space of time, however, the Finnish authorities urged Sweden to take him back. They said he was 'terribly nervous and fearful' that he was to be transferred to the Soviet

19    *... han anser sig veta mer on tingen än de flesta andra.* Excerpt from § 32, 'Protokoll' 18 april 1946, Länsstyrelsen i Östergötlands Län, central dossier of B45.
20    Central dossier of B45.
21    Various documents from 1947 and 1948 within central dossier of B45.

Union. They also claimed that the situation could rapidly change and that, as a consequence, the Finnish authorities could find themselves compelled to expatriate him to the Soviet Union.[22] Additionally, they swiftly concluded that they had no evidence that this Estonian-Swede had in fact ever resided in Finland and as such, did not acknowledge any responsibility for accepting him. Thus, in October 1948 he was deported back to Sweden.[23]

A threat of expulsion hung over this Estonian-Swede until 1961. However, no more attempts were made to implement it. Despite his stubborn refusal to reveal his true identity, he was protected from referral to the Soviet authorities and could thus remain in Sweden. This solution was reached with great reluctance on the part of the Swedish authorities, however. The man in question represented one of many individuals the authorities deemed as 'unwanted' in Sweden, but found themselves having no legal possibility to remove from the country due to their status as political refugees and because of the international situation at the time.[24]

### 5.1.2 Suspected Balts: to Remove or not Remove?

The security police had the Soviet legation under constant surveillance during the Cold War, and increasingly so when the international tensions intensified. They regularly shadowed Soviet representatives and kept a close track on those with whom they came into contact. This is how they discovered that an Estonian accountant had visited members of the Soviet legation staying at a hotel in Gothenburg in March 1950. As a result, both the Commission and the security policy began to monitor his doings. Over the course of a year it was observed that he had had two encounters with Soviet representatives, and one dinner with a 'well-known Swedish communist' (a student secretary of the Swedish-Russian organisation in Gothenburg) during which he was seen to take notes. Additionally, a search in the man's private home had revealed his

22   *... ett förändrat läge kunde mycket snabbt komma till stånd, i vilket de finska myndigheterna kunde se sig nödsakade att överlämna [XX] till Sovjetunionen.* 'PM' by Rättsavdelningen, Utrikesdepartementet, 16 september 1948, central dossier of B45.
23   Central dossier of B45.
24   *Ibid.*

ownership of 21 wrist watches and three cameras, one of which had been found within an envelope which the security police, based on the handwriting and the design, interpreted as being sent by the Soviet Embassy in Stockholm. A few names and addresses of Balts had also been discovered in his calendar. However, no evidence of illegal activities was revealed.[25]

When examining their former espionage cases in search for any links to the accountant, the security police had noticed that the previously mentioned 42 year-old, who had been expelled to the Soviet Union as a result of his spying activities, had once – in 1949 – been seen walking somewhat 'confusedly' on a street in Gothenburg, as if he was looking for something. This location, the police now observed, was in fact the street on which the accountant lived. Thus, this information was also added to the dossier. So too was the fact that the man had refused to take on permanent work positions, since he wanted to be 'free in order to come and go as he wanted'. The police considered this, plus the evidence of the cameras and multiple timepieces in his possession as indications that he might be receiving money from another source – including, perhaps, the Soviet legation.[26]

The accountant was also subject to several interrogations. He was, among other things, questioned in careful detail about the trips to foreign countries he had made during the past few years. His untraditional lifestyle intrigued the police. He was also asked about his encounters with the Soviet legation and the 'well-known communist'. Obviously incensed, he defended himself vigorously, and claimed to be a democrat. He complained that he was subject to state persecution in Sweden similar to that of a dictatorship like the Soviet Union. He also maintained, however, that he was a socialist and based his ideas concerning the ideal human society on several philosophers and scientists. The intellectual debate in Sweden was limited, he argued, and the information available on the Soviet Union was deeply biased. In order to get more information on the situation in the Soviet Union, and to discuss politics, he had approached other like-minded Swedish citizens as well as Soviet representatives. He pointed out that, as a free citizen in a

25   Central and control dossier of B74.
26   *Ibid.* Quote from note dated 4 June 1952 in central dossier.

democratic country, this should not be rendered illegal. He had, however, no thoughts on returning to the Soviet Union, since he believed his personal safety would be endangered there.[27]

Thus, in 1951, the security police had come no further in their attempt to prove that he was engaged in unlawful activities. However, they remained exceedingly suspicious of him and regarded him as an unwanted element in Swedish society. Therefore, they suggested to the National Alien Commission that he be considered for political expulsion according to paragraph 37 of the Aliens Act. The Commission referred the matter to the Aliens Appeals Board which consented to the idea. It stated that there were 'reasonable grounds' to assume that he had 'forwarded information to Russian representatives… that should not be brought to a foreign power's attention'. They also declared that the facts he had alleged regarding the danger he faced should he be returned to the Soviet Union '[did] not deserve consideration'.[28] Thus they concurred with both the police and the Commission, which believed that he was not to be considered a political refugee, since he, by his own admission, had fled from the war rather than from the Russians, and had not at that time expressed an opinion on either of the occupying regimes. When referred to the government, however, the idea of his expulsion on political grounds was refused. It would go against the principles pursued regarding Balts over the past few years, they argued. Additionally, there was no evidence of him pursuing anything unlawful. So, in the end, this Estonian accountant was allowed to remain in Sweden. No expulsion decision was ever issued.[29]

This was the only time during the research period that paragraph 37 of the Aliens Act was discussed with reference to a Balt, according to available sources at least. A similar conclusion is reached when examining expulsions according to other reasons stated in the legislation. One such was, as mentioned above, 'sexually immoral behaviour'. Within the group of Balts chosen for closer examination, one individual has been found whose manners, at least according to the law, could have made him eligible for expulsion on that ground. This regarded a young Estonian, who

27   Central and control dossier of B74.
28   'Stockholm den 29 september 1951', vol. 10, B 1, Utlänningsnämnden, Ra.
29   Central dossier and control dossier of B74. See also protocols dated 8 and 21
      March, 3 July, 16 and 23 October in vol. 3, A 1 A, Kanslibyrån, SUK, Ra.

had arrived in Sweden on his own as a 19 year-old, after serving within the Finnish army. He had been badly injured during the war and spent his first months in Sweden in hospital. His injuries left him partially disabled for the rest of his life, and limited the type of employment he could take on.

Between 1947 and 1949, when he was in his early twenties, he was repeatedly interrogated by the police due to incidents of indecent exposure. Twice, he was also sentenced in court to financial punishments. In 1949 he agreed to being hospitalised in a mental care unit to receive treatment for his sexually deviant behaviour. He claimed he was depressed over his situation, his injuries and the absence of female company in his life. The treatment seems to have helped him, because there are no more reports of him offending again after this date. Indeed, subsequent reports reveal that he got married and became a much appreciated worker at various Swedish companies.

Due to his behaviour, the young Estonian's personal dossier contains a substantial amount of information. However, there is no evidence of expulsion or deportation ever being discussed as a possibility at any time. His status as a political refugee never seems to have been questioned.[30]

Thus, when it came to Balts, serious criminal offences which challenged internal or external security constituted the only reason removals were brought to the fore (with the exception of the Estonian-Swedish recidivist). Additionally, whereas both the security police and the immigration authorities were prepared to expel to the Soviet Union a self-proclaimed socialist Estonian whose supposed espionage activities had not been proven, the government was reluctant to do so and put a stop to these plans.

## 5.2 The Management of 'Unwanted' Ingrians

Apart from the decision in September 1945 to gradually deport 542 Ingrians (a resolution which was later withdrawn), the sources reveal only a handful of deportation decision regarding Ingrians during the entire research period. Thus, as with the treatment of

30   Central dossier of B50.

the Balts, the evidence suggests that this tool was not that often used.[31]

Two examples demonstrate what sort of circumstances could lead to this decision. A troublesome youngster, convicted for assault and battery, was regarded as an 'unwanted' foreigner by the authorities, and was deported back to Finland in 1953 as a negative response to his application for a renewed residence permit. After this, he was refused entry a couple of times when he tried to return. By then, the National Alien Commission and the Ministry for Foreign Affairs believed that the risk of him being sent to the Soviet Union from Finland was slight, and they thus decided to wash their hands of him.[32]

The second case regards his sister who was deported the year before, in July 1952. She was 18 years old and had been granted a residence permit in 1951. The police in Gothenburg had been in contact with her friend (also Ingrian), with whom she had stayed for a while. The friend told the police that the young woman 'supports herself through temporary liaisons with men'. In other words, she accused her of being a prostitute, which, according to the Aliens Act could constitute grounds for expulsion. The woman also claimed that she believed the 18 year-old had a venereal disease.[33]

A cleaning lady in the house in which the female friend lived confirmed this picture. She claimed that it was obvious that the 18 year-old engaged in an 'improper lifestyle', and that she herself had refused her entry to the building many times. She also alleged that the 18 year-old had tried to make her friend join her in her profession. The accused young woman's former employer – an owner of a Tea Salon – was also invited to give her opinion. She stated that the girl had managed her work well, but that she had been of the impression that she was 'loose'.[34]

31  On the withdrawn deportation decision, see chapter four, part 4.3.1.
32  Nr 1455, 5 september 1953, vol. 1, A 2, 2:a byrån, SUK, Ra. He had also been refused entry once in 1952, see 20 maj 1952 vol. 3, A 1 A, Kanslibyrån, SUK, Ra. See also 'Helsingfors den 12 maj 1952', vol. 6, F 2 B, Hemliga arkivet, SUK; and control register card of I24.
33  'Protokoll', 4 juli 1952, vol. 8, A 2, Kontrollbyrån, SUK, Ra; and various documents, including police protocols ('förhörsprotokoll') in control dossier of I23.
34  'P.M.', 26 juni 1952 in control dossier of I23.

After being reported as possibly infectious, the woman in question was forced to visit medical services. A member of staff there
told the police that she had refused treatment. The police took her
into custody and added to her report that she was 'untruthful and
untrustworthy'.[35] Thus, the matter of her deportation was brought
up within the National Alien Commission. It made some efforts to
find out from the Ministry for Foreign Affairs what dangers were
faced by Ingrians in Finland. The Ministry reported back that any
such risks were now negligible. Soon after that, the 18 year-old was
deported to Finland. Aspects of social control – and particularly
sexual morality and *skötsamhet* (conscientiousness) – thus clearly
determined the case.[36]

Similar aspects nearly caused the deportation of another Ingrian.
This concerned a man who suffered from alcoholism. Although he
managed his work to the satisfaction of his employer, the question
of his possible deportation was discussed by the Commission in
1950 after the courts had sentenced him repeatedly for drunkenness in public. A deportation was never issued, however. Still,
though, reports testify how medical staff threatened him with
expulsion to the Soviet Union if he did not stop drinking. In the
end, he was hospitalised for medical care to tackle his addiction.[37]

These three Ingrians clearly challenged societal norms, and
the treatment of them ought to be understood as a consequence
of this. In particular, the management of the young prostitute
and the alcoholic evidently correspond to general state attitudes
towards such sexual and moral health issues during this period, as
was discussed in chapter one.[38] What is noteworthy, however, is
the fact that in the two implemented deportation decisions, some
effort was made to evaluate whether or not the individuals were
likely to be deported to the Soviet Union should they be sent back
to Finland. When the risk was described as 'low', the deportations
were carried out. This demonstrates that the individuals' status
as political refugees was taken into some consideration before the
decisions were issued.

35  *Ibid.*
36  Central register card, control register card and control dossier of I23. See also
    'Helsingfors den 12 maj 1952', vol. 6, F 2 B, Hemliga arkivet, SUK.
37  Central dossier of I10.
38  Chapter one, part 1.1.5.

### 5.2.1 *The Orderly Ingrians*

Only three expulsion decisions have been found regarding Ingrians during the entire research period. They were all issued by the County Administrative Board as a consequence of crimes committed. Misdemeanours such as theft, violence and burglary led to this outcome. All such determinations, however, came with the 'home country proviso' that prohibited their being sent back to the Soviet Union, or to a country from which they risked being so sent. Consequently, they were never implemented.[39] Thus, just as with the Balts, the protection of the Ingrians' refugee status seems to have taken precedence over the wish to remove criminals from Swedish society.

Apart from these individuals, the Ingrians in Sweden seem to have being law-abiding. No other expulsion decisions have been found. It is possible to conclude, therefore, that no Ingrians seem to have been sentenced in court for unlawful intelligence activities of any kind during the period in question.

## 5.3 The Management of 'Unwanted' Russians

During the first years of the research period, the sources reveal only a few deportation decisions of Russians with previous residence permits. They all seem to have pertained to individuals transferred to West European countries. A young Russian woman, for example, was deported after overstaying her temporary tourist visa which had brought her to a Swedish holiday home.[40] A 60 year-old Russian was sent back to his former home country of Spain (despite his Swedish family connections), when the influential Swedish company at which he had worked for over a year declared that they were no longer pleased with his services.[41] Neither of these individuals were characterised as political refugees, nor were they sent to what might be called grey zone countries. Thus, a sudden *increase* of the deportation tool from 1949 onwards regarding Russians constitutes a change of attitudes which contrasts with the results of the examinations of both Balts and Ingrians.

39  Control register cards of I2, I24, and central dossier and central register card of I41.
40  Central register card of R82.
41  Central dossier and central register card of R78.

Initially, social control aspects pertaining to contemporaneous ideals of *'skötsamhet'* (conscientiousness) seemed to have been a factor. One example of this is constituted by the treatment of a 28 year-old Russian photographer. He had arrived in 1947 from the Russian zone of Germany where he, according to own account, had assisted refugees to flee. In 1949, the Commission was receiving reports from the police that this man was behaving in a way the authorities found inappropriate. His landlord had reported that he was negligent and slovenly, and his employer claimed that he had taken days off work without permission. Thus, they were both dissatisfied with him. Additionally, he was in conflict with his wife and, when interrogated by the police, she claimed that he had lied about his past and had actually lived in France during those years he had claimed to have resided in East Germany. As a result, the National Alien Commission decided to reject his application for a renewed residence permit in August 1949 and issued a deportation decision. It was not, however, to be implemented through his referral to the Soviet Union.[42]

The subsequent years were difficult for the photographer. He divorced the woman who had reported him to the police, entered into another relationship and had a child. Even so, the National Alien Commission continued to pressurise him into leaving Sweden through the acquisition of an entry permit to some other country. He was granted only short prolongations to his resident permit and had to apply for renewals ones repeatedly. He became suicidal, as he makes clear in his own pleading letters to the Commission, and was eventually admitted to a mental hospital in the beginning of the 1950s. He tried but failed to receive an entry permit to France. This treatment of him by the Commission continued until 1958, when the deportation decision was withdrawn by the Ministry for the Interior. By then, he was married to another Swedish woman.[43]

In 1949 similar treatment was accorded to an elderly illiterate Russian farmer and his wife. They had arrived from Finland the previous year with several adult children who were Finnish citizens but who wanted to accompany their parents. After spending some

42　Central dossier of R5. See also 'Protokoll', 23 augusti 1949, vol. 1, A 1, Hemliga arkivet, SUK, Ra.
43　Central dossier of R5.

time at a textile factory in the town of Norrköping, they were all provided forestry work and residence in a small, poorly equipped crofter's holding in a provincial area of Sweden. The farmer averred that they were severely underpaid, and that the inadequately-sized cottage they had been provided was not suitable for winter lodging. He also claimed that, when they had complained about this, their employers had informed them that they would pay 'what they wanted to refugees'.[44]

Reports about the family were soon received. In a letter to the Commission from a company that distributed radios it was reported that the man had not been able to pay for a receiver he had bought on credit. A police examination was begun which came to the conclusion that the family's inability to support itself was due to 'reluctance to work' and refusal to take on assigned work duties. It was claimed that some of the adult family members were not working and had received poor relief. Thus, the police officer stated, it was likely that the family would be an on-going burden to the local poor relief and suggested deportation according to paragraph 25 of the Aliens Act, which provided the authorities with the right to remove foreigners from the country if they believed them incapable of supporting themselves in an 'honest manner'.[45]

The Aliens Appeals Board agreed, and recommended deportation for the entire family, regardless of the fact that the parents were Soviet citizens. The National Alien Commission, however, decided to deport only the adult children, who were Finnish citizens, but to allow the elderly parents a continued right to stay.[46]

In the 1950s, similar cases can be traced where purely social factors, such as financial troubles or an inability to adjust to current social norms (in other words aspects pertaining to *social control and morality* and *economics*), rather than illegality or political untrustworthiness, have clearly been the decisive factors for the

<hr>

44   Various documents from 1949 and 1950 within central dossier of R68. Quote from handwritten letter, 'Ärade Kung Gustaf Adolf', undated, though presumably written in January or February 1949.

45   Various documents from 1949 and 1950 within central dossier of R68. Quote from 'Till Konungens Befallningshavare i Värmlands län', dated 25 January 1949, and 'Till Länsstyrelsen i Värmlands län', dated 7 March 1949.

46   'Till Statens utlänningskommission', dated 4 April 1949, and 'Utdrag ur Protokoll, fört vid statens utlänningskommissions sammanträde den 12 april 1949' in central dossier of R68.

authorities' decisions. One example is a 45 year-old Russian who had lived in France since the 1920s and married a Swedish female artist in 1949 during a temporary visit in Sweden. He then applied for a residence permit in Sweden, and his wife pleaded for this too by providing his applications with a number of certificates from prominent members of the Swedish art elite, such as superintendents of various art museums and the director of the Royal College of Fine Arts. Their letters certified the excellence of the female artist, and her need of having her husband by her side. Mention was also made of her mental wellbeing, suggesting that she was 'one of those sensible Swedish artist geniuses, whose state of mind oscillates between health and illness'. Therefore, one of the art experts stated, it was 'utterly important' that her husband should be allowed to stay with his by now pregnant wife, 'at least until the child is born'.[47]

However, the Commission required a special examination of the man's character, as well as that of his wife. This was pursued by the police through an interrogation with him and several others. Investigations of his past in France were also pursued. The findings resulted in a memorandum, from which it is clear that neither the police nor the National Alien Commission were impressed with what had been found.

First and foremost, the man lived off his wife. She supported him financially and he had not taken on the work that he had been allocated. The couple's explanation was that, as he had supported her while they lived in France, it was now time for his wife to return the favour. Additionally, as a fairly successful artist, she could afford it, and her husband was currently working on his plans to start a business in Sweden. The police, however, apparently did not approve of this solution. As a result, they questioned the woman's mother who, according to the constabulary, had 'admitted' that she had sometimes helped out.

Secondly, it had been noticed that the man called himself a 'prince' due to his alleged relations with a century-old Russian principality. The police questioned him about this. He submitted a written exposition to the Commission which seemingly revealed

---

47 Various documents from 1949 and 1950 within central dossier of R35. Quote from 'Till Kungl. Socialstyrelsen, Utlänningsbyrån', dated 8 October 1949.

his extensive family history. After pursuing some additional lines of enquiry, however, the police concluded that his 'social status was false'. They claimed that there had never been any princes carrying his name in Russia.[48]

Thirdly, a careful examination revealed that in France during the 1930s he had been found guilty of paying bills with invalid cheques. During the German occupation, he had also been sent to prison for 'illegally' leaving his allocated residence area. Much attention was devoted to these crimes, as well as to allegations of an attempted expulsion order during the 1940s. This prompted the couple to hire a lawyer to challenge the veracity of the allegations – particularly the incident which had taken place during the German occupation of France.[49]

Fourthly, the police had acquired character statements from individuals in France. They were, as they said, 'not complimentary for him'. He had a 'very well-known brother', a French reservist. This man's two lawyers – who personally did not know the artist's husband – had been contacted. They had certified that the alleged prince's brother 'was angry with him', that he was 'dishonest', and that 'no important business' should be entrusted to him. They called him a dreamer, and regarded his business plans as 'jokes'. They also revealed that his personal life had been messy, and that 'his mother is the only person who has supported him'. The police also noticed, somewhat mockingly, that neither his mother nor his brother 'prided themselves with a title'.[50]

Other aspects of the man's life on which the police commented was the fact that, prior to coming to Sweden, the couple had lived together in France 'as if they had been married'; that the female artist had been admitted to a mental hospital twice in her life; that her husband had apparently also undergone psychiatric treatment at least once in France; that his old mother was 'fleeting' and 'very disliked' at the home for the elderly where she lived in France; and that a loud argument had once been heard from the couple's apartment in Stockholm (a matter referred to by a landlady who had

48   'P.M.' (undated, however from spring 1950), and 'Förhörsanteckningar', dated 3
       April 1950, in central dossier of R35.
49   *Ibid*; and 'Stockholm den 7 juli 1950', in central dossier of R35.
50   'P.M.' (undated, however from spring 1950), and 'Förhörsanteckningar', dated 3
       April 1950, in central dossier of R35.

been asked to provide the police with a statement about her tenants). Within citation marks, the report's compilers also remarked that the woman's alleged pregnancy had apparently led to a '"miscarriage"', as if they found this piece of information unconvincing. In the final part of their report, the police concluded that the man was 'an adventurer' and 'a swindler' who had 'abused the trust he had gained within the Swedish colony in Menton' in France, but that this had been 'hushed-up' due to the colony's sympathies for the Swedish female artist (although the report makes no mention of the source of this allegation).[51]

Consequently, the police advised against a prolonged residence permit for the artist's Russian husband. And the National Alien Commission seems to have concurred. It sent the case to the Aliens Appeals Board for a statement. The Board, in its turn, recommended immediate deportation according to paragraph 28 of the Aliens Act.[52]

The decision was postponed, however. Instead, more investigations were pursued. The couple continued to seek legal assistance in order to convince the Swedish authorities that the allegations dating from Nazi-occupied France were untrue. They also submitted certificates from various individuals in France affirming the man's good nature. It is striking, in fact, that nearly all the hundreds of documents that have been saved in this individual's personal dossier pertain exclusively to his character. Copious details about his personal life are provided. And numerous individuals – civilians and officials – provided statements about the man. In order to be granted a residence permit as a non-political refugee, he had to be an individual regarded as 'wanted' in Sweden, regardless of the fact that he was married to a Swede. His unusual personality clearly did not match the authorities' ideas of a proper lifestyle at this time.[53]

After pursuing more lines of enquiry the Aliens Appeals Board was asked to give a statement once again. Almost a year had now passed since the man had submitted his application. The Board saw no reason to change its mind. However, at this time, France no longer permitted him re-entry. No other country would have

51   *Ibid.*
52   'Till Statens utlänningskommission', dated 4 May 1950, in central dossier of R35.
53   Various documents from 1950 and 1951 in central dossier of R35.

him either. As a result, in late 1950, approximately fifteen months after he had submitted his application, he was granted a short, three month residence permit. As shall be demonstrated further in chapter seven, however, this plus his continuous, short permits were attached with various limitations – a state of affairs that would continue for several years.[54]

The handling of this case was obviously determined by aspects of *social control and morality*. Nowhere was the artist's husband defined as a threat to the state or the society, either directly or indirectly. Even so, he was clearly defined as an 'unwanted' foreigner. The reason seems to have been purely a matter of the bureaucrats' personal opinions of the man's personality and lifestyle. The fact that he lived off his wife, was regarded as professionally untrustworthy, called himself a prince and was possibly – like his wife – mentally unstable seem to have constituted more important triggers for the authorities' endeavours to remove him from the country than his possible fraudulent activities in France twenty years earlier. The case was thus characterised by a significant portion of arbitrariness. However, it was the fact that he was not a political refugee in Sweden (given that he had arrived from France) that opened up possibilities for the authorities to try to remove him in the first place.

Other deportation decisions were made out of unambiguous concerns for national security. At least three individuals were deported due to having been in touch with the Soviet legation in Sweden in 1950–51. One of them, a 50 year-old Russian sailor with anti-communist views, had resided in Sweden as a refugee since 1938. In the 1940s, he had been fined repeatedly for 'offensive behaviour'. Once he had apparently spat in the face of an Orthodox priest who he felt was guilty of spreading communist propaganda. On a couple of other occasions he had appeared drunk in public. A local police officer, who encountered him as he signed on and off various ships, described him as 'an original character' but 'decent and harmless', who 'would not hurt a human being' – even if he enjoyed a drink or two. This officer's character assessment that formed part of the sailor's application for a prolongation of his residence permit concluded that, politically speaking, he was

54  Central dossier and central register card of R35.

'surely harmless'. He was, in short, an 'old white Russian' who was 'constantly angry with the communists'.[55]

However, about one year earlier, the Swedish security services claimed that they had noticed this supposed anti-communist visit the Soviet Embassy no fewer than fourteen times in the space of just a few months. Additionally, an anonymous messenger had reported the sailor to the security services and claimed that he was engaged in unlawful spying activities. The informant claimed he was receiving alcohol and cigarettes for his services. Another person to express an opinion was an Estonian colleague at the factory where the man currently worked. He felt sure that the seaman had provided the Soviet Embassy in Stockholm with his address on the grounds that it had begun sending him post shortly after the accused had started working at the factory. It was also noted that in 1944, while he and other Russians were phone-tapped, the sailor had been discovered to have contacted the Embassy on one occasion.[56]

These accusations and suspicions prompted the security services to open an investigation and keep the sailor under surveillance. No evidence of espionage activities was forthcoming. Nor, however, was the exact nature of his repeated visits to the Embassy. And, one year later, the security services reported that the man was still in contact with the Russian consulate, and that he had changed employment several times during the past year. They therefore insisted that the sailor should be removed from the country due to 'security reasons'.[57]

Thus, after hearing the Aliens Appeals Board, which recommended deportation and stated that the man should no longer be regarded as a political refugee, the Commission decided that the man had to leave.[58] Where he would go, however, was another question. The Commission decided that it could not be *confirmed* that he should no longer be regarded as a political refugee and,

---

55   Central dossier and control dossier of R52. Citation from
     'Förhörsanteckningar', 12 februari 1951 in central dossier.
56   Control dossier of R52.
57   Various documents from 1950 and 1951 in control dossier of R52.
58   He was issued a so called 'departure decision' (*utresebeslut*), which can be
     regarded as a milder form of deportation, even if the consequences were the
     same.

as such, it was not possible to send him to the Soviet Union. As a consequence the removal decision was never implemented. Be that as it may, the decade-long suspicions that hung over him were to have wide-reaching ramifications, as will be demonstrated further in chapter seven.[59]

Maintaining contact with Soviet authorities got at least two other individuals in trouble in 1951. One was a 40 year-old Russian who had fought in the Finnish army during the Second World War. In 1951, the Swedish security services had collated evidence suggesting that he had had 'dealings with Soviet authorities' in Sweden. No illegal activities could be proven, but he was suspected of having reported the names and contact details of other Soviet citizens in Sweden in exchange for money. As a result, the authorities regarded him as untrustworthy and unwanted, and a deportation order was issued. However, due to his past in the Finnish army, the Commission considered his life to be in jeopardy should he be expelled to the Soviet Union. His case was therefore brought to the government for assessment. As a result, his deportation decision was not implemented, but repeatedly postponed. In 1956, however, he left Sweden voluntarily for the Soviet Union.[60]

Similar suspicions were raised against another Russian who had been granted status as a political refugee. His contacts with the Soviet Embassy in the early 1950s were interpreted by the security services as a sign of potential espionage. They believed he was informing on other refugees in exchange for money. Corroborating evidence was lacking, but his contacts with the Embassy made him 'apparently an unwanted foreigner' in the eyes of the security services, and they urged the National Alien Commission to remove him from the country. The Commission obliged and in April 1951 a formal deportation decision was issued. Nine months later, however, a home land country proviso was added to the decision. In contrast to the individuals mentioned above, however, this decision was indeed implemented. Under pressure from the authorities, the man signed onto a Swedish ship in 1952. When the vessel returned in 1953 and 1954, he was refused entry, despite the

59   Central dossier and control dossier of R52.
60   Control dossier of R56.

fact that he could not gain an entry permit to any other country. He was forced to continue to live at sea.[61]

At least one deportation decision which was implemented through referral to the Soviet Union has, however, been found, this dating from 1952. Again, this stemmed from suspicions of 'dealings with Soviet authorities'. However, in contrast to the above-mentioned individuals who all denied having committed anything unlawful or, in particular, being communists, this man seems to have voluntarily admitted that he had changed his political views during the eight years he had stayed in Sweden. He had grown positive towards the Soviet regime, and had started to spread his views among other Soviet refugees, trying to persuade them to return to the Soviet Union. He denied having committed any unlawful intelligence services for the Soviet authorities. According to the files in his personal dossiers, no such evidence was found either. However, due to the suspicions and the man's apparent enhanced appreciation for his homeland, both he and his wife were deported to the Soviet Union in the summer of 1952.[62]

This indicates that, from 1949 onwards, perceived communist world views and, especially, suspicions of unlawful contact with the Soviet Union resulted in several deportation decisions. As such, they clearly stem from concerns for national security, regarding both external and internal aspects. This correlates with previous research on the security services' perceptions of threats linked to Swedish citizens who were suspected of similar things, and the resulting surveillance and other measures directed against such individuals. It also coincides in terms of timing, as previous research has demonstrated that these fears and consequential state surveillance activities increased dramatically from 1948 onwards.[63]

### 5.3.1 Expelling Russians – Political Refugees or not?

All the expulsion decisions issued to Russian refugees between 1945 and 1954 were delivered as a consequence of a committed crime. As was the case with the Balts, they were issued both as a result of non-

---

61 Control dossier of R59.
62 Central dossier and control dossier of R65.
63 See chapter 1, part 1.1.2.

political crimes, such as theft and burglary, and crimes considered to threaten national security, such as espionage or other unlawful intelligence activities beneficial to the Soviet authorities.[64]

In contrast to the management of the Balts and the Ingrians, however, a small number of the Russians who had this decision delivered as a consequence of a non-political crime were indeed also removed from the country. Rather than being attached with a homeland clause, they were carried out. Contrary to the management of the other categories, thus, some of the Russians were regarded by the authorities as having forfeited their right to asylum as a consequence of their deeds.

In one such case, the authorities made a substantial effort to persuade the Soviet authorities to grant a 40 year-old Ukrainian priest a visa to re-enter the Soviet Union. He had been granted political asylum in December 1944, after fleeing from Lisma and informing the authorities of the political persecutions (including deportation to Siberia) that he had endured in the Soviet Union. However, during his years in Sweden he had committed theft and burglary on several occasions and had been sentenced to multiple prison sentences plus expulsion. Additionally, he had been found guilty of 'fornication', after having a sexual relation with a young man aged between 18 and 21 years of old.[65]

The implementation of his first expulsion sentence had been postponed. In 1948, however, the National Alien Commission decided that his right to asylum had been forfeited and he was sent to Finland. The Finnish authorities refused to accept him. Instead, they sent him to the Soviet zone of Germany, from where it was envisaged he would travel on to Ukraine. However, the authorities in the Soviet zone of Germany did not recognise his identity documents, and in early 1949 they sent him back to Sweden. The fact that he came back from there made the Swedish security police fear that he might have been sent on a spying mission. Their suspicions increased when, later that year, he was found guilty of breaking into a hotel room in which some members of the armed forces were staying. They believed he might have been searching for military

64   No examples of expulsion according to § 37 of the Aliens Act (such as in the
      case with above-mentioned Estonian accountant) have been found in this
      group.
65   Control dossier of R66.

documents. The police confiscated a 52-page handwritten document that was in his possession at the time of his arrest. It revealed no intelligence activities, however. Russian interpreters considered the 'confused notes' to have been written by a 'mentally disordered person' on such matters as religion, dreams and history. Given that no further indications of espionage activities were identified, the National Alien Commission saw no other solution but to issue continuous postponements to his deportation.[66]

He quickly returned to crime and, in 1952, was sentenced to two years in a high security prison. When his sentence had expired, the question of the implementation of the decision was discussed again. The Commission and the Aliens Appeals Board were now both of the opinion that the man should be transferred to the Soviet Union since he constituted a 'serious danger to public order and security'. With regard to his status as a political refugee, they now felt that if what he said was true – that he was a priest, had been imprisoned both in Siberia and in a German prisoner of war camp and had fled to Sweden from Lisma – then the man should probably still be considered a political refugee. As such, he was likely to be punished upon a return to the Soviet Union. However, the Commission now argued that his 'punishment or persecution' would 'probably not be of such a fierce kind'. This reasoning was based on the fact that the Russian authorities had had a chance to 'get to him' already during his short period of stay in the Russian zone of Germany in 1948. Since he had come back, however, the Commission believed that he was not going to be punished all that seriously. Even so, due to the special circumstances of this case, the decision was referred to the government.[67]

The government, in its turn, concurred. It was decided that this nefarious priest was to be referred to the Soviet Union. Thus, the Ministry for Foreign Affairs was granted the task of persuading the Soviet authorities to issue all necessary documents to enable his return. The Soviet authorities were not that keen to have him back, however, and the process was repeatedly delayed. Several years later

66   Various documents from 1948 and 1949 within control dossier of R66. Quotes
     from 'Promemoria onsdagen den 21 juli 1954' including attachment.
67   Various documents from 1952–55 within control dossier of R66. Quotes
     from a letter to the government from the National Alien Commission, 'Till
     Konungen', 8 september 1955.

– in 1960 – they declared that the cleric was not considered a Soviet citizen and could thus not be granted an entry permit to the Soviet Union. The Ukrainian thus remained in Sweden, and continued to yo-yo in and out of prison throughout his life. Equally vacillating were the National Alien Commission's postponed expulsion decisions.[68]

This example reveals that political refugee status could indeed be withdrawn or simply cease to matter even when the crimes committed were not deemed to impinge on matters of internal or external security. As a serial offender and portrayed as a threat to 'public order and security' (or, in other words, *societal security*), a Soviet refugee could lose his previous protection from the Soviet authorities. However, the fact that this particular individual was of Russian-Ukrainian ethnicity rather than, for example, a Balt, seems to have weakened his asylum rights even further. It should be noted that, in comparison, none of the over 40 Balts served with expulsion orders due to non-political crimes was referred to the Soviet Union, as has been demonstrated in the discussion above.[69]

A similar treatment was dealt out to a Russian man who had been sentenced to prison twice for fraud and embezzlement. Already after the first sentence, in 1948, an expulsion decision was issued. A homeland proviso was initially attached to the decision, rendering its completion impossible. However, after the security police reported that he had been noticed having 'diligent relations' with Soviet representatives in Sweden, the assessment of his case changed. The security police believed there were reasons to suspect that he might be a Russian agent. In any case, they argued, his relations with the Soviet representatives meant that he ought not to be regarded as a political refugee, regardless of what he had previously stated about his personal background. He had been seen when visiting Russian and Polish ships in Swedish harbours, and according to one of the security police's reporters, the man was believed to collect and transfer information about Baltic refugees to the Soviet authorities.

The individual in question denied all allegations of unlawful activities and complained that he felt 'politically persecuted' in

68   Control dossier and control register cards of R66.
69   One was, however, transferred to Finland in 1948, as mentioned in part 5.1.1.

Sweden: 'No matter what he did or whom he met, accusations of illegal activities were produced about him' was his lament recorded by the police report in their interview notes.[70]

In 1951, the assessment of the case was referred to the government. The Commission, supported by the Aliens Appeals Board, argued vigorously for an implementation of the decision through referral to the Soviet Union. However, since they had 'not previously referred individuals against their own will to the Soviet Union' (a statement that would require some qualifying, as the results so far have demonstrated), the Commission believed the government ought to decide.

The government, in its turn, found the evidence for the security services' claims of the man's suspicious contacts with Soviet representatives compelling. In 1952, his deportation decision was implemented and he was put on the infamous *Beloostrov*, for a sea transportation to the Soviet Union.[71]

Thus, an individual with a deportation decision, whose crimes had *not* been national security-related, could indeed be referred to the Soviet Union despite a previous postponement if he was seen liaising with Soviet representatives in Sweden. Any such contact increased the perception that an individual posed a threat to national security. Not surprisingly, therefore, individuals who *were* in fact found guilty of some espionage activities were not protected from expulsion to the Soviet Union either.

However, even in such situations implementation was not always possible. Such was the case with a man who was sentenced to prison for espionage already in 1944. He had arrived in Sweden as early as 1914 in his capacity as marine attaché for Tsarist Russia. After the revolution, he had remained in Sweden. The security police had kept him under surveillance for decades. Suspicions that he might be a spy dated back to the First World War. In 1944, illegal information activities were proven in court and he was sentenced to prison. Upon his release in 1947 he was to be sent to the Soviet Union. However the authorities there refused to recognise him as a Soviet citizen and withheld an entry visa. Again, the Commission was forced to grant him continued postponements. Nonetheless,

70   'P.M.' dated 5 October 1951, quote from p. 19, in control dossier of R60.
71   Control dossier of R60.

the security police held him under constant surveillance and he was subject to other measures.[72]

From the preceding examples a conclusion can be drawn, namely that the authorities appeared to have been keener to remove political refugee status from known Russian criminals than from transgressors who happened to be Ingrians or Balts. This, plus a readiness to send them to the Soviet Union, applied even if the crimes committed were not of a political nature. As such, the protection of Russians' refugee status appears to have been weaker throughout the whole research period than that for the other two groups.

That said, however, there were also non-political offenders who the authorities did *not* try to remove. Examples of expulsion decisions with 'home country proviso' (*hemlandsklausul*) have been found too (even if some such clauses were only issued after discussion).[73] Some cases also suggest that the Aliens Appeals Board was somewhat keener to withdraw the protection from offending political refugees than was the Commission. This includes the case of a Russian felon who had been sentenced to prison and subsequent expulsion in 1948. In 1950 and again in 1952 the Board was of the opinion that the decision ought to be implemented and the individual expelled to the Soviet Union. The Commission, however, granted a postponement. Even when the Swedish security police again contacted the Commission in 1954 to inform them that he had had been seen visiting Soviet ships and urged that they remove him from the country due to the 'suspicion of political untrustworthiness', he remained protected. As a Lisma escapee, he had been mentioned in a Soviet expatriation demand, which according to the logic regarding political asylum that had been developed in Sweden at this time made his status as a political refugee inviolate. Even so, the Commission pressurised him to find another country to which to move. This was easier said than done, however. Thus, the postponements continued.[74]

<hr>

72  Central and control dossier of R81. See also chapter seven.
73  Central and control dossiers of R10 and R31.
74  Control dossier of R21.

## 5.4 Conclusion

The examination has revealed that, in general, Soviet refugees with residence permits were protected from referral to the Soviet Union even when their behaviour in Sweden led to them being regarded as 'unwanted'. Deportation and, in particular, expulsion decisions were indeed made, signalling clearly to the individual that his presence in Sweden was unwelcome, but if he was considered a political refugee the implementation of the decision was most often postponed or, in cases where it was possible, implemented through referral to another country. The only circumstances that certainly prompted the removal of an individual were where there was evidence of unlawful intelligence activities – in other words crimes that had challenged *external* and/or *internal security*. This was the case even with those individuals whose espionage activities had been directed at other refugees rather than towards the Swedish state. In instances where espionage had not been proven or only suspected the results reveal that the government was less keen on expelling individuals to the Soviet Union than were the security police and the immigration authorities (specifically the Aliens Appeals Board).

The findings also demonstrate that Balts, Ingrians and Russians were treated differently. Whereas Balts' political refugee status seems to have been thoroughly protected (apart from when unlawful intelligence activities had been proven), Russians were comparatively more likely to lose this status when committing crimes, irrespective of whether these offences related to national security or not. Under such circumstances the government's attitude does not seem to have hindered any such processes. This means that removal decisions to Finland and the Soviet Union were implemented for reasons which would not have been the case had they been Balts. However, the difficulties of carrying out such decisions was compounded by the Soviet Union's unwillingness to receive these offenders.

As with the results in chapter four, these findings suggest that Russians' refugee rights were less acknowledged than were the Balts'. Again, there is reason to assume that this had to do with *ethnic prejudice*. Russians with suspected communist sympathies seem to have been particularly regarded as more untrustworthy and 'unwanted' than their Baltic counterparts. It is also possible that the old habit of rendering Russians as collectively less worthy of refugee status than the Balts influenced this behaviour. However, in contrast to the management of new arrivals, in which the differences levelled out in 1948, these discrepancies characterised policies during the entire research period. In fact, they are most clearly apparent in the early 1950s when international Cold War tensions were at their height.

This timing is itself revealing. The fact that all the removal decisions involving concerns for external and internal security took place after 1948 suggests that these processes were a result of the increasing fears of Soviet and communist infiltration that – as previous research has illuminated – prompted the Swedish security services to increase its surveillance over its domestic citizens too. So whereas international Cold War developments influenced the strengthening of asylum rights for new arrivals after 1948, they also made Soviet refugees more vulnerable to suspicions of untrustworthiness. In some cases, this lead to the forfeiture of those asylum rights as the Swedish security services became more vigilant of the Soviet refugee population. The Russians, however, were regarded as a more likely threat than were the Balts.

Aspects of *social control and morality,* including demands of '*skötsamhet*' (conscientiousness), and, to some extent, *economics*, also strongly influenced the authorities' interpretation as to who was regarded as 'wanted' and 'unwanted'. It is perhaps unsurprising that removal decisions were issued to criminals. But this was also the case with those individuals believed to challenge societal norms in other ways. Alcoholics, prostitutes, individuals struggling to support themselves or persons whose personalities the authorities found objectionable for other reasons could be issued (or threatened with) such decisions too. However, the noticeable difference between issued removal decisions and implemented ones clearly demonstrate that such concerns were not in the end given priority over the ambition to protect political refugees' asylum rights. This, again, suggests an influence from *international juridical developments* which reinterpreted the relationship between the refugee and the state during this decade, strengthening the refugee's position as a holder of rights against the state. 'Unwanted' refugees' rights were thus protected, provided that they were not believed to have endangered Sweden's external or internal security. The authorities could make substantial efforts, however, to remove unwanted individuals who were not regarded as political refugees, such as the self-proclaimed Russian prince or the young Ingrian prostitute.

All the potential influencing factors outlined in chapter one thus seem to have had some bearing on the attitudes and the policies regarding those refugees deemed to be 'unwanted'. However, *external* and *internal security concerns* and *international juridical developments* emerge as the most significant in terms of the outcomes of the policies pursued.

# The Demanded

From 1944 onwards, the Soviet Union sought to force the return of dispersed Soviet citizens from Western territories. This was partly motivated by Moscow's desire of circumventing the establishment of anti-Soviet exile enclaves abroad. Aside from reaching the exiles through infiltrating their communities, strategies were also directed at Western regimes. Previous researchers have claimed, however, that the Soviet administration preferred exerting informal pressure on the latter rather than risking their prestige by issuing official demands that might not be reciprocated.[1]

When it came to Soviet citizens in Sweden, however, the Soviet authorities seem to have adopted a slightly bolder approach. Apart from the 2,700 Germans and Balts who were extradited during the winter of 1945–46, several others were requested too. It is true to say that most of the Soviet authorities' efforts to bring the 30,000 civilian Balts back to the Soviet Union from Swedish territory were exerted through informal pressure.[2] Nonetheless, during the following years, several hundred Soviet citizens were demanded for extradition. These demands challenged both moral values and aspects of national interest. Principles relating to refugee rights and

---

1    Berge 1992, pp. 11 and 39. See also Bethell 1974 and Tolstoy 1977. On Soviet exile communities, see, for example, *Anti-Communist minorities in the United States: political activism of ethnic refugees,* Ieva Zake (ed.), Palgrave Macmillan, New York 2009.

2    Ekholm 1995, and various documents, such as, for example, 'Telegram', 3 juni 1945, and 'Stockholm den 5 juni 1945', in vol. 77, P 40 R, 1920 års dossiésystem, UD, Ra.

rule of law were contested. So too were presumably concerns for Swedish national security, given Sweden's sensitive foreign policy relations with the Soviet Union.

Further complications arose from the clash of national and international regulations and principles. As Deland has pointed out, some of the individuals the Soviet Union wished to see extradited during the first post-war years were indeed guilty of war crimes, including civilian murder. As a member of the United Nations from December 1946, Sweden was mandated to track down and punish war criminals and traitors.[3] Thus, the Soviet Union could and did refer to the regulations of the UN when presenting some of its claims. At the same time, Swedish national legislation prohibited the extradition of foreigners to countries where they risked becoming subject to political persecution. As such, the extradition of Soviet citizens to the Soviet Union, regardless of the various circumstances, undoubtedly constituted a challenge to this set of principles as Cold War tensions and the international refugee regime developed in tandem. Thus, taken together, the 1945 Aliens Act, the 1913 Extradition Law and the newly established international UN conventions regarding genocide and war crimes entailed several inconsistencies. During the following years, therefore, Swedish jurists were tasked with trying to make Swedish legislation more coherent – both internally and in comparison with international regulations.[4]

Regarding the pursued practices, historian Mats Deland has confirmed that no Baltic war criminals were extradited to the Soviet Union after the forced return of the 2,700 Germans and Balts in 1945–46.[5] In this chapter, the Ministry for Foreign Affairs' management of Soviet extradition demands is studied in more detail. This also includes demands that regarded many other individuals than accused war criminals, such as, for example, newly arrived refugees. How did Sweden react to these? What factors determined the pursued policies? As in previous chapters, special attention is accorded

---

3    Particularly *UN resolution of the 13 February 1946, regarding Extradition and Punishment of War Criminals.* http://daccess-dds-ny.un.org/doc/RESOLUTION/ GEN/NR0/032/54/IMG/NR003254.pdf?OpenElement (accessed 15 September 2013); and Deland 2010, pp. 358–368.

4    Deland 2010, pp. 350–357.

5    Deland 2010.

the six potential influential aspects that were identified in chapter one, namely *external* and *internal security; economics; ethnicity; social control and morality;* and *international juridical developments.*


## 6.1 From Compliance and Pragmatism to Principles and Perseverance, 1945–47

In 1945, Sweden had specific extradition treaties with a number of countries. The Soviet Union was not one of them. The 1913 Extradition Law, moreover, mainly regulated cases regarding civilians accused of crimes of a non-political kind. Thus, the affair involving the 2,700 German and Baltic military personnel was managed as an administrative measure outside of juridical frameworks.[6]

This was not the case with other extradition demands. Already in 1941, for example, the Soviet Union had demanded the extradition of five Soviet mariners who had deserted from their military service. The Soviet authorities claimed that they had murdered their officers, and thus referred their petition to the regulations within the Swedish 1913 Extradition Law. The case dragged on throughout the Second World War and attracted much media attention. In 1946, it was finally settled in a Swedish court which deemed the evidence of the supposed crime to be insufficient. Thus, the mariners were granted continued permission to remain in Sweden. This verdict displeased the Soviet authorities and they made a point of raising it in discussions over the course of the next few years.[7]

Around the same time, extradition requests were made for three young women. The first was a promising 15 year-old motherless Estonian pianist who had fled to Sweden with relatives in 1944 and been placed in the care of a Swedish family. In early 1945, the Soviet legation notified the Swedish authorities that her father was alive and wanted her to return home. The girl, however, refused to leave. She made it clear that she wanted to live neither in the Soviet Union nor with her father.

6   Deland 2010, p. 351; Ekholm 1995.
7   There are  hundreds of documents describing this affair within del I, vol. 204, R
    70, 1920 års dossiésystem, UD, Ra; See also an undated memorandum ('P.M.')
    in vol. 2, E 4, Hemliga arkivet, SUK, Ra.

The extradition demand that followed prompted many discussions both within the National Alien Commission and the Ministry for Foreign Affairs, and was covered by several newspapers. On the one hand, the young pianist was not of age to decide over her own destiny. This spoke in favour of her father's claims to decide on behalf of a minor. On the other hand, she was a Balt who was resistant to the idea of returning to the Soviet Union. As such, she was looked upon as a political refugee. This did not prevent the Soviet Embassy being given her address, leading to a personal visit which deeply troubled the young woman. A removal decision was never issued, however. This caused indignation among Soviet officials who continued to make appeals about her for some years to come.[8] She was also mentioned in Swedish-Soviet discussions over the missing Swedish diplomat Raoul Wallenberg, as an inexplicit blackmailing factor.[9]

A second extradition demand concerning young women who had recently arrived concerned two Polish Jewish teenage sisters, descending from an area now under Soviet control. They had been saved from a German concentration camp and received medical treatment in Sweden. They were demanded for extradition with reference to them being underage. The girls, however, did not wish to live in the Soviet Union. Instead, they wanted to go to Palestine where they had a surviving aunt. The Ministry for Foreign Affairs forwarded the case to the National Alien Commission, which in its turn asked the Aliens Appeals Board for a statement. The Board believed the sisters ought to be granted continued permission to stay in Sweden because they had both 'behaved very well' since arriving. Thus, the Commission granted them continued residence permits and the Ministry for Foreign Affairs rejected the extradition requests. In contrast to the above-mentioned cases, however, this does not seem to have caused any further diplomatic disputes.[10]

8    Central and control dossier of B69; Protocols dated 21 August 1945, 30 August 1945, 11 September 1945, 18 September 1945, 22 September 1945, in vol. 1, A 1 A, Kanslibyrån, SUK, Ra; 'P.M.', 19 november 1946, vol. 68, P 40 I, 1920 års dossiésystem, UD, Ra; and various documents from 1945 and 1946 in within vol. 77 and 78, P 40 R, 1920 års dossiésystem, UD, Ra.

9    As a consequence, the case has also been described in later research and literature. See SOU 2003:18; Susan Lisa Carruthers, *Cold War captives: imprisonment, escape and brainwashing*, University of California Press 2009, pp. 65–66.

10   Central dossiers of B54 and B118. Quote from 'Stockholm den 5 september 1946, Till Statens utlänningskommission', vol. 5, B 1, Utlänningsnämnden, Ra.

In February 1946, an extradition demand regarding a larger group of Soviet citizens was presented. This concerned 89 mainly Russian individuals who, the Soviet legation claimed, had 'unlawfully escaped' from the refugee camp Lisma. The legation demanded that they should be 'handed over to the Soviet Union with or against their own will'.[11]

The Ministry for Foreign Affairs once again asked the National Alien Commission for a statement. For the first time, the Commission now expressed the opinion that refugees' activities while in Sweden – such as a flight from Lisma – could possibly constitute a criterion for political asylum.[12] It also emphasised that only a few of the individuals mentioned were likely to be deportable. A short examination was submitted, in which the Commission had attempted to identify all the alleged individuals. Some had left the country, others were reported as missing, but most of them had been granted residence permits.[13]

It is somewhat surprising perhaps that no more details on the continued assessment of this case have been found, either within the National Alien Commission's archive or the Ministry for Foreign Affairs. If the latter responded to the demand after receiving the required information from the Commission, it has left no archival trace. However, no evidence that any of the individuals were extradited has been revealed either. A spot test of a random sample of the 89 individuals mentioned in these documents shows no indication that the authorities intended to bend to the demands of the Soviet administration this time. On the contrary, the individuals' confirmed status as political refugees and their granted residence permits seem to have been accorded precedence.[14]

Another case reveals that the Ministry for Foreign Affairs was in no rush to deal with fresh extradition demands following the extradition of the military Balts and Germans in 1945–46. In June 1946 the Soviet Embassy delivered a formal note demanding the extradition of 33 out of a total of 40 military Balts who had been exempted

11   'P.M.', 19 februari 1946, vol. 3, E 4, Hemliga arkivet, SUK, Ra and vol. 68, P 40
     I, 1920 års dossiésystem, UD, Ra.
12   This document has also been mentioned in chapter four, part 4.4.2.
13   'Till Kungl. Utrikesdepartementet', 26 mars 1946, vol. 3, E 4, Hemliga arkivet,
     SUK, Ra.
14   Central and control dossiers of R6, R8, R12, R21, R34, R50, R55, R71, R87.

from the forced repatriation on health grounds. The Ministry, however, appears to have made little effort to respond. In November,
therefore, a representative from the Soviet Embassy, Basarov, made
a personal visit to the Ministry for Foreign Affairs and demanded
a reply. He claimed that he had interpreted the exclusion of these
40 remaining individuals as temporary until they had recovered.

Contrary to the assessment of the demand presented the previous year, this case was now handled not by the Minister for Foreign
Affairs, but by one of his officials, Sverker Åström. It was not
referred to any other authority for a statement either. In an oral
meeting, alluded to in a secret memorandum later that day, Åström
simply explained that the Swedish government's decision to allow
the exempted individuals to stay in Sweden was permanent. None
of the remaining military Balts would be extradited. Basarov was
evidently displeased with this response. He asked incredulously
how it was that some of these supposedly unwell men had now
sailed from Sweden to the United Kingdom in 'open boats with
all the risks such a journey entails?' Åström answered that 'even
very ill individuals can choose to do so' adding pointedly: 'There
is a difference between travelling of one's own free will and being
expelled'. Basarov countered by demanding to be informed of
the names and personal details of all Balts who had left Sweden.
Åström politely declined this request.[15]

This management of a Soviet extradition demand thus differs
substantially from previous such examples. That it was refused was
perhaps not that surprising. The recent expatriation of the 146
Balts had been experienced as a traumatic experience for elements
of Swedish society and several of the politicians responsible. This
time, however, the Swedish response was conspicuously more
intransigent and non-cooperative towards the Soviet authorities.
The fact that it was assessed single-handedly at a lower level of
the bureaucracy and by an individual official also strengthens the
assumption that a change in approach had occurred.

New demands soon followed, however. Shortly after Basarov's
visit, the Soviet legation despatched two separate formal notes to
the Swedish Ministry for Foreign Affairs insisting that it identify
and extradite all Russian former prisoners of war who had fled to

15   'P.M.', strängt förtroligt, 1 november 1946, vol. 3, E 4, Hemliga arkivet, SUK, Ra.

Sweden in contravention of the Finnish-Soviet armistice agreement. They similarly demanded back a total of 260 named Russians and Ingrians who had enlisted in the Finnish army.[16]

This time the assessment was not delayed. On the contrary, the Ministry for Foreign Affairs immediately asked the National Alien Commission for an examination. The Commission tackled this assignment by using a Finnish list of 1,357 Soviet citizens who were to be extradited to the Soviet Union from Finland but had gone missing after the signing of the armistice agreement. With assistance from this document, the Commission now tried to map out which of these had reached Sweden. Nearly 500 such individuals were identified. This included 169 of the 260 individuals who had been named in the second appeal, and details of their whereabouts were submitted to the Ministry for Foreign Affairs.[17]

The examination does not seem to have led to a response to the two Soviet missives, however. Instead, in February 1947, Sweden received another formal extradition request regarding Soviet 'war criminals'. This time, however, it came from Finland. A total of 327 individuals who had fled to Sweden from Finland to avoid repatriation were listed. Another investigation was initiated as a result, and about half of the individuals mentioned were confirmed as residing in Sweden. A month later, the Finnish minister Gripenberg visited the Ministry for Foreign Affairs to remind it of the matter and to request an answer. According to the memorandum that was written as a result of the visit, Gripenberg 'hinted that Finland feared the consequences that would follow if the Russian Control Commission received the impression that the matter was not pursued with appropriate intensity by the Finnish authorities.'[18]

16 Formal note 17 December 1946 from the Soviet Union's legation to the
Ministry for Foreign Affairs, vol. 68, P 40 I, 1920 års dossiésystem, UD, Ra; 'Till
Kungl. Utrikesdepartementet' (including three attachments), 8 januari 1947,
vol. 68, P 40 I, 1920 års dossiésystem, UD, Ra; various documents within vol. 9,
F 4, Hemliga arkivet, SUK, Ra.

17 'Till Kungl. Utrikesdepartementet' (including three attachments), 8 januari
1947, vol. 68, P 40 I, 1920 års dossiésystem, UD, Ra; various documents within
vol. 9, F 4, Hemliga arkivet, SUK, Ra.

18 *Han antydde att man i Finland fruktade konsekvenserna, därest kontrollkommis-
sionen finge uppfattningen att saken icke drevs med tillbörlig kraft av finska vederbö-
rande.* 'P.M.', 11 mars 1947, vol. 68, P 40 I, 1920 års dossiésystem, UD, Ra. See
also 'Stockholm 10 februari 1947', vol. 68, P 40 I, 1920 års dossiésystem, UD, Ra.

Even so, a formal reply to the Soviet notes was still not issued. The Finnish demand was met with a belated response, but only in the form of numerical information regarding how many of the requested individuals resided in Sweden.[19] This does not seem to have come as a surprise to the Finnish authorities, however. That becomes clear in a written conversation between the Finnish Major V. Teutari, who was responsible for tracing missing Soviet citizens, and R. Hansen, the head of the Control Bureau at the National Alien Commission. Hansen had previously assisted the Major in his search, and provided him with information on which of the demanded escapees resided in Sweden, and which had left the country or died. This information had then been forwarded to the Soviet Union by Teutari. The letters between them were generally characterised by a friendly, personal tone. An illustration of this is a penned note to Hansen by Teutari: 'Even though one knows the result, it sometimes happens that one has to do a thing or two.'[20] Thus, there seems to have been an informal agreement between Hansen and Teutari, and perhaps also between Sweden and Finland, that no Soviet citizens would be extradited to Finland, but that the formal diplomatic process needed to go on as usual in order to maintain appearances to the Soviet authorities.

Basarov at the Soviet Embassy seems to have been excluded from this arrangement. Almost a year later, in December 1947, he made a repeat visit to the Ministry for Foreign Affairs insisting on a reply. The official who took the call promised to investigate the case, but informed him that 'the answer will probably be negative'.[21]

This is the last documented conversation regarding these cases that has been found. No formal reply seems to have been produced. No evidence has been discovered either that would suggest that any of the Soviet citizens listed on the documents provided by the

19    'Till beskickningen i Moskva' (including three attachments), 8 april 1947, vol. 68, P 40 I, 1920 års dossiésystem, UD, Ra.

20    *Trots, att man vet resultatet, händer det ju ibland, att man är tvungen att göra ett och annat.* Handwritten letter from V. Teutari to R. Hansen at the National Alien Commission dated 31 January 1947, nr 249, vol. 9, F 4, Hemliga arkivet, SUK, Ra. See also various other letters between Teutari and Hansen in the same volume, for example those dated 4 July 1946, 14 January 1947, and 6 March 1948 with attachments.

21    'P.M.', (letter from the Ministry for Foreign Affairs to the Swedish representative in Moscow), 15 december 1947, vol. 68, P 40 I, 1920 års dossiésystem, UD, Ra.

Finnish or Soviet (or, indeed, Swedish) authorities were extradited from Sweden. Soviet traitors and war criminals (as defined by the Soviet Union) who were found in Finland, however, were quickly brought over to the Soviet border. Just such a case is outlined in another handwritten letter that Teutari sent to Hansen. This concerned an Ingrian man who had fought against the Soviet Union within the Finnish army and fled to Sweden in 1944. In January 1946 he had secretly returned to Finland to search for his wife who had been left behind. Discovered by the Finnish police he was subsequently transferred to the Soviet Union. Similar things occurred to others who attempted to return, even when moving under false identities.[22]

Thus far, Sweden seems to have protected the rights of political refugees from Soviet extradition demands after January 1946 – regardless of what kind of accusations were directed against them. It even seems to have maintained a rather unflustered attitude, including evading formal responses to several of the demands. It did, however, go to considerable lengths to identify the demanded individuals and passed some details on to the Finnish and Soviet authorities.

The Swedish authorities were not quite so unflappable when it came to its handling of a Soviet NKVD-agent (previously mentioned in chapter five). He had deserted his ship and applied for asylum in September 1946. The matter was immediately attended to by the Soviet legation in Stockholm, which demanded him for extradition. This was evidently a sensitive issue for the Soviets, which put severe pressure on the Ministry for Foreign Affairs. Soviet representatives stressed that Swedish-Soviet relations could be damaged if the man was not returned.[23]

The Swedish government, including the Minister for Foreign Affairs Östen Undén, paid heed to these admonitions. Undén argued that the man should be refused entry and sent back to the Soviet Union forthwith. A similar conclusion was reached by the National Alien Commission. Both it and the security police

22  Handwritten letter from V. Teutari to R. Hansen at the National Alien
    Commission dated 23 February 1946, nr 249, vol. 9, F 4, Hemliga arkivet, SUK, Ra.
23  He was also mentioned during discussions about the missing Swedish diplomat
    Raoul Wallenberg. As a result, his case has also been discussed in later research.
    See SOU 2003:18 pp. 440–446; Krister Wahlbäck, *Wallenberg-ärendet 1945–47*,
    unpublished memorandum, Utrikesdepartementet, Stockholm 2001; Krister
    Wahlbäck, *Undén, Granovskij och Wallenberg-ärendet 1946*, unpublished memo-
    randum, Utrikesdepartementet, Stockholm 2001.

had pursued an extensive investigation of the agent, leading to a report of over 100 pages covering his background and work for the NKVD. There was a risk, they stated, that the man still worked for the Soviet security services. And, even if he did not, a residence permit would deeply annoy the Soviet administration. In other words, the Commission and the security police practically argued that granting him permission to stay would endanger external *or* internal security, although which of the two was at greatest risk was uncertain.[24]

The man was held in custody and interrogated several times while the investigation was pursued. One day he was visited by Soviet officials, although having stated clearly to the Swedish authorities that he did not wish to have any contact with representatives of his home country. The officials threatened him in various ways, among other things by mentioning his mother. This event annoyed Undén. Not out of concern for the man's well-being, though, but because the incident in itself strengthened his claims to be a political refugee. According to the diplomat Sven Grafström, however, Undén continued to resist bestowing him this status.[25]

Due to the political implications of the case, the Commission referred the NKVD agent's residence permit application to the government. It transpired that Undén's harsh attitude was not shared by all its members. Although they did not want to keep him in Sweden, they were not prepared to deny him the mantle of political refugee. On 8 November 1946, therefore, the government decided to issue him a deportation decision including a prohibition to return to Sweden. However, it was attached with a home country proviso. Arrangements had by then been made with Denmark, which was prepared to receive him. Shortly therefore he left the country. The Soviet legation complained vociferously when it realised what had occurred.[26]

---

24  Various documents within control dossier of R26; See also 'Protokoll', 14 november 1946, vol. 1, A 1, Hemliga arkivet, SUK, Ra; and a themed volume about him in the secret archive, vol. 7, F 4, Hemliga arkivet, SUK, Ra.

25  'Stockholm den 17 oktober 1946' (letter from state police to the National Alien Commission) in control dossier of R26. See also SOU 2003:18 *Ett diplomatiskt misslyckande*, p. 441.

26  See documents dated 21 November 1946, 22 November 1946, 23 November 1946, 25 November 1946, 26 November 1946, 27 November 1946, 4 December 1946, in vol. 68, P 40 I, 1920 års dossiésystem, UD, Ra; 'Telegram' (from am-

Nonetheless, Sweden had reached a compromise that benefited its interests. It took national security concerns into consideration by refusing residence, while at the same time paying heed to humanitarian concerns by making sure his rights to protection as a political refugee were safeguarded. It achieved this by deporting the problem to Denmark. If the Minister for Foreign Affairs had had it his way, however, the man would have been refused entry and sent back to the Soviet Union – in effect an extradition.

In 1947, a similar affair unfolded. A Russian locksmith fled from the Soviet ship he was currently working on while it harboured in Gothenburg. He told the police he had been locked up on board due to an argument he had had with the ship's 'political commissioner'. Through a friend he had found out that the commissioner planned to send him to Moscow where he faced punishment. He had thereafter managed to jump ship and now applied for asylum.[27]

In Gothenburg he was placed in custody for several months. During his imprisonment the Swedish authorities allowed Soviet representatives to visit him three times. During these visits he was threatened, intimidated and told that, if he did not come voluntarily now, he would be punished upon his enforced arrival. The locksmith remained steadfast, however. In a last-ditch attempt the Soviet officials accused him of theft and used this as a reason for him to be handed over in accordance with the Swedish 1913 Extradition Law relating to criminal offences.[28]

What happened next is unclear. A few months later, however, the man enlisted on a Swedish ship and left the country. This contradicted his initially stated intention of returning to work in his original profession. He was at a later date refused both an entry permit and a Swedish Aliens' Passport. The Ministry for Foreign Affairs and the National Alien Commission made it abundantly clear that the locksmith was to be forbidden from returning. They wrote to several Swedish legations with specific instructions that

---

bassador Sohlman in Moscow to the Ministry for Foreign Affairs), 25 februari 1946, del VIII, vol. 78, P 40 R, 1920 års dossiésystem, UD, Ra; and various documents in control dossier of R26.

27 Various documents in central and control dossier of R74, such as, for example, 'Rapport', 24 juli 1947, in control dossier.

28 Various documents dated 1947 in central and control dossier of R74.

they were not to grant him an entry permit should they be so asked.[29]

The archival documents make it impossible to determine whether or not the decision to board was freely made or at the behest of the Swedish authorities. However, despite having evident reasons for political asylum, and no other 'uncomplimentary information' in his dossiers, the Swedish administration made sure he would not be allowed to return once his ship had departed. It had also allowed Soviet representatives access to him. This is suggestive of the fact that it was Swedish officials who persuaded him to leave the country. In doing so they sought to 'export the problem', just as they had done with the NKVD agent. That being the case, the Soviet pressure also had an influence in this case. It challenged bilateral relations, including concerns of external security.

## 6.2 1948 Onwards – Refugee Rights Increasingly in Focus

During the years that followed more extradition demands were presented, both regarding newly arrived refugees and larger groups of long-term residents. At least one demand concerned individuals once again categorised by the Soviets as 'war criminals'. Occurring in February 1948, it related to 556 individuals who the Soviet authorities claimed were 'engaged in hostile propaganda against the Soviet Union and of carrying out every kind of subversive activity against the USSR on the territory of Sweden'. As such it insisted on their repatriation.[30]

The Ministry for Foreign Affairs asked the National Alien Commission for a thorough examination of the list, which was then pursued by the Control Bureau. It identified 395 of the alleged individuals and passed on their personal details to the Ministry. Most of them were Ingrians who had enlisted in the Finnish army. But there were also other Soviet citizens, including a considerable number of Balts. Some of these were already well known to the Swedish authorities since they were included in the security police's

29   Central and control dossier of R74.
30   'Telegram', 3 mars 1948, vol. 68, P 40 I, 1920 års dossiésystem, UD, Ra; and del II, vol. 204, R 70, 1920 års dossiésystem, UD, Ra.

examination of suspected Nazi perpetrators. As Deland has pointed out, some of them were quite rightly branded as war criminals. Keenly aware of Sweden's international commitments, the Soviet administration cited the UN resolution of the 13 February 1946 in support of its case.[31]

As on previous occasions, the Swedish Ministry for Foreign Affairs sought to prevaricate for as long as possible. Deland has emphasised that Sweden did indeed know that it would be forced to extradite some of these individuals (namely those Balts that stood accused of war crimes) if the Soviet Union furnished them with legal documentation as stipulated under the 1913 Extradition Law. A refusal to respond to such a claim could have presaged a diplomatic crisis. Therefore, Sweden moved to meet its responsibilities with delaying tactics that ranged from silence to evasive juridical statements, argues Deland. He also points out that certain questions cannot be answered without recourse to the Soviet sources. This includes why the Soviet Union failed to provide the correct legal documents or why it sought to include several individuals it must have known could not be extradited. The latter included Ingrians, a pair of refugee smugglers plus exiled politicians. They, it was claimed, were equally guilty of serious war crimes.[32]

Demands were also continuously presented regarding newly arrived refugees. All of them included accusations of criminality, thus falling within the remit of the Swedish 1913 Extradition Law. This, for example, was the case with nine mariners (mainly Balts) who in early 1948 had arrived to the island of Gotland on a Soviet ship. The Soviet Embassy accused them of theft. It insisted on the right to see them in person and demanded their extradition. This time, both requests received a response. However, in its replies, the Ministry for Foreign Affairs now referred to the National Alien Commission on the basis that the assessment of new arrivals was the Commission's responsibility. And when the Commission opted

---

31 'Telegram', 3 mars 1948, vol. 68, P 40 I, 1920 års dossiésystem, UD, Ra; 'Till Chefen för Rättsavdelningen', 30 juni 1948, nr 251, vol. 10, F 4, Hemliga arkivet, SUK, Ra. The list of individuals is also to be found in del II, vol. 204, R 70, 1920 års dossiésystem, UD, Ra. See also Deland 2010, pp. 359–368.

32 Deland 2010, pp. 359–368. See also various documents within nr 251, vol. 10, E 4, Hemliga arkivet, SUK, Ra.

to grant the mariners residence permit, the Ministry claimed there was nothing else it could do. The insistence on personal visits was denied on the grounds that the individuals involved did not wish for this to happen.[33]

This kind of reasoning was novel. Previously, the responsibility for asylum and, in particular, extradition matters had been acknowledged as a political matter. As such it came under the purview of the government as the highest authority. Although the Ministry for Foreign Affairs had previously asked the Commission for statements, it had never referred to it in this manner in its response to extradition demands from the Soviet legation. The Aliens Act continued to allow the government to have a final say in how asylum law should be interpreted on a case by case basis. Indeed, as has been demonstrated particularly in chapter four, it was diligently used during the first post-war years. Now, however, it was argued that legal and institutional practices left the government with no other option than to defer to the National Alien Commission. A similar rhetoric was utilised a few weeks later, when the Ministry refused to extradite a 19 year-old Estonian stewardess who had fled from the ship on which she was working while it rested in a Swedish harbour.[34]

The following year, in the summer of 1949, a similar approach was attempted. This time, however, the government had to be interventionist, since the new arrival was an escaped Russian military officer who landed at a small airport outside Stockholm in a plane belonging to the Soviet armed forces. As such, the case was more sensitive and, indeed, prestigious, to the Soviet authorities. It generated considerable media attention, and within hours of landing, the Soviet legation in Stockholm contacted the Ministry for Foreign Affairs and insisted on a meeting with the officer. They also asked when he could be sent back. The officer, however, claimed to be a political refugee and refused to see the Soviet authorities. He asserted that he had secretly been a lifelong opponent of the Soviet regime, in part due to the persecutions inflicted on members of his

33   'Telegram', 4 mars 1948, del IX, vol. 79, P 40 R, 1920 års dossiésystem, UD, Ra.
     See also documents dated 8 January 1948, 22 January 1948, 29 January 1948,
     and 4 February 1948, del VIII, vol. 78, P 40 R, 1920 års dossiésystem, UD, Ra.
34   See documents dated 19 February 1948, 23 February 1948, and 25 February
     1948, del VIII, vol. 78, P 40 R, 1920 års dossiésystem, UD, Ra.

family. He himself had now begun to be subject to the same sort of intimidation due to his marriage to a Jewish woman. Thus, he had decided to go into exile.[35]

The Ministry denied the Soviet legation permission to visit the officer, who was kept in custody while his asylum application was assessed. As a result, the Soviets attempted another strategy. With reference to the Swedish Extradition Law of 1913, the legation now accused the man of having raped a young girl before fleeing to Sweden. Various documents were provided to prove the case this time, and he was formally demanded for extradition.[36]

The Swedish authorities seem to have regarded these documents as unreliable. Possibly as a way of gaining time, the Ministry asked the Soviet legation to provide them with supplementary documentation. However, before the Soviet legation had managed to submit the required paperwork, the Swedish authorities settled his case. The juridical department of the Ministry for Foreign Affairs put together an examination of Soviet Criminal Law, and established that 25 years of penal servitude (imprisonment with hard labour) awaited an individual who escaped from the armed forces. The family members of such individuals were also likely to be punished if there were reasons to suspect that they had had prior knowledge of the escape and not reported these to the authorities. Based on this information, the National Alien Commission granted the pilot political refugee status and a residence permit. Additionally, it added a prohibition stating that the decision, as well as any information relating to it, was not to be communicated to anyone outside the Swedish authorities.[37]

Knowing that the Soviets were searching for him, however, the officer soon left for West Germany. Whether or not he was encouraged to do so by the Swedish authorities remains unknown. However, when the Soviet legation returned to the Ministry with

35   Documents dated 18 May 1949, 19 May 1949, 21 May 1949, 25 May 1949, 11
     June 1949, 20 June 1949 in nr 254, vol. 10, F 4, Hemliga arkivet, SUK, Ra.
36   Documents dated 18 May 1949, 19 May 1949, 20 May 1949, 21 May 1949, 23
     May 1949, 25 May 1949, 28 May 1949, 4 June 1949, 7 June 1949, 14 June 1949,
     18 June 1949, 21 June 1949, 22 June 1949, 9 July 1949, 10 July 1949, 11 July
     1949, 8 August 1949, 13 August 1949, 17 August 1949, in vol. 204 del II, R 70
     Er, 1920 års dossiésystem, UD, Ra
37   *Ibid.*

the required additional documents, allegedly constituting evidence of his committed crime, the man had already left the country. This prompted a wave of protests from the Soviet authorities, including the sending of an official complaint to the Ministry for Foreign Affairs.[38]

The treatment of this case differs substantially from the handling of the NKVD-agent who arrived under similar circumstances in 1946. He too was ultimately granted protection from being repatriated to the Soviet Union. However, he was not protected from harassment from the Soviet authorities in Sweden, and he was denied a residence permit and officially deported to Denmark. Additionally, several elements of the Swedish administration (including the Minister for Foreign Affairs) had recommended that he should be sent back to the Soviet Union. Thus, in comparison, the officer landing in Sweden in 1949 was granted significantly more protection, as the authorities now adopted a more coherent and far less cooperative stance towards the Soviet legation.

The same perseverance, in favour of refugee rights, characterises the management of Soviet extradition demands during the 1950s. Overall, they were reduced in numbers, but those that did occur were dealt with along the same lines as applied in the cases of the mariners, the stewardess and the pilot. Most concerned asylum seekers who had escaped from the ships on which they worked. The Soviet legation persisted in accusing such individuals of criminal activities. The Ministry for Foreign Affairs, in its turn, continued to assess all demands according to usual diplomatic standards, requesting formal evidence and so forth. Yet from then on it regularly referred both responsibility and assessment to other parts of the Swedish bureaucracy. The National Alien Commission was left in peace to grant the individuals residence permits and confirm their status as political refugees. The Ministry for Foreign

---

38    There are numerous of documents relating to this event, particularly within the archives of the Ministry for Foreign Affairs, but also within the National Alien Commission's archive. See, for example, documents dated 18 May 1949, 19 May 1949, 21 May 1949, 25 May 1949, 11 June 1949, 20 June 1949 in nr 254, vol. 10, F 4, Hemliga arkivet, SUK, Ra; and documents dated 18 May 1949, 19 May 1949, 20 May 1949, 21 May 1949, 23 May 1949, 25 May 1949, 28 May 1949, 4 June 1949, 7 June 1949, 14 June 1949, 18 June 1949, 21 June 1949, 22 June 1949, 9 July 1949, 10 July 1949, 11 July 1949, 8 August 1949, 13 August 1949, 17 August 1949, in vol. 204 del II, R 70 Er, 1920 års dossiésystem, UD, Ra.

Affairs then used the verdict of the Commission as grounds for rejected extradition demands. At times it buttressed its position by declaring accusations of criminality as either inadmissible or lacking sufficient corroborating evidence to warrant extradition. On those occasions when the Soviet authorities had supplied legal documentation, a court of justice was charged with handling the juridical aspects as set down in the 1913 Extradition Law. Thus, in its formal responses to the Soviet legation the Ministry for Foreign Affairs now generally referred to legal and institutional procedures outside of its direct control as the main reason why it was unable to comply with the demand.[39]

## 6.3 Conclusion

Overall, the examination in this chapter demonstrates that Swedish authorities went from an, at least partly, compliant and pragmatic attitude to Soviet extradition demands in 1945–46, to an unyielding one in the 1950s. The first and perhaps most important shift took place already during the spring of 1946 directly after the severely criticised extradition of the military Balts. From this date onwards, no evidence that any Soviet citizens were in fact extradited has been found. The Soviet Union's continued attempts to get hold of individuals it characterised as war criminals failed, as did its efforts to lay claims on 'normal' refugees. By lingering processes, and, sometimes, making somewhat opaque juridical

39  See, for example, an Estonian seaman who absconded from his ship during the spring of 1950. Example of documents relating to his case dated 15 April 1950, 30 May 1950, 26 July 1950, 1 September 1950, 1 November 1950, 3 November 1950, 4 November 1950, in del 11, R 70 Er, 1920 års dossiésystem, UD, Ra. Another example is constituted by a Russian escapee who disappeared from his vessel in February 1951. See documents dated 2 February 1951 and 7 February 1951 in del 11, R 70 Er, 1920 års dossiésystem, UD, Ra. A third example is constituted by three Lithuanian seamen escaping from their fishing trawler during the summer of 1951. See documents dated 18 July 1951, 20 July 1951, 21 July 1951, 25 July 1951, 26 July 1951, 27 July 1951, 27 July 1951, 28 July 1951, 30 July 1951, 2 August 1951, 3 August 1951, 4 August 1951, 24 August 1951, 24 September 1951, 26 September 1951, 6 October 1951, 20 October 1951, 20 October 1951, 16 November 1951, 29 November 1951 in R 70 Er, 1920 års dossiésystem, UD, Ra. See also various documents on 'Kustin' in vol. 47, R 58 Eö, 1920 års dossiésystem, UD, Ra.

statements, the government managed to circumvent potentially difficult situations. Thus, the room for manoeuvre that the Swedish government presumably sought to establish for itself in matters regarding refugees through its compliance with the extensive extradition demands of 1945 seems to have been perceived as successful. Subsequent extradition demands were not interpreted as being so closely entwined with external security concerns that no option other than compliance was available. In fact, Soviet dissatisfaction with Swedish attitudes seems to have been regarded as increasingly less disquieting. A statement from an official at the Ministry for Foreign Affairs illuminates this further. In a letter to the Swedish representative in Moscow in 1948, he wrote that Russian accusations regarding Sweden's administration of refugee matters was something 'we [should] not worry about'.[40] As a result, refugees' rights were protected. So too, however, were several serious war criminals of particularly Baltic origin.

Nevertheless, it was not until 1948 that this protection can be considered to have reached a stable state. The extradition of an escaped NKVD-agent was close at hand in 1946, and the Swedish administration provided the Soviet legation with names and other details of requested individuals plus, on occasions, permission to visit them until 1947. This semi-cooperative attitude towards the Soviet legation's wishes illuminates a desire to demonstrate an at least partly obliging approach, to the detriment of the personal safety of the refugees. Thus, with this policy the Swedish administration seems to have sought to simultaneously pay heed to both its foreign policy ambitions and humanitarian refugee concerns.

Apart from constituting a shift between concerns for foreign policy and considerations for refugee rights, however, the change that took place in 1948 also bears witness to a new approach to the division of responsibility within the state administration. A considerably more juridical and administrative interpretation of management procedures of extradition demands is evident both in and the way decisions were reached and motivated. This replaced a previously almost exclusively political framing, where the government had issued all decisions regarded as politically important.

---

40 *De ryska påståendena om vår behandling av dessa ärenden tycker jag vi bör taga lugnt.* 'Stockholm den 16 mars 1948', del II, vol. 204, R 70, 1920 års dossiésystem, UD, Ra.

From then on, however, it referred responsibility to the law-interpreting authorities and 'excused' itself to the Soviet legation with references to bureaucratic procedures over which it claimed to have no authority.

So far, therefore, this suggests an adaptation to *international juridical developments* in two ways. First of all, the increasing respect for refugees' right to protection tallies with the general transformation in thinking on refugees that took place within the Western international UN based refugee regime at this time. Secondly, the changing formal reasoning about the division of responsibility within the state administration regarding refugee and extradition matters correlates with this regime's reinterpretations of refugee rights as a matter more of *law* than *politics*. Refugee rights were increasingly protected when they were no longer interpreted as an issue for the political administration to assess from time to time according to its own current political ambitions, but as a matter for state bureaucracies to consider according to the applicable legislation. However, although this interpretation is a probably accurate description of the developments overall – in particular since it correlates with results in chapters 4 and 5 – it can also be questioned at a detailed level, especially when it comes to the assessment of the extradition demands. First and foremost, this regards the management of war criminals. Because, as Deland has pointed out, Sweden might very well have been placed in a very difficult situation had the Soviet Union kept insisting on the extradition of suspected Baltic Nazi perpetrators. A delivery of the correct juridical documents would have placed *law* on their side – both the Swedish 1913 Extradition Law and the international conventions Sweden was bound to through its UN membership of 1946. A *political* determination, however, seems to have made the Swedish authorities take measures to avoid this. Domestic and international opinion, and the fresh and traumatic memory of the extradition of the 146 military Balts, would probably have made it almost impossible for the government to pursue such an act. Perhaps that is also why the Soviet Union never decided to press the demands any further. Too much prestige was involved on both sides.

Thus, in terms of the potential influential factors identified in chapter one, the examination of Sweden's handling of the demanded – and their demander – has demonstrated the following. The importance of *external security concerns* clearly diminished after the extradition of the military Balts and Germans in 1945–46. They still compromised the procedures in 1946–47, but were not allowed to determine the outcomes. From 1948 onwards, their impact was further reduced. *Internal security concerns* could influence specific cases (such as the NKVD-agent), but did not play a prominent role. None of the results indicated a strong influence of *ethnicity* or *economic* aspects either. What seem to have mattered significantly, however, and particularly from 1948 onwards, are *international juridical developments*. Refugee rights were from now on fully protected from any challenges that Soviet extradition demands posed. It is also possible that this was in part a result of a consideration of public opinion.

This raises a number of supplementary questions, however. One of them regards how this transformation came about. What caused the reduction of external security concerns? How could extradition demands – regarded as so intimately connected with foreign policy relations and external security in 1945 – be interpreted as so disconnected from such concerns in 1948 that they no longer needed to be taken into serious consideration?

One possible answer has been hinted above. This regards the possibility that the extradition of the military Balts had demonstrated enough 'good intentions' towards the Soviet Union to create future room for manoeuvre. However, it is also conceivable that it had just as much to do with Sweden's changing foreign policy ambitions, as insinuated in previous chapters. When the bridge building ambitions were abandoned in 1948, due to a changed attitude towards the Soviet Union, the government no longer felt the need to adjust its domestic policies to Soviet demands to the same extent. Thus, there was more scope for other influences – like the international refugee rights developments – to have an impact.

It is also likely, however, that the increasing autonomy partly came about as a (perhaps unforeseen) benefit from the legal and administrative reinterpretation of refugee policies that these developments inspired. The Ministry for Foreign Affairs could now refer the responsibility of sensitive matters to the administrative structures, not just in practice but also within its communications with Soviet authorities. This reduced to some extent the political framing of refugee matters, even when it concerned such a sensitive and potentially confrontational issue as extradition demands.

# The Residence Permits

So far, this thesis has demonstrated that Swedish asylum policies stabilised in 1948, as practically all Soviet citizens fleeing from the Soviet Union or grey zone areas were from then on recognised as political refugees. Influences from *international juridical developments* were identified as an important reason behind this transformation, as were generally hardening attitudes towards the Soviet Union. However, it has also been revealed that whereas *external security concerns* as a direct influence on pursued policies lessened after 1948, the importance of *internal security factors* increased, leading to an escalation of individuals perceived as unwanted due to political untrustworthiness. Additionally, aspects of *ethnicity* were suggested as an explanation for the different treatment of Balts, Ingrians and Russians. How do these developments relate to the continuous treatment of those who were granted a right to stay?

Communications between the National Alien Commission and those in political power during this period suggest that the progressively more generous asylum policies did not reflect an increasingly more positive estimation of the Soviet refugees. In a letter from the National Alien Commission to the Ministry for the Interior in April 1948, for example, its chairman Nils Hagelin clearly stated that the increasing traffic of Eastern European refugees that spring (a substantial percentage of which were Soviets) in combination with the new more generous policies entailed a 'security risk'. 'Unwanted' foreigners could not be returned due to their status as political refugees. Additionally, the sudden increase had enforced abandonment of the normal procedures which prescribed keeping new arrivals in police custody until the National Alien Commission had made a decision regarding their future destiny. Now, new arrivals were being housed in four different reception camps in various parts of Sweden. From these, Hagelin pointed out, they had access to the local population as well as to other foreigners both inside and outside the camps throughout those critical first weeks in Sweden. Instances of asylum-seeking foreigners suspected of being spies had arisen, Hagelin confirmed. Such dubious individuals' possible interface with the surrounding society constituted a threat. During the days or weeks which preceded the settling of the individual's asylum application, he or she might 'obtain and give away information that could harm the country or other refugees'. Additionally, a newly arrived foreigner, who was later to be rejected, could take with them valuable information about other refugees, and/or information about the Swedish asylum process, such as what questions the police would ask and what reasons should be presented to ensure a successful assessment.[1]

In agreement with the security police, therefore, the National Alien Commission pleaded to the government for more resources to be allocated to the Commission in order to enable it to increase its control over illegally arrived refugees. It suggested that 'security reasons' should lead to them being held in isolation upon their arrival and until the Commission had reached a decision. The refugee camps ought to be managed by superintendents directly responsible to the Commission, and they should contain 'specially trained and qualified police', who could pursue 'careful interrogations' with the newcomers.[2]

A second point of concern that Hagelin believed needed to be attended to regarded foreigners who refused to obey the restrictions on movement that were sometimes attached to their residence permits. The law had become 'obsolete' since the end of the war, argued Hagelin, since it now only allowed for the deportation of 'disorderly' foreigners if 'specific reasons' existed. As a result, the police's only 'real legal possibility to punish such

---

1    'v.p.m.' (by Nils Hagelin), 26 april 1948, attachment to 'Protokoll'. 27, april 1948 § 1, vol. 1, A 1, Hemliga arkivet, suk, Ra.
2    *Ibid.*, pp. 2–3.

misbehaviour' was to levy fines. As a solution, Hagelin suggested the introduction of new legal measures to empower the authorities to restrain and deport such individuals.[3] Finally, he also argued that the Commission was in need of additional staff in order to enable a more effective surveillance of all foreigners.[4]

The chairman's letter thus reveals an unmistakable security framing of Soviet and other East European refugees in 1948, oscillating around concepts such as 'security', 'threat', 'control' and 'surveillance'. However, it was not concerns over Swedish-Soviet relations and potential Soviet reactions that constituted the main problem, which – as chapter four demonstrated – was a troubling issue in 1945–46. It was instead rooted in the characters and intentions of the refugees themselves. The fear of spies and agents is palpable. Thus, *internal security concerns* stand out as an acute apprehension in the National Alien Commission's plea.

Similar concerns were expressed by the Commission two years later. In a letter to the government in January 1950, three groups of 'unwanted' individuals whose apparent right to reside in Sweden was protected due to their political refugee status were now identified: 1) criminals, 2) individuals who were 'suspected of pursuing illegal activities' and 3) individuals who 'refuse to adjust to normal living circumstances', but chose instead to 'lead a wandering life'. The Commission proposed increased legal possibilities to keep such suspected and/or disorderly foreigners in custody. Some members even argued that the administrative internment practices of suspected foreigners without court trials and for indefinite periods of time of the sort used during the Second World War ought to be re-established. They acknowledged that this risked contradicting 'prevailing ideas on the humane treatment of individuals', but maintained that 'in the current situation' it was nevertheless necessary to 'protect society from particularly dangerous foreigners'.[5] The Commission also argued for an intensification of the usage of

---

3    *Ibid.*, pp. 3–4. Hagelin referred to the discontinuation in 1946 of the *1945 Law regarding taking foreigners' into custody*. See chapter three, part 3.3.

4    *Ibid.*, pp. 4–5.

5    Other members of staff, however, averred that the 'liberal policies' that Sweden had tried to attain regarding foreigners during the last few years hindered the return of such practices, and argued that only those foreigners who had been issued removal decisions ought to be included in the new interment regulations.

imprisonment as punishment for foreigners who exceeded their designated area of residence. Additionally, it suggested an establishment of particular 'work centres' where roving young male foreigners could be taken care of, disciplined and educated.[6]

The timing of these remarks is noteworthy, coinciding as they did with the final planning stages of the 1951 Refugee Convention which, among other things, prohibited discrimination and arbitrary imprisonment of refugees. This jarring juxtaposition suggests that the severe international tensions around 1950 had a deep impact on the Swedish authorities' attitudes towards refugees stemming from communist countries.[7] General (external) security concerns prompted by the bipolar conflict thus seem to have amplified the *internal security* framing of Eastern European refugees.

However, it also reveals a discernible concern with the social behaviour of the foreigners. Criminals evidently constituted a threat to law, order and societal stability, but the National Alien Commission also expressed striking concerns over those refugees branded as just 'disorderly', including not only those who disobeyed their specific geographical restrictions but also the 'wanderers' in general. Their deviant lifestyle seems to have rendered them as societal threats, which the Commission wanted to ameliorate through interning, socialising and disciplining them.[8] Thus, aspects of *social control and morality* appear to have played a significant part in this evaluation.

No new legislation was initiated as a result of the National Alien Commission's pleas. Nor is there any evidence of the establishment of 'work centres'. However, increasing internal security concerns relating to Eastern European refugees led to a renewal in 1951 of another Second World War phenomenon – the so called 'wartime

---

6    § 2 in attachment to 'Protokoll', 24 januari 1950, vol. 3, A 1 A, Kanslibyrån, suk, Ra; § 4 in attachment to 'Protokoll', 6 september 1949, vol. 2, A 1 A, Kanslibyrån, suk, Ra. For more about the wartime regulations on keeping suspected foreigners interned without court trials, see chapter three.

7    For more on anti-communism and fears of the Soviet Union in Sweden around 1950, see Cronqvist 2004; Salomon 2007; Oredsson 2003; Hjort 2004 and Schmidt 2002.

8    This third group mostly included Poles according to the Commission – particularly a group of around twenty individuals. § 2 in attachment to 'Protokoll', 24 januari 1950, vol. 3, A 1 A, Kanslibyrån, suk, Ra.

lists' (*krigsfallslistor*).[9] The aim was to establish a comprehensive register of foreigners who, 'during war or danger of war' needed to be taken into custody. This was a pressing concern. War was anticipated, and these foreigners were regarded as possible fifth columnists. 'With regards to the tense international situation, the Commission reckons that the work in establishing such registers ought to be initiated as soon as possible', it emphasised in January 1951.[10] It also urged the government to make sure that these foreigners could be placed in custody already during a *preliminary stage* of any future conflict.[11]

With the approval of the government, the lists were set up through cooperation and information sharing between the National Alien Commission, the security police and the Department of Counterintelligence of the Swedish Armed Forces. Staff at the Commission examined all Eastern Europeans' control dossiers in detail and started to group individuals in accordance with how dangerous they were considered to be for Swedish national security. In August 1951, a first version was presented, containing the names of 1,360 foreign citizens.[12]

The individuals identified were divided into three groups. The first included Eastern Europeans who were strongly suspected of harbouring communist ideas, and 'with reason could be suspected to serve foreign states' interests' in the event of war. It also included all holders of passports of communist states (generally not refugees who most often held Swedish Aliens' Passports) and foreigners who were employed at companies in which communist states were represented or had significant interests, in case there were any doubts regarding their 'trustworthiness in political respect'.[13]

The second comprised those foreigners 'regarding which suspicions of untrustworthiness exists, particularly in political terms,

---

9   On the war-time lists of the Second World War, regarding both Swedish and foreign citizens, see Eliasson 2006, p. 18, and Hallberg 2001, p. 79 (about 'nationalitetsregister').

10  'Till Konungen', 15 januari 1951, vol. 4, E 4, Hemliga arkivet, SUK, Ra.

11  'Till Konungen', 24 januari 1951, vol. 4, E 4, Hemliga arkivet, SUK, Ra.

12  The second version, finished in February 1952, included only some minor amendments. 'Herr Statspolisintendenten G. Thulin', 9 augusti 1951, vol. 4, E 4, Hemliga arkivet, SUK, Ra; and 'Till Statens Utlänningskommission', 1 februari 1952, vol. 4, E 4, Hemliga arkivet, SUK, Ra.

13  'Till Konungen', p.4, 22 april 1952, vol. 4, E 4, Hemliga arkivet, SUK, Ra.

but where the suspicions are not sufficiently founded to be referred to group I.' It also contained names of some of the more serious criminals and recidivists.[14]

Group three, finally, seemed to have been regarded more as a register to keep close at hand in case it was needed. It included *all* citizens or former citizens of Eastern European communist states, aged 16 to 65, who had control dossiers within the archive of the National Alien Commission, regardless of their contents, and who had not been included in the first two groups. It is important to note, however, that *Balts* and *Ingrians* were excluded unless they had been issued with deportation or expulsion decisions, or already featured in groups I or II.[15]

Groups I and II consisted of slightly over 500 individuals. The plan was to place them all in custody immediately in the event of war or during a preliminary stage of any conflict.[16] The security police also urged the National Alien Commission to 'work towards [the goal] that foreigners belonging to groups I and II should leave the country as soon as possible'.[17]

The design of the lists is revealing. First of all, it demonstrates the strong security framing of refugee issues during these first critical years of the 1950s. The quickly deteriorating international situation, which witnessed heightened rhetoric between the superpower blocs, violence in Korea, the Soviet Union's tightening grip on Eastern Europe, the communist takeover of China and the chilling realisation that both superpower blocs had now mastered the technology of nuclear weapons, prompted the Swedish authorities to expect and plan for war. Communism was interpreted as menacing and aggressively expansive. This turned Eastern European refugees into potential internal security threats.[18]

14   *Ibid.*

15   *Ibid.*, p. 4–5.

16   'Till Konungen', 22 april 1952, vol. 4, E 4, Hemliga arkivet, SUK, Ra; 'Herr Statspolisintendenten G. Thulin', 9 augusti 1951, vol. 4, E 4, Hemliga arkivet, SUK, Ra.

17   'Till Statens Utlänningskommission', 1 februari 1952, p. 2, vol. 4, E 4, Hemliga arkivet, SUK, Ra.

18   On the fears of communism and the Soviet Union in Sweden during the 1950s, see chapter one, parts 1.1.1 and 1.1.2, and for example, Bjereld, Johansson & Molin 2008; Kronvall & Petersson 2012; Cronqvist 2004; Salomon 2007; Oredsson 2003; SOU 2002:87 and Hjort 2004.

Secondly, the lists suggest that *Russians* – alongside Albanians, Bulgarians, former Danzig-citizens, Yugoslavs, Poles, Romanians, Czechoslovakians and Hungarians – were generally regarded as being inherently less politically trustworthy than *Balts* and *Ingrians*, regardless of the specific circumstances of their lives, backgrounds and personalities. Simply by originating from these countries, these individuals were apparently considered more unreliable and therefore automatically included in group III if they had control dossiers. In other words, it seems as though Balts and Ingrians were regarded as less likely to be communists, and possibly also less likely to be *susceptible* to communist ideology and Soviet infiltration in general, even though Soviet agents were undoubtedly active among these groups as well.[19]

Taken together, the two pleas and the construction of the wartime lists mentioned above demonstrate a significant interpretation of refugee matters as closely intertwined with aspects of *internal security* from 1948 onwards – and particularly so during the early 1950s. However, *ethnic preconceptions* seem to have influenced these perceptions too as some Eastern Europeans were apparently regarded as more likely internal security threats than others. Aspects pertaining to *social control and morality* obviously also concerned the National Alien Commission, as testified by their anxieties about the roving young men who refused to adjust to 'normal living standards'.

What consequences did such comprehensions have on the National Alien Commission's management of Soviet refugees' residence permits? As was demonstrated in chapter three, such permits could be granted for varying periods of time and applied with different geographical limitations. The immigration legislation, however, did not define what sort of circumstances would lead to what type of permit or restriction. As such, the National Alien Commission was furnished with considerable room for manoeuvre. Thus, the potential scope of influence for various possible influential aspects was significant.

19  On Soviet agents' activities within the Ingrian and Baltic refugee groups, see, for example, 'ang. Heimoveljet', vol. 5, F 2 B, Hemliga arkivet, SUK, Ra; and several documents within vol. 47, R 58 Eö, 1920 års dossiésystem, UD, Ra.

## 7.1 Residence Permits as Control Tools

Among the 260 individuals who have been chosen for closer examination in this chapter the duration of their residence permits differed considerably. Some were given three months, others five, eight, or sometimes one or two years. From 1949 onwards a number of individuals began to be granted five-year permits. When the document expired, the individual had to apply for a renewal.

In the same manner, a general overview reveals that the issuing of geographical limitations varied markedly as well. Whereas some individuals never experienced any geographical limitations to their residence permits, others began their lives in Sweden with a 'big city restriction'. This banned them from residing in Sweden's three largest cities, namely Stockholm, Gothenburg and Malmö. Others, however, were compelled to reside in a specified area only, such as a small town or district. Only with written permission from the National Alien Commission could he or she reside elsewhere. The restrictions could last for a few months or many years. Normally, however, such constraints were gradually lifted, thus allowing the individual more freedom of movement. Some recipients, however, had this strict geographical constraint introduced later on in their stay as a result of a changed attitude towards them within the National Alien Commission.

A general examination of the assessment procedures demonstrate that they ought to be understood in terms of *control*. Because, what shorter permits brought to the Commission, except for a heavier workload, was control over the applicant. Every time a refugee applied for a renewal of his or her residence permit, an investigation was pursued. The Commission processed all information gathered in an individual's sometimes very comprehensive personal dossier.[20] It also involved the local police and the County Administrative Board, which were asked to go through police registers before submitting a statement. The overall aim of this process was to ensure that nothing 'disadvantageous' (*ofördelaktigt*) was known about the person. If there were reasons to suspect something 'dubious' (*tveksamheter*), those in close contact with the refugees – such as employers and landlords – were asked to give a statement too. This was called a 'standard investigation' (*standard-*

20   Regarding the contents of these, see chapter 1, part 1.3.3.

*utredning*) and was to be pursued in all renewal assessments.[21]

Sometimes, however, a 'special investigation' (*specialutredning*) was requested. This was more extensive. It was to be based upon an individual interrogation of the immigrant regarding his or her personal history including criminal records, financial position, plans for the future, reasons for residing in Sweden, and the likelihood of their moving to another country. These questions were similar to those that were always asked upon a foreigner's first application for asylum in Sweden. Nevertheless they were invariably repeated in any special investigation. Additionally, a compulsory ingredient was hearings with individuals who could give a statement about the immigrant's *skötsamhet* (conscientiousness). Again these often focused on the subject's employer and landlord. They were asked questions about the individual's character and conduct. For example, were they satisfied with the refugee's performance and behaviour? Had he or she conducted themselves satisfactorily at their workplace, paid their rent on time, or ever caused a problem of any kind? Other persons such as neighbours, work colleagues and teachers could also be asked to provide statements. All the information gleaned was then sent to the Commission, which gathered it in the personal dossiers of the individual. It was on the basis of this information that new decisions were reached.[22]

The more often this procedure was conducted, the larger was the body of information the authorities were able to gather about the individual. Thus, the procedures aimed at facilitating control over the immigrant population in Sweden. It was a tool to separate the well behaved from the disorderly – and, indeed, to reward the former and reprimand the latter. It therefore corresponds well with the definition of *surveillance* in modern society developed by sociologist David Lyon as connoting 'any collection and processing of personal data, whether identifiable or not, for the purposes of

---

21   *Råd och anvisningar rörande förfarandet hos polismyndighet med ärenden om uppehålls- eller arbetstillstånd för utlänningar,* SUK 1947, p. 5, vol. 1, B 4 C, Kanslibyrån, SUK, Ra.

22   *Råd och anvisningar rörande förfarandet hos polismyndighet med ärenden om uppehålls- eller arbetstillstånd för utlänningar,* SUK 1947, vol. 1, B 4 C, Kanslibyrån, SUK, Ra; 'Till samtliga polismyndigheter', 5 december 1947, vol. 1, B 4 C, Kanslibyrån, SUK, Ra; 'Till polismyndigheterna', 20 mars 1952, vol. 1, B 4 C, Kanslibyrån, SUK, Ra; 'Cirkulär till polismyndigheterna 1/55' (dated 16 December 1954), vol. 1, B 4 C, Kanslibyrån, SUK, Ra.

influencing or managing those whose data have been garnered'.[23]

Likewise, the geographical restriction also facilitated control. This was especially the case with the stricter type which enabled the Commission, with the help of the local police, to keep a better track of a person's whereabouts. Additionally, it was intended to hinder him or her from integrating into other geographical parts of Swedish society.

An individual granted a short permit with a strict geographical constraint should, therefore, be interpreted as a person that the Commission for some reason found it had stronger grounds to control than someone with a longer permit and larger freedom of movement. The length of the residence permit as well as the possible geographical constraints attached to it constituted *control tools* used by the Commission to monitor refugees and other foreign citizens. As such, the extensive bureaucratic procedures outlined above served as a *control system*.[24] Aspects of *social control* and, indeed, *security concerns* (both external and internal) thus supposedly induced this process.

From late 1947 onwards, the system was partly decentralised, leaving the local police with the authority to assess the renewal applications of those individuals deemed to be well-behaved. Individuals currently under the strict geographical constraint, and/or marked with an 'A' due to some specific troubling circumstances, continuously demanded central immigration authority attention and was to be sent to the National Alien Commission. So too were all applications involving permits longer than two years.[25]

What factors, then, determined the policies pursued in practice

23  David Lyon, *Surveillance society: monitoring everyday life,* Open University Press, Buckingham 2001, p. 2.

24  This interpretation is further strengthened by the Commission's own statements about the system. See, for example, attachment 2 to 'Protokoll', 5 mars 1946, vol. 2, A 1 A, Kanslibyrån, SUK, Ra; 'Protokoll', 19 februari 1946, vol. 2, A 1 A, Kanslibyrån, SUK, Ra; 'Protokoll', 14 maj 1946, vol. 2, A 1 A, Kanslibyrån, SUK, Ra; 'Kontrollbyråorder nr 2', 16 januari 1950, vol. 1, B 2 A, Kontrollbyrån, SUK, Ra; 'Till Riksåklagarämbetet', 16 januari 1950, vol. 1, B 2 A, Kontrollbyrån, SUK, Ra.

25  'Till samtliga polismyndigheter', 5 december 1947, vol. 1, B 4 C, Kanslibyrån, SUK, Ra; 'Meddelande till rikets samtliga polismyndigheter', 21 december 1950, vol. 1, B 4 C, Kanslibyrån, SUK, Ra; 'Till polismyndigheterna', 20 mars 1952, vol. 1, B 4 C, Kanslibyrån, SUK, Ra; and 'Cirkulär till polismyndigheterna 1/55' (dated 16 December 1954), vol. 1, B 4 C, Kanslibyrån, SUK, Ra.

regarding Soviet refugees' residence permits? Who was granted what type of residence permit, and why? How long did it take for various individuals to be granted a two- and five-year permit or, indeed, full freedom of movement?[26] And what circumstances led to the issuing of shorter permits and geographical restrictions later on?

## 7.2 Baltic Refugees' Residence Permits

The extensive group of Balts who arrived in the autumn of 1944 seem to have received coherent treatment. All of the individuals in the chosen study group belonging to this category were granted a so-called 'normal visa for Baltic refugees'. This included a six month first permit upon arrival, and a big city restriction. The rest of Sweden was fully accessible to them.[27]

Most of the Balts who arrived in 1945 were handled in the same manner.[28] Only in specific cases does the stricter geographical constraint seem to have been used on this group upon arrival. One such example was an Estonian man who had moved to Germany in 1939 and become a military pilot within the German Luftwaffe. The Commission suspected that he was actually a German citizen. Therefore, his first five months were spent confined to a refugee camp for military personnel, and his following residence permits came with a strict geographical restraint. This remained the case for three years, before a 'normal' big city restriction was issued.[29]

A few examples have been found in which individuals arriving in

26  Individuals who became Swedish citizens will fall into the 'five-year-permit' group. The rationale for this is that citizenship is not a beneficial analytical category in itself in this context, simply because not all refugees wanted to become Swedish citizens and therefore did not apply for this status. Additionally, the Ministry of Justice (which issued citizenships) cooperated with the National Alien Commission in this matter. Thus, those who were granted citizenship were generally only individuals who could come into consideration for five-year permits.

27  B4, B12, B13, B16, B18, B19, B20, B23, B24, B37, B39, B49, B50, B53, B55, B58, B64, B65, B69, B71, B72, B74, B76, B77, B78, B81, B82, B88, B92, B94, B96, B97, B102, B108, B115, B117.

28  B27, B48, B54, B73, B62, B105, B111, B118.

29  Central dossier of B59.

1945 were initially issued shorter three months permits, albeit with
the normal main city constraint. This was the case with the Latvian
refugees who arrived in a boat in the middle of the extradition affair
in November 1945 and were issued a postponed deportation decision by the government with reference to the 'security paragraph'
56 of the Aliens Act (mentioned in chapter four). They all seem to
have been issued shorter first permits.[30] So too was, for example,
an Estonian sailor who abandoned his Soviet ship in August 1945
and applied for asylum.[31] The other 1945 new arrivals of Baltic
origin included in this study however – two teenage girls, a few
Latvian lawyers, a former government representative, an engineer,
a company owner and a newspaper director – were granted the six
months 'normal visas for Baltic refugees'.[32]

Fresh practices were introduced in 1946. Baltic refugees arriving from then on and until 1949 were issued the shorter three
to five months permit. In addition, all of them received a strict
geographical constraint to start with, regardless of from where
they had arrived.[33] This was a result of a principal decision the
Commission had made in May 1946 which stated that all illegally
arrived Balts should receive shorter three months first permits and
strict geographical restrictions before being allowed more freedom
later on, provided that the police unearthed no problematical facts
about them.[34]

In 1950, these instructions changed. Blanket geographical
constraints could no longer be issued to all new arrivals, the
Commission now stated. Instead, it was only to be used for such
individuals where it 'from a surveillance point of view' was regard-

30    See, for example, central dossier and central register card of B79.

31    Central dossier of B113.

32    B27, B48, B54, B73, B62, B105, B111, B118. This was despite the fact that at
      least two of these (B27 and B111) had been identified in the police investigation
      of the Baltic community as having committed war crimes during the Nazi occu-
      pation, as will be further discussed below.

33    B5, B6, B8, B14, B17, B21, B22, B28, B35, B46, B56, B60, B83, B85, B103, B112.

34    This therefore did not pertain to foreigners arriving legally with valid entry
      visas. They were generally not subject to any geographical restrictions at all.
      'Protokoll', 14 maj 1946, vol. 2, A 1 A, Kanslibyrån, SUK, Ra. See also attach-
      ment 2 to 'Protokoll', 5 mars 1946, vol. 2, A 1 A, Kanslibyrån, SUK, Ra;
      'Protokoll', 19 februari 1946, vol. 2, A 1 A, Kanslibyrån, SUK, Ra.

ed 'absolutely necessary'.[35] And, indeed, an examination of a group of Balts arriving in the early 1950s suggests that the new directions were followed. Only a few were now granted a strict geographical constraint. They were generally regarded as suspicious for some reason. A deserted Estonian agent, for example, who claimed to have been sent to Scandinavia by the NKVD on a secret mission, but who had instead chosen to desert and apply for asylum, was handled with extra care. A shorter permit and a strict geographical constraint, combined with police surveillance, characterised his first year in Sweden before the security services and the National Alien Commission decided to trust his intentions.[36]

Others were treated with more discretion by being granted either a main city constraint only or permission to reside in all of Sweden immediately upon arrival. The responsible official's own personal views seem to have decided which one it was to be, as no apparent differences have been traced between these individuals. The 1950s arrivals in this study group who had the main city constraint, however, had this removed within a year.[37]

Aside from a few individuals arriving in 1953–54, there were some other individuals in the Baltic study group who never experienced a geographical constraint of any kind. They were, for example, diplomats, professors, newspaper editors and even a student and a sailor. These had all arrived before 1944 (in other words before the second, and sometimes even the first, Soviet occupation of their home countries).[38]


### 7.2.1 *Continued Residence Permits*

Generally speaking it took a Balt between one and four years to receive a two year permit. For those arriving in the 1950s, this document was generally granted within two years. Receiving a five year permit normally took between four and seven years.[39]

---

35  'Kontrollbyråorder no. 2', 16 januari 1950, vol. 1, B 2 A, Kontrollbyrån, SUK, Ra.
36  Central dossier and central register card of B68.
37  See, for example, B42, B43, B63, B91, B110. Due to the archival situation at the National Alien Commission, no names of Balts arriving in 1950–52 have been found. These examples are all individuals arriving in 1953–54.
38  B3, B15, B40, B51, B80, B116.
39  B1 – B120.

Those in this study group who had to wait longer for their five year permit – between nine and seventeen years – included some individuals accused of grave war crimes during the German occupation of their home countries; some individuals suspected of conducting espionage on behalf of the Soviet Union; some of the individuals included in the November 1945 deportation decision; a few sailors; and individuals who had committed crimes (ranging in severity from drunkenness to murder). It could also include individuals who were believed to have engaged in criminal activities in their home countries.[40]

This cohort also included individuals considered problematical for other reasons. This concerned, for example, alcoholics; individuals who travelled about within the country more than the Commission found suitable; and individuals suspected of criminal activities other than those pertaining to the security of the state, such as drug dealing. It could also pertain to someone about whom employers or landlords had reported misdemeanours of some description, such as loud arguments from within the accommodation and delayed rental settlements.[41]

Far from all individuals suspected of war crimes during the Nazi regimes in their home countries had to wait for their five year permit, however. Out of the total of 33 suspected war criminals and/ or highly ranked Nazi collaborators within the study group at least ten were dealt with according to the same principles as other Balts in terms of the issuing of five year permits.[42] However, six of the others emigrated within a few years (often to Latin America or the United States) before the five year permit had started to be issued. Some of these had held central positions within the Nazi regime, including within the Gestapo or the Nazi courts, and were accused of very serious crimes, such as multiple murders, the deportation of thousands of individuals to concentration camps and the confiscation of Jewish property.[43]

Balts who arrived after 1945 and were issued a strict geographical constraint upon arrival had to wait between six months and two and a half years to have this exchanged for a 'normal' main city

40	B4, B19, B37, B53, B72, B74, B82, B79, B87.
41	See, for example, central dossiers and control dossiers of B66, B85, B112.
42	See, for example, B18, B20, B49, B65, B73, B88, B94, B97.
43	B13, B39, B40, B64, B71, B116,

restriction. The only individual who had to wait somewhat longer was the above-mentioned suspected German citizen, who had been a pilot in Nazi Germany.[44]

Receiving a permit to reside in all of Sweden, without any geographical constraints, generally took a Balt between two to seven years. Those who had to wait longer – between eight and fifteen years – were constituted of the same group as that mentioned above, namely a few of the former Nazi collaborators, individuals suspected of communist views and/or illegal collaboration with Soviet authorities, and individuals with a criminal record.[45]

Again, however, several of the individuals who were suspected of war crimes during the Nazi occupation of their home countries were also permitted to live anywhere in Sweden within the same timeframe as other Balts. Among them was, for example, a Latvian lawyer accused of having deported 9 000 fellow countrymen to concentration camps, and other infamous Nazi collaborators, some of who had committed serious war crimes.[46]

Why some of these Nazi-accused Balts were subject to some limitations – mostly a delayed five year permit – whilst others were not cannot be determined for certain. It does not seem to correlate with the seriousness of the accusations, or their reliability. It might well have had to do with which official handled the case at the National Alien Commission. However, *none* of the 33 individuals accused of war crimes faced any more serious consequences, and most of them were granted the right to reside in Stockholm. They were generally well educated and found themselves good positions in various parts of Sweden, unless, of course, they decided to emigrate. The refusal to grant some of them the longer five year permit appears to have been used as a sort of arbitrary punishment rather than as a stringent control measure, since all of them enjoyed at least two year permits and full freedom of movement.[47]

---

44  Central dossier of B59.

45  See, for example, B19, B55, B85. The seamen, however, generally received all of Sweden permits before everyone else through the issuing of *sailors' visas* – which included the right to reside in all of Sweden's harbours. See 'Angående inresebehandlingen m.m. av utländska sjömän', vol. 1, B 2 A, Kontrollbyrån, SUK, Ra.

46  B71, B73, B88, B94, B96, B97.

47  B3, B4, B15, B18, B19, B20, B27, B36, B37, B39, B40, B49, B56, B58, B62, B64, B65, B71, B72, B73, B76, B87, B88, B92, B94, B96, B97, B102, B105, B108,

Thus, the National Alien Commission does not seem to have regarded the former Nazi war criminals as individuals whom it needed to control to any more extensive degree than other Balts. They do not appear to have been regarded as specific *threats* – neither to social stability nor Swedish national (internal or external) security. The aim of the security police's two extensive examinations seems mostly to have been to collect information. These results thus correlate well with Mats Deland's research regarding this group, which established that most of these individuals were free to live normal lives in Sweden after the war.[48]

### 7.2.2 *Shorter Permits and/or Geographical Restrictions Issued Later On*

Shorter permits and geographical restrictions could also be issued later on in an individual's life. In such cases, it always constituted a response to something the individual had done – or something the authorities believed he or she *might* have done – and of which the Commission did not approve. A criminal act could lead to stricter residence permits after the punishment had been issued. This was indeed the case with some individuals in the Baltic group. In 1945, for example, two young men stood accused of rioting and violent behaviour in a refugee camp. This led to the imposition of a strict geographical restriction.[49] A couple of bank robbers were dealt with in a similar manner after they had served their prison sentence.[50]

Among the Balts there were, however, several individuals who had been granted exceptions from the big city constraint and been allowed residence in one of the main cities (often Stockholm) on employment grounds. Thus, in some cases an individual who had previously been granted permission to reside in a city could be forced to leave it should some 'uncomplimentary information' be revealed about him or her. Such was, for example, the case with the young Estonian sentenced to fines and later mental care due to a num-

---

B111, B115, B116. See also 'Ang. av Statens utlänningskommission begärd utredning rörande vissa balt. förhållanden', vol. 10, F 4, Hemliga arkivet, suk, Ra. Balts accused of war crimes were generally refused so-called 'archival work', however.

48   Deland 2010.
49   Various documents dated 1945–47 in central dossiers of B34 and B1.
50   Various documents dated 1945–48 in central dossiers of B10 and B72.

ber of incidents of 'indecent exposure' (as discussed in chapter five).[51]

The group that was affected the most, however, were those individuals suspected of illegal contacts with the Soviet authorities, even if the supporting evidence was slight.[52] One example is constituted by a Latvian teenager who visited the Soviet Embassy in 1947. He claimed that this was in order to seek information about his father who had been deported to Siberia. This visit was discovered by the security police, which had the Embassy under surveillance. As a consequence, the teenager was expelled from Stockholm (where he lived with his mother and studied at the technical college) and had his following residence permits limited to periods of three months. Years of arguing with the Commission followed, since he believed he had been unjustly treated. Despite the fact that he acquired both a job and a wife in Stockholm, the Commission continued to persistently refuse him permission to reside there for many years. In this they were supported by the security police who wanted to hinder him from socialising further with Soviet representatives. Additionally, he had to wait thirteen years to receive his first two year permit, and fifteen years for his five year permit. By then, the authorities had ceased to regard him as a security risk.[53]

A 40 year-old socialist accountant (also mentioned in chapter five), received a similar treatment. The security services and the National Alien Commission failed in their ambition to have him expelled due to the government's unwillingness to remove an individual without evidence of pursued illegal activities. Nevertheless, his 'free thinking approach' to socialism, his contacts with Soviet representatives – and a well-known Swedish communist – as well as his lack of interest in permanent employment led the authorities to exert other forms of pressure. He was repeatedly issued short residence permits of a few months only, had to wait fifteen years before

51   Central dossier of B50.
52   Whilst contacting the Soviet Embassy *per se* was, obviously, not illegal, the exchange of information on particularly sensitive Swedish matters or about refugees was.
53   Various documents dated 1947–60 within central dossier and control dossier of B82. See also, for example, protocols dated 28 September 1948, 22 February 1949, 12 April 1949, 23 August 1949, 1 November 1949, vol. 2, A 1 A, Kanslibyrån, SUK, Ra.

he was allowed to visit the main cities again, and a similar amount of time elapsed before his application for a five year residence permit was approved. His application to buy property (an obligatory process for all foreigners at the time) was denied, as was his applications for Swedish citizenship and several of his applications for travel permits. He was registered in group I on the wartime lists. Not until 1970 was he granted Swedish citizenship.[54]

Similarly, a young Estonian locksmith had his residence permits shortened to six months in 1952 when the security police reported that they suspected that he might be a communist and/ or a 'Russian sympathiser'. This was based on his contacts with another questionable individual, and reports from other Estonians to the security police a couple of years earlier suggesting that he might not be trustworthy. Some Russian magazines and an issue of the Swedish syndicalist magazine *Arbetaren* ('The Worker') had been discovered in his home. During an interrogation, he denied being a Russian sympathiser or engaging in any unlawful intelligence activities. On the contrary, he claimed that 'the conditions in Sweden are the best imaginable'. However, according to the security police he had confessed to sympathising with *some* parts of the communist ideology, as well as to occasionally reading both Russian and Swedish communist magazines.[55]

As a result, his residence permits were drastically shortened, and his files were stamped with an 'A', meaning that all decisions about him were to be handled by the central immigration authorities (rather than the local police) with assistance from the security police. In 1954, however, suspicions against him lessened, and he was eventually granted Swedish citizenship.[56]

All of the above examples occurred in the 1950s. No traces of such measures against Baltic refugees' residence permits due to

54  Various documents dated 1950–70 in central dossier and control dossier of B74; 'Herr Statspolisintendenten G. Thulin', 9 augusti 1951, vol. 4, E 4, Hemliga arkivet, suk, Ra; and 'Till Statens Utlänningskommission', 1 februari 1952, vol. 4, E 4, Hemliga arkivet, suk, Ra.

55  Various documents dated 1951–4 in central dossier and control dossier of B16. Citations from 'Rapport', 24 oktober 1952, in central dossier of B16; 'Förundersöknngsprotokoll', Statspolisen 7 juni 1951, and several documents titled 'p.m.' in control dossier of B16.

56  Various documents dated 1951–54 in central dossier and control dossier of B16. See also B67, who was subject to similar treatment.

suspicions of communist world views or unlawful contacts with Soviet authorities have been found from the 1940s. On the contrary, during the first two post-war years, similar restrictions were issued against some individuals who had *criticised* the Soviet Union. A journalist who was found guilty of having engaged in political activities after writing articles condemning the democratic Latvians in a Sweden-based Latvian magazine lost his permission to reside in Stockholm in early 1947 as well as his job after the Commission's involvement. He was abruptly granted short three months permits only. According to the Commission, he had contravened the rules prohibiting foreigners from engaging in political activities. In 1948, however, he regained the right to reside in Stockholm and was issued a one-year permit. In 1951 he received full freedom of movement and a two year permit. The undesirability of his continued political activities now seems to have mattered less.[57]

That Baltic citizens' political activism against the Soviet Union was regarded less problematic in the 1950s compared with 1945–46 is averred indirectly in a letter sent by the National Alien Commission to the Swedish parliament's legal ombudsman in 1950. The latter had enquired about the treatment of certain refugees in the 1940s in response to accusations levelled against the Commission in a newspaper article. Among those refugees mentioned were two newspaper editors in whose right wing magazine 'rancorous attacks' against a social democratic Latvian academic had been published in Sweden in 1945. As a result the editors had been warned that, if they continued to break the prohibition on foreigners engaging in political activities, they would be taken into custody or removed from the country. They had also been granted a strict geographical constraint. In 1946, new warnings had been issued when one of them wrote another article which the Commission interpreted as political propaganda. In 1948, however, their strict geographical restrictions had been removed and they had been treated according to normal standards for Balts.

57   Central dossier and control dossier of B26.

In its response to the legal ombudsman in 1950, the Commission made the following remark about the case:

> The letter to [x] should be seen against the background of the sensitive situation which then prevailed regarding the refugees from the Soviet occupied Baltic States, which was accentuated by the famous repatriations of certain military personnel who had fled from there at the time of the armistice. In this context it appeared essential that political agitation among the Baltic refugees be hindered, particularly since one could fear that such agitation could provoke Russian demands regarding the Baltic refugee group as a whole.[58]

Hindering Balts from making political statements about the Soviet Union had constituted a way for Sweden to try to mitigate further Soviet pressure. Thus, Swedish-Soviet relations (relating to *external security concerns*) were the reason why politically active Balts who criticised the Soviet Union (including some fascism-orientated agitators) were subject to stricter geographical constraints and shorter residence permits in 1945–46. From 1947–48, however, the authorities apparently stopped troubling themselves as much with such kinds of expressions from the Baltic community. For example, a priest defined as 'one of the most dangerous and most active antidemocratic elements in Uppsala' by the security police in 1947, was not subject to any sort of consequences despite the 'fascist sermons' he was holding.[59] Thus, at that time, Baltic refugees' right-wing political activism no longer seemed to have been interpreted as constituting a specific threat to Swedish national security. Sweden's shifting attitude towards the Soviet Union, and

58    *Skrivelsen till [x] den 18 april 1946 bör ses mot bakgrund av det ömtåliga läge, som då rådde beträffande flyktingarna från det Sovietockuperade Balticum, vilket läge särskilt accentuerade av de bekanta återtransporterna av viss därifrån i samband med vapenstilleståndet flyktad militärpersonal. Det framstod i denna situation som angeläget, att politisk agitation bland de baltiska flyktingarna förhindrades, framför allt med hänsyn till att en sådan agitation kunde befaras utlösa krav från rysk sida beträffande den baltiska flyktinggruppen i sin helhet.* Attachment 1 to 'Protokoll', 23 augusti 1950, § 1, vol. 3, A 1 A, Kanslibyrån, SUK, Ra.
59    Central dossier and control dossier of B20. See also also 'Ang. av Statens utlänningskommission begärd utredning rörande vissa balt. förhållanden', vol. 10, F 4, Hemliga arkivet, SUK, Ra.

the abandonment of its formal bridge-building ambitions, apparently left more room for freedom of speech for the Baltic refugees – including extreme right-wing agitators.

In addition, of course, the fall of Nazi Germany meant that such individuals no longer had a superpower to support them. The potential damage they could cause to Swedish national security was thus limited.[60] Communist-influenced refugees, however, could potentially collaborate with the Soviet Union. During the jittery early 1950s in particular, this was regarded a critical security threat. And it was well known by the authorities at this time that officials at the Soviet Embassy frequently sought to persuade refugees into secretly working for them by offering inducements or promising improved conditions for their relatives at home.[61] Thus, suspected communists – even on the basis of flimsy evidence – were subject to far greater sanctions than former Nazi collaborators and war criminals. Particularly from 1948 onwards, it was the suspected communists who were regarded as potential *internal security threats* – not the former Nazis. Together with the criminals and the socially maladjusted – in other words individuals who challenged *social and moral norms* – it was such Balts who were subjected to shorter permits and considerable restrictions to their freedom of movement.


## 7.3 Ingrian Refugees' Residence Permits

The Ingrian refugees experienced a somewhat different reception than the Balts. Out of those within the study group who arrived during the 1940s, less than half was granted six months residence as their first permit. The others received a three to five month permit.

---

60  This correlates with results in Ekengren & Oscarsson 2002, p. 148, 197–198.

61  The security police, as well as the Ministry for Foreign Affairs, often received reports of their activities from refugees who had been contacted by the Soviet Embassy. See, for example, 'ang. Heimoveljet', vol. 5, F 2 B, Hemliga arkivet, SUK, Ra; 'ang. Ryska legationens repatrieringsverksamhet', vol. 9, F 2 B, Hemliga arkivet, SUK, Ra; and several reports within vol. 40, R 58 Er, 1920 års dossiésystem, UD, Ra; vol. 47, R 58 Eö, 1920 års dossiésystem, UD, Ra. A few such reports are also to be found in vol. 77–79, P 40 R, 1920 års dossiésystem, UD, Ra; and vol. 67–69, P 40 I, 1920 års dossiésystem, 1920 års dossiésystem, UD, Ra. On Polish agents' activities among refugees, see several documents within vol. 4, E 4, Hemliga arkivet, SUK, Ra.

The difference within this category has, however, no connection with their dissimilar arrival dates in the same obvious way as it had with the Baltic group.[62]

Additionally, nearly all of them were granted a strict geographical constraint upon arrival, rather than the main city constraint which was the norm for newly arrived Balts. Only four out of thirty of those in the chosen study group who arrived during the 1940s and were granted a right to stay were issued the main city restriction only. The difference cannot be accounted for by their arrival dates. Nor can any particular details in their personal dossiers pertaining to their behaviour and personal backgrounds explain the difference.[63]

In the 1950s, however, this practice changed. All the individuals in the Ingrian study group who arrived in 1953–54 were issued a main city restriction only upon arrival, according to the new directions. Their first permits lasted between six months and one year.[64]

### 7.3.1 *Continued residence permits*

The Ingrians who arrived in the 1940s had to wait between nine months and three and a half years before their strict geographical restraint was exchanged for a normal big city ban, and six to eleven years before their residence permit gave them recourse to the whole of Sweden.[65] This thus contrasts with the Balts who were generally granted full freedom of movement after two to seven years, unless the Commission perceived any particular reasons to refuse them this on personal grounds.

In addition, none of these individuals were granted exceptions to the big city constraint in order to work within one of the main

---

62  I1, I5, I9, I7, I10, I11, I13, I14, I15, I17, I19, I22, I26, I27, I28, I30, I31, I32, I33, I36, I37, I38, I39, I40, I41, I45, I46, I48, I49.

63  Three of these four arrived in 1944, and one in 1946. See I11, I13, I22, I32. The others arrived at various times between 1944 and 1949. See I1, I5, I9, I7, I10, I14, I15, I17, I19, I26, I27, I28, I30, I31, I33, I36, I37, I38, I39, I40, I41, I45, I46, I48, I49.

64  I3, I6, I8, I16, I21, I23, I25, I44, I50, I51. Due to the methodological difficulty of finding names of new arrivals from 1950–1952 within the National Alien Commission's archive, no examples of Ingrians arriving during those years have been included.

65  I1, I5, I9, I7, I10, I11, I13, I14, I15, I17, I19, I22, I26, I27, I28, I30, I31, I32, I33, I36, I37, I38, I39, I40, I41, I45, I46, I48, I49.

cities (such as was often the case with the Balts). They were all placed at various work positions in smaller communities around the country, where they seem to have remained.

In terms of longer residence permits, a more considerable difference emerges. Whereas the Balts, as mentioned, generally waited four to seven years for their five year permits, the Ingrians normally had to wait between seven and eleven years. The two year permit was generally granted the Ingrians within two to five years, however.

Nothing specific can be found in these Ingrians' personal dossiers that could explain why they were treated less generously than their Baltic counterparts. In fact only a few of the Ingrians in the chosen study group had any so-called 'uncomplimentary information' gathered about them at all – significantly fewer than in the Baltic group.[66] Thus, the Ingrians' *behaviour* cannot explain the harsher treatment of them as a group in comparison with the Balts. It seems, therefore, that Ingrian refugees in general were controlled to a larger extent than the Balts, and that this was not due to any specific traits that can be traced to them personally.

One apparent difference between the groups has to do with their respective social and financial status, however. Whereas many of the Balts were well educated with high social positions in their home countries, most of the Ingrians who arrived were only educated to primary school level. Many of them were farmers and factory workers. However, those few who had attended higher education – such as an architect and a teacher – do not stand out in comparison with the treatment of the other Ingrians in the study group.[67] At least in terms of differences *within* the Ingrian group, status and education do not seem to have constituted the decisive factor.

This also indicates that the reason for the variation between the Balts and the Ingrians probably had more to do with *ethnic aspects*. Simply because they were Ingrians, the authorities seem to have treated them less generously than the Balts.

A few individuals were dealt with more harshly than the other Ingrians due to particular reasons pertaining to their own behav-

66  I2, I10, I36, I40, I41.
67  Central dossiers of I33 and I13.

iour. One alcoholic had his five year permit delayed for thirteen years as a result of his addiction.[68] A couple of other Ingrians who had been sentenced for drunkenness and affray had to wait around ten years. As such, however, their treatment did not differ that much from that of other Ingrians who lacked any such negative details in their personal dossiers.[69]

The most parsimonious treatment was received by a former NKVD agent. He had switched sides during the war and started working for the Finnish military administration. The authorities were suspicious about the man's character and granted him short permits and strict geographical restrictions only. His multiple convictions for drunkenness in public (which was a criminal offence during this time) and 'violation of the privacy of the home' did nothing to improve his standing. In an attempt to put pressure on him to make him 'more keen on leading a decent life' and 'not make him feel so certain about his residence here', the police recommended that the Commission continued to grant him short permits only. As a result, he never had his strict geographical constraint removed, and never received a permit longer than six months. He disappeared in 1951, after having lived in Sweden under those conditions for seven years.[70]

Among those who arrived in the 1950s, waiting periods were shorter. However, as mentioned, they were all served with big city constraints upon arrival, which differs somewhat in comparison with the Baltic group. Within one to three years they were removed. By then they had also generally received a two-year permit. Within three to seven years, they received the five year permit.[71]


### 7.3.2 Shorter Permits and/or Geographical Restrictions Issued Later On

Few Ingrians within this study group had their residence permits shortened or restricted later. One who did, however, was the alcoholic mentioned above. In 1950, after being convicted several times for public drunkenness, his residence permit was shortened to only

68   Central dossier and central register card of I10.
69   Central dossiers of I36, I40 and I41.
70   Central and control dossier of I15. Citations from attached police statement to residence application dated 23 January 1948 in central dossier.
71   I3, I6, I8, I16, I21, I23, I25, I44, I50, I51.

three months. He was also threatened with deportation, both by the social services and the National Alien Commission.[72] Urged by the social services, he submitted himself to a medical institution for alcoholics. Later on, he was also admitted to a mental home. His problems escalated, however, and he spent most of the rest of his life in various institutions. At one point during the 1950s he was convicted of attempted manslaughter and sentenced to further compulsory institutional care. As a result, he had to wait thirteen years before being granted longer residence permits again.[73] A couple of other Ingrians who were convicted for committed crimes, such as theft, burglary and a knife fight, received similar consequences to their residence permits.[74]

Apart from these examples, no other Ingrians have been found who had residence permits shortened or restricted as a result of their own behaviour.[75] An Ingrian engineer who was suspected of being a communist was freed from these suspicions before they could impact on his residence permits. Anonymous accusations had been reported to the security police suggesting that he might be a communist and a spy. The allegation was based on two claims: 1) that he read Russian magazines; and 2) that he travelled the country extensively. After investigating the matter, however, the security police stated that the suspicions were most likely groundless. The resulting 22-page report was nevertheless kept in his file. In it are the statements of several individuals, including his landlord who had complained that his tenant sometimes brought women to his room. None of the interviewed individuals thought he was a communist however. On the contrary, he was known to be strongly opposed to the Soviet regime. Nevertheless, one man with a passionate disliking for the engineer told the security police that the Ingrian was 'definitely a communist'. In this case, however, the security police did not believe the informant. Be that as it may, he had

---

72  Deportation was not issued, however, and even if it had, it probably could not have been implemented due to his status as a political refugee. See chapter five.

73  Central dossier and central register card of I10.

74  Central dossiers of I2 and I40.

75  However, the chosen study group includes one man who had his residence permit shortened to six months in 1949, without any apparent reasons discernible from his personal dossier. Central dossier of I9.

already been included in group I in the above-mentioned 'wartime' lists of 1951.[76]

Overall, few Ingrians seem to have been suspected of the type of activities and ideologies that could have made them regarded as internal security threats. Instead, aspects pertaining to *social control and morality*, in particular societal norms of *skötsamhet* (conscientiousness), stand out as one of the most important factor influencing the Ingrians' residence permits. Alcoholics and criminals were subject to stricter geographical constraints and shorter residence permits than the other Ingrians. On the whole, however, significant differences have been illuminated between the Ingrian and the Baltic group. These should in all likelihood be interpreted as outcomes of *ethnic preconceptions*, to the detriment of the Ingrians which were more harshly treated.


## 7.4 Russian Refugees' Residence Permits

*All* Russian refugees included in this analysis who arrived in Sweden in the 1940s were issued a strict geographical constraint upon arrival. The majority was also issued the shorter three to five months as their first permit.[77] Only five individuals had six months permits issued at the outset. These were all civilians rather than members of the military – a locksmith, a doctor, a photographer, a shoemaker and a farmer – and arrived at various dates during the second half of the 1940s.[78] However, far from all civilian Russians in the study received this introductory permit. Thus, the military/ civilian aspect does not seem to have been the only determining factor (even though all the former soldiers were issued three months only).[79]

---

76  Central and control dossier in I13. See particularly police reports dated 9
    February 1953 and 25 February 1953 in control dossier. On the wartime lists,
    see 'Herr Statspolisintendenten G. Thulin', 9 augusti 1951, vol. 4, E 4, Hemliga
    arkivet, SUK, Ra; and 'Till Statens Utlänningskommission', 1 februari 1952,
    vol. 4, E 4, Hemliga arkivet, SUK, Ra.

77  R5, R6, R7, R8,R10, R12, R13, R14, R15, R16, R18, R20, R21, R22, R24, R25,
    R30, R31, R32, R34, R38, R39, R43, R45, R46, R47, R48, R51, R54, R55, R62,
    R63, R64, R65, R68, R71, R72, R73, R75, R76, R77, R84, R86, R87, R88.

78  R5, R47, R65, R68, R75.

79  Two Soviet Russian citizens in the study group were issued no geographical

Thus, in comparison with both the Balts and the Ingrians, the Russians were definitely subjected to the harshest treatment upon arrival. As with the Ingrian group, most of them had not attended higher education or enjoyed high social status. There were exceptions, however. A medical doctor, an architect, an interpreter, an engineer, a photographer and a few highly ranked military officials are to be found within the study group. In terms of their first permit, however, their status made little difference.[80]

In the 1950s, however, these practices changed. In line with the new directions, mentioned in part 7.2, the new arrivals were now generally granted a six months permit with a big city constraint only upon arrival, provided that the Commission saw no particular reason to grant them a stricter constraint.[81] An example of such reasons can be found within the handling of the case of an iron worker arriving from Finland in 1950. The security police did not approve of the fact that he was a member of a Finnish communist organisation. The man himself, however, claimed that he had joined that organisation only because he had been advised to do so by other Soviet citizens in Finland. Should he be forced to return to the Soviet Union, that membership was supposed to help him avoid the hardest punishments. Moreover, he claimed to have fled to Sweden to escape from harassments from communists in Finland. The security police remained unconvinced. As a result, he was issued a strict geographical constraint as an attachment to his three month permit.[82]

---

restrictions at all (R35 and R78). However, they arrived from France and Spain with valid entry visas as a tourist and a businessman respectively. Thus, as the Commission had stated in 1946, such individuals were not to be restricted geographically during their stay in Sweden. (See attachment 2 to 'Protokoll', 5 mars 1946, vol. 2, A 1 A, Kanslibyrån, SUK, Ra; and 'Protokoll', 19 februari 1946, vol. 2, A 1 A, Kanslibyrån, SUK, Ra.) Despite the fact that they were not refugees, they have been included in the study since the Commission later considered deporting them from the country. As such, they have both been discussed in chapter five.

80   R5, R25, R30, R51, R75, R88.
81   R9, R61, R70.
82   Central dossier, control dossier and central register card of R1. See particularly a police report dated 14 June 1950 in the control dossier.

### 7.4.1 *Continued Residence Permits*

The time it would take for the Russians who had arrived in the 1940s to have their strict geographical constraints exchanged for a normal big city restriction varied from between one and eight years. Thus their wait was significantly longer than that of both the Balts and the Ingrians.[83] None of the Russians who had to wait for more than three years were criminals, however.[84] But most of them had been involved in the Soviet army in one way or another, and had managed to escape the mass deportations in 1944–46. In fact, *none* of the former Red Army soldiers included in the study group of Russian refugees were issued a normal city constraint in under three years of residence. Most of them waited five to ten years.[85] To receive full freedom of movement took the Russians between six and thirteen years. This was particularly longer than both the Balts and the Ingrians. And again, it was the former Red Army personnel who had to wait the longest. That included individuals who had deserted the Red Army and joined the Finnish or German forces (or the Vlasov army), and individuals who had held higher positions within the military, such as, for example, the man who had worked at the Finnish headquarters.[86]

In terms of lengths of the permits, the examination reveals a similar result. Whereas 'unproblematic' civilians could be granted a two year residence permit within three to six years of residence, the former soldiers often had to wait between ten and fifteen years. Receiving the five year permit took a long time for all the Russians. Whereas a few managed this within seven to nine years, most of them had to wait between ten and twenty years. And again it was the former soldiers – and an increasing number of individuals suspected of political untrustworthiness of some kind during the 1950s – who were repeatedly denied this permit.[87] Individuals who

83   R5, R6, R7, R8, R10, R12, R13, R14, R15, R16, R18, R20, R21, R22, R24, R25, R30, R31, R32, R34, R38, R39, R43, R45, R46, R47, R48, R51, R54, R55, R62, R63, R64, R65, R68, R71, R72, R73, R75, R76, R77, R84, R86, R87, R88.

84   Although some of them would be suspected for communist world views later on.

85   R5, R7, R12, R13, R16, R18, R20, R22, R30, R31, R34, R51, R54, R55, R65, R71, R73, R87.

86   R7, R12, R13, R16, R18, R30, R31, R54, R55, R71, R73, R87.

87   R5, R6, R7, R8, R10, R12, R13, R14, R15, R16, R18, R20, R21, R22, R24, R25, R30, R31, R32, R34, R38, R39, R43, R45, R46, R47, R48, R51, R54, R55, R62, R63, R64, R65, R68, R71, R72, R73, R75, R76, R77, R84, R86, R87, R88.

had by then been convicted of a crime now belonged to this group as well.[88]

As a group, the Russians were thus significantly more constrained in terms of residence permits than both the Balts and the Ingrians. However, those who had served in the Soviet armed forces seem to have lost out the most. For some reason, these individuals were subject to more control by the National Alien Commission than all other Soviet refugees who were not criminal offenders and/or suspected of communist world views or espionage. The former soldiers who had changed sides during the war were not regarded as more trustworthy either – in some cases quite the opposite.

A few civilians had to wait for a similar amount of time for longer residence permits and full freedom of movement. They all had some so-called 'uncomplimentary information' in their personal dossiers.[89] One such man was the photographer mentioned in chapter five. A 'special examination' carried out by the National Alien Commission in 1948 discovered that he was 'negligent and non-conscientious' according to his employer and landlord, and a liar according to his wife. He was to be deported due to his 'defective morals and mode of life', but since no other country than the Soviet Union would accept him the Commission saw no other solution than to postpone the implementation. As a consequence, however, he was continuously issued short residence permits with strict geographical constraints. Although the constraints were removed during the middle of the 1950s (in line with the general developments at that time) he had to wait until the early 1960s before he was issued his first two-year permit. He had then resided in Sweden for fourteen years. In 1964, he became a Swedish citizen, at which point his central dossier within the National Alien Commission, containing several hundreds of pages of reports, letters, pictures, examinations and statements was archived.[90]

Aspects of *social control and morality*, particularly those pertaining to ideals on *skötsamhet* (conscientiousness), thus clearly constituted a determinant factor for the treatment of this man in terms of the conditions to his residence permit. Similar concerns guided

88   See, for example, central dossiers, central register cards and control dossiers of R10 and R31.
89   See, for example, R5, R8, R21, R34.
90   Central dossier of R5. Citations from 'Rapport', 5 november 1948.

the authorities' treatment of another Russian civilian. As a member of the troublesome category of 'young men who [led] a wandering life', he was subject to a strict geographical constraint for ten years. The security police found it worrying that he moved from one place to another (despite his geographical restriction), stayed for only short periods of time at each work place, seemed to receive money from women and enjoyed the occasional 'luxury'. They stated to the Commission that he was 'untrustworthy' and interrogated him many times – particularly in the 1950s. When he at one point spent time with a female secretary at a mobilisation department, it was noted that this secretary had started to make mistakes at work. The security police then suspected that she made them 'on purpose' at the youth's behest in order to sabotage a future possible mobilisation. Thus, the man's lifestyle was not only interpreted as an undesired societal behaviour – it also caused the security police to suspect him of Soviet/communist infiltration. A failure to adjust to *social demands* was thus interlocked with *internal security concerns*. According to his control dossier, however, the evidence against him was very vague. It seems that the facts mentioned above – the itinerant lifestyle, the money and the women – were enough to incur the security police's disapprobation. As a result, the man had to wait fifteen years before he could enjoy his first two years residence permit. Additionally, he was subject to constant police surveillance.[91]

The third Russian civilian who was treated just as strictly as the former Red Army soldiers was a Russian doctor who had worked for the Finnish army and fled to Sweden in 1944. Upon arrival – and much to his displeasure – he was placed in custody for a few months in the northern town of Haparanda. This prompted him to write several letters of complaint to the National Alien Commission. According to a member of prison staff, however, the doctor was a 'peculiar type'. And in early 1945, he was transferred to an internment camp to receive 'special care'. The reason for this was a reported incident whilst in custody in Haparanda, in which a Norwegian man, who had shared his cell, accused him of 'abnormality'. The Norwegian claimed he had seen the Russian doctor

---

91	Control dossier and central register card of R34. Citations from 'Stockholm den 18 september 1950', 'Stockholm den 16 november 1950' and 'Rapport lördagen den 24 mars 1951' in control dossier.

kissing and hugging a young Ingrian man 'as if he was a woman'. Additionally, he had found several 'stains of sperm' in his bed and received an unwelcome approach from him as well. A Finnish man had also witnessed the kiss, and described the doctor as looking at the young Ingrian man as if 'in love'. According to the Finn, the doctor was 'weird' and 'not quite right in the head' – something which he felt was proven further by the fact that he believed he had seen the doctor masturbate during the night.

The events were carefully described in a report, which was sent to the Commission and saved in the man's control dossier. The Commission now stated in its own reports that the Russian doctor was a homosexual and in need of compulsory institutional mental health care. It was also suggested that he was psychotic. But the Swedish doctor who was to treat him did not agree. He claimed that the Russian showed no signs of mental illness and was not in need of care. Thus after two months he was discharged from the internment camp and granted a three months residence permit with a strict geographical restriction. He was assigned a position as a hotel assistant in a small Swedish town.[92]

Nevertheless, the suspected homosexual doctor would struggle with the National Alien Commission for years to come. After some time he was permitted to reside in Stockholm to pursue archival work at a veterinary university college – but still with short residence permits of a few months only and the continuance of a strict geographical restraint. He was not allowed to work as a doctor, even though one of the hospitals in Stockholm offered him a position as such. 'Special examinations' were regularly pursued regarding him, in which his employers and landlords certified that he was conscientious, cooperative, calm and sober-minded and paid his rent on time. Even so, it took him nearly six years to have his strict geographical restraint exchanged for a normal big city constraint. Full freedom of movement was not granted him until 1954, when the Ministry of Justice decided to grant him Swedish citizenship. He had by then resided in Sweden for ten years.[93] Again, however, aspects of *social control and morality* constituted the determinant

92  Numerous documents dated 1944–45 in central dossier and control dossier of
    R51. Citations from 'Rapport' dated 5 December 1944 in control dossier.
93  Various documents dated 1945–54 in central dossier and control dossier of R51.

factor for the National Alien Commission's treatment of this man during his first decade in Sweden. In his case, it had predominantly to do with ideas on *sexual morality*.

The only Russian within this study group who managed to attain full freedom of movement within the same time span as the (non-criminal and trusted) Balts was another doctor who arrived from Norway in the autumn of 1945. Contacts within Swedish society, his own intelligence and knowledge of how to communicate with the authorities meant that he managed not only to have his deportation decision withdrawn (as mentioned in chapter five), but also to receive full freedom of movement after four years of residence. He worked for free at a Swedish hospital and managed to make himself so appreciated among the staff and other members of the Swedish society with influential positions that he eventually received permission to work as a doctor – despite the Board of Medicine's initial reluctance. His personal dossier contains numerous certificates and testimonials from friends and colleagues, all affirming his qualities. His many letters to the authorities were very polite and well-articulated, often emphasizing his 'gratefulness' towards Swedish society and the National Alien Commission in particular. Among the Russian refugees included in this examination, he was the one who was most generously treated. He married a Swedish woman and got permission to reside in Stockholm already in 1946. In 1949, he obtained the right to reside in all of Sweden and in 1954, he became a Swedish citizen. Thus, his own capacity to convince the authorities of his excellent morality, *skötsamhet* (conscientiousness) and social character, led him to be treated far more generously than other Russians.[94]

This was an exception, however. Overall the Russian refugee group contrasts markedly with both the Ingrians and the Balts. Whereas the Balts were more generously treated in terms of lengths and restrictions than the Ingrians, the Ingrians were still not subject to as many short permits and strict geographical constraints as the Russians. The differences remain standing regardless of the inclusion or exclusion of individuals convicted of crimes and/or suspected of espionage or communism. Thus, *ethnic preconceptions* emerge as a likely determinant factor here.

94   Central dossier and central register card of R75.

In the 1950s, however, newly arriving Russians and Ingrians seem to have been treated more equitably in comparison with the Balts. Main city constraints were removed within six months and two and a half years, and five year permits were generally issued within four years. Individuals suspected of political untrustworthiness, however, such as the Russian who had been a member of a Finnish communist organisation, had to wait longer.[95]

### 7.4.2 Shorter Permits and/or Geographical Restrictions Issued Later On

Similar to the Balts and the Ingrians, some Russians had shorter permits and tighter geographical constraints introduced (again) later on. Given the initially stricter treatment of this group, some incidents just led to the continuance of constraints rather than the issuing of new ones (they were simply not lifted). And, similar to the previous groups, it was criminal offences and suspicion of communist views and/or Soviet fifth columnist activities that led to this result.

However, such apprehensions seem to have been more readily applied to the Russian cohort than the Balts and the Ingrians. A supposed witness could, for example, have heard an individual say something positive about the Soviet Union during a lunch break at work, and reported it to the security police. For others, it was their 'wandering lifestyle' or regular travels that awoke their suspicions. Subscriptions to certain magazines constituted another criterion, or, as has been demonstrated, contacts with the Soviet Embassy, for whatever reason. Similarly problematical were individuals who were thought to have personal contacts with communists in Sweden. For many people – and the Russians in particular – this led to shorter residence permits and stricter geographical constraints over a prolonged period, as well as to police surveillance and interrogations. And it was during the early 1950s that suspicions were at their height. Often, however, the indications were rather vague.[96]

95  See, for example, R1, R9, R61, R70, and I51 whose Russian or Ingrian ethnicity has not been possible to determine. The results account for individuals arriving in 1950, 1953 and 1954. Due to the archival situation, names of Russian new arrivals from the years 1951 and 1952 have been difficult to gather.

96  See, for example, central and particularly control dossiers of R7, R10, R18, R19, R21, R57.

One example of these practices is constituted by a Russian artist who was friends with a Swedish professor of physics and his wife in Uppsala. The scientist was a member of the Swedish National Committee of Atomics (*Atomkommittén*). In 1950, an anonymous informant reported to the security police that the artist sometimes lived in the professor's house, supposedly to paint a portrait of his wife. This, it was claimed, meant that he could easily spy on the professor's work, by copying research papers and so forth. This was highly likely, continued the informant, since the suspect was apparently involved with the Soviet legation and had had dealings with a known Swedish communist. The anonymous accuser also suggested that the painter was having an affair with the professor's wife.[97]

There was nothing apart from this unidentified person's testimony to substantiate any of these claims. On the contrary, the security police's interrogations with him and other individuals who knew him suggested that he was a fierce opponent of the Soviet regime. Even so, however, the National Alien Commission expelled him from Uppsala, forced him to move to a small town and issued him a strict geographical constraint. Additionally, his residence permit was shortened from two years to six months. As a former Russian citizen, contact with a family that included an expert on nuclear fission apparently led him to be regarded as a security risk, regardless of the evidence suggesting that he was anything but a communist or a Soviet sympathiser.[98] He was also included in group I in the first version of the wartime lists that were drawn up in August 1951.[99]

Not surprisingly the painter complained vehemently about his ill-treatment and informed the Commission that the man who had reported him was a notorious Russian blackmailer who had tried to extort money from him by threatening to feed the police false accusations. The professor and his wife supported his version of events and criticised the authorities for their handling of this sorry affair.[100]

---

97  Various documents dated 1950 and 1951 in control dossier of R18.

98  Central register card, central dossier and various documents dated 1950 and 1951 in control dossier of R18.

99  'Herr Statspolisintendenten G. Thulin', 9 augusti 1951, vol. 4, E 4, Hemliga arkivet, SUK, Ra.

100 Various documents dated 1950 and 1951 in central dossier and control dossier of R18.

Their efforts were successful. The National Alien Commission reversed the strict geographical constraint that prohibited his presence in the city. Nevertheless, his residence permits were kept short for a further five years, despite the fact that the following special examinations revealed nothing derogatory about him. Not until eleven years later – in 1962 – was he granted his first five year permit.[101]

Thus, it appears that disparaging other refugees and fellow countrymen through reporting 'uncomplimentary information' about them to the security police – particularly in relation to their political orientation – was relatively easy. It constituted a straightforward way to render their lives more difficult. No verification of the information seems to have been required in order for it to have a negative effect on the subject's life, and perhaps particularly if that person happened to be Russian. The National Alien Commission took measures against individuals to be on the safe side.

Indeed, Cold War anxieties and fears of Soviet infiltration apparently pervaded the refugee community itself to a significant degree. Several other cases reveal that the suspicions against Soviet refugees leading to restrictions to their residence permits often originated from other refugees. A housekeeper who had resided in Sweden since 1938 experienced this in 1947 when an Estonian reported her to the security police. She had raised their suspicions already in 1940–41 when she had adhered to the Soviet Union's exhortation and exchanged her former Estonian passport for a Soviet-Russian and taken up employment at the house of a representative of the Soviet legation in Stockholm. Although the suspicions of intelligence activities had soon been dismissed, the immigration authorities had continued to treat her applications with caution, refusing her residence permits longer than twelve months. Similarly, her application for Swedish citizenship had been turned down in 1946.[102]

---

101 Central register card, and various documents dated 1951–1964 in central dossier and control dossier of R18.

102 Since she had arrived before the war, she was never subjected to any geographical constraints and lived in Stockholm (which in itself might also partly explain the shorter residence permits). Various documents dated 1942, and 'p.m.' (by the State Police) dated 4 July 1950, in control dossier of R19; and central register card and various documents dated 1942–46 in central dossier of R19.

In 1947, however, her fellow countrymen's statement about her rendered her life difficult. The fact that she had 'voluntarily' obtained a Soviet-Russian passport had become known by other Estonians and was regarded with the utmost scepticism. One man reported her to the security police, claiming that all Estonians in Sweden who had Russian passports were 'in all likelihood' Russian agents. The housemaid had appeared nervous, added the informant, which he interpreted as a sign that she collected information on other Estonians before passing it to the Russians. Additionally, she had revealed an interest in Estonian anti-communist literature.[103]

Another Estonian, who had been a colleague of hers at the Central Bureau of Statistics, revealed to the security police that he often found her crying, which he interpreted as an indication that she was tormented by 'serious conditions'. A third co-worker reported that she was both unintelligent and uneducated, but that she 'despite this' managed to ingratiate herself with her superiors at work, for example by sending them flowers. He also claimed that she tried to give the impression of being an Estonian national, but gave an evasive answer on any direct questions regarding her citizenship. She had also 'pretended' to be religious, he argued, and visited the Estonian Baptist Community. However, the informant added, it was obvious that she did not pay an interest in this community for only religious reasons, since she had enquired who was funding the movement.[104]

Another event which the informant wished to report regarded a time when he had found her in a room at work one evening. Upon entering she had hastily closed a box into which she had been looking. When he asked her what she was doing, she had claimed to be searching for an eraser. This he had regarded as highly suspicious. However, there was no confidential information kept in that room, the informant admitted. A few weeks later, however, he had found her in an official's office without any due cause, and interpreted this as another sign that she was involved in some unlawful intelligence work for the Soviet authorities.[105]

103 *Ibid.*
104 'P.M.' (by the State Police) dated 4 July 1950 in control dossier of R19.
105 *Ibid.*

The informant admitted that he could not find any more distinct evidence of her illegal activities. However, he claimed with confidence that his opinion was that, as a Russian citizen, it was certain that the woman would have no choice but to work for the Soviet intelligence service. She was likely to be subject to coercion.[106]

No other evidence than these rather nebulous suggestions, seemingly based on the Estonians' deep aversion towards a former compatriot willingly adopting Soviet nationality, was found of her supposed illegal activities. Even so, when the woman applied for Swedish citizenship again in 1950 the security police put this information together in a report and sent it to the National Alien Commission and the Ministry of Justice. As a consequence, she was denied citizenship.[107]

Additionally, in 1951, she was brought in for interrogation due to her application for a Swedish alien's passport. She claimed to want to change her Soviet passport for a Swedish one, in order to put an end to the rumours about her supposed espionage activities. It would also reduce the risk of her getting an order to return to the Soviet Union, she argued. She claimed to regret the decision to change her passport, not least because of all the hassle it had caused her in terms of vicious rumours and ill treatment from other Estonians in Sweden. She had been enticed to do it at the time, she said, and had had no one to talk to for advice. She vigorously denied having been engaged in any intelligence services for the Russians, and when asked about her political views she claimed to be uninterested in politics, although she was opposed to the current regime in Estonia. She was asked detailed questions about her visits to the Soviet Embassy, which she had been forced to pursue when her passport needed to be renewed, since her previous applications for a Swedish alien's passports had been refused. When asked if she wanted to return to the Soviet Union, she started crying and claimed, according to the police protocol, that 'one does not travel to Siberia out of one's own free will'.[108]

106 *Ibid.*
107 *Ibid.*; and 'Underdånigt utlåtande' dated 10 March 1949, 'Underdånigt utlåtande' dated 6 September 1950, and 'Till överståthållarämbetet' dated 27 October 1950, in central dossier of R19.
108 'P.M.' (by the State Police) dated 6 July 1951 in control dossier of R19.

                                                            

The police officer somewhat spitefully declared that the woman, who was now in her fifties, 'took to tears, as soon as the interrogation touched upon individuals or events that had gone against her'. He also stated that 'he could not help getting the impression that she engaged in some kind of acting'.[109]

As a result, the housekeeper was yet again refused a Swedish alien's passport. In addition, she had her residence permit (which was already short compared to refugees with Swedish alien's passports) shortened to six months. No geographical restrictions were issued, however.[110] When the wartime lists were set up, nonetheless, she too was included as a group I individual.[111]

Another example occurred in the case of a 23 year-old Russian circus artiste who fled to Sweden from Poland in 1948. He was seconded to work in a metal factory in northern Sweden where he encountered several Swedish communists. He even happened to be assigned to cohabit with one of them for a short period as he recovered from tuberculosis. He later told the police that, as an act of friendliness towards his host, he had followed this Swede to a number of communist meetings. They had paid him to perform his circus act and he had enjoyed the dancing that took place afterwards. He attracted considerable attention at work due to his nationality. This, he claimed, did not prevent him from disagreeing with his communist-minded colleagues when they praised the conditions in the Soviet Union. Not wishing to anger them, however, he had let himself be persuaded to sign his name on an appeal they had formulated.[112]

A few of his Polish colleagues, however, did not approve of his overly sympathetic attitude towards the Swedish communists, and reported him to the security police. They claimed he too was a communist and that he had tried to read their personal letters during a visit to their home. This led them to suspect that he was involved in espionage.[113]

109 *Ibid.*
110 Central dossier and central register card of R19.
111 'Herr Statspolisintendenten G. Thulin', 9 augusti 1951, vol. 4, E 4, Hemliga arkivet, s u k, Ra; and 'Till Statens Utlänningskommission', 1 februari 1952, vol. 4, E 4, Hemliga arkivet, s u k, Ra.
112 Various documents (mostly police reports) dated 1950 and 1951 in control dossier of R10.
113 *Ibid.*

The young Russian was interrogated, but denied having anything to do with Soviet agents. He also disavowed being a communist. He had encountered trouble in Poland due to his refusal to join the communist party. Moreover, he had fled to Sweden when the Polish authorities discovered his Russian citizenship and claimed they were seeking to repatriate him to the Soviet Union, where he knew he would be punished for his illegal departure. He gave a detailed account for how he had been persuaded to go to the communist meetings in northern Sweden, and how he had tried to avoid provoking the Swedish communists at work whilst also acting in a courteous manner to his Swedish host during his convalescence. However, the suspicions remained with him and he had his residence permits shortened to three months in the autumn of 1950.[114] And on the wartime lists, he was registered as a group I individual.[115]

That accusations of this kind were taken particularly seriously during the 1950s is emphasised further by the treatment of another group I individual on the wartime lists: a 60 year-old Russian who had resided in Sweden since 1913. The security police believed him to be a communist. His agitation for communist ideas was well known, and he apparently subscribed to both the communist magazine 'Ny Dag' (*New Day*) and the syndicalist 'The Worker' (*Arbetaren*). This had been known since 1939 and, during the war, police examinations had taken place in order to try to establish whether or not he worked for the Soviet authorities. Nonetheless, the resultant examination proved inconclusive. In 1950, however, his residence permits were suddenly shortened. No new information about him had been discovered, as far as his personal dossiers can reveal. Nevertheless, the information now seems to have been interpreted as more 'uncomplimentary' than before.[116]

The evidence of communist sympathies appears to have been more well-founded in the case of the 60 year-old than in the previ-

---

114 Central register card, central dossier and various police reports dated 1950 and 1951 in control dossier of R10.

115 'Herr Statspolisintendenten G. Thulin', 9 augusti 1951, vol. 4, E 4, Hemliga arkivet, SUK, Ra; and 'Till Statens Utlänningskommission', 1 februari 1952, vol. 4, E 4, Hemliga arkivet, SUK, Ra.

116 In 1949 he was also denied Swedish citizenship. Central register card, control register card and central dossier of R23.

ously mentioned cases. There were also individuals whose links with the Soviet Embassy were indisputable, even if the nature of that contact was uncertain. This was the case with the 50 year-old Russian anti-communist sailor mentioned in chapter five. In 1945 he had spat in the face of an Orthodox priest who he felt was spreading communist propaganda. Some years later this very same assailant paid fourteen visits to the Soviet Embassy. A subsequent deportation decision, issued in 1951, could not be implemented since he was regarded as a political refugee. As a result, he was expelled from Stockholm and had his following residence permits shortened to a few months. And he was indeed included in group I on the wartime lists. His alcohol abuse, which he sometimes failed to disguise, did not help his cause either.[117]

Perhaps not surprisingly, individuals against whom there were stronger indications of illegal intelligence activities were subjected to similar restrictions. A Russian who was known to have been in close contact with several individuals who had been sentenced in court for espionage, as well as members of other countries' legations (of both East and West) who were known to engage in unlawful espionage activities, constitutes one such example.[118]

However, due to the authorities' practices during the 1950s, which seems to have been characterised by a 'better safe than sorry'-attitude, far more individuals than those of whom one can actually confirm that indications of unlawful activities *were* significant, were subject to the same kind of treatment. In particular, those who were believed to embrace communist opinions were subjected to an arbitrary kind of discrimination and the removal of their freedom of movement by the National Alien Commission. The security police's and the National Alien Commission's joint endeavours thus constituted an extensive process of registration of (possible) political opinions and the issuing of increased control and 'punishments' of supposed wrong thinking. And had the threat of war become acute in Sweden, they would have been immediately interned.

Thus, the fears of communist infiltration and Soviet aggression that characterised Swedish society during this period clearly influ-

117 Central dossier and control dossier of R52.
118 Control dossier and control register card of R42. See also control dossier of R56.

enced the authorities' handling of these individuals. It is, therefore, reasonable to argue that the increasing *external security concerns* that the international Cold War developments brought to Sweden during the early 1950s exacerbated the interpretation of Russian refugees as potential *internal security threats*. This, in its turn had a direct bearing on their treatment.

In comparison with the Balts and the Ingrians, however, Russians appear to have been more likely to be suspected of communist world views and espionage. If taking into account the fact that the Balts and the Ingrians constituted a significantly larger refugee group in Sweden than the Russians, the difference becomes even more striking. It is difficult to ascertain, of course, whether more Russians than Balts and Ingrians actually *were* communists. The examples above demonstrate, however, that suspicions arose more easily regarding Russians – and were taken more seriously – than those in relation to Balts and Ingrians. It seems to have been easier for a Russian to be the subject of rumours of political untrustworthiness – and, indeed, for this to have consequences for their residence permits. The way the security police and the National Alien Commission handled the, to say the least, rather imprecise accusations levelled against the Russian painter and the Estonian-Russian housekeeper, suggests that the authorities kept a significantly more watchful eye over the Russian refugees than their Baltic and Ingrian neighbours. In tandem with the design of the wartime lists, this indicates that Russians were in themselves regarded as more likely to be communists – or to *become* communists should they be influenced by the 'wrong' company – than Balts and Ingrians. Although all the Soviet refugees had supposedly fled from the communist regime in the Soviet Union, the Russians seem to have been regarded as more likely to be ideologically influenced by it – just by the simple fact that their nationality was Russian. It is, thus, reasonable to assume that *aspects of ethnicity* influenced these attitudes and policies too.

However, as with the Balts and the Ingrians, some Russians were also subject to limitations of their residence permits as a consequence of aspects of *social control and morality*. The illiterate Russian (described in chapter five) who failed to pay his bills after a year of residence constitutes one such example. His residence permits were shortened to three months.[119] The self-proclaimed Russian prince (also mentioned in the same chapter), who married and was financially supported by a Swedish female artist of reputedly instable mind, and whom the authorities revealed strong antipathies against, was subject to similar consequences.[120] (Here, *economic aspects* can be shown to be at play too.) And, finally, the issuing of restrictions to Russians convicted of various 'ordinary' crimes matched the treatment of analogous Balts and Ingrians.[121]

## 7.5 Conclusion

This examination has revealed a number of things. First of all, the results demonstrate clearly that among the Soviet refugees of whom no particular so-called 'uncomplimentary information' existed, the National Alien Commission treated Balts more generously than Ingrians and Russians. They were issued fewer strict geographical restraints, and enjoyed full freedom of movement and longer residence permits significantly faster than individuals belonging to the other two categories. In other words, Balts were considerably *less controlled* than the other two categories.

The Ingrians take a middle position. Initial permits were stricter and shorter, and waiting periods for full freedom of movement and five year permits were longer than for the Baltic group. However, they were still more generous than those granted to the Russians. This group had to wait the longest for both freedom of movement and longer residence permits, and were thus the category among the Soviet refugees that were *most controlled*. The waiting period between Balts and Russians could differ by up to fifteen years. Former Red Army soldiers were treated with a particular lack of generosity. Short permits and strict geographical constraints could characterise the lives of these individuals for up to ten years, without any 'uncomplimentary information' relating to their personal behaviour being discovered. The Russian civilians were treated in a significantly more hard-hearted manner in comparison with

---

119 Central dossier and central register card of R68.
120 Central dossier and central register card of R35.
121 See, for example, R8, R10, R21, R31. It should be noted that some of these were subsequently suspected of illegal intelligence activities.

the Balts too. Only one individual within the Russian study group managed to obtain full freedom of movement within the same period as was standard for the Balts. He was an educated, articulate medical doctor with an excellent capacity to communicate with the authorities and an ability to use his many contacts among the Swedish elite.

The differences between the three groups can be summarised in the following graph.

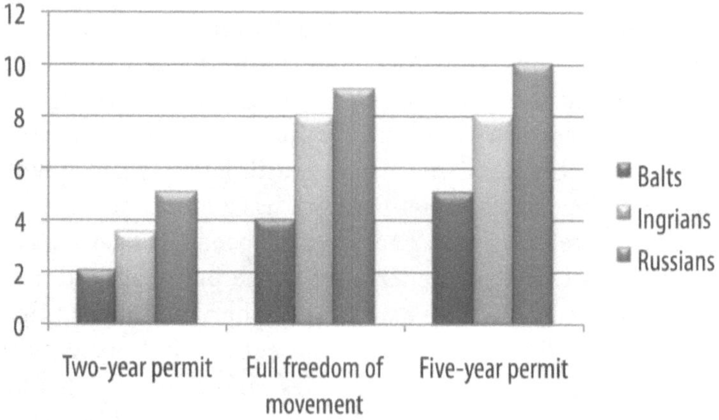


*Caption: Number of years that a refugee (not suspected or convicted for criminal or antisocial behaviour or political untrustworthiness) arriving in 1945–49 could generally expect to wait before being granted two and five year residence permits and full freedom of movement*

No reasons for the differences pertaining to the refugees' personal behaviour can be identified in their personal dossiers. As collectives, though, the Baltic group differed from the Ingrians and the Russians somewhat in terms of social status, financial position and education, since a significant portion of the Baltic refugees had belonged to the middle and upper classes in their home countries.[122] However, *within* the Ingrian and Russian category, such factors mattered less as the few with higher social status and education tended to be treated in the same manner as other individuals of the

122 Byström claims that the Swedish authorities classified 20% of the Baltic refugees as 'intellectuals'. Byström 2012, p. 122.

same category, unless they made a substantial effort to persuade the authorities of their trustworthiness and excellent character.

The results thus indicate that *aspects of ethnicity* constituted the most significant reason for this difference. Previous research has, as mentioned in chapter one, demonstrated a significant antipathy towards Eastern Europeans in Sweden during the first half of the 20th century. It seems, however, that Balts were not considered to belong to that group to the same extent as Russians. Although hostility definitely prevailed against the Balts within Swedish society (particularly within the factories and labour unions, as Horgby has demonstrated) they were clearly regarded as more acceptable than both Russians and Ingrians. Although factors such as social status possibly mattered too, they cannot solely explain the conspicuous differences between the Balts' and the Russians' residence permits. The treatment the Russians received ultimately came down to the fact that they were *Russians*. Ingrians, who according to the Minister for Foreign Affairs had after all been 'Russians for 200 years', were not treated as generously as the Balts, but still not as harshly as the Russians.[123] Their Finnish heritage and Lutheran religion in all likelihood influenced the authorities' perception of the Ingrians as more 'similar' to Swedes (and therefore also more trustworthy) than the Russians. In fact, it is possible that the Swedish 17th century heritage of both the Balts and the Ingrians in the end meant that they were not considered to be as culturally and ethnically dissimilar to Swedes as Russians. As a result, they were treated more generously.

Aspects of both *external* and *internal security* were deeply involved in these practices too. This is apparent particularly from 1948 onwards as the Cold War conflict intensified. Potential communists and Soviet infiltrators now came to be regarded the most significant threat to Sweden's political stability. External security concerns thus turned refugees into potential internal security threats, and individuals suspected of being spies, agents or just supporters of left wing / socialist / communist ideas often had severe restrictions placed on their residence permits, even in cases where the evidence was indeed vague. And as international tensions heightened even further in the early 1950s, so too did the

---

123 On the Minister's statement, see chapter four, part 4.3.1.

security police's hunt for suspicious foreigners in Sweden.

These fears seem to have had more consequences for the Russian refugees than for the other two categories, however. The authorities watched them more carefully than the others and reacted more robustly to the surfacing of any 'uncomplimentary information' of a political nature. All in all, they seem to have regarded the Russians as more politically untrustworthy *in themselves* – including an interpretation of them as more susceptible to communism and Soviet pressure than the occupied Balts and oppressed Ingrians. Reinforcing this interpretation is the design of the wartime lists from 1951 and 1952. These omitted Balts and Ingrians from the third group but included Russians and all other Eastern European nationalities. This also suggests that these preconceptions were not only determined by the political history of the three categories, but also by aspects of *ethnic prejudice*. The results thus indicate that the *security concerns* that determined these practices were also influenced by *ethnic preconceptions* towards Eastern Europeans, rendering Balts and Ingrians as less likely to constitute a threat to Swedish national security than Russians.

The results also reinforce the sense that it was the potential communists rather than the confirmed Nazis that were regarded as a pressing threat to the Swedish state and society. This had consequences for the issuance of residence permits. Former Nazi collaborators among the Balts were generally not subjected to any particular consequences apart from, in some cases, a longer wait for the five year permit. This did not affect all of them, however, and in terms of geographical constraints and two year permits, they were all treated according to the same principles as other Balts.

Aspects of *social control and morality*, however, influenced the authorities' treatment of all three categories' residence permits. The rigorous assessment procedure – here taken to constitute a system of surveillance – was designed not only to expose possible security threats among the foreigners, but to facilitate social control over them too. Questions pertaining to personal behaviour were specifically emphasised in the National Alien Commission's instructions to the police. And, evidently, social behaviours perceived as degenerate, such as alcohol abuse or an itinerant disposition, as well as, obviously, criminal offences, led to stricter and shorter residence permits. However, even matters such as personal sexual behaviour, unusual personalities and financial agreements between spouses challenging the norm of the male breadwinner could be penalised by the National Alien Commission through the issuing of stricter residence permits. The state's interference in the individual refugee's life can thus be considered to have been significant – at least in those cases where it found behaviour deemed to be inferior.

The other two influential factors identified in the first chapter – economics and international juridical developments – seem to have played a secondary but not insignificant role. *Economic aspects* were to some degree involved in the management of individuals who could not or did not support themselves – particularly if they were men. *International juridical developments*, on the other hand, were by all likelihood the most important reason for the discontinuation of the usage of the strict geographical constraint as a standard for all newly arrived refugees from 1950 onwards. This made practices regarding new arrivals somewhat less discriminatory. The international juridical developments were in all likelihood also the reason why new internment legislation, similar to that which had been in use during the Second World War, was never established in the early 1950s, despite the increasing internal security concerns relating to refugees and the security police's and the National Alien Commission's resulting appeals. The 1951 Refugee Convention forbade such arbitrary restrictions to refugees' freedom of movement. Even so, however, geographical constraints remained in place for the most suspect of individuals long after this date.

# CHAPTER EIGHT

# Conclusion: Security, Ethnicity, Morality or Human Rights?

What factors determine refugee policies in liberal democracies? That was the wide-ranging question with which this thesis began. Its aim has been to contribute to the diverse scholarly debate pertaining to this issue. Its objective has been to conduct a detailed examination of the factors that governed Sweden's policies towards Soviet refugees between 1945 and 1954. The Swedish authorities' management of 260 Soviet refugees has been scrutinised with attention being given to two facets in particular. Firstly when it came to their right to reside in Sweden and, secondly, in terms of the continuous treatment of those who were granted leave to remain through the issuance of various residence permits. The spatial and temporal choices governing this study were motivated primarily by the specific Cold War conditions that characterised Swedish society during the first post-war decade. They made it conducive to an exploration of conflicting interests affecting a refugee policy regimen that itself appears to have undergone considerable change at this time. Six potential influential aspects were identified in the introductory chapter, namely: *external security*; *internal security*; *economics*; *ethnicity*; *social control and morality*; and *international juridical developments*. It transpired that they all, in various ways and to different degrees, influenced the pursued policies. In the following, the results of the study will be summarised and situated within a wider scholarly context. Prompted by these results, a theoretical discussion about the relationship between security and refugee policies will conclude the chapter.

## 8.1 Adjustment to International Juridical Developments

The examination has revealed rapidly developing policies directed towards Soviet refugees between 1945 and 1954. The *first* important change regards the *strengthening of asylum rights*. Whereas guiding principles were still unsettled in 1945, leading to the removal of several Soviet citizens from Swedish territory, basically all Soviet refugees were granted asylum towards the end of the research period, provided that they had arrived from the Soviet Union or the grey zone areas of Eastern Europe. A further safeguard applied to those refugees who had resided in Sweden for some time but become regarded as 'unwanted' due to their (assumed) political beliefs, unconventional lifestyles and/or criminal offences; and individuals who were demanded for extradition by the Soviet authorities. During the second half of the research period only persons sentenced in court for unlawful intelligence activities were removed from the country by referral to the Soviet Union. Although the immigration authorities (including the National Alien Commission, the Aliens Appeals Board, and, not the least, the security police) sometimes attempted to remove certain individuals regarded as politically untrustworthy, the government proved to be more unwilling to do so and put a halt to these plans.

The strengthening of refugees' asylum rights occurred gradually during the first three post-war years. A definite watershed year was 1948. Prior to that date, Soviet refugees could be removed from Swedish territory for a variety of reasons. The grounds for this might pertain to themselves as individuals, such as criminal behaviour or a failure to convince the authorities of their reasons for political asylum. But it could also be determined, in part at least, by bilateral Swedish-Soviet relations. However, after the infamous extradition of the military Balts and Germans in 1945–46, those individuals issued removal decisions were still protected either through postponement of their extradition or by virtue of their referral to another Western country. From 1948 onwards, practically all Soviet refugees were regarded as political refugees and their asylum rights were fully protected.[1]

---

1    It was also revealed, however, that this does not seem to have applied to all

The analysis suggested several reasons for this changing picture. One regarded the Swedish administration's fluctuating estimation of the Soviet Union. Post-war Sweden evinced an initial admiration for the Soviet Union, and a wish to establish friendly relations for reasons of future stability and (external) security. However, this appraisal turned rapidly sour as the Soviet Union tightened its grip over Eastern Europe. Initial bridge building ambitions were gradually abandoned. This probably influenced the Swedish government's willingness to recognise Soviet citizens' refugee rights. At the same time, non-aligned Sweden's membership of the United Nations and its wish to (at least on an ideational basis) belong to the democratic bloc encouraged it to fall into line with the developing human rights standards, even as they were themselves influenced by the Cold War conflict. Indeed, already by 1948 Sweden had adjusted fully to the asylum regulations in the form of the new international refugee convention then taking shape. Thus it appears that practices changed before the actual legislation was drawn up to govern them.

The *international juridical developments* on refugee rights thinking within the UN thus stand out as the most important influential factor for Swedish asylum policies during the first post-war decade. Reinforcing this interpretation is another change that took place at this time, namely a noticeable depoliticization of refugee issues. The results revealed in this thesis show that the extensive government involvement that characterised the individual asylum cases of particularly Ingrian and Russian refugees in 1945–47 came to a definite halt in 1948. From then on, the law-implementing authorities were left to assess asylum cases according to predetermined principles. This in itself made asylum policies less politically sensitive, as it reduced those potential external security concerns that were previously inherent. When the government no longer considered itself as directly responsible for the assessment of individual cases, it could seek protection from any resultant Soviet pressure. Thus, as asylum policies became more a juridical than a political matter, they were notably liberated from

Eastern Europeans. Correspondence exists that tells of some Poles and Eastern Germans still being refused entry by the turn of the decade due to the Swedish authorities' wish to try to control the numbers of new arrivals by means of deterrence.

bilateral tensions. The handling of the extradition demands demonstrates this further. A semi-cooperative attitude in 1946–47, which included refusing to expatriate demanded individuals to the Soviet Union but allowing Soviet authorities access to them on Swedish territory, was replaced by an intractable refusal to accede to any such requests from 1948 onwards. In addition, they were from that point on dealt with by an administrative section of the Ministry for Foreign Affairs rather than, as previously, by government representatives.

## 8.2 National Security and Social Control

The strengthening of asylum rights meant that the Swedish authorities lost some control over its borders. They were now more or less compelled to grant asylum to new arrivals if they were categorised as political refugees, even if they found them 'unwanted' for some reason. The results of this study reveal, however, that control was maintained in other ways. Accordingly, the *second* significant result of this thesis is the light it casts on the ways in which the Swedish immigration authorities used the *residence permit as a control tool* for the monitoring of refugees' lifestyle and behaviour. And it was primarily concerns for national security and social control that governed these practices.

Residence permits were issued for differing periods of time and attached with various geographical constraints throughout the research period. These procedures enabled the authorities to control the foreigners, both through the extensive information collection procedure that was pursued every time a foreigner applied for a renewal of the residence permit, and through the physical restraint that often came with such a permit. The Alien's Law did not define what sort of circumstances should lead to what type of residence permit. This left the National Alien Commission with a substantial room for manoeuvre.

The examination of these practices revealed several reasons for the issuing of stricter permits. The most important pertained to *internal security*. Through its residence permit application system and a far-reaching collaboration with the security services, the National Alien Commission kept the Soviet refugee group under surveillance. From 1948 onwards, when international tensions grew, the Swedish authorities perceived an increasing need to maintain a close watch on this cohort. The hunt for potential spies, communists and/or (future) fifth columnists had severe consequences for several individuals. Confirmed or suspected socialist or communist sympathies could lead to shorter permits, drastically reduced freedom of movement, police surveillance and even expulsion from one's city of residence. Any confirmed contacts with the Soviet legation had similar consequences. Even rather nebulous and unverified rumours of possible political untrustworthiness could lead to such measures. No evidence was required. The security services had several informants among the refugee groups. As the international situation grew tenser, the perceived seriousness of any allegations increased.

So, increasing international *external* security concerns from 1948 onwards had two somewhat contradictory consequences for Swedish refugee policies. On the one hand they influenced Sweden's ideational move towards the West which brought depoliticization and thus *'de-securitisation'* to its asylum policies, making them more stable and coherent for Soviet refugees. On the other hand they caused an increased *internal* security framing of refugee issues, rendering all Soviet refugees potential security threats in the eyes of the Swedish authorities. While their right to asylum was strengthened, they were exposed to a higher risk of having their freedom of movement drastically reduced.

The other important reason for stricter residence permits pertained to *social control and morality*. The results demonstrate the extent to which the permit was deployed as means of monitoring and influencing the behaviour of refugees who were regarded as socially deviant. This remit included sexual conduct, work morals, drinking habits, financial solvency and general conscientiousness. It was also influenced by ideas on gender, which became clear from the authorities' hostile treatment of a Russian man who, rather than taking up employment, was financially supported by his Swedish wife; and by the deportation of an Ingrian female prostitute in the early 1950s. Morality issues were thus monitored to the same extent as internal security issues. The residence permit application procedure provides abundant evidence of this. It became routine for landlords, employers and others to provide detailed statements about the applicant's character and personal behaviour before his or her permit was renewed and any restrictions lifted. Individuals who did not conduct themselves according to contemporaneous social norms were granted shorter permits and stricter constraints. This enabled the authorities to maintain their surveillance with the aim of trying to compel them to change their ways. Contemporaneous ideals of *skötsamhet* (conscientiousness) proved to be at the heart of these practices. Thus, the interventionist aspects that characterised the social policies of the early Swedish welfare state (broadly outlined in chapter one, part 1.1.5) coloured its management of foreigners too.

Some aspects of this control structure eased towards the end of the research period. Permits became gradually longer, and more generous in terms of freedom of movement. By the 1950s, the practice of placing strict geographical constraints on all newcomers was abolished. This was clearly influenced by international juridical developments on refugee rights, which rendered such measures anachronistic. Still, however, these instruments were used when the authorities perceived there to be a need. Individuals who fell under specific suspicion remained continually restricted, especially if this pertained to dubious political points of view. Practices such as these ran counter to the regulations set down in the 1951 Refugee Convention, which states that foreigners should enjoy the same freedom of movement as other citizens, and that this liberty must not be restricted without a court mandate.[2]

## 8.3 The Securitisation of Ethnic Prejudice

The control system outlined above demonstrates that the Swedish authorities regarded *all* foreigners as untrustworthy to some extent, and thus in need of monitoring. However, the results of this thesis have also made clear that some foreigners were regarded as significantly more unreliable than others. The grounds for determining this ran largely along ethnic lines. Thus, the *third* important result of this study is its illumination of how significantly differently the Swedish authorities treated Balts, Ingrians and Russians, and how

2    *1951 Convention relating to the Status of Refugees,* Article 26.

*perceptions of threat and security were influenced by ethnic prejudice.*
This was true both for new arrivals and those who had resided in
Sweden for some time.

In terms of new arrivals, the first post-war years saw the continuance of practices inherited from the Second World War. The
recognition of Baltic nationals as political refugees on the basis of
their experience of recent occupation was largely sustained, with
only a few exceptions. As such, incoming Balts were continually
granted asylum if arriving from the Soviet Union or any grey zone
areas. Ingrians and Russians, on the other hand, had to struggle
harder. Unusually clear guidelines based on individual assessment
were established for the Ingrians in 1945, with the aim of drawing a
distinction between those who were to be sent back to Finland and
those who were to be protected. As a result, several Ingrians were
refused entry up until the summer of 1946, when policies changed
in their favour. Not until 1948, however, were their asylum rights
fully recognised.[3]

It was the Russians, however, who had to really fight for a right
to asylum. In contrast to Allied policy, Sweden granted protection to some Russians in 1945. Yet this governed only 'hard core'
political refugees such as those who had fought against their own
country. The others were repatriated regardless of other mitigating
circumstances. This included prisoners of war, deserters and others
deemed to be traitors in the eyes of the Soviet authorities.

As in other Western countries, these policies changed gradually.
Already in 1946 officials within the National Alien Commission
began to recognise a Russian's flight within Sweden as a potential
ground for asylum. In late 1947, the same guidelines that had been
used for the Ingrians since 1945 were applied to the Russians. Up
until 1948, however, Russians were collectively regarded as less
worthy of political asylum than the other two categories.

To a significant degree, these discriminatory practices were
guided by the collective approach to asylum that governed refugee policies internationally as well as in Sweden both before and
during the Second World War. Asylum was granted to national
or ethnic groups based on their shared experiences. As such, Balts

3   However, in the early 1950s some 'unwanted' individuals were again removed
    on the grounds that the Swedish authorities now regarded the risk to Ingrians
    in Finland as insignificant.

were accorded asylum regardless of their individual circumstances on the basis that they belonged to three national groups that had recently experienced occupation by a foreign power. Ingrians took a middle position. They were regarded as legitimate Soviet citizens since they had belonged to Russia for two centuries. However, recognition of their particularly severe circumstances as well as, in all likelihood, their Finnish-Swedish heritage, prompted the government into drawing up individual guidelines for the Ingrians. The Russians could draw on no such collective experiences. However, as the Cold War conflict developed and refugee policies became more individualised, recognising both reasons for flight and risk of persecution led to a re-evaluation of the Russians' right to asylum.

Evidence also suggests, nonetheless, that these policies were influenced by perceptions of the supposed 'inherent' characteristics of these three groups (in other words ethnic prejudice). This is because, in terms of the residence permit practices at least, the results clearly reveal the Balts to have been regarded with more trust than both Ingrians and, in particular, Russians. Here, a general antipathy towards Russians seems to have taken its full toll. During the entire research period, Russians were granted significantly shorter residence permits with considerably stricter geographical restraints than both Balts and Ingrians. Whereas Balts generally had to wait between four and five years for the longer five-year residence permit and full freedom of movement, the Russians waited on average nine to ten years, regardless of whether or not there was any 'uncomplimentary information' gathered about them in their files within the National Alien Commission. Initial permits were significantly more generous towards the Balts than the Russians too. Only one Russian included in the examination – an articulate medical doctor who diligently used all his social capital to persuade the authorities of his excellent character – enjoyed the same generous conditions as those which were standard for the Balts. Ingrians were treated somewhat more generously than the Russians, but still substantially more harshly than the Balts, often waiting around seven or eight years for their longer, restriction-free permits. This was despite the fact that, as a collective, the Ingrians had remarkably fewer pieces of 'uncomplimentary information' in their dossiers.

Despite the extensiveness of their individual dossiers, no reasons for these conspicuous differences pertaining to the refugees as individuals could be found. As collectives, distinctions pertaining to social status were identified, as the Baltic refugees were often more educated and had been in possession of stronger financial and social capital within their home countries than had the Ingrians and the Russians. However, within the Russian and Ingrian refugee groups, such differences mattered less, as erudite and non-educated individuals alike were mostly issued similar kinds of permits. Instead, these practices by all means stand out as being based on a different evaluation of individuals depending on to which ethnic and/or national group they were deemed to belong. Consequently, Balts were regarded as more trustworthy *in themselves* than Ingrians, who in their turn were still regarded as more trustworthy than the Russians, who constituted the most monitored group among the three. This appears to have been simply because they were Russian. The inclusion of suspected Nazi-collaborators among the Balts made little difference, as these individuals still generally enjoyed more freedom of movement and longer residence permits than both Ingrians and Russians.

Aspects of ethnicity thus influenced perceptions of security. The authorities' management of those regarded as raising particular security concerns reinforces this interpretation. Russians were looked upon as more likely to be – or to become – communists and/or Soviet agents, than Balts. Although it was fairly well known that Soviet agents had infiltrated all the Soviet refugee groups, the authorities kept a closer eye on the Russians than the Balts. Allegations of potential political untrustworthiness could have severe consequences for any Soviet refugee, but particularly if they happened to be Russian. The design of the 'wartime' lists drawn up in the early 1950s against a backdrop of international tensions reinforces this impression. Extra surveillance was accorded all Russians (together with other Eastern Europeans) that were subject to non-political 'uncomplimentary' information. This was not the case with the Balts and Ingrians. The authorities (not least the security police) thus appear to have perceived that they had more reason to watch over the Russians in general than they had the Balts and the Ingrians. And, as a result, the residence permits issued to the former were also collectively shorter and stricter in terms of freedom of movement.

Another similar intersection of influential aspects regards morality and security. Individuals perceived as socially untrustworthy, such as roving young men who refused to adjust to contemporaneous social expectations, were regarded as more likely to be, or to become, spies. The extra monitoring of this group was thus not only triggered by a wish to compel them to adjust to a moral code; it was also a result of the interpretation of them as likely potential internal security threats.

## 8.4 Adding Complexity to Previous Research

The results of this thesis challenge previous scholarly interpretations of the mechanisms of refugee policies. One important insight it offers is constituted by its illumination of the *complexity* of this policy area. Every aspect of refugee policies under scrutiny revealed influences from more than one factor. No single variable could explain any of the major developments that took place. Whereas both aspects of external security and international juridical developments had a profound impact on the changing asylum policies, internal security, ethnicity, social control and morality had a bearing on the issuing of residence permits. In addition, a number of exceptional, time-and-place-specific circumstances were proven to have impacted on pursued policies. The legacy of the controversial extradition of the military Balts, for example, impinged on the management of subsequent demands and, not the least, the Ingrians' asylum claims. Similarly, the structural heritage of a collective approach to asylum, with roots stemming back to the First World War and the origins of the refugee regime, continued to influence policies right up until 1948.

Thus, although confirming previous researchers' assertions that aspects of *ethnicity* were a major influential factor on refugee related decisions in Sweden during the mid-20th century, this thesis also demonstrates clearly that ethnicity alone cannot provide sufficient explanation of the pursued policies. In particular, national security concerns (internal and external) and Sweden's relationship with the international community emerge as areas that have previously been overlooked. The extent to which aspects of social control and morality influenced residence permit practices also generates further questions about how such issues were dealt with both prior to, and after, the time period examined in this study.

Additionally, the study sheds some light on previous scholarly debates on the timing and organisational structure of refugee policies in Sweden during and slightly after the Second World War. It supports Byström's and others argument that a transformation of attitudes in Swedish refugee policies occurred *after* rather than *during* the war. A structural and ideational change took place in 1948, when Sweden adjusted its asylum policies fully to prevailing juridical developments. In terms of organisational structures and the division of power between politicians and bureaucrats (mentioned in chapter two), this study demonstrates that it was the government that had the upper hand when it came to *asylum* policies. Prior to 1948 it orchestrated practices regarding Soviet (particularly Russian and Ingrian) refugees by means of a close involvement in individual cases, often through the issuing of precedential decisions. The bilateral tensions that were intertwined with these decisions rendered it essential for the government to retain power. After 1948, the juridical reinterpretation of asylum policies depoliticised the assessment of individual cases. That said, however, the new principles that were then established were in all likelihood provided by the political administration. Nevertheless, when it comes to the practices of the *continuous residence permits*, this study has revealed a significant room for manoeuvre for individual bureaucrats, with decisions being made on subjective grounds.

Although specifically relating to the Swedish early Cold War context, the results of this thesis have relevance at a more general level. This is because refugee policies are inherently enmeshed in other aspects of the societal and political life of liberal democracies. Granting asylum to another state's citizen is to make a solemn political verdict about that state. As such, it is inextricably entwined with bilateral relations.[4] This can be fairly uncomplicated for the host state in some situations, and deeply troublesome in others, not least in times of severe international tension and military threat. Additionally, within the nation state in particular, the refugee's cultural background may be perceived in various ways

---

4   Salomon 1991, ch.1.

depending on several circumstances. Domestic policies, populism and humanitarian concerns can also influence or be influenced by the state's management of refugees. This undoubtedly also includes the national economy of the host state. Refugees can both contribute to the financial system and weaken it. The comparatively small numbers of refugees that came to Sweden during the first decade of the Cold War meant that such factors mattered less. That economic arguments are nearly always present in debates over refugee policies in modern, liberal democracies is, however, underlined by the fact that they continued to feature when it came to those Balts who arrived from Western countries, and still to some Poles and East Germans in 1949 (according to the Minister of the Interior, as was revealed in the introduction to chapter four). Moreover, since the birth of the modern international refugee regime in 1951, liberal democracies cannot refuse to confer protection on political refugees without losing a significant portion of international prestige. Refugee policies, therefore, interrelate with multiple concerns in modern liberal democracies.

Consequently, this thesis can be regarded as an example of how a variety of factors operate together to influence refugee related decisions made by the state under specific circumstances. In particular, it can be used to exemplify how refugee policies function in times of severe international tension. Contemporaneous international juridical developments on human rights and refugee rights obliged Sweden to adjust its policies. Even so, a strong security framing of the Soviet refugees – and the Russians in particular – persisted, and had profound consequences for the individuals involved. It is likely that similar measures were taken in other Western refugee-receiving countries at this time. As such, the study also provides an instance of how expressly ideas on ethnicity and security can conspire to alienate foreigners. This is obviously not an exclusively Swedish phenomenon and could thus potentially be used for international comparison.

Additionally, the thesis illuminates with clarity the sense in which refugee policies consists of far more than simply border controls and asylum practices. Statistical accounts on the numbers of admissions could not have revealed the strong influence stemming from internal security concerns when it came to the issuing of residence permits. They were managed as administrative measures implemented by bureaucrats at the National Alien Commission, rather than as politically governed decisions regarding a person's right to reside in Sweden. The international reputation accorded to Sweden when it comes to its refugee policies needs to be set against such detailed scrutiny. As such, this study reveals the need for further research that goes beyond official statements and numerical accounts of permits and removals. Only in this way will it become possible to fully understand the pursued policies. This should also serve as a reminder that control over the foreign stock in a country can be, and often is, carried out in other ways than at the border.

As such, the thesis constitutes an example of how historians' research methods provide necessary complements to social scientists' ways of approaching similar data. In this case, the historical research method has allowed for a detailed study of the policy formation and implementation that drills down to the level of individual bureaucrats' handwritten notes in an effort to establish their motives. More macro-analytically orientated methods can obviously elucidate other things. However, they could probably not have revealed the shift from extensive government involvement to a more juridical approach in individual asylum and extradition affairs in the late 1940s, or the way in which morality and internal security mattered when it came to individuals' residence permits. Thus, the thesis illuminates the usefulness of historical research into subjects often handled by social scientists.

## 8.5 The Relationship Between National Security and Refugee Policies

The study has revealed an intimate relationship between refugee policies and concerns for national security in Sweden during the beginning of the Cold War. As a result it can contribute to a wider scholarly debate regarding security and migration. In this section, therefore, I will dwell on these issues and explore how the results compare with various theoretical and factual statements on this intricate matter.

The most fundamental point(s) of disagreement within this diverse field regards if, when, where and how migration became 'securitised'. The responses are varied indeed and stem from a broad range of academic disciplines. One commonly presented argument is that migration and security intersected only recently, namely after '9/11' (11 September 2001). To support this claim, scholars point towards the rigorous anti-terrorism measures that have been introduced in the 21st century. These have included stricter border control, restrictions on asylum claims, increased domestic surveillance of immigrants, and increased legal power to detain or deport foreign citizens. It has also witnessed the establishment of new authorities such as the Department of Homeland Security in the United States in 2002, which now monitors both border control and naturalisation issues, and new legislation such as the Patriot Act in the United States and the ATCSA (*Anti-Terrorism, Crime and Security Act*) in Britain.[5] Elsewhere in the European Union, similar developments have taken place, although the responses have been more mixed. Collective EU plans to consolidate immigration policies and to make them more generous and observant of the regulations set down in the 1951 Refugee Convention and other such documents were articulated at the European Council meeting held in Tampere in 1999. These were abandoned after the 9/11 attacks. As Adam Luedtke has demonstrated, cooperation plans after this date instead turned towards security measures, border control and coming to terms with illegal immigration.[6]

Studying the causal backgrounds for 21st century political decisions and legal amendments, many scholars thus argue that migration policy has been reframed as a security issue after the collapse of the Twin Towers in New York in 2001.[7] Other scholars come to the

5    James Hampshire, 'Disembedding liberalism?: Immigration politics and security in Britain since 9/11' in *Immigration policy and security: U.S., European, and Commonwealth perspectives*, Terri E. Givens, Gary P. Freeman and David L Leal (eds), Routledge, New York 2009, pp. 109–129; Marc J. Rosenblum, 'Immigration and U.S. National Interests' in *Immigration policy and security* 2009, p. 20. See also http://www.legislation.gov.uk/ukpga/2001/24/contents (accessed 11 Nov 2013); and *Major challenges facing the Department of Homeland Security*, Department for Homeland Security, OIG-13-09 (Revised) December 2012. Published on the internet: http://www.oig.dhs.gov/assets/Mgmt/2013/OIG_13-09_Dec12.pdf (accessed 10 November 2013).

6    'Introduction' in *Immigration policy and security* 2009, pp. 1–10; Luedtke, Adam: 'Fortifying Fortress Europe?: the effect of September 11 on EU immigration policy' in *Immigration policy and security* 2009, pp. 130–147.

7    *Immigration, integration, and security: America and Europe in comparative perspective*, Ariane Chebel d'Appolonia & Simon Reich (eds), University of Pittsburgh

same conclusion by examining the debate and/or the discourse surrounding migration and asylum policies. Some of them turn to the
notion of *securitisation*, as it is formulated within the Copenhagen
School and critical security studies.[8] Here, securitisation is a *speech
act*, and refers to the process in which political actors are articulat-
ing a particular issue as a security threat in order to justify certain
– often state empowering – extraordinary measures.[9] Regardless of
whether focusing on actual policies or the language in which they
are embedded, however, a number of scholars come to more or
less the same conclusion in terms of timing at least: immigration
policies (including refugee policies) have been *securitised* in the 21st
century, as a response to the terrorist threat. Before the turn of the
century, they often argue, migration and security were seen as, and
treated like, two different spheres of society.[10]

Other researchers claim that this process of 'securitisation' of
immigration occurred earlier in time. They focus, for example,
on counter-terrorism measures and the generally stricter asylum
policies and increased border controls that were introduced within
the European Union already during the middle of the 1990s, and
date the beginning of this 'securitisation' process to that period.[11]
The same chronological framing is also presented by some other
researchers who focus on what they see as the changing discourse
on immigration that took place in the aftermath of the Cold War.[12]
Negative attitudes towards immigration based on perceptions of

<br>

Press, Pittsburgh 2008 (ref: *Immigration, integration and security* 2008);
*Immigration policy and security* 2009; John Tirman, *The maze of fear: security and
migration after 9/11*, New York Press, New York 2004 (ref: Tirman 2004).

8    See, for example, *Immigration policy and security* 2009.

9    Ole Wæver, 'Securitization and Desecuritization' in *On Security*, Ronnie D.
     Lipschutz (ed.), Columbia University Press, New York 1995, pp. 46–86 (ref:
     Wæver 1995); See also Buzan, Wæver & de Wilde 1998.

10   *Immigration, integration and security* 2008; Tirman 2004; *Immigration policy and
     security* 2009.

11   'Introduction' in *Immigration, integration and security* 2008; Jef Huysmans, *The
     politics of insecurity: fear, migration and asylum in the EU*, Milton Park, Abingdon,
     Oxon, New York 2006 (ref: Huysmans 2006). However, Huysmans embraces a
     holistic approach and focuses on discursive practices as well.

12   On the changing discourse within UNHCR, for example, see Anne
     Hammerstad, 'Whose Security?: UNHCR, refugee protection and state security
     after the Cold War', in *Security Dialogue*, 2000 vol. 31(4), pp. 391–403 (ref:
     Hammerstad 2000); Abiri 2000.

identity and/or (false) accounts on the economy and the labour market created a discursive securitisation of immigration which portrayed refugees and immigrants as a threat to their host societies, it is argued. Some contrast this disapproving interpretation of 'foreigners' to the (in their view) more positive image that prevailed after the Second World War, when immigrants were seen as assets to the growing Western economies.[13] Didier Bigo, who is employing the Copenhagen School's concept of securitisation, blames this discursive post-Cold War development on the interests of what he calls the 'security professionals' (the intelligence services, national and local police, military professionals, border patrols and even politicians) who, according to him, needed to invent new threats after the end of bipolarity, in order to 'affirm their role as providers of protection and security and to mask some of their failures', and so as to secure their jobs and sources of funding. With good help from the media, the hijacking of the immigration debate succeeded, he argues.[14]

A related perspective, also dating the intertwining of security and immigration to the 1990s, was introduced already in 1993 by Buzan, Kelstrup, Lemaitre and Wæver in their book, *Identity, migration and the new security agenda in Europe*.[15] In this work the authors predicted that the main security issues of the post-Cold War world would be generated by notions of identity and culture, which were to be challenged by increasing migration flows. The notion of 'societal security' was introduced, which in its turn initiated the debate on the widening of the concept of 'security' among scholars of international relations and political science. The same year also witnessed the publication of Samuel Huntington's pessimistic but

---

13 Ayse Ceyhan & Anastassia Tsoukala, 'The securitization of migration in Western societies: ambivalent discourses and policies' in *Alternatives* 2002: 27, Special Issue, pp. 21–39; Scott D. Watson, '*The securitization of humanitarian migration: digging moats and sinking boats*', Routledge, New York 2009 (ref: Watson 2009).

14 Bigo 2002, pp. 63–92. Citation from p. 65. See also Huysmans 2006, for an extended discussion on (a Foucaultian understanding of) the process of 'security framing'.

15 *Identity, migration and the new security agenda* 1993. This work triggered the development of Critical Security Studies and constituted the foundation for the Copenhagen School on security, which would later grow extensively and develop, among other things, the concept 'securitisation'.

widely read and discussed article 'The clash of civilizations?' in *Foreign Affairs*, in which he similarly claimed that the main driving force of conflicts in the post-Cold War era would be cultural and religious. He thereby rejected liberal thinkers' more positive hopes for a future world characterised by free trade, democracy and human rights, such as, for example, the rather radical approach by Francis Fukuyama in *The end of history and the last man*.[16]

A further, alternative view on the relationship between security and refugee policy is presented by scholars who have examined the threats to both national and personal security that comes from the complicated and protracted existence of large refugee camps in the Middle East and the Developing World. They mostly date the intertwining of security and refugee policies to the 1980s and the emergence of mass migration from war zones, internal conflicts and famines in the Third World.[17] The security threats analysed here are regarded as highly factual, rather than products of a discursive framing project.[18] They also point towards the fact that the Western world's response to rapidly increasing migration and refugee flows from the 1980s onwards has been increased immigration and border control, state surveillance, usage of improved surveillance technologies and stricter visa, asylum and immigration policies in general.[19] Additionally, this 'securitisation' of immigration and refugee policies is claimed to have brought about the merging together of *internal* and *external* security. These constitute two spheres of society traditionally looked upon as separate, they argue, being handled by different pillars of the state (the police

16  Samuel Huntington, 'The clash of civilizations?' in *Foreign Affairs*, 1993(72):3, pp. 22–49; Francis Fukuyama, *The end of history and the last man*, Hamish Hamilton, London 1992.

17  According to UNHCR statistics, the number of refugees in the world rose from 1.66 million in 1960, to 15.75 million in 1994. In 2009, UNHCR registered 10.4 million refugees in the world, including both so-called Convention-Refugees and De Facto-Refugees. UNHCR Statistical Online Population Database, United Nations High Commissioner for Refugees (UNHCR) www.unhcr.org/statistics/populationdatabase (accessed 10 November 2013).

18  Gil Loescher & James Milner, *Protracted refugee situations: domestic and international security implications*, Routledge, Abingdon, Oxon 2005.

19  This excludes travels and migration *within* the EU, which has witnessed the gradual abolition of internal borders, in line with the EU's ambition to encourage free movement of capital, goods, services and labour/individuals. The EU's *external* borders have been fortified, however.

versus the armed forces), and studied by different academic disciplines (criminology and sociology versus international relations). The Cold War, in particular, is seen by many scholars as a period of time when the dividing line between internal and external security was clear cut.[20]

Thus, all these above-mentioned perspectives, although disparate, have something important in common. They all portray security and refugee policy as two political areas that have coalesced rather recently. They describe the intertwining as something which has occurred in the post-Cold War world, or, if the date is set to the 1980s, at least *outside* of the Cold War conflict. The years 1945–90, according to most of these scholars, represented an era when migration issues were 'relegated to the realm of low politics and off the security agenda, which was associated primarily with military security'.[21] Instead, refugee policy has become securitised due to problems originating from the context of the Third World, some argue, or due to cultural or religious clashes between the Western world and Muslim countries, the emergence of international terrorism, or, as Bigo argues, as a result of the financial and occupational needs of the 'security professionals'. In the historical context of the Cold War, though, security and immigration issues were altogether separate, just as external and internal security affairs.

The results of this thesis challenge these interpretations. It cannot be questioned, of course, that migration policies have transformed a great deal during recent decades and that security aspects have been increasingly emphasised.[22] However, this study has revealed that security aspects (both external and internal) played an important role in refugee related matters several decades before the emergence of international terrorism and mass migration. Additionally, by utilising Buzan, Kelstrup, Lemaitre and Wævers'

20  Didier Bigo, 'The Möbius Ribbon of Internal and External Security(ies)'
    *Identities, borders, orders: rethinking international relations theory*, Mathias
    Albert, David Jacobson & Yosef Lapid (eds), University of Minnesota Press,
    Minneapolis 2001; Derek Lutterbeck, 'Between police and military: the new
    security agenda and the rise of gendarmeries' in *Cooperation and Conflict* 2004
    (39):45.
21  Watson 2009, p. 15.
22  Although there are scholars who claim this too. See, for example, Christina
    Boswell: 'Migration, security and legitimacy: some reflections" in *Immigration
    policy and security*, 2009, pp. 93–108 (ref: Boswell 2009).

concept of 'societal security', both the ethnicity aspects and the morality factors that were demonstrated to have strongly influenced the continuous treatment of refugees in Sweden during the early Cold War can be understood in terms of 'security' too. This would perhaps be particularly appropriate given that the results also revealed a conspicuous influence from aspects of ethnicity and morality on perceptions of threat and (internal) security.

As such, the results of this thesis give credence to those scholars who claim that security concerns have played a longstanding role in refugee and immigration policies. Although not specifically about the concept of security, this includes researchers such as the previously mentioned Loescher and Scanlan, who have illuminated the United States' usage of refugees as political weapons during the Cold War; and Salomon, who has explored the way in which the international refugee regime became a component in the conflict. They would probably agree with the argument that refugee policies were intimately connected with concerns for security during the Cold War.[23] So too would scholars such as Christopher Rudolph, who has explored immigration policy in the US, France, Britain and Germany, and claims that these two political areas have had an intimate relationship in the Western democratic states at least since the end of the Second World War. Similar to Buzan, Kelstrup, Lemaitre and Wæver, he focuses, among other things, on aspects of 'social' security and demonstrates how immigration can challenge a society's perceived 'identity' if the ethnic makeup of the migrant group is perceived as significantly different from that of the host country. Outbreaks of xenophobia and social unrest and/ or stricter migration policies can be triggered as a result. He also argues that 'material' security plays an important role as liberal democratic states tend to welcome immigration in general in times of economic growth, and halt it in times of economic stagnation.[24]

Political scientist Marc R. Rosenblum, however, goes even further back in time when arguing that immigration has often been 'defined as a national security priority during periods of international conflict'. He presents examples of this in the US dating back as far as the First World War and Woodrow Wilson's Espionage

23   Loescher & Scanlan 1986; Salomon 1991, pp. 13–42.
24   Rudolph 2006.

and Sedition Acts of 1917 and 1919, as well as the Federal Bureau of Investigations' arrest and deportation of hundreds of foreign-born communists during the Palmer Raids of 1919–1921. Similar policies were again adopted during the Second World War as 120,000 Japanese Americans were forcibly interned. And later on the Cold War witnessed, for example, the establishment of the Internal Security Act which made aliens deportable if they were members of the Communist Party and/or advocated communist or anarchist ideologies.[25] Similar developments took place in other countries during the 20th century.[26]

Thus, could it be that the intersection of migration matters with concerns for security is innate within the nation state? That is the argument presented in Elspeth Guild and Joanne van Selm's *International migration and security: opportunities and challenges*. Security concerns, they argue, are inherently intertwined with immigration policies within the nation state, since immigration is so closely connected with aspects of border control and challenges the very idea of the nation state as a culturally, politically and territorially defined area.[27] The strong connection between migration and security illuminated in this thesis supports these thoughts. Regardless of whether discussing these issues in terms of ethnicity, identity, morality or security, human societies' tendency to alienate members of other groups appear to constitute an essential factor that governs, in various ways and to various degrees, all interaction between collectives and, in particular, nation states.

Terminology, however, seems to constitute at least one of the reasons why the above-mentioned scholars come to such conspicuously diverse conclusions regarding when and how migration became securitised. They are, to say the least, employing sometimes strikingly different definitions of 'security'. The aforementioned Rudolph, for example, embraces a liberal definition which includes several aspects of society as the referent object of security (that

---

25  Rosenblum 2009, pp. 16–17.

26  For example, in Canada. Ken Adachi, *The enemy that never was: a history of the Japanese Canadians*. McClelland and Stewart Ltd., Toronto 1977; Roger Daniels, *Concentration camps, North America: Japanese in the United States and Canada during World War II*, R.E. Krieger Pub. Co., Malabar 1981.

27  *International migration and security: opportunities and challenges*, Elspeth Guild & Joanne van Selm (eds), Routledge, London 2005, ch. 1.

which is being secured), namely 'military', 'material' (economic), and 'societal' security. Such a concept opens up for an interpretation of several different phenomena as 'security threats' too. Hence, ethnicity, racial prejudice and outbreaks of xenophobia are interpreted as falling within the domain of 'security', just as do the needs of the labour market.[28] This concept is in line – although not identical – with the one adopted in the above-mentioned Copenhagen School, which, however, was later reworked so as to include five sectors of 'security': the military, environmental, economic, societal and political sectors.[29] Rosenblum's concept of security is not as explicitly defined, but seems to refer to a more classical concept, defining security in terms of state sovereignty and the defence of the state's territory. In other words, it appears to adjust more to the views held by the members of the so-called traditional school, which identifies only the state as the referent object of security, and the threats as those deriving from other actors within the international arena. Luedke, who is exploring adopted policies and the factual motivations behind them at an EU level, adopts a similar, territorial concept. Others, however, focus exclusively on discursive processes.[30] Additionally, there are other scholars who wish to redirect attention to a considerably different understanding of the concept in which the role of the state should be withdrawn in order to make space for individuals, often by using the concept *human security*. Examples of such views can be found among the scholars exploring the mass migration movements of the Third World, for example, and scholars illuminating the particular risks to which women are generally exposed during times of conflict.[31]

Hence, it is evident that any results of scholarly work on the relationship between security and refugee and immigration issues

28  Rudolph 2006.
29  Buzan et al, 1993; Buzan, Wæver & de Wilde 1998; Buzan 1991.
30  See, for example, Boswell 2009.
31  For a more thorough discussion on the theoretical foundations of concept of security, see, for example, Buzan & Hansen 2009, ch.1; Buzan, Wæver & de Wilde 1998; Kjell Goldmann, 'Miljöhot, migration och terrorister i Tokyo – om begreppet säkerhetspolitik' in *Brobyggare: en vänbok till Nils Andrén*, Leif Leifland (ed.), Nerenius & Santérus, Stockholm 1997 (ref: Goldmann 1997); Tickner 1992; Myron Weiner (red), *International security and migration*, Westview, Boulder, Colorado 1993; Huysmans 2006; Hammerstad 2000; *Gendered states* 1992.

will depend substantially on what concept of 'security' is being applied. The exuberant menu of concepts available originates from academic fields as diverse as, for example, international relations, political science, feminist studies, sociology and psychology.

Although not intending to make bold statements on the issue of what security actually is and should be, the results of this thesis can be used to suggest that a wider definition, pertaining more to the concept utilised by liberal thinkers (sometimes called 'modernisers') than traditionalists, is more useful in this context as it by all means appears to pertain more to the reality such as it was (is) perceived and understood by the main 'security actors'. Government representatives and, indeed, state bureaucrats looked upon certain individuals as more untrustworthy – in other words as more likely to be or to become *threats* to Swedish national security – because of their ethnic origin as well as their social behaviour during the first decade of the Cold War. If not allowing for such aspects to be included in the concept of 'security', the analyst loses an important tool in his or her attempt to understand the past (and, indeed, the present).

As such, this approach relates to the constructivist theoretical stance, briefly mentioned in chapter one, which perceives foreign politics as greatly influenced by cultural traits and state actors' perceptions of identity. Generally speaking, they leave it to the actors themselves to define what security actually is. Whatever is being understood and treated as a security issue by relevant state actors at a certain moment in time is included in the concept. In other words, according to this understanding, no issue is inherently about security outside of its specific context in time and space. This enables an open approach to the historical reality without losing too much analytical and theoretical capacity. The apparent intersection of ethnicity aspects and security perceptions revealed in this examination suggest that such an understanding and employment of the concept of 'security' is both useful and appropriate in order to understand the pursued policies.[32]

If this study can be used to encourage thinkers on security to contemplate ethnicity and identity aspects (as well as, indeed,

---

32    *The culture of national security* 1996; Wendt 1999; Wæver 1995; Rousseau 2006.
      An example of a concept influenced by these ideas is the above-mentioned
      Copenhagen School's concept of *securitization*.

social control and morality), it can also, hopefully, inversely be used to inspire scholars of ethnicity to reflect on security too. The thesis has provided a focused example of how perceptions on ethnicity, morality and security can work together to alienate non-nationals. As foreigners, the refugees were all regarded as untrust-worthy to some extent. However, a general antipathy towards Russians within Swedish society, in combination with the tense Cold War context and Swedish-Soviet relations, rendered this group particularly suspect in the eyes of the Swedish authorities. Placed in a wider scholarly context, these results have ramifications that extend far beyond the national borders of Sweden.

# Bibliography

## I. Primary sources


UNPUBLISHED

### *Riksarkivet, Ra (The Swedish National Archives)*

*Inrikesdepartementets arkiv, 1947–73 (The archives of the Ministry of the Interior)*

    A II, vol. 1–8: Föredragningslistor

*Statens utlänningskommissions arkiv (SUK), 1944–69[1] (The archives of the National Alien Commission)*

ANDRA BYRÅN, 1953–69 (THE SECOND BUREAU)

    A 2, vol. 1–3: Specialprotokoll
    B 1, vol. 1–2: Skrivelser till Kungl. Majt
    E 1 A, vol. 1–2: Korrespondens med Kungl. Utrikesdepartementet

FÖRSTA BYRÅN, 1953–69 (THE FIRST BUREAU)

    A 2, vol. 1–3: Specialprotokoll


---

1    A list of the real names behind the pseudonyms used in this thesis, as well as the exact location of the personal dossiers and register cards, has been deposited at the Swedish National Archives in Stockholm. A copy can also be solicited from the author of this book, as well as from the Department of History at Stockholm University.

344

HEMLIGA ARKIVET, 1944–69 (THE SECRET ARCHIVE)

A 1, vol. 1: Pleniprotokoll
D 2: Kontrollregister över utlänningar
E 4, vol. 2–4: Kontrollbyråns korrespondens
E 8, vol. 1: Andra byråns korrespondens
F 2 A: Kontrolldossiéer
F 2 B, vol. 4–6, 9–10: Kontrolldossiéer angående ämnen
F 4, vol. 1, 3, 6, 9–10: Kontrollserie H-reg, kassavalvet
F 8, vol. 1–2: Yttranden från Försvarsstaben och andra militära myndigheter
F 11 A (serie 3418), vol. 34–56: Arkivdossiéer

KANSLIBYRÅN, 1944–69 (THE SECRETARIAT)

A 1 A, vol. 1–4: Pleniprotokoll
B 4 C, vol. 1: Cirkulär och utlänningsmeddelanden till polismyndigheter
D 2: Centralregister över utlänningar
E 1 A, vol. 1: Betänkanden
F 1: Centraldossiéer över utlänningar
H1, vol. 1: Diverse utlänningsstatistik
H3, vol. 1: Administrativ utlänningsstatistik
H4, vol. 1–2: Övrig statistik

KONTROLLBYRÅN, 1944–52 (THE CONTROL BUREAU)

A 2, vol. 2–8: Protokoll rörande förpassningar och utresebeslut
B 1, vol. 1: Skrivelser till Kung. Maj:t
B 2 A, vol. 1: Cirkulär (kontrollbyråorder)
B 2 B, vol. 1–2: Cirkulär och spärrar till passkontrollerna
B 2 C, vol. 1: Meddelanden till passkontrollerna
B 4, vol. 1: Kopior av utgående handlingar
E 1 A, vol. 1: Kungliga brev
F 3, vol. 1: Handlingar rörande ryssar och ingermanländare

PASSBYRÅN, 1944–52 (THE PASSPORT BUREAU)

A 2, vol. 1–11: P-protokoll

*Statspolisens Tredje Rotel/Säkerhetspolisens arkiv (SÄPO), 1938– (The archives of the Swedish security police)*

P4818: Utredning rörande vissa baltiska flyktingar
JWK 10.1, vol. 493–502: Politiska flyktingar

*Utlänningsnämndens arkiv, 1944–78 (The archives of the Aliens Appeals Board)*

A 1, vol. 3–7: Protokoll

A 2, vol. 1–4: Förhörsprotokoll (hemliga protokoll)
B 1, vol. 3–12: Kopior av nämndens yttranden
F 2 A, vol. 4–6, 22–24: Föredragningspromemorior

*Utrikesdepartementets arkiv, (UD), 1840-, 1920 års dossiésystem (The archives of the Ministry for Foreign Affairs)*

P 40 I, vol. 67–69: Hjälp åt flyktingar från Polen och Ryssland
P 40 R, vol. 77–80: Hjälp åt flyktingar från de baltiska länderna
R 58 Eö, vol. 47: Flyktingar, Östersjöländerna (Balticum)
R 58 Er, vol. 40–42: Flyktingar, Ryssland
R 70 Er, vol. 240: Av utländska myndigheter begärda extraditioner, Sovjetunionen

PUBLISHED

*Befolkningsrörelsen*, Statistiska Centralbyrån, Stockholm 1945–54
*Dagens Nyheter*, 2012
International conventions and statutes relating to refugees, 1938–57
Lindencrona, G: *Utlänningshandbok, årgång 1949. Utlänningslagen och därmed sammanhängande författningar jämte anvisningar och förklaringar.* P.A. Norstedt & Söner Förlag, Stockholm 1949
Myrdal, Gunnar: *Varning för fredsoptimism*, Bonnier, Stockholm 1944
*Riksdagens protokoll år 1949*, Första Kammaren, Riksdagen, Stockholm 1949
*Sociala Meddelanden*, Norstedt, Stockholm 1945–54
SOU 1945:1, *Betänkande med förslag till utlänningslag och lag angående omhändertagande av utlänning i anstalt eller förläggning*, 1943 års utlänningssakkunniga, Norstedt, Stockholm 1945
SOU 1946:36, *Parlamentariska undersökningskommissionen angående flyktingärenden och säkerhetstjänst. 1, Betänkande angående flyktingars behandling*, Parlamentariska undersökningskommissionen angående flyktingärenden och säkerhetstjänst, Stockholm 1946
SOU 1951:42, *Betänkande med förslag till utlänningslag m.m.*, 1949 års utlänningskommitté, Stockholm 1951 *Svensk författningssamling (SFS)* 1937, 1945–54
Undén, Östen: *Anteckningar: 1918–1952*, Kungl. Samf. för utgivande av handskrifter rörande Skandinaviens historia, Stockholm 2002

## Reference literature

Hallberg, Lars: *Källor till invandringens historia i statliga myndigheters arkiv 1840–1990*, Riksarkivet, Stockholm 2001.
Nationalencyklopedin, NE
Oxford English Dictionary, OED

*Riksarkivets beståndsöversikt. D. 5, Centrala myndigheter och domstolar, internationella organ*, Riksarkivet, Stockholm 1999.


## II. Literature

Abiri, Elisabeth: *The securitisation of migration: towards an understanding of migration policy changes in the 1990s: the case of Sweden*, Göteborg University, Göteborg 2000.

Adachi, Ken: *The enemy that never was: a history of the Japanese Canadians*, McClelland and Stewart Ltd., Toronto 1977.

Agrell, Wilhelm: *Fred och fruktan: Sveriges säkerhetspolitiska historia 1918–2000*, Historiska media, Lund 2000.
— *Konsten att gissa rätt: underrättelsevetenskapens grunder*, Studentlitteratur, Lund 1998.
— *Underrättelseanalysens metoder och problem: medan klockan tickar*, Gleerup, Malmö 2009.

Ambjörnsson, Ronny: *Den skötsamme arbetaren: idéer och ideal i ett norrländskt sågverkssamhälle 1880–1930*, 4 ed., Carlsson, Stockholm 2001.

Andersson, Lars M.: *En jude är en jude är en jude: representationer av "juden" i svensk skämtpress omkring 1900–1930*, Nordic Academic Press, Lund 2000.

Andræ, Carl Göran: *Sverige och den stora flykten från Estland 1943–1944*, Gustav Adolfs akademi, Uppsala 2004.

Andrew, Christopher M. & Mitrochin, Vasilij Nikitič: *The sword and the shield: the Mitrokhin archive and the secret history of the KGB*, 1. ed., Basic Books, New York 1999.

*Anti-Communist minorities in the United States: political activism of ethnic refugees*, Ieva Zake (ed.), Palgrave Macmillan, New York 2009.

Appelqvist, Örjan: *Bruten brygga: Gunnar Myrdal och Sveriges ekonomiska efterkrigspolitik 1943–1947*, Santérus, Stockholm 2000.

Berge, Anders: *Det kalla kriget i Tidens spegel: en socialdemokratisk bild av hoten mot frihet och fred 1945–1962*, Carlsson, Stockholm 1990.
— *Flyktingpolitik i stormakts skugga: Sverige och de sovjetryska flyktingarna under andra världskriget*, Centre for Multiethnic Research, Uppsala University, Uppsala 1992.
— *Socialpolitik och ansvarsmoral*, Bertil Ohlin-institutet, Stockholm 1995.
— 'Sveriges politik mot de ungerska flyktingarna 1956–1959', in *Historisk tidskrift*, 1993:113, pp. 332–349.
— 'Urholkad frivillighet: Sveriges repatriering av sovjetryska f d krigsfångar 1944–1945' in *Militärhistorisk tidskrift.*, 1990:12, pp. 217–233.

Berglund, Tobias & Sennerteg, Niclas: *Svenska koncentrationsläger i Tredje rikets skugga*, Natur & Kultur, Stockholm 2008.

Bethell, Nicholas: *The last secret: forcible repatriation to Russia 1944–7*, Deutsch, London 1974.

Bigo, Didier: 'Security and immigration: toward a critique of the governmentality of unease' in *Alternatives*, 2002:27, Special Issue, pp. 63–92.
— 'The Möbius Ribbon of Internal and External Security(ies)' in *Identities, borders, orders: rethinking International Relations theory*, Mathias Albert, David Jacobson & Yosef Lapid (eds), University of Minnesota Press, Minneapolis 2001.

Bjereld, Ulf: *Hjalmarsonaffären: ett politiskt drama i tre akter*, Nerenius & Santérus, Stockholm 1997.

Bjereld, Ulf, Johansson, Alf W. & Molin, Karl: *Sveriges säkerhet och världens fred: svensk utrikespolitik under kalla kriget*, Santérus, Stockholm 2008.

Bjereld, Ulf & Demker, Marie: *Utrikespolitiken som slagfält: de svenska partierna och utrikesfrågorna*, Nerenius & Santérus, Stockholm 1995.

Björklund, Fredrika: *Samförstånd under oenighet: svensk säkerhetspolitisk debatt under det kalla kriget*, Uppsala University, Uppsala 1992.

Björkman, Jenny: *Vård för samhällets bästa: debatten om tvångsvård i svensk lagstiftning 1850–1970*, Carlsson, Stockholm 2001.

Bogatic, Wirginia: *Exilens dilemma: att stanna eller att återvända*, Linneus University Press, Växjö 2011.

Bon Tempo, Carl J.: *Americans at the Gate: the United States and refugees during the Cold War*, Princeton University Press, Princeton 2009.

Boswell, Christina: 'Migration, security and legitimacy: some reflections' in *Immigration policy and security: U.S., European, and Commonwealth perspectives*, Terri E. Givens, Gary P. Freeman and David L Leal (eds), Routledge, New York 2009.

Breitman, Richard & Kraut, Alan M.: *American refugee policy and European Jewry, 1933–1945*, Indiana University Press, Bloomington 1987.

Buzan, Barry: *People, states and fear: an agenda for international security studies in the post-cold war era*, 2. ed., Harvester Wheatsheaf, London 1991.

Buzan, Barry & Hansen, Lene: *The evolution of International Security Studies*, Cambridge University Press, Cambridge 2009.

Buzan, Barry, Wæver, Ole & de Wilde, Jaap: *Security: a new framework for analysis*, Lynne Rienner, Boulder Colorado 1998.

Byström, Mikael: *En broder, gäst och parasit: uppfattningar och föreställningar om utlänningar, flyktingar och flyktingpolitik i svensk offentlig debatt 1942–1947*, Acta Universitatis Stockholmiensis, Stockholm 2006.
— *Utmaningen: den svenska välfärdsstatens möte med flyktingar i andra världskrigets tid*, Nordic Academic Press, Lund 2012.

Byström, Mikael & Geverts, Karin Kvist: 'Från en aktivism till en annan: hur ska Sveriges agerande i flyktingfrågan under andra världskriget förklaras?' in *Sverige och Nazi-Tyskland: skuldfrågor och moraldebatt*, Lars M. Andersson & Mattias Tydén (eds), Dialogos, Stockholm 2007.

348

Carlgren, Wilhelm: *Svensk utrikes-politik 1939–1945*, Allmänna förlaget, Stockholm 1973.

Carlsson, Carl Henrik: *Medborgarskap och diskriminering: östjudar och andra invandrare i Sverige 1860–1920*, Acta Universitatis Upsaliensis, Uppsala 2004.

Carruthers, Susan L.: *Cold War captives: imprisonment, escape and brainwashing*, University of California Press, California 2009.

Ceyhan, Ayse & Tsoukala, Anastassia: 'The securitization of migration in Western societies: ambivalent discourses and policies' in *Alternatives* 2002:27, Special Issue, pp. 21–39.

Choucri, Nazli: 'Migration and security: some key linkages' in *Journal of international affairs* 2002:(56)1, New York 2002, pp. 97–122.

Cohen, Stanley: *Visions of social control: crime, punishment and classification*, Polity press, Cambridge 1985.

*Constructivism and international relations: Alexander Wendt and his critics*, Guzzini, Stefano & Leander. Anna (eds), Routledge, London 2006.

*Criminally queer: homosexuality and criminal law in Scandinavia 1842–1999*, Rydström, Jens & Mustola, Kati (eds), Aksant, Amsterdam 2007.

Cronqvist, Marie: *Mannen i mitten: ett spiondrama i svensk kallakrigskultur*, Carlsson, Stockholm 2004.

Dalsjö, Robert: *Life-line lost: the rise and fall of "neutral" Sweden's secret reserve option of wartime help from the west*, Santérus Academic Press Sweden, Stockholm 2006.

Daniels, Roger: *Concentration camps, North America: Japanese in the United States and Canada during World War II*, R.E. Krieger Pub. Co., Malabar 1981.

*De första båtflyktingarna: en antologi om balterna i Sverige*, Eriksson, Lars-Gunnar (ed.), Statens invandrarverk (SIV), Norrköping 1986.

De Geer, Eric: *Ingermanland, vad är det och vilka är ingermanländarna?* Finsk-ugriska seminariet, Göteborgs universitet, Göteborg 2000.

Deland, Mats: *Purgatorium: Sverige och andra världskrigets förbrytare*, Atlas, Stockholm 2010.

Demker, Marie & Malmström, Cecilia: *Ingenmansland:? svensk immigrationspolitik i utrikespolitisk belysning*, Studentlitteratur, Lund 1999.

Dufwa, Sune G.: 'Våra systrar snart här' in *Sveriges mottagning av flyktingar – några exempel. Årsbok 2007 från forskningsprofilen Arbetsmarknad, migration och etniska relationer (AMER) vid Växjö universitet*, Ekberg, Jan (ed.), Växjö University Press, Växjö 2007.

Edman, Johan: *Torken: tvångsvården av alkoholmissbrukare i Sverige 1940–1981*, Almqvist & Wiksell International, Stockholm 2004.

Ekecrantz, Stefan: *Hemlig utrikespolitik: kalla kriget, utrikesnämnden och regeringen 1946–1959*, Santérus, Stockholm 2003.

Ekengren, Ann-Marie & Oscarsson, Henrik: *Det röda hotet: de militära och polisiära säkerhetstjänsternas hotbilder i samband med övervakning av svenska medborgare*

*1945–1960*, Nordic Academic Press, Lund 2002.

Ekengren, Ann-Marie: *Sverige under kalla kriget 1945–1969: en forskningsöversikt*, Göteborg 1997.

Ekholm, Curt: *Balt- och tyskutlämningen 1945–1946: omständigheter kring interneringen i läger i Sverige och utlämningen till Sovjetunionen av f d tyska krigsdeltagare, parts 1 and 2*, 2 ed., Uppsala University, Uppsala 1995.

Eliasson, Ulf: *Politisk övervakning och personalkontroll 1945–1969: säkerhetspolisens medverkan i den politiska personalkontrollen: forskarrapport till Säkerhetstjänstkommissionen*, SOU 2002: 88, Fritzes offentliga publikationer, Stockholm 2002.

— *I försvarets intresse: säkerhetspolisens övervakning och registrering av ytterlighetspartier 1917–1945*, Nordic Academic Press, Lund 2006.

*En problematisk relation?: Flyktingpolitik och judiska flyktingar i Sverige 1920–1950*, Andersson, Lars M. & Kvist Geverts, Karin (eds), Historiska Institutionen, Uppsala Universitet, Uppsala 2008.

*Encounter with strangers: the European experience*, Persson, Hans-Åke (ed.), Lund Univ. Press, Lund 1997.

Eneberg, Kaa: *Tvingade till tystnad: en okänd historia om några svenska familjeöden*, Hjalmarson & Högberg, Stockholm 2000.

— *Förnekelsens barn: svenskarna som drog österut*. 1. uppl. Hjalmarson & Högberg, Stockholm 2003.

Enquist, P.O.: *Legionärerna: en roman om baltutlämningen*, Norstedt, Stockholm 1968.

Eriksson, Johan: *Kampen om hotbilden: rutin och drama i svensk säkerhetspolitik*, Santérus, Stockholm 2004.

*Ett diplomatiskt misslyckande: fallet Raoul Wallenberg och den svenska utrikesledningen*, Kommissionen om den svenska utrikesledningens agerande i fallet Raoul Wallenberg, Statens offentliga utredningar, SOU 2003:18, Fritzes offentliga publikationer, Stockholm 2003.

*European Union non-discrimination law: comparative perspectives on multidimensional equality law*, Chiek, Dagmar & Chege, Victoria (eds), Routledge-Cavendish, London 2009.

Faist, Thomas: *The migration-security nexus: international migration and security before and after 9/11*, IMER, Malmö högskola, Malmö 2003.

*Familjeangelägenheter: modern historisk forskning om välfärdsstat, genus och politik*, Bergman, Helena & Johansson, Peter (eds), B. Östlings bokförlag Symposion, Eslöv 2002.

Flink, Toivo: *Kotiin Karkotettavaksi: Inkeriläisen siirtoväen palautukset Suomesta Neuvostohiittoon 1944–1955*, Suomalaisen Kirjallisuuden Seura, Helsinki 2010.

Flyghed, Janne: *Rättsstat i kris: spioneri och sabotage i Sverige under andra världskriget*, Federativ, Stockholm 1992.

*Forced migration in Central and Eastern Europe, 1939–1950*, Rieber, Alfred J. (ed.), Frank Cass, London 2000.

Forsberg, Tore: *Spioner och spioner som spionerar på spioner: spioner och kontraspioner i Sverige*, 2 ed., Hjalmarsson & Högberg, Stockholm 2004.

Forsberg, Tore & Grigorjev, Boris Nikolaevič: *Spioner emellan*. Efron & dotter, Saltsjö-Duvnäs 2006.

Frykman, Jonas & Löfgren, Orvar: *Den kultiverade människan*, Liber Läromedel, Lund 1979.
— 'På väg – bilder av kultur och klass' in *Modärna tider: Vision och vardag i folkhemmet*, Jonas Frykman (ed.), Liber Förlag, Malmö 1985, pp. 20–139.

Fukuyama, Francis: *The end of history and the last man*, Hamish Hamilton, London 1992.

Gaddis, John Lewis: *The cold war: a new history*, Penguin Press, New York 2005.

*Gendered states: feminist (re)visions of international relations theory*, Peterson, V. Spike (ed.), Lynne Rienner, Boulder, Colorado 1992.

Gerner, Kristian: 'Svenskars syn på Sovjetryssland: myten om antisovjetismen' in *Östersjö eller Västerhav? Föreställningar om tid och rum i Östersjöområdet*, Karlsson, Klas-Göran & Zander, Ulf (eds), Östersjöinstitutet, Karlskrona 2000.

Goldmann, Kjell: 'Miljöhot, migration och terrorister i Tokyo – om begreppet säkerhetspolitik' in *Brobyggare: en vänbok till Nils Andrén*, Leif Leifland (ed.), Nerénius & Santérus, Stockholm 1997.

Goldmann, Kjell, *Identitet & politik: nationellt, övernationellt, semi-nationellt*, SNS förlag, Stockholm 2008.

Goodwin, Guy S.: 'The Politics of Refugee Protection' in *Refugee Survey Quarterly*, 2008: (27)1, pp. 8–23.
— *The refugee in international law*, 2. rev.ed., Clarendon, Oxford 1996.

Guild, Elspeth: *Security and migration in the 21st century*, Polity, Cambridge 2009.

Hafström, Gerhard: 'Ingermanländarna och asylrätten' in *Svio-Estonica: Studier utg. av svensk-estniska samfundet*, vol. XX, Stockholm 1971.

Hallberg, Lars: *Källor till invandringens historia i statliga myndigheters arkiv 1840–1990*, Riksarkivet, Stockholm 2001.

Hammar, Tomas: *Sverige åt svenskarna: invandringspolitik, utlänningskontroll och asylrätt 1900–1932*, Stockholm University, Stockholm 1964.
— 'Flyktingpolitiken i hetluften' in *Brobyggare: en vänbok till Nils Andrén*, Leif Leifland (ed.), Nerénius & Santérus, Stockholm 1997.

Hammarström, Uno: *Ingermanländarna som flydde till Sverige: en minnesberättelse*, Finsk-ingermanländarnas centralförbund, Borås 1984.

Hammerstad, Anne: 'Whose Security?: UNHCR, refugee protection and state security after the Cold War', in *Security Dialogue*, 2000:(31)4, pp. 391–403.
— *Refugee protection and the evolution of a security discourse : the United Nations High Commissioner*

*for Refugees in the 1990s,*
University of Oxford, Oxford
2002.

Hampshire, James: 'Disembedding
liberalism?: Immigration politics
and security in Britain since
9/11' in *Immigration policy and
security: U.S., European, and
Commonwealth perspectives,*
Givens, Terri E., Freeman, Gary
P. and Leal, David L (eds),
Routledge, New York 2009.

*Handbok om förfarandet och kriteri-
erna vid fastställande av flyktingars
rättsliga ställning: enligt 1951 års
konvention och 1967 års protokoll
angående flyktingars rättsliga ställning,* 1. ed., UNHCR, Publica,
Stockholm 1996.

Hansen, Peo: EU*:s migrationspolitik
under 50 år: ett integrerat perspektiv
på en motsägelsefull utveckling,*
Studentlitteratur, Lund 2008.

Hathaway, James C.: *The rights of
refugees under international law,*
Cambridge University Press,
Cambridge 2005.
— 'A Reconsideration of the
Underlying Premise of Refugee
Law', in *Harvard International
Law Journal,* 1990:(31)1, pp.
29–183.

Haynes, John Earl & Klehr, Harvey:
*Early Cold War spies: the espionage
trials that shaped American politics,*
Cambridge University Press,
Cambridge 2006.
— *Venona: decoding Soviet espio-
nage in America,* Yale Univ. Press,
New Haven, Connecticut 1999.

Hellner, Kerstin: *De landsflyktiga
och Sverige,* Bonnier, Stockholm
1952.

Hirdman, Yvonne: *Att lägga livet tillrätta: studier i svensk folkhemspo-*

*litik,* 2 ed., Carlsson, Stockholm
2000.

Hjort, Magnus: *Den farliga fredsrörelsen: säkerhetstjänsternas
övervakning av fredsorganisationer,
värnpliktsvägrare och FNL-grupper
1945–1990: forskarrapport till
Säkerhetstjänstkommissionen,* SOU
2002:90, Fritzes offentliga publikationer, Stockholm 2002.
— *Hotet från vänster: säkerhetstjänsternas övervakning av
kommunister, anarkister m.m.
1965–2002: forskarrapport till
Säkerhetstjänstkommissionen,* SOU
2002:91, Fritzes offentliga publikationer, Stockholm 2002.
— *'Nationens livsfråga': propaganda och upplysning i försvarets tjänst
1944–1963,* Santérus, Stockholm
2004.

Holborn, Louise W.: *Refugees: a
problem of our time: the work of the
United Nations High Commissioner
for Refugees, 1951–1972,* Scarecrow
P., Metuchen, N.J. 1975.

Holmström, Mikael: *Den dolda
alliansen: Sveriges hemliga NATO-
förbindelser,* Atlantis, Stockholm
2011.

Horgby, Björn: *Dom där: främlings-
fientligheten och arbetarkulturen i
Norrköping 1890–1960,* Carlsson,
Stockholm, 1996.

Huntington, Samuel: 'The Clash of
Civilizations?' in *Foreign Affairs,*
1993:(72)3, pp. 22–49.

Huysmans, Jef: *The politics of insecu-
rity: fear, migration and asylum in
the* EU, Milton Park, Abingdon,
Oxon, New York 2006.

Hylland Eriksen, Thomas: *Ethnicity
and nationalism: anthropological
perspectives,* 3rd ed., Pluto Press,
London 2010.

*Identity, migration and the new security agenda in Europe*, Wæver, Ole, Buzan, Barry, Kelstrup, Morten and Lemaitre, Pierre (eds), Pinter, London 1993.

*Immigration, integration, and security: America and Europe in comparative perspective*, d'Appolonia, Ariane Chebel & Reich, Simon (eds), University of Pittsburgh Press, Pittsburgh 2008.

*Immigration policy and security: U.S., European, and Commonwealth perspectives*, Terri E. Givens, Gary P. Freeman and David L Leal (eds), Routledge, New York 2009.

*International migration and security: opportunities and challenges*, Guild, Elspeth & Selm, Joanne van (eds), Routledge, London 2005.

*International refugee law*, Lambert, Hélène (ed.), Ashgate, Farnham, Surrey England 2010.

*International security and migration*, Weiner, Myron (ed.), Westview, Boulder, Colorado 1993.

Johansson, Alf : 'Regeringen och tysk- och baltutlämningen 1945–1946' in *Säkerhet och försvar: en vänbok till Kent Zetterberg*, Artéus, Gunnar, Molin, Karl & Petersson, Magnus (eds), Abrahamsson, Karlskrona 2005.

Johansson, Christina: *Välkomna till Sverige?: svenska migrationspolitiska diskurser under 1900-talets andra hälft*, Bokbox, Malmö 2005.

Kadhammar, Peter: *De sammansvurna*, 2 ed., Fischer, Rimbo 2002.

Keeley, Charles B.: 'The International Refugee Regime(s): The End of The Cold War Matters' in *International Migration Review*, Spring 2001:(35)1, Special Issue: UNHCR at 50: Past, Present and Future of Refugee Assistance, pp. 303–314.

Karlsson, Klas-Göran, *Terror och tystnad: sovjetregimens krig mot den egna befolkningen*, 2 ed., Atlantis, Stockholm 2005.

Koblik, Steven: *The stones cry out: Sweden's response to the persecution of the Jews 1933–1945*, Holocaust Library, New York 1988.

Kronvall, Olof: *Den bräckliga barriären: Finland i svensk utrikespolitik 1948–1962*, Försvarshögskolan, Stockholm 2003.

Kronvall, Olof & Petersson, Magnus: *Svensk säkerhetspolitik i supermakternas skugga 1945–1991*, 2 rev. ed., Santérus Academic Press Sweden, Stockholm 2012.

Kvist Geverts, Karin: *Ett främmande element i nationen: svensk flyktingpolitik och de judiska flyktingarna 1938–1944*, Acta Universitatis Upsaliensis, Uppsala 2008.

Lampers, Lars Olof: *Det grå brödraskapet: en berättelse om IB: forskarrapport till Säkerhetstjänstkommissionen*, Statens offentliga utredningar, SOU 2002:92, Fritzes offentliga publikationer, Stockholm 2002.

Langkjaer, Jenny: *Övervakning för rikets säkerhet: svensk säkerhetspolisiär övervakning av utländska personer och inhemsk politisk aktivitet, 1885–1922*, Acta Universitatis Stockholmiensis, Stockholm University, Stockholm 2011.

Lavenex, Sandra: *The Europeanisation of refugee policies: between human rights and internal security*, Ashgate, Aldershot 2001.

Leino, Olle: *Vem tackar Yrjö Leino? Ett mänskligt och politiskt doku-*

ment om Finlands kommunistiske inrikesminister 1945–48, Askild & Kärnekull, Stockholm 1973.

Levine, Paul: *From indifference to activism: Swedish diplomacy and the Holocaust, 1938–1944*, Uppsala University, Uppsala 1998.

Hans Lindberg: *Svensk flyktingpolitik under internationellt tryck 1936–1941*, Allmänna förlaget, Stockholm University, Stockholm 1973.

Lindencrona, Gustav: *Utlänningshandbok: utlänningslagen och därmed sammanhängande författningar jämte anvisningar och förklaringar*, Årg. 1949, Norstedt, Stockholm 1949.

Loescher, Gil & Scanlan, John A.: *Calculated kindness: refugees and America's half-open door 1945 – present*, Free Press, New York 1986.

London, Louise: *Whitehall and the Jews, 1933–1948: British immigration policy, Jewish refugees and the Holocaust*, Cambridge University Press, Cambridge 2000.

Luedtke, Adam: 'Fortifying Fortress Europe? The Effect of September 11 on EU Immigration Policy' in *Immigration policy and security: U.S., European, and Commonwealth perspectives*, Givens, Terri E., Freeman, Gary P. and Leal, David L (eds), Routledge, New York 2009.

Lundberg, Urban & Tydén, Mattias: 'Stat och individ i svensk välfärdspolitik' in *Staten som vän eller fiende? Individ och samhälle i svenskt 1900-tal*, Hedin, Marika *et al.* (eds), Institutet för framtidsstudier, Stockholm 2007, pp. 17–39.

Lundh, Christer & Ohlsson, Rolf: *Från arbetskraftsimport till flyktinginvandring*, 2 ed., SNS, Stockholm 1999.

Lundgren, Hans: *Krampen: ryssläger i Sverige under andra världskriget*, Västmanlands läns museum, Västerås 2008.

Lutterbeck, Derek: 'Between police and military: the new security agenda and the rise of gendarmeries' in *Cooperation and Conflict* 2004:(39)45.

Lyon, David: *Surveillance society: monitoring everyday life*, Open University Press, Buckingham 2001.

Lööw, Heléne: *Hakkorset och Wasakärven: en studie av nationalsocialismen i Sverige 1924–1950*, Göteborg University, Göteborg, 1990.

Malmborg, Mikael: *Den ståndaktiga nationalstaten: Sverige och den västeuropeiska integrationen 1945–1959*, Lund University Press, Lund 1994.

Marrus, Michael: *The Unwanted: European refugees from the First World War through the Cold War*, 2 ed., Temple University Press, Philadelphia 2002.

Melander, Göran: *Flyktingar och asyl*, Norstedt, Stockholm 1972.
— *Asyl: svensk praxis i ärenden om politiskt flyktingskap: undersökning utförd på uppdrag av utlänningsutredningen*, Allmänna förlaget, Stockholm 1972.
— *Politiskt flyktingskap enligt utlänningslagen* 1969 (unpublished report)

*Migrants, refugees, and foreign policy: U.S. and German policies toward countries of origin*, Müntz, Rainer & Weiner, Myron (eds),

Berghahn Books, Providence 1997.

Molin, Karl: *Övervakningen av "SKP-komplexet": forskarrapport till Säkerhetstjänstkommissionen*, Statens offentliga utredningar, SOU 2002: 93, Fritzes offentliga publikationer, Stockholm 2002.
— *Hemmakriget: om den svenska krigsmaktens åtgärder mot kommunister under andra världskriget*, Tiden, Stockholm 1982.

Montesino, Norma: 'Flyktingmottagning en fråga om hälsa och arbete' in *Sveriges mottagning av flyktingar – några exempel. Årsbok 2007 från forskningsprofilen Arbetsmarknad, migration och etniska relationer (AMER) vid Växjö universitet*, Ekberg, Jan (ed.) Växjö University Press, Växjö 2007.

Morgenthau, Hans J.: *Politics among nations: the struggle for power and peace*, McGraw-Hill, New York 1993.

*Nationalism and exclusion of migrants: cross-national comparisons*, Gijsberts, Mérove Isabelle Léontine, Hagendoorn, A. & Scheepers, Peer (eds) Ashgate, Aldershot, Hants, England, 2003.

Nelhans, Joachim: *Utlänningen på arbetsmarknaden: de rättsliga förutsättningarna för utlännings tillträde till den svenska arbetsmarknaden*, Studentlitteratur, Lund, 1973.

Nilsson, Sture: *Rysskräcken i Sverige: fördomar och verklighet*, Samspråk, Örebro 1990.

Nilsson, Åke: *Efterkrigstidens invandring och utvandring*, Demografiska rapporter 2004:5, Statistiska Centralbyrån, Stockholm 2004.

*Nordisk flyktingpolitik i världskrigens epok*, Persson, Hans-Åke & Johansson, Rune (ed.), Lund Univ. Press, Lund 1989.

*Norsk innvandringshistorie. Bd 3, I globaliseringens tid, 1940–2000*, Tjelmeland, Hallvard & Kjeldstadli, Knut (eds) Pax, Oslo 2003.

Notini, Cecilia: *Säkerhetspolitisk flyktingpolitik: ingermanländare i Sverige 1945–47*, (unpublished Master's thesis) Department of History, Stockholm University 2006.

Olsson, Lars: *På tröskeln till folkhemmet: baltiska flyktingar och polska koncentrationslägerfångar som reservarbetskraft i skånskt jordbruk kring slutet av andra världskriget*, Morgonrodnad, Lund 1995.

O'Nions, Helen: *Minority rights protection in international law: the Roma of Europe*, Ashgate, Aldershot 2007.

*On security*, Lipschutz, Ronnie D. (ed.), Columbia University Press, New York 1995.

Oredsson, Sverker: *Svensk oro: offentlig fruktan i Sverige under 1900-talets senare hälft*, Nordic Academic Press, Lund 2003.
— *Svensk rädsla: offentlig fruktan i Sverige under 1900-talets första hälft*, Nordic Academic Press, Lund 2001.

Palm, Thede: *Några studier till T-kontorets historia*, Kungl. Samf. för utgivande av handskrifter rörande Skandinaviens historia, Stockholm 1999.

Persson, Sune: *Vi åker till Sverige: de vita bussarna 1945*, Fisher & Co, Rimbo 2002.

Petersson, Bo: *Med Moskvas ögon: bedömningar av svensk utrikespolitik under Stalin och Chrusjtjov*, Arena, Stockholm 1994.

Petersson, Magnus: ”*Brödrafolkens väl*”: *svensk-norska säkerhetsrelationer 1949–1969*, Santérus, Stockholm 2003.

*Protracted refugee situations: political, human rights and security implications*, Loescher, Gil (ed.), United Nations University Press, New York 2008.

Radzilowski, John: 'Ethnic Anti-Communism in the United States' in *Anti-Communist minorities in the United States: political activism of ethnic refugees*, Ieva Zake (ed.), Palgrave Macmillan, New York 2009.

*Reaching a state of hope: refugees, immigrants and the Swedish welfare state, 1930–2000*, Byström, Mikael & Frohnert, Pär (eds), Nordic Academic Press, Lund 2013.

*Redefining security: population movements and national security*, Poku, Nana & Graham, David T. (eds), Praeger, Westport, Connecticut 1998.

*Refugees and international relations*, Loescher, Gil & Monahan, Laila (eds) Clarendon, Oxford 1990.

*Rikets säkerhet och den personliga integriteten: de svenska säkerhetstjänsternas författningsskyddande verksamhet sedan år 1945: betänkande*, Säkerhetstjänstkommissionen, Statens offentliga utredningar, SOU 2002: 87, Fritzes offentliga publikationer, Stockholm 2002.

Rosenblum, Marc J.: 'Immigration and U.S. National Interests' in *Immigration policy and security: U.S., European, and Commonwealth perspectives*, Givens, Terri E., Freeman, Gary P. and Leal, David L (eds), Routledge, New York 2009.

Rothstein, Bo: *Vad bör staten göra?: om välfärdsstatens moraliska och politiska logik*, 3 ed., SNS förlag, Stockholm 2010.

Rousseau, David L: *Identifying threats and threatening identities: the social construction of realism and liberalism*, Stanford University Press, Stanford California 2006.

Rudolph, Christopher: *National security and immigration: policy development in the United States and Western Europe since 1945*, Stanford University Press, Stanford California 2006.

Runcis, Maija: *Steriliseringar i folkhemmet*, Ordfront, Stockholm 1998.

Ruthström-Ruin, Cecilia: *Beyond Europe: the globalization of refugee aid*, Lund University Press, Lund 1993.

Rydström, Jens: 'Piska och morot. HBT mellan stat och folkrörelse' in *Staten som vän eller fiende?: individ och samhälle i svenskt 1900-tal.*, Hedin, Marika *et al* (eds) , Institutet för framtidsstudier, Stockholm 2007, pp. 157–92.

Salomon, Kim: *Refugees in the Cold War: toward a new international refugee regime in the early postwar era*, Lund University Press, Lund 1991.

— *En femtiotalsberättelse: populärkulturens kalla krig i folkhemssverige*, Atlantis, Stockholm 2007.

Schmidt, Werner: *Antikommunism och kommunism under det korta 1900-talet*, Nordic Academic Press, Lund 2002.

Security and identity in Europe: exploring the new agenda, Aggestam, Lisbeth & Hyde-Price, Adrian (eds), Macmillan, Basingstoke 2000.

Sjöberg, Tommie: *The powers and the persecuted: the refugee problem and the Intergovernmental Committee on Refugees (IGCR), 1938–1947*, Studentlitteratur, Lund 1991.

Sjögren, Mikael: *Fattigvård och folkuppfostran: liberal fattigvårdspolitik 1903–1918*, Carlsson, Stockholm 1997.

*Social kontroll: övervakning, disciplinering och självreglering*, Larsson, Bengt & Engdahl, Oskar (eds), Liber, Malmö 2011.

Svanberg, Johan: *Arbetets relationer och etniska dimensioner: Verkstadsföreningen, Metall och esterna vid Svenska stålpressnings AB i Olofström 1945–1952*, Linnaeus University Press, Växjö 2010.

*Svensk invandrar- och flyktingpolitik*, Arbetsmarknadsdepartementet, Stockholm 1988.

*Sverigeingermanländarnas historia*, Sveriges ingermanländska riksförb., (SIR), Västra Frölunda 2000.

Svensson, Anders: *Ungrare i folkhemmet: svensk flyktingpolitik i det kalla krigets skugga*, Lund University Press, Lund 1992.

*Sverige och Nazityskland: skuldfrågor och moraldebatt*, Andersson, Lars M. & Tydén, Mattias (eds), Dialogos, Stockholm, 2007.

*Sveriges mottagning av flyktingar – några exempel: årsbok 2007 från forskningsprofilen Arbetsmarknad, migration och etniska relationer (AMER) vid Växjö universi-tet*, Ekberg, Jan (ed.) Växjö University Press, Växjö 2007.

*Säkerhetspolitik och historia: essäer om stormaktspolitiken och Norden under sjuttio år : vänbok till Krister Wahlbäck*, Bergquist, Mats & Johansson, Alf W. (eds), Hjalmarson & Högberg, Stockholm 2007.

Söderblom, Tomas: *Horan och batongen: prostitution och repression i folkhemmet*, Gidlund, Stockholm 1992.

Tempsch, Rudolf: *Från Centraleuropa till folkhemmet: den sudettyska invandringen till Sverige 1938–1955*, Göteborg University, Göteborg 1997.

*The culture of national security: norms and identities in world politics*, Katzenstein, Peter J. (ed.), Columbia University Press, New York 1996.

*The Refugee Convention at fifty: a view from forced migration studies*, Selm, Joanne van (ed.), Lexington Books, Lanham, Md. 2003.

*The uprooted: forced migration as an international problem in the post-war era*, Rystad, Göran (ed.) Lund University Press, Lund 1990.

Thor, Malin: *Hechaluz – en rörelse i tid och rum: tysk-judiska ungdomars exil i Sverige 1933–1943*, Växjö University Press, Växjö 2005.

Thor, Malin: 'Det är billigare att bota ett TBC-fall än att uppfostra en svensk' in *Sveriges mottagning av flyktingar – några exempel: årsbok 2007 från forskningsprofilen Arbetsmarknad, migration och etniska relationer (AMER) vid Växjö universitet*, Ekberg, Jan (ed.) Växjö University Press, Växjö 2007.

Thor, Malin & Montesino, Norma: 'Migration och folkhälsa: tuberkulos i den svenska flyktingmottagningen under 1940- och 1950-talen', unpublished paper presented at *Svenska Historikermötet i Lund*, May 2008.

Tickner, Ann J.: *Gender in international relations: feminist perspectives on achieving global security*, Columbia University Press, New York 1992.

Tirman, John: *The maze of fear: security and migration after 9/11*, New York Press, New York 2004.

Tolstoy, Nikolai: *Victims of Yalta*, Hodder and Stoughton, London 1977.

Towns, Ann: *Asyl i Sverige? En analys av asylpolitiken i Sverige under 1990-talet*, Göteborgs Universitet, Göteborg 1996.

Twain, Mark: 'Chapters from My Autobiography', in *North American Review*, 7 September 1906.

Tydén, Mattias, *Från politik till praktik: de svenska steriliseringslagarna 1935–1975*, 2 rev. ed., Almqvist & Wiksell International, Stockholm, 2002.

Uggla, Nils Andrzej: *I nordlig hamn: polacker i Sverige under andra världskriget*, Centrum för multietnisk forskning, Uppsala Universitet, Uppsala 1997.

Van Munster, Rens: *Securitizing immigration: the politics of risk in the EU*, Palgrave, Basingstoke 2009.

Wahlbäck, Krister: *Wallenberg-ärendet 1945–47*, (unpublished memorandum) Utrikesdepartementet, Stockholm 2001.

— *Undén, Granovskij och Wallenberg-ärendet 1946*, (unpublished memorandum) Utrikesdepartementet, Stockholm 2001.

Wallentin, Hans: *Lösdriveri och industrialism: om lösdriverifrågan i Sverige 1885–1940*, Högskolan i Östersund, Östersund 1989.

Walt, Stephen M: 'The Renaissance of Security Studies' in *International Studies Quarterly*, 1991: (35)2.

Watson, Scott D.: *The securitization of humanitarian migration: digging moats and sinking boats*, Routledge, New York 2009.

Widén, Jerker: *Notkrisen och dess efterspel: USA:s relationer med Sverige under en av kalla krigets höjdpunkter, oktober 1961–mars 1962*, Göteborg University, Göteborg 2004.

Wæver, Ole: 'Securitization and Desecuritization' in *On Security*, Ronnie D. Lipschutz (ed.), Columbia University Press, New York 1995, pp. 46–86.

Wendt, Alexander: *Social Theory of International Politics*, Cambridge University Press, Cambridge 1999.

Westad, Odd Arne: *The global Cold War: third world interventions and the making of our times*, Cambridge University Press, Cambridge 2005.

Åmark, Klas: *Hundra år av välfärdspolitik*, Boréa, Umeå 2005.

— *Att bo granne med ondskan: Sveriges förhållande till nazismen, Nazityskland och förintelsen*, Bonnier, Stockholm 2011.

— 'Recension av Tobias Berglund, Svenska koncentrationsläger i

Tredje rikets skugga' in *Historisk tidskrift*, 2009:(129)4, pp. 776–778.

— 'Ansvar och moral: flyktingforskningens problematik', in *Arbetarhistoria.*, 2006(30):2/3(=118/119), pp. 5–9.

## Internet


http://www.arkisto.fi/se/news/228/358/Nya-uppgifter-om-ingermanlaendarnas-repatriering-efter-fortsaettningskriget
http://www.arkisto.fi/se/news/228/358/Nya-uppgifter-om-ingermanlaendarnas-repatriering-efter-fortsaettningskriget
http://conventions.coe.int/treaty/Commun/ChercheSig.asp?NT=024&CM=8&DF=&CL=ENG
http://www.ibiblio.org/pha/policy/1943/431109a.html
http://www.icrc.org/ihl/INTRO/305
http://www.humanrights.gov.se/dynamaster/file_archive/040414/6562845
6c55c5444dfc7beca3d6f26f6/konventioner_komplett.pdf
http://www.legislation.gov.uk/ukpga/2001/24/contents
http://www.narc.fi/Arkistolaitos/inkerilaissiirtolaiset/statistik.html
http://www.narc.fi/Arkistolaitos/inkerilaissiirtolaiset/flyttar.html
http://www.oig.dhs.gov/assets/Mgmt/2013/OIG_13-09_Dec12.pdf
http://www.refworld.org/docid/3ae6b37810.html
http://www.refworld.org/docid/3dd8cF 374.html
http://www.refworld.org/docid/3dd8d12a4.html
http://www.unhcr.org/3b66c2aA 10.html
http://www.unhcr.org/refworld/docid/3ae6b3628.html
www.unhcr.org/statistics/populationdatabase


## Radio


'Baltutlämningen', 26 April 2009, P3, Sveriges Radio, available at: http://sverigesradio.se/sida/artikel.aspx?programid=2519&artikel=3587226